Understanding
Global Security

Fully revised to incorporate recent developments, this fourth edition of *Understanding Global Security* analyses the variety of ways in which people's lives are threatened and/or secured in contemporary global politics. The traditional focus of Security Studies texts – war, deterrence and terrorism – are analysed alongside non-military security issues such as famine, crime, disease, disasters, environmental degradation and human rights abuses to provide a comprehensive survey of how and why people are killed in the contemporary world.

This new edition features:

- Greater coverage of the evolving theoretical literature on security, including more analysis of critical theory perspectives and emerging schools of thought.
- Reflections on recent developments in the conflicts in Syria and Ukraine.
- New data and cases on poverty, hunger and depression and greater analysis of the social and political implications of the prolonged period of stagnation the global economy has gone through.
- New content reflecting the recent resurgence in populist nationalism evident in the election of Trump in the USA, the UK's exit from the EU and the authoritarian turn taken in many countries.
- Analysis of the 2015 Paris climate change treaty and the international responses to recent pandemics such as Ebola.
- A new section has been included on suicide, plugging a gap evident in the earlier editions.

User-friendly and easy to follow, this highly acclaimed and popular academic textbook is designed to make a complex subject accessible to all and will continue to be essential reading for everyone interested in security.

Peter Hough lectures in International Relations and heads up this subject at Middlesex University.

Understanding Global Security

4th edition

Peter Hough

Routledge
Taylor & Francis Group

LONDON AND NEW YORK

Fourth edition published 2018
by Routledge
2 Park Square, Milton Park, Abingdon, Oxon, OX14 4RN

and by Routledge
711 Third Avenue, New York, NY 10017

Routledge is an imprint of the Taylor & Francis Group, an informa business

First edition published by Routledge 2004

Third edition published by Routledge 2013

British Library Cataloguing in Publication Data
A catalogue record for this book is available from the British Library

Library of Congress Cataloging-in-Publication Data
Names: Hough, Peter, 1967- author.
Title: Understanding global security / Peter Hough.
Description: Fourth edition. | New York : Routledge, 2018. |
Includes bibliographical references and index.
Identifiers: LCCN 2017043815| ISBN 9781138726826 (Hardback) |
ISBN 9781138726833 (Paperback) | ISBN 9781315191164 (E-book)
Subjects: LCSH: Security, International.
Classification: LCC JZ5595 .H68 2018 | DDC 355/.033—dc23
LC record available at https://lccn.loc.gov/2017043815

ISBN: 9781138726826 (hbk)
ISBN: 9781138726833 (pbk)
ISBN: 9781315191164 (ebk)

Typeset in Century Old Style and Futura
by Florence Production Ltd, Stoodleigh, Devon, UK

To my mate Chris from 'Peter Sprout'

Contents

CONTENTS

Boxes

Tables

Acknowledgements

The idea for the first edition of this book arose out of a general discussion with editorial staff from Routledge and I must thank them, and in particular Craig Fowlie, for putting their faith in me and for marketing the book so well that it has now gone to a fourth edition.

Many people have helped in the process of developing this work through three editions over the past ten years by offering advice and/or support, including the following: Mohammed Al-Amin; Tunç Aybak; June Burnham; Heather Deegan; Paula Dunbar from the National Oceanic and Atmospheric Administration of the US government; Andy Frary; Jeff Haynes; David Hough; Roy and Sandra Hough; Dave Humphreys; Angela and Paul Lambillion; Lloyd Pettiford; Norman and Frances Say; Jeroen Warner; Lindsay Wright; and Peter Willetts.

Numerous seminar discussions with students (too many to name) have also informed my thinking on many of the topics covered in the book. Finally, I must thank Lisa, Daisy and Rosie for their patience, support and inspiration.

Abbreviations

AAA	American Anthropological Association
AIDS	Acquired Immune Deficiency Syndrome
ANC	African National Congress
ASEAN	Association of South East Asian Nations
AU	African Union
CAFOD	Catholic Agency for Overseas Development
CEDAW	Convention on the Elimination of all forms of Discrimination Against Women
CERD	Convention on the Elimination of all forms of Racial Discrimination
CFCs	chloro-fluoro-carbons
CIA	Central Intelligence Agency (USA)
CICP	Centre for International Crime Prevention (UN)
CJD	Creutzfeld-Jakob Disease
CND	Commission on Narcotic Drugs (UN)
CTBT	Comprehensive Test Ban Treaty
DDT	dichloro-diphenyl-trichloroethane
EADRCC	Euro-Atlantic Disaster Response Coordination Centre (NATO)
EAPC	Euro-Atlantic Partnership Council
EC	European Community
ECA	Earth Crossing Asteroid
ECOSOC	Economic and Social Council (UN)
ECOWAS	Economic Community of West African States
EFTA	European Free Trade Association
ETA	(Basque Fatherland and Unity)
EU	European Union

FAO	Food and Agriculture Organization
FARC	Revolutionary Armed Forces of Colombia
GDP	gross domestic product
GHS	Globally Harmonized System of Classification and Labelling of Chemicals
GNI	gross national income
GOARN	Global Outlook and Alert Response Network
GPEF	Global Programme to Eliminate Filiarisis
GPHIN	Global Public Health Intelligence Network
GPPPs	global public-private partnerships
HDI	Human Development Index
HIV	human immunodeficiency virus
HNP	Health, Nutrition and Population division (World Bank)
HOLN	Health Organization of the League of Nations
ICC	International Criminal Court
ICFTU	International Confederation of Free Trade Unions
ICIDI	Independent Commission on International Development Issues
ICJ	International Court of Justice
IDNDR	International Decade for Natural Disaster Reduction
IGO	intergovernmental organization
IHR	International Health Regulation (WHO)
ILC	International Labour Conference
ILC	International Law Commission (UN)
IMF	International Monetary Fund
INCB	International Narcotics Control Board
INGO	international non-governmental organization
IO	international organization
IPE	International Political Economy
IR	International Relations
IRA	Irish Republican Army
ISDR	International Strategy for Disaster Reduction
LDC	less developed country
LIEO	Liberal International Economic Order
MAD	Mutually Assured Destruction
MARS	Major Accident Reporting System (EU)
MERCOSUR	Common Market of the South (America)
MIC	methyl-isocyanate
MNC	multi-national corporation
MRTA	Tupac Amaru Revolutionary Movement
MSF	Médecins Sans Frontières
NAALC	North American Agreement on Labor Cooperation
NAFTA	North American Free Trade Agreement
NAM	Non-Aligned Movement
NATO	North Atlantic Treaty Organization
NCB	National Crime Bureau

NEO	Near Earth Object
NIC	National Intelligence Council (USA)
NIEO	New International Economic Order
NPT	Non-Proliferation Treaty (nuclear weapons)
OECD	Organization for Economic Cooperation and Development
OIHP	L'Office Internationale d'Hygiene Publique
OPEC	Organization of Petroleum Exporting Countries
OSCE	Organization for Security and Cooperation in Europe
PCIJ	Permanent Court of International Justice
PHARE	Poland and Hungary: Assistance for Reconstruction of the Economy
PKK	(Kurdish Workers Party)
PLO	Palestinian Liberation Organization
POPs	persistent organic pollutants
PSCs	private security companies
SALT	Strategic Arms Limitation Talks
SARS	severe acute respiratory syndrome
SAS	Special Air Service
SDI	Space Defence Initiative
SIPRI	Stockholm International Peace Research Institute
TCP	trichlorophenol
UN	United Nations
UNCED	United Nations Conference on the Environment and Development
UNCHE	United Nations Conference on the Human Environment
UNCLOS	United Nations Conference on the Law of the Sea
UNDCP	United Nations International Drug Control Programme
UNDP	United Nations Development Programme
UNEP	United Nations Environment Programme
UNESCO	United Nations Educational Scientific and Cultural Organization
UNFPA	United Nations Population Fund
UNICEF	United Nations Children's Fund
UNITA	National Union for the Total Independence of Angola
UN-OCHA	United Nations Office for the Coordination of Humanitarian Affairs
UNODC	United Nations Office for Drugs and Crime
UNSC	United Nations Security Council
WFP	World Food Programme

Chapter 1

Security and securitization

> *Nearly all other earthly benefits are needed by one person, not needed by another; and many of them can if necessary be cheerfully foregone, or replaced with something else; but security no human being can possibly do without . . .*
>
> John Stuart Mill (Mill 1863: 251)

Defining security

Security Studies

The study of security in the global context is a sub-discipline of the wider subject usually still referred to as *International Relations*. International Relations is the study of all political interactions between international 'actors', which include: states (represented by governments), international organizations (either inter-governmental or non-governmental[1]) and, to a lesser extent, some influential private individuals. Security Studies concerns itself with a sub-set of those political interactions marked by their particular importance in terms of maintaining the security of the actors and people. Where the line demarking this International Relations (IR) sub-discipline is to be drawn is increasingly contentious, as indeed is the demarcation of IR in relation to the wider realms of political and social science. Increased political interaction between actors, other than through the traditional state-to-state route, has served to blur the distinction between domestic and foreign policy and widened the scope of IR. The process commonly referred to as globalization has led to once internal political issues becoming increasingly externalized and once external political issues becoming increasingly internalized. Traditionally domestic policy concerns, like health and rights, are more prominent than ever on the global political agenda and events occurring in other states, such as disasters or massacres, are more often than ever deemed to be of political significance for people not personally affected. In light of these changes, and the reduced prevalence of inter-state war, it has become a matter of contention amongst theorists of IR whether Security Studies should maintain its traditional emphasis on military threats to the security of states or widen its focus. Alternative perspectives have argued increasingly that the discipline should either: (1) extend its reach to include non-military threats to states and, perhaps, other actors or, (2) go further and bring within its remit the security of all people in relation to a range of threats, both military and non-military.

The main *paradigms* of International Relations offer alternative conceptual frameworks for comprehending the complexity that emerges from attempting to study the huge volume of interactions between actors that makes up the contemporary global political system. These different 'lenses' for making sense of this political complexity focus in very different ways when it comes to thinking about issues of security in International Relations.

Realism

Realists are the traditionalists in International Relations and Security Studies and still the dominant paradigm, both academically and in the 'real world' as the approach favoured by most governments in conducting their foreign policies. Classical Realism emerged in the 1940s and dominated the young discipline of International Relations with a straightforward and almost unchallenged view of how and why politics on the world stage was conducted. The 'actors' were states. Intergovernmental organizations (IGOs) were merely alliances of convenience between states whilst international non-governmental organizations (INGOs) were considered irrelevant (and indeed, by comparison with today, were so at the time). Hence the world, in political terms, was a state system. The interactions between the states in the system could be characterized as 'power politics'. A pessimistic view of human nature permeates Realism, meaning that, on the world stage, it is assumed that states should not trust other states and therefore seek to 'look after number one' by extending their own power wherever possible in order to secure themselves.

This promotion of the self-interest of states is captured in the term 'national interest' (see Box 1.1). For Realists, governments making a clear distinction between 'high' and 'low' politics in their policy-making best serve their national interest. Individual concerns with health, welfare and other 'low politics' issues are the stuff of domestic politics and need to be kept separate from the 'high politics' of state security. This approach was justified on the premise that failing to deter or losing a war would undermine the satisfaction of low politics aspirations. Individual interests were inextricably tied up in the national interest. Hence in the UK in the late 1940s society tolerated food rationing whilst the socialist government poured the country's shrunken exchequer into developing atomic weapons. Individual hardship was considered a price worth paying to avert the potentially catastrophic hardship of failing to deter invasion from the Soviet Union.

The conundrum that emerges from assuming that a state's security is achieved by it pursuing the maximization of its own power is that all states cannot simultaneously follow this prescription. The security of one's own state is likely to be enhanced at the expense of another state in what has been termed the 'security dilemma'. For Realists the security dilemma is averted by their faith in the balance of power. The balance of power keeps a sense of order to the *anarchy* of the state system as there is a mutual interest for the most powerful amongst them to work together and preserve the status quo. The security of the most powerful states rests on not allowing any one of them to tip the balance by becoming too powerful. For classical Realists, then, Security Studies was pretty much synonymous with International Relations.

The rise in significance of economic interactions between states and their increased involvement in IGOs in the 1960s and 1970s broadened the focus of IR

BOX 1.1 **The national interest**

The idea of the national interest being pursued in foreign policy was central to the development of Realism in the post-Second World War years and continues to be very influential both in academic circles and in governments. The term seeks to encapsulate the point that governments need to act according to the interests of their own people even if this conflicts with the interests of other states and peoples. Hence the term tends to be employed by politicians when seeking to offer a justification for a policy considered by some to be immoral, such as a lucrative arms deal with a government known to oppress its population. Morgenthau brought the concept to prominence, stating that the fundamental aim of foreign policy must be to ensure 'the integrity of the nation's territory, of its political institutions and of its culture' (Morgenthau 1982: 973). In a world of self-serving states this was best pursued by policies which seek to maintain or increase the power of the state.

The amorality of national interest is criticized by those who consider that morality can and should inform foreign policy just as it does in domestic policy. Additionally, the concept presupposes that sovereignty is the ultimate of all political goals, which does not accord with the European experience, where it has been concluded by a number of governments that the voluntary 'pooling of sovereignty' is in the best interest of their administrations and their peoples. Defining what is and is not in the best interests of a state is also far from straightforward given the range of options open to governments in conducting their foreign affairs. Morgenthau and fellow arch-Realist the US Foreign Minister Henry Kissinger famously argued over whether the war in Vietnam was in the US national interest.

In defence of the concept of national interest, for all its analytical shortcomings, it cannot be denied that many governments today do continue to use it as a basis for the conduct of their foreign policy. The Foreign Minister of Australia, in a 2002 speech in advance of the publication of a government paper, 'Advancing the National Interest', stated that: 'The Government has ensured that Australia's national interest is advanced in an ambitious yet pragmatic and clear-minded fashion. Because if we don't . . . no one else will' (Downer 2002).

beyond military power politics to incorporate economic power issues. Realist thought metamorphosized into 'Neo-realism', which maintained the focus on states and the pursuit of power but accepted that not everything that happens in the world is determined by military might. States could also become powerful by concentrating on their economies (such as West Germany and Japan), being lucky enough to possess a key economic resource (such as the major oil-producing states) or by exerting diplomatic influence in the world via IGOs (as the US had done through the IMF, World Bank or NATO, for example). In light of this a new sub-discipline of IR emerged considering such matters, *International Political Economy (IPE)*. For (Neo-)realists then, Security Studies became the military arm of International Relations and IPE its economic sister.

Liberal-Pluralism

Liberal-Pluralism emerged as a paradigm of IR from the 1960s, made up of scholars unconvinced that Neo-realism had evolved far enough from Realism to take account of the changes that had occurred in the world since the 1940s. It began to be argued that adding the pursuit of economic power to the pursuit of military power by states and factoring in IGOs was still too simplistic an understanding of world politics. Pluralists, as the term implies, consider that a plurality of actors, rather than just states, exert influence on the world stage. State dominance of international relations was being eroded from above and below, the Liberal-Pluralists contended. IGOs (such as the European Community and organizations of the United Nations) had become more than expedient alliances and were moulding state policies together into common interests which sometimes redefined or contradicted national interests. INGOs, such as pressure groups and multi-national corporations (MNCs), were also becoming significant players on the world stage in their own right and were not necessarily acting in accord with their 'home' government. In addition, Pluralists built on the political philosophy of Liberalism, which had been very much to the fore in early IR thinking before the ascendance of Realism, to argue that the amorality of the national interest was not an appropriate guide to foreign policy. Individual people prosper from the mutual benefits inherent in cooperation and would find their interests better served in a world in which states and their interests, as defined by their governments, ceased to dictate their lives.

For Liberal-Pluralists these developments were making the interactions of politics in the world more complex and varied. 'Low politics' issues, such as environmental change or controlling diseases, were becoming international as well as domestic political issues. IR could no longer assume all that happens in the world was related to a military – or even an economic – balance of power between states. This aspect of international affairs was important but not all-subsuming and an issue-by-issue-based approach was necessary. This approach accepts that many non-military issues are legitimate concerns of IR and that they might be contended over without reference to military power on an increasingly busy world stage.

For Liberal-Pluralists then, Security Studies – in the traditional sense of the military defence of the state – was but a small sub-set of the broad subject that is International Relations.

Marxism

The Marxist paradigm of International Relations is related to but not synonymous with Marxist political thought. Proponents of the Marxist paradigm of International Relations are usually also ideological Marxists, but not necessarily so and, in political practice, Marxist governments have often pursued foreign policies broadly Realist in character, such as in the USSR's maintenance of a sphere of influence in Eastern Europe. For such Marxist, or *Structuralist*, thinkers the Neo-realist and Liberal-Pluralist conversion to appreciating the importance of economic factors in the conduct of politics in the world was both belated and insufficient. Economic concerns, rather than military or issue-specific power, determine the fate of the world's peoples and always have done. In this view globalization is nothing new, it is merely the latest phase of the world's 'haves' exploiting the 'have nots'. Imperialism is not a relic of a bygone age but a persistent feature of a global system built on the capitalist logic of ever-increasing profit. From a Marxist perspective, inter-state competition is a side-show to the 'competition' between the wealthy peoples of the world (most of the developed world and a small fraction of elites in the less-developed world) and the poor, in which there is consistently only one winner.

Marxists thus see IR as largely synonymous with IPE. Security Studies, as it has evolved, is superfluous since human and global security can only ever come through global, structural change. Military strategy serves global economic rather than national security interests. Wars are fought to preserve or maintain exploitative economic systems (for example over colonies or over the economic mastery of the whole system, as with the Cold War). In this view the fates of individuals are determined not so much by their states but by the wider global system, and only world socialist revolution could improve their prospects.

'Reflective theories'

From the 1980s dissatisfaction with the three main paradigms of IR, and their myriad offshoots and hybrid theories, produced a range of theoretical challenges influenced by a new wave of post-modernist thinking on *methodology* (how you study a subject). The 'scientific method' – seeking to understand the behaviour of actors by the objective testing of theories and concepts (broadly accepted by the three main IR paradigms) – came to be questioned by a new breed of IR scholars. *Critical Theorists*, such as Booth and Cox, questioned the premise that studying human behaviour can ever be objective and scientific and that the study of IR inevitably reflected a Western bias (Booth 1991; Cox 1981). Since 'theory is always for someone' (Cox 1981: 128), the job of the Critical Theorist is to detect bias in concepts and analysis and seek to correct them. Critical Theory hence became a home for many IR thinkers on the political left who had grown disillusioned with the rigid 'economic structuralism' of Marxism, which left little room for the consideration of human agency ('people power'). Hence 'critical schools' have emerged in IR seeking to give greater voice to the traditionally marginalized, such as in Development Studies where post-development theory reasons that the whole discipline was framed from the neo-imperialistic perspective of the developed world. The required response to this was to construct new theory, from the perspective of the less developed world, to counter this orthodoxy.

In a similar vein, feminist scholars, such as Tickner and Enloe, came to argue that IR had an inherent male bias and that concepts like sovereignty and power were in need of re-appraisal in order to achieve an understanding of the political world based on all of its people (Tickner 1992; Enloe 1990). Since both the 'real' and academic worlds of politics have been dominated by men, the theories and concepts of IR reflect a 'masculinist epistemology' (male way of thinking about the subject), emphasizing abstract concepts and aggression over human and social realities. Sovereignty, for instance, could be said to be traditionally constructed in political discourse in a possessive manner, legitimizing a government's right to control 'it's people' as they choose without considering the human cost of maintaining law and order. For feminist IR thinkers this notion of sovereignty is analogous to the 'public-private dichotomy' in patriarchal societies where a masculinist notion of family-life as being private (and so not a 'public', legal matter) can lead to the legitimization of domestic abuse and female subjugation.

Social Constructivism

For some critics of the scientific method (or *post-positivists*), building new reflective theories, though welcome, was not enough. Instead of just seeking to knock down the established approaches, Social Constructivists sought to build a new, all-encompassing theory of IR which saw validity in both the traditional and post-positivist approaches.

Changes in the 'real world' of international relations, as well as in thinking on how to study it, also stimulated the new theories. The way in which the Cold War ended, and the panning out of the 'New World Order' which followed, prompted a number of scholars to challenge many of the assumptions of the discipline across the paradigms. In particular Social Constructivism argued that understanding political events in the world necessitated more introspection and less grand abstract theorizing. The paradigm favours a more sociological approach and advocates a greater appreciation of the cultural dimensions of policy-making. It began to be argued that maybe the actors on the world stage do not really follow any kind of rational script, be it written in the language of self-interest, mutual interest or dictated by economic circumstance. Perhaps, at least some of the time, foreign policy reflects parochial ideological or moral guidelines rather than the pursuit of objective gains. By the 1990s, Ruggie, a lifelong Liberal, contended that that paradigm and Neo-realism had come to share so much common ground, in assuming states to be rational gain-driven actors (only differing in *how* they gain), that they should henceforth be considered as a single paradigm of 'neo-utilitarianism' (Ruggie 1998: 1–39).

The USSR's voluntary 'defeat' in the Cold War, when Gorbachev negotiated a 'surrender' with the enemy for what he considered to be the good of his country, appeared to defy the logic of Realism and the national interest.[2] In the proceeding years the reluctance of the newly reunified Germany to use its enhanced physique to exert greater power in Europe, preferring instead to throw its weight behind European integration, appeared to offer greater evidence of a government acting according to ideas rather than interests. Constructivists (and reflective theorists) consider that the three established paradigms all downplay the normative element of politics in attempting to build 'value-free' 'scientific' models to explain the actions of international actors. Thinking purely about 'who gets what' in reference to particular actors ignores the role that can be played by human agency. The 1989 anti-communist revolutions in East Europe had demonstrated that ideas and people power could overcome the interests of states and mould events.

Whereas Liberal-Pluralists and Marxists tended to focus on other aspects of IR, largely leaving Security Studies to the Realists, Critical Theorists and Social Constructivists mounted the first concerted attack on the logic of Security Studies as it had developed during the Cold War years. *Ontological* questions largely ignored between 1940 and 1990 began to be asked. Who are being secured? Who are doing the securing? What is it to be secure?

Wide and narrow conceptions of security

This book adopts a broad and deep interpretation of security encompassing a varied range of perceived threats to human life, which takes the subject area well beyond the framework of traditional treatments of international security politics which have tended to focus on military threats to states emanating from other states. This broader approach to conceptualizing global security gained ground in the 1990s when the ending of the Cold War seemed, to many statesmen, academics and members of the general public, to herald a new era of international politics. In this 'New World Order' the threat of global nuclear Armageddon had subsided, allowing previously marginalized issues to emerge from the shadow of superpower rivalry and register on the international political agenda. Such an approach to the subject was, however, articulated as far back as 1983 when Ullman defined a threat to security as:

> an action or sequence of events that (1) threatens drastically and over a relatively brief span of time to degrade the quality of life for the inhabitants of a state or (2) threatens significantly to narrow the range of policy choices available to a government of a state, or to private, nongovernmental entities (persons, groups, corporations) within the state.
>
> (Ullman 1983: 133)

Such an expansive interpretation of security found many critics amongst Realists, who were not shaken from their belief in maintaining a narrower focus on what constitutes Security Studies by the ending of the Cold War. Walt forcefully argued this case: 'security studies may be defined as the study of the threat, use and control of military force' (Walt 1991: 212). Walt and the traditionalists fear that widening the definition of security risks rendering the concept redundant by making it too all-encompassing and diluting the important task of analysing military threats and inter-state conflict. Underlying this fear is the belief of many Realists that military threats are actually more apparent in a post-Cold War world devoid of that traditional guarantor of state security, the military balance of power. This 'anti-New World Order' thesis was epitomized by Mearsheimer's lament in 1990 that 'we will soon miss' the Cold War (Mearsheimer 1990). These traditionalists asserted that the demise of the Cold War actually necessitated Security Studies going 'back to basics' rather than broadening its base, since international politics shorn of the nuclear balance of power imposed by the two superpowers would find the need to rediscover lost arts of multilateral diplomacy, conflict resolution, fighting limited wars and conventional defence (Chapman 1992).

Although there is a case to be made that military threats in the twenty-first century are as apparent as ever, and maybe even greater than during the Cold War, wideners and deepeners of security contend that they are not the only threats that face states, people and the world as a whole. Indeed, they never have been. Throughout history most people have been killed by things other than soldiers and weapons, and many states have been weakened or destroyed by things other than military conflict. Ullman argued that the security implications for states of demographic pressures and resource depletion needed to be taken on board alongside military threats from other states (Ullman 1983). This logic was developed further in a seminal article by Mathews towards the end of the Cold War which highlighted the need for states to give proper concern to the newly-apparent threats posed by environmental problems such as ozone depletion and global warming (Mathews 1989). With the shadow of the Cold War lifted, many other 'wideners' emerged in Security Studies literature in the 1990s. Ayoob highlighted that internal rather than external threats were the principal security concern of most less developed countries (LDCs) (Ayoob 1997). Peterson and Sebenius made the same point with reference to that most developed and powerful state, the USA, positing that a crisis in education and a growing economic 'underclass' should be understood as security threats (Peterson & Sebenius 1992). Lynn-Jones and Miller addressed the need to give attention to a range of previously neglected internal and external threats such as virulent nationalism and the social impact of migration (Lynn-Jones & Miller 1995). Although viewed as unwelcome by traditionalists, such as Walt and Mearsheimer, this widening of security did not necessarily undermine the Realist logic of conventional Security Studies. The focus was still on the state system and seeing relationships between states as governed by power. Security 'widening' was simply a case of extending the range of factors which affect state power beyond the confines of military and trade affairs.

An argument for a more profound widening of security than tacking on some non-military issues to the range of threats to states emerged through the 1990s in a new approach that came to be characterized as the 'Copenhagen School', after the Copenhagen Peace Research Institute. Buzan trailblazed this approach in the early 1990s (Buzan 1991), but it crystallized later in the decade, when he teamed up with Waever and de Wilde in producing the groundbreaking work *Security*.

> Threats and vulnerabilities can arise in many different areas, military and non-military, but to count as security issues they have to meet strictly defined criteria that distinguish them from the normal run of the merely political. They have to be staged as existential threats to a referent object by a securitizing actor who thereby generates endorsement of emergency measures beyond rules that would otherwise bind.
>
> (Buzan, Waever & de Wilde 1998: 5)

TABLE 1.1 Narrow, wide and deep conceptions of security

Referent object

Individual	Human (narrow)		
Non-state actor	Copenhagen School		Human (wider)
State	narrow	widened	
	military	using military	non-military

Issue type

Hence the Copenhagen School went further than the 'wideners' in partially *deepening* the meaning of security by arguing that issues can be considered matters of security even if they are not threatening states (see Table 1.1). Buzan and the Copenhagen School were not Critical Theorists or Social Constructivists[3] but, nevertheless, were influenced by post-positivist methodology and argued that issues could become matters of security through societal pressure being put on the government to 'do something'. A key influence on this was the largely unforeseen revival in nationalism being played out in the post-Cold War landscape of Central and Eastern Europe, particularly in Yugoslavia. The fact that conflict and the disintegration of a state occurred not as a result of a state security dilemma but because of internal 'societal security' dilemmas (rivalry between different nationalities within the state) prompted an attempt to incorporate sub-state groups into security analysis. Elsewhere, heightened anxieties over the perceived societal threats posed by migration and globalization have since manifested themselves in an upsurge in populist nationalism in many countries. This was epitomized by the UK beginning the process of exiting the European Union in 2016 despite such a move being considered contrary to the national interest by the government and all major political parties. The Copenhagen School approach thus sees 'securitization' as a process in which human agency, alongside government interests, plays a role.

The deepening of security

Going beyond the Copenhagen School in extending the domain of Security Studies is the 'deepening' approach led by Liberal-Pluralists, Reflective Theorists and Social Constructivists. Deepeners embrace the concept of 'human security' and argue that the chief 'referent object' of security should not be the state or certain sub-state groups, such as stateless nations within societies, but the individual people of which these institutions/groups are comprised. For Liberal-Pluralists the emphasis on the individual over the state is a predictable position to take both ontologically and ethically. Falk, for example, considers that security ought to be defined as: 'the negation of insecurity as it is *specifically* experienced by individuals and groups in concrete situations' (Falk 1995: 147). This is a significant leap from widening which, as Falk describes; 'still conceives of security largely from the heights of elite assessment, at best allowing the select advisor to deliver a more enlightened message to the ear of the prince' (Falk 1995: 146).

Critical Theorists furthered this deepening of security by challenging not only the referent object of security but also what it takes to make people secure. Ken Booth, a self-styled 'fallen Realist', led this challenge by arguing in contradiction to the assumptions he once shared that: 'Security and emancipation are in fact two sides of the same coin. It is emancipation, not power and order, in both theory and practise, that leads to stable security' (Booth 1991: 539).

The root of the problem with the traditional approaches to security politics is what Wyn-Jones, like Booth a Critical Theorist, describes as the 'fetishization of the state' (Wyn-Jones 1999: ch. 4). This tendency in IR is not resolved by the Copenhagen School approach. The Copenhagen School approach accepts the idea that non-military issues can be securitized and that the referent object of this can be something other than a state but maintains the logic that only the state can be the 'securitizing actor' (i.e. decide whether the issue is acted upon as a matter of urgency). Hence statecentricism is maintained, if in a subtler form. The practical limitation with this is that not only are the traditional security agents of the state (i.e. the armed forces and the police) often inadequate for dealing with security problems affecting the people of that state, they are often a chief cause of those problems. Buzan accepts that states can be the source of threats rather than protection for individual people but considers that this is a property of only certain types of states. 'Strong states' co-existing in 'mature anarchy', which have increasingly become the norm through democratization and the development of international human rights law, can be relied upon to secure individuals (Buzan 1991: 98–111). Hence Buzan and Waever are principally wideners rather than deepeners, albeit of a much more refined form than those wideners who preceded them.

Whilst the practical concern that widening the focus of Security Studies should not distract attention from military threats has some validity, the intellectual rationale for maintaining a narrower focus is weak. In a book taking a widened approach to security (though not as wide as the Copenhagen School), Wirtz contends that, 'if the threat of force, the use of force or even the logistical or technical assistance that can be supplied by military units does little to respond to a given problem, it probably is best not to treat the specific issue as a security threat' (Wirtz 2002: 312). He also scoffs at the idea that global warming should be construed as a security issue in stating, 'It is not exactly clear . . . how military forces can help reduce the build-up of greenhouse gases in the atmosphere' (Wirtz 2002: 311). This view gives an indication of how blinkered the mainstream study of security can be. Defining an issue as one of security on the basis of whether or not it involves military forces strips the term of any real meaning. Security is a human condition. To define it purely in terms of state bodies whose aim it is to help secure their state and people in a certain dimension, rather than the people whose security is at stake, is both odd and nonsensical. This way of framing what is and what is not a security issue is akin to saying that children being taught to read by their parents are not being educated or that happiness does not exist unless it is induced by the performances of state-sponsored clowns. A security issue, surely, is an issue which threatens (or appears to threaten) one's security. Defining a security issue in behavioural terms rather than excluding certain categories of threats because they do not fit conventional notions of what defines the subject area gives the term some objective meaning. If people, be they government ministers or private individuals, perceive an issue to threaten their lives in some way and respond politically to this, then that issue should be deemed to be a *security* issue.

This notion of *human security* is best known for its adoption by the United Nations Development Programme (UNDP):

> The concept of security must change – from an exclusive stress on national security to a much greater stress on people's security, from security through armaments to security through human development, from territorial to food, employment and environmental security.
>
> (UNDP 1993)

Hence human security is a profound shift in thinking from national security, even in a widened or partially deepened form.

It should be noted, though, that human security itself is a contested concept with more and less expansive versions having come to be employed in both academic and political discourse. Wider human security is often characterized as combining 'freedom from want' and 'freedom from fear' (from the UNDP definition) in that it considers any issues with direct or indirect life-threatening consequences for individuals to be matters of security. Concerns among some advocates of an individual-focused approach to security that 'existing definitions of human security tend to be extraordinarily expansive and vague' (Paris 2001: 88) led them to favour a more restricted version based purely on 'freedom from fear'. This narrow version of human security concentrates on direct and deliberate violent threats, excluding less directly human-caused forms of insecurity like diseases and disasters. Recent Canadian governments have been supportive of such an approach in their advocacy of human security as a pragmatic determinant of when specific, concrete foreign policy actions – such as taking part in a humanitarian intervention or developing international human rights conventions – should be undertaken. In contrast, the Japanese government's endorsement of human security has tended to be more in line with the expansive version as favoured by the UNDP and employed in this volume. From this perspective there is a fatal fatalism in assuming that only direct and deliberate threats to life can be deemed worthy of security status. Such a restriction might make the concept easier to deal with but does so by simply choosing to ignore the insecurities of most of the world's people, even when the means of securing them are apparent.

One consequence of this bifurcation of how human security is conceptualized has been a lack of coherence amongst the 'deepeners', with Critical Security Studies tending to distance itself from the more mainstream Liberal deepening approach. In essence Critical Theorists came to be irritated by what they saw as 'bandwagoning' and a dilution and sell-out of an idea first nurtured by a new breed of Liberal scholars. For Booth, the Human Security approach has been 'co-opted and incorporated into statist discourses' (Booth 2005: 266). The popularization of the concept – in its narrower form – has led Critical Theorists to become suspicious that it has come to be used to advance state, rather than human, interests. McCormack, for example, argues that the concept 'allows powerful states or international interests greater freedom to intervene in and regulate weaker states in a number of different ways. This serves to disempower the citizens of weak or impoverished states' (McCormack 2008: 114).

This Human Security–Critical Security Studies schism is unfortunate since the two approaches have much in common. The Liberal focus on the individual is, ultimately, in accord with Critical Theory despite the latter's more socialist and social orientation. As Booth acknowledges, 'the only transhistorical and permanent fixture in human society is the individual physical being, and so this must naturally be the ultimate referent in the security problematique' (Booth 2005: 264). Similarly, Liberal thinkers, long before the emergence of human security, have stressed that the state can be a primary source of harm to human interests and needs (Newman 2010).

Hence, by adopting the wide human security framework, the notion of security is recast as a social construct, stripping away the need for the analyst to speculate on what *they* think is the most threatening of the myriad issues on the contemporary international political agenda and concentrate instead on analysing how and why certain issues actually are perceived of as vital and responded to in extraordinary ways. This approach is appropriate since it is clear that people do think of their security in different terms today than they did during the Cold War (see Table 1.2). It is also observable in various ways that the international political agenda has become far more diverse since 1990, with governments giving greater priority to issues such as environmental change, drugs and public health. Even explicitly military organizations, like NATO, are increasingly focusing on non-military activities such as disaster relief.

Who's securing whom?

The preoccupation of Security Studies with the state is very much a relic of the Cold War. In some ways this is understandable since the discipline of IR, and its sub-discipline Security Studies, only emerged in the 1930s and was thus very much forged in an era of unprecedented military threats. Realism was in the ascendancy at the

TABLE 1.2(a) Most important problem in the world (%)

Crime	32
Environment	7
Terrorism	7
War	5
Human rights	5
Education	3
Health	1
Others	2

Note: 66,806 people in 65 countries were asked: 'What do you think is the most important problem facing the world today?' The responses are collated into the categories used here by the author.

Source: *Win/Gallup International Annual Survey 2013* (Win/Gallup 2014).

TABLE 1.2(b) Biggest fears for EU citizens (%)

1	Crime	93
2	Economic	50
3	Terrorism	49
4	Human Rights	20
5	War	11
6	Environment	7
7	Natural disaster	6
8	Accidents	4

Note: 28,082 people were asked to choose up to three of the most important challenges to security of EU citizens today. The responses are collated into the categories used here by the author.

Source: Internal Security Special Eurobarometer 432 Wave EB 83.2, April 2015, Brussels (Eurobarometer 2015).

close of the Second World War since the application of force had proved its worth in curbing aggression and restoring order in Europe and Asia. Pre-war international cooperation, in the form of the League of Nations, and appeasement diplomacy *vis-à-vis* aggressors, comprehensively failed to keep the peace. In addition, the total war of the Second World War and the 'total phoney war' of the Cold War, whereby whole populations were threatened by state quarrels in ways not previously seen, bound individuals to the fates of their governments like never before.

Hence in the 1940s the twin concepts of 'national interest' and 'national security' took centre stage in IR and Security Studies. Walter Lippmann, an American journalist who popularized the term 'Cold War', also defined the nature of security that would characterize that era: 'A nation has security when it does not have to sacrifice its legitimate interests to avoid war and is able, if challenged, to maintain them by war' (Lippmann 1943: 32). The USA's new pre-eminence and preparedness to act on the world stage in 1945 was an additional key factor in promoting this approach. The government of the USA found itself in a position of unprecedented dominance and compelled to utilize its power in a way that it had shown no inclination to do in the 1920s and 1930s. Using the precursor 'national' in a government's political rhetoric is always a device to rally society behind it and garner legitimacy for a potentially controversial policy. The US government was embarking on a radical new direction in its foreign policy and needed its society united and on board for the journey (McSweeney 1999: 20–1). American academic, and godfather of Realism in the 1940s and 1950s, Hans Morgenthau summarized this new dynamic:

> The nation state is to a higher degree than ever before the predominant source of the individual's moral and legal valuations and the ultimate point of reference for his secular loyalties. Consequently, its power among the other nations and the preservation of its sovereignty are the individual's foremost concerns in international affairs.
>
> (Morgenthau 1972: 32)

The scale of the threat posed by nuclear war in the second half of the twentieth century served to weld the security of individual people in the USA and elsewhere to that of their governments. The state would assume the responsibility for protecting its citizens and demand their loyalty in return in a strengthened version of the *Social Contract* relationship articulated by political philosophers such as Hobbes and Locke from the seventeenth century. Hobbes's advocacy of the need for the *Leviathan* (meaning a strong state) to save individuals from the dangerous anarchy that would otherwise result from the pursuit of their own selfish interests was a major influence on Morgenthau and the Realists. In the late twentieth century, the anarchy was the international state system, and the dangers came, to a greater extent than ever before, from other states. Hence the Realist approach to IR represented a revival of the understanding that the state was crucial to securing the lives of its citizens in a different guise.

In between Hobbes and Morgenthau, however, political philosophy and state governance in Europe and North America were more influenced by Liberalism and a very different notion of security. Eighteenth-century Liberal philosophers were alarmed that the social contract had become overbalanced and that the Leviathan was endangering rather than protecting its individuals. Paine, Montesquieu, Mill and Smith all referred to 'security' in their notable works and Bentham saw security and liberty as synonymous, declaring that, 'without security equality could not last a day' (Bentham 1876: 96).

McSweeney observes that security over time had come to be defined in IR solely as a noun rather than an adjective, or as 'a commodity rather than a relationship' (McSweeney 1999: 15). The human part of a human condition had been lost and the term had become synonymous with *realpolitik*, the interest of the state. Military might and the application of the national interest can secure lives but it can also, of course, imperil them. Additionally, human lives can be imperilled by a range of issues other than military ones. A thorough application of security in the study of global politics surely must recognize this or else admit that it is a more limited field of enquiry: 'War Studies' or 'Strategic Studies', for example. The conceptualization of International Relations, like the conduct of International Relations, was very much frozen in time between 1945 and 1990.

The international political agenda

The meaning of 'security' is not just an arcane matter of academic semantics. The term carries significant weight in 'real world' political affairs since threats to the security of states have to be a priority for governments and threats to the lives of people are increasingly accepted as more important than other matters of contention. The need to widen the meaning of security in global politics was recognized by prominent statesmen long before it achieved a certain fashionability following the end of the Cold War. In the late 1970s the Independent Commission on International Development Issues (ICIDI), chaired by former West German chancellor Willy Brandt and including the former premiers of the UK and Sweden, Heath and Palme, concluded in their influential report that:

> An important task of constructive international policy will have to consist in [sic] providing a new, more comprehensive understanding of 'security' which would be less restricted to the purely military aspects. . . .
>
> Our survival depends not only on military balance, but on global cooperation to ensure a sustainable biological environment based on equitably shared resources.
>
> (ICIDI 1980: 124)

The Brandt Report helped raise the profile of poverty as an international issue (see Chapter 4), but global security politics continued to be focused on military matters in general, and the Cold War in particular, until the passing into history of that conflict at the end of the 1980s. As with the academic treatment of security, however, it is important to remember that the notion that the conduct of international security politics should be about non-military as well as military issues was not born of the 1990 peace dividend. Rather, it first emerged in those two previous eras of Liberal optimism which followed the twentieth century's other two global conflicts. Though its chief historical legacy is a failure to keep the peace, the League of Nations first implemented the idea that some lateral thinking was required to avert war by incorporating within its system of organizations, alongside conflict resolution mechanisms, 'specialized agencies' focusing on health and welfare. The Second World War, which prompted the dissolution of the League, led the United Nations to change the military approach to security of its predecessor, more in line with Realist logic (see Chapter 2), but it still persisted with the lateral approach. The specialized agencies were retained and the UN Charter openly declares as an aim 'the creation of conditions of stability and well-being which are necessary for peaceful and friendly relations among nations' (Article 55). In addition the Constitution of the World Health Organization (WHO), the largest in the widened roster of specialized agencies taken under the UN's wing, explicitly states that human well-being is a precondition for world peace (see Chapter 7). The UN also went further than the League of Nations in for the first time giving international expression to the idea of keeping the peace for individual people as well as states through the enshrinement of human rights (see Chapter 5), thus moving towards a deepened understanding of security.

In the 1990s elements within the UN system were able to revive and further develop this line of thinking with the concept of human security. Most notably the UNDP incorporated the concept into their Human Development Reports from 1993, influenced in particular by the thinking of Pakistani economist Mahbub ul Haq (see Box 1.2).

The UNDP line has been endorsed by other UN agencies, in the General Assembly and by former Secretary-General Kofi Annan. Probably the first articulation of human security in international politics, though, came two years earlier at a Pan-African conference co-sponsored by the UN and the Organization for African Unity.

BOX 1.2 Mahbub ul Haq

Haq was a Pakistani Liberal economist who worked for the World Bank and as finance minister in his home government before joining the UNDP in the late 1980s. Here he launched the influential Human Development Reports and, with his Indian counterpart Amartya Sen (see Box 4.1), created the Human Development Index (HDI) to help quantify economic growth that is in the human interest. He died in 1998 but these initiatives ensure that his legacy will live on for a long time as maybe the principal founding father of the concept of human security.

> The concept of security goes beyond military considerations. [It] must be construed in terms of the security of the individual citizen to live in peace with access to basic necessities of life while fully participating in the affairs of his/her society in freedom and enjoying all fundamental human rights.
>
> (African Leadership Forum 1991)

The more 'Realist' element of the UN system, the Security Council, has been less radical but has become a 'widener', if not a 'deepener'. In 2000 the Security Council passed a resolution on a non-military issue for the first time when it debated the global HIV/AIDS pandemic, and others have since followed (see Chapter 7).

Many states have come to take a widened approach to security since the 1990s. The US Clinton administration made extensive use of academic advisers and a burgeoning literature on the national security imperative of taking on board non-military concerns now that the Soviet threat had receded. The impact of this was made explicit in the 1994 'National Security Strategy', an annual foreign policy manifesto: 'Not all security risks are military in nature. Transnational phenomena such as terrorism, narcotics trafficking, environmental degradation, rapid population growth and refugee flows also have security implications for both present and long term American policy' (White House 1994: 1). Clinton's widening approach to security owed much to his special adviser Strobe Talbot who, in turn, was inspired by Joseph Nye's concept of 'soft power' (Nye 1990). Soft power for Nye denotes the non-military and non-economic dimensions of state power, derived from possessing good information and a positive international reputation. For the US government, being 'on top' of information on global issues was useful not only for better comprehending problems like AIDS and transnational crime, but also for advancing the US's standing in the world. Explicit recognition that the protection of US citizens was a domestic as well as foreign policy matter then came in the aftermath of the September 11th 2001 terrorist strikes on New York and Washington, with the launch of a new government department for 'Homeland Security'.

Whilst many other governments have come to be 'wideners', few have taken the more radical step of deepening as well as widening in embracing human security. The Canadian government like their southern neighbour were influenced by Nye but have gone further and repeatedly expressed their support for (narrow) human security in their foreign policy statements. Canada's Foreign Minister from 1996 to 2000, Lloyd Axworthy, advanced the concept rhetorically in the UN General Assembly and other global forums and practically, by being a leading advocate for the creation of the International Criminal Court. Cynics have suggested that this strategy was just a tactical move by the Canadian government to raise the diplomatic profile of a middle-ranking power in an exercise of populism (McDonald 2002: 282). Axworthy's advocacy of 'soft power' gives some credence to this since Nye's concept ultimately is concerned with the advancement of state interests rather than altruism or the global interest, but the Canadian government has done much to further global political responses for the common good. The Canadians, for example, have been at the forefront of campaigns to ban the use of land mines and reform the UN Security Council so that it is less constrained by power politics.

Perhaps most significantly for the advancement of deepened security, the Canadian government signed a declaration with their Norwegian counterparts at the 1998 Lysøen Conference launching the Human Security Network. This network advocates the development of global policies focused on the human interest, whether or not these happen to coincide with state interests. By 2017 the network included eleven other states, both geographically and politically diverse (Austria, Chile, Costa Rica, Greece, Republic of Ireland, Jordan, Mali, Netherlands, Slovenia, Switzerland and Thailand).

> Human security has become both a new measure of global security and a new agenda for global action. Safety is the hallmark of freedom from fear, while well-being is the target of freedom from want. Human security and human development are thus two sides of the same coin, mutually reinforcing and leading to a conducive environment for each other.
>
> (Human Security Network 1999)

As previously mentioned, the wider 'freedom from want' variant of human security, favoured by the UNDP (and acknowledged by the Human Security Network), has only one clear governmental backer: Japan.

The securitization of issues

It is clear that designating an issue as a matter of security is not just a theoretical question but carries 'real world' significance. The traditional, Realist way of framing security presupposes that military issues (and certain economic issues for Neo-realists) are security issues and as such must be prioritized by governments above other 'low politics' issues, important though these might be.

As stated earlier, most governments do tend to be somewhat Realist in their foreign policies and this high-politics/low-politics distinction is evident in the level of state expenditure typically allocated to the achievement of military security as opposed to other issue areas. Africa is the continent that has had the highest growth in military expenditure in recent years (an increase of 65 per cent between 2004 and 2014), after a previous decade of stagnation (*Economist* 2014). This, though, does not reflect an escalation of military security concerns. Contrary to much popular assumption, Africa, in intergovernmental terms, is a comparatively peaceful continent with only a limited history of classic state-to-state wars. In this regard the continent stands in good comparison to more developed and democratic Europe and has even prompted some to refer to an 'African peace' (Henderson 2008). The only major inter-state wars since the continent began to largely rule itself from the 1960s have been the 1978–9 invasion of Uganda by Tanzania (which is often viewed as a humanitarian intervention) and the wars between Ethiopia and Eritrea (1998–2000) and Sudan and South Sudan (2013–), both of which followed the secession of the latter. In addition, whilst there is huge variation across the continent, it is very hard to argue that hunger and famine do not represent greater threats to life in Africa than armed conflict, either intergovernmental or civil.

Military threats are, of course, more apparent for some countries than others, so global figures give a better insight into the balance between health and defence expenditure. You could posit, for example, that African peace is a measure of the success of national defence policies. However, the scale of threats to the world as a whole is quantifiable and, as a result, the misprioritizing of expenditure becomes obvious. World military expenditure accounts for 2.3 per cent of global GDP (World Bank 2017), whilst world health expenditure makes up 9.9 per cent of global GDP (WHO 2017). Over a third of the world's health expenditure is private and so cannot be considered as government prioritizing of health (except in so far as it is considered as an alternative to public health). Overall, then, governments allocate two to three times as much money to health as to military security. Consider this is relation to the relative threat to people's lives posed by military and health threats (Table 1.3).

In considering the figures in Table 1.3 a few qualifications need to be taken into account. It is entirely natural to die of ill health since we all die in the end and 'old age' or 'natural causes' make up a significant proportion of the deaths by 'disease'. However, a third of all deaths are from communicable diseases which cannot be thought of as inevitable. In addition, many of the people who die from

TABLE 1.3 Global causes of death, 2015 (million)

Disease/ill health	51.07
Accidents	3.31
Suicide	0.83
Criminal violence	0.41
War/political violence	0.17
Natural disasters	0.02

Source: *Lancet* 2016.

non-communicable diseases die 'prematurely' from ailments like cancer which are, at least partially, avoidable. Furthermore, 'disease' incorporates deaths from malnutrition which most certainly are politically avoidable (see Chapter 4). Also, while some accidents may be unavoidable and, to a certain extent, 'natural', this is, in fact, a pretty small proportion even for so-called 'natural disasters' (see Chapter 9).

It is an indication of how the study of security in IR has become skewed over time that the issue most associated with the discipline is a comparatively minor threat to most people in the world. Of all of the security threats considered in this book the average citizen of the world is least threatened by military action from another state or a foreign non-state actor. Threats are invariably close to home and familiar. This is exemplified by the fact that more people kill themselves each year than are killed in both homicides and 'political killings' combined (see Chapter 7).

Security 'wideners', including some Realists, accept that non-military issues can become 'securitized' and be privileged with 'national security' status. The issues securitized in this way, however, are usually arbitrarily defined. The tendency has been, on the one hand, to select non-military issues which military forces can help deal with, such as fighting drugs barons abroad or assisting in civil emergency operations. On the other hand, 'securitization' has sometimes been granted to external non-military problems on the basis that they have domestic military repercussions. Issues such as AIDS or environmental degradation in distant countries may de-stabilize regional balances of power and trigger military conflict which the onlooking government may be drawn into or affected by in some capacity. Hence, with widening, the logic of national interest and prioritizing high politics is not really challenged. It is more of a refinement of the way in which external threats are calculated and a case of allowing 'low politics' to rise to prominence in the absence of major 'high politics' threats. Military defence is still being prioritized and security is still being defined as a very specific noun rather than as an adjective.

The Copenhagen School approach takes a step forward from widening in using the methodology of the 'speech act' to define when an issue becomes a security issue. In this approach, security issues can be military or non-military but are distinguishable by the urgency that is attached to them in political discourse. 'If by means of an argument about the priority and urgency of an existential threat the securitizing actor has managed to break free of procedures or rules he or she would otherwise be bound by, we are witnessing an act of securitization' (Buzan, Waever & de Wilde 1998: 25). This methodology allows for a more behavioural definition of security than 'conventional widening' since issues given priority by people other than the government are included in the framework. However, this approach still leaves the act of securing threatened people to the state. This can result in life-threatening issues being excluded from consideration because the government still chooses not to prioritize them or because the voices speaking for securitization are insufficiently loud. Security threats particular to women, for example, tend to be marginalized because of difficulties in 'being heard' amongst the 'speakers of security' in society (see Chapter 5). Non-military issues are more easily accommodated by the speech act approach but there is still a large measure of subjectivity and relativism in leaving the demarcation to governments rather than objective analysis.

The political practice of widening security has sometimes proved counter to the interests of the people affected by the issue due to a clumsy militarization of tasks previously performed by more appropriate personnel. Recent post-conflict 'nation-building' exercises in Afghanistan and Iraq have been notable for a militarization of development projects, with remaining armed forces being redeployed to reconstruction tasks and 'winning the hearts and minds' of the locals. Such 'humanitarian' roles may have some beneficial results for local populations, but are, of course, ultimately driven by military expediency rather than human security. The disillusionment of pressure groups with this phenomenon was made clear in 2004 when Médecins Sans Frontières pulled out of Afghanistan, with its President, Dr Rowan Gillies, declaring: 'we refuse to accept a vision of a future where civilians trapped in the hell of war can only receive life-saving aid from the armies that wage it' (Gillies 2004). One consequence of this phenomenon has been a backlash against the concept of human security by many Critical Theorists and Development Studies specialists as merely representing the militarization of development. Many academic applications of the concept have, indeed, taken the approach that it is a 'merging of development and [military] security' (Duffield 2001), but, for the concept to have real meaning, it is important not to conflate it with 'widened security' and to recognize that a proper application of human security to development puts the security of the vulnerable centre stage, not the geopolitical interests of states.

Security *is* subjective in that individual fears do not necessarily tally with the reality of threats, but individual needs are a better guide to the issues that matter than the priorities of governments. The security of governments often does not equate with the security of the people they are meant to represent. This has already been acknowledged by governments in sanctioning the development of global human rights law, and is still evident in the existence of global systemic failings such as the widespread persistence of hunger and treatable diseases in a world with sufficient food and medicine to counter them (see Table 1.4).

TABLE 1.4 Security threats

Threats	The threatened			
	Individuals	Societal groups	Government	The world
Individuals	crime, 'hate crimes'	'hate crimes'		
Societal groups	'hate crimes'	genocide	civil war	
Government	human rights abuses	genocide, politicide	war, economic sanctions	nuclear war
Global structures	poverty, industrial accidents, pollution	global warming	global warming	
Non-human	disease, natural disasters			asteroid/ comet collision

Conclusions

If politics is about the 'authoritative allocation of values' (Easton 1965: 96), issues arise over contention over certain values. In International Relations the traditional assumption has been that the core value is the preservation of state sovereignty and that this automatically takes pride of place at the top of domestic and international political agendas. However, it has become increasingly evident over the years that values other than this are becoming prioritized and that the pursuit of state security can often undermine human security. Political issues are myriad but can ultimately be distilled down to contention over the allocation of certain core values such as security, economic gain and altruism.

It is perfectly natural to give priority to security over the other values since it is a precondition for realizing their allocation. If security is considered from the perspective of individual people, however, issues are less easily compartmentalized. Most issues of state altruism, such as the granting of emergency foreign aid, are matters of life and death to the people affected. Many issues of state economic gain, such as the altering of the terms of international trade, are security matters for people in other states affected by the change. State altruism exists in the world, as do some limitations to the pursuit of economic gain, but not to the same prominence as in the domestic politics of states where individual people are empowered with votes and/or rights of citizenship. Individual security is recognized in democratic states as overriding other values (at least most of the time), as is evidenced by health and safety laws restricting business activities, and 'social security' laws. In global politics, though, issues of life and death frequently are not treated as priorities because they do not coincide with state gain or security. The blinkered pursuit of profit can enrich some but imperil others. If saving others from abuse or disaster is seen as an act of charity, rather than political duty, it will only happen infrequently and selectively. Actual threats to people (Table 1.3) and perceived threats (Table 1.2) are so far removed from the way in which issues are conventionally ordered on the political agenda by states that International Relations theory and international political practice need to find ways of accommodating them, or cease to be connected in any meaningful way with human behaviour and needs.

Human rights policies have developed significantly in recent decades but this has not yet come close to securing *all* humans (see Chapter 5). Governments tend to prioritize the rights and lesser interests of their own citizens over the fundamental rights of others, and human rights are still routinely treated as secondary to 'national security' issues where the two are perceived to clash. The tightening up of migration laws and the increased surveillance of foreign citizens in the present 'war against terror' in the US and Western Europe represent cases in point. The lives of far more people in today's world, however, are imperilled by human rights abuses than by terrorist and conventional military attacks. Throughout the total war era of the twentieth century a case could be made that the security of individuals was inextricably tied up with that of their states, but that era has now passed into history. Today the issues that threaten people's lives bear such little relation to those issues that dominate the international political agenda that statecentricism is impeding both the study and the practice of that most fundamental of political concerns: securing people. The word security derives from the Latin *sine cura*, meaning 'without care'.

As such it is a fairly elastic term since the 'cares' may be major fears or minor frustrations. Complete freedom from care is both impractical and undesirable. Human life that does not have any everyday concerns is unimaginable, and a complete absence of risk-taking in society would eliminate much beneficial scientific progress and entertainment from life. As such this enquiry into security in global politics focuses on the most meaningful fears there are: threats to the lives of people.

 **Key points**

- The study of global security is a sub-set of the discipline of International Relations.
- The Realist paradigm of International Relations traditionally has dominated the study of security and focused enquiry on military security in inter-state relations.
- The end of the Cold War brought about a re-appraisal of the Realist orthodoxy in Security Studies since the scale of military threats had receded and the logic of the balance of power as a necessary condition for peace had been undermined.
- Some Neo-realists contend that Security Studies should still be preoccupied with state security and military issues or risk becoming too diverse a subject to give proper treatment to these still vital concerns.
- 'Wideners' in Security Studies (including some Neo-realists) favour extending the subject to incorporate non-military issues which affect the security of the state.
- A 'deepening' approach to Security Studies, favoured by the Liberal-Pluralists, Critical Theorists and Social Constructivists in International Relations, widens the range of issues to be considered but also shifts the focus of the discipline to the security of people rather than of states: that is, human security.

 Notes

1   Non-governmental actors are taken to include all private organizations with political influence. Hence, alongside those groups conventionally thought of as 'NGOs', pressure groups, the term also covers multi-national corporations (MNCs), non-state 'terrorist' groups, organized crime groups and organized religions.
2   Although it can be argued that, unusual though this 'surrender' was, it was essentially a victory for the power politics approach of the USA in the 1980s which compelled the USSR to capitulate.
3   Buzan is generally characterized as an 'English School' theorist: a branch of Realism characterized by a rejection of the scientific method and, so, receptive to the idea that social and cultural factors – as well as state interests – can influence international affairs.

 **Recommended reading**

Buzan, B., Waever, O. & de Wilde, J. (1998) *Security. A New Framework for Analysis*, Boulder, CO & London: Lynne Rienner.
Collins, A. (ed.) (2013) *Contemporary Security Studies*, 3rd edn, Oxford: Oxford University Press.
Hough, P., Malik, S., Pilbeam, B. & Roberts, A. (2014) *International Security Studies: Theory and Practice*, London: Routledge.

McSweeney, B. (1999) *Security, Identity and Interests: A Sociology of International Relations*, Cambridge: Cambridge University Press.

Morgenthau, H. (1972) *Politics among Nations*, 5th edn, New York: A. Knopf.

Ullman, R. (1983) 'Redefining Security', *International Security*, 8(1): 129–53.

Wyn-Jones, R. (1999) *Security, Strategy and Critical Theory*, Boulder, CO: Lynne Rienner.

 Useful web links

- Human Security Network: www.humansecuritynetwork.org/

- Stockholm International Peace Research Institute (SIPRI): www.sipri.se/

- United Nations Development Programme Human Development Reports: http://hdr.undp.org/

- World Health Organization's *World Health Report*: www.who.int/whr/en/

Military threats to security from states

War between states has always been central to the study of International Relations and widely accepted as an inevitable feature of state-to-state interactions. This is understandable given that, historically, this form of conflict has been so prominent and so costly in lives. The Realist model of powerful states vying for supremacy, restrained only by the countervailing power of other states, seems to be borne out by considering the scale and nature of the major wars in history. Most of the conflicts listed in Table 2.1 were 'clashes of the Titans' involving the world's premier military powers. The four biggest clashes had a catalytic effect on international relations beyond their direct human and governmental impact in the states directly involved. These wars were infernos in which new international orders, normatively altering state relations, were forged. The Korean and Vietnamese wars, however, were only indirect clashes of the Titans and, in fact, great power collisions have not been seen since the ultimate of such clashes in 1939–45. That the potential 'mother' of all clashes of the Titans, the Cold War, should end with a peaceful transition to a new order, rather than military victory, served to challenge the ascendancy of Realism in the study of military security. Incidences of inter-state war, in general, have also receded over recent decades. The spectre of this sort of war, however, still looms large over much of the conduct of government foreign policies.

TABLE 2.1 The ten bloodiest inter-state wars in history

	War	Years	Battle deaths
1	Second World War	1939–45	20,000,000
2	First World War	1914–18	8,500,000
3	Thirty Years War	1618–48	2,071,000
4	Napoleonic War	1803–15	1,869,000
5	War of the Spanish Succession	1701–13	1,324,300
6	Korean War	1950–3	1,200,000
7	Vietnam War	1965–73	1,200,000
8	The Crusades	1095–1272	1,000,000
9	Iran–Iraq War	1980–8	850,000
10	Seven Years War	1755–63	500,000

Source: White 2001.

Is war inevitable?

Understanding the causes of war – and consequently also the bases for peace – must be the fundamental concern of the study of military security and, many would say, of International Relations as a whole. The precise causes of war are, of course, myriad, but they can be distilled down to some general explanatory factors about the nature of the political world. A landmark IR text in this regard was Kenneth Waltz's 1959 *Man, the State and War* which pioneered the widely adopted and adapted explanatory framework of three levels of analysis: man, the state and the international system (Waltz 1959).

TABLE 2.2 Waltz's levels of analysis

	Level of analysis	Cause of war
1	Man	Human nature
2	State	Socio-political factors
3	International system	Anarchy

Source: Waltz 1959.

Realists

Waltz, as a Realist, held a Hobbesian view of human nature as being aggressive and selfish and, hence, was of the view that armed conflict over clashes of interest was inevitable. Notwithstanding some improvement in the last two decades, wars have become more frequent and more deadly as time has proceeded, contradicting the idea that humanity has become less savage as it has evolved. From this, Realists conclude that violent conflict is an inevitable feature of international politics. They laud Clausewitz for his famous dictum that war is 'a continuation of political intercourse, with the addition of other means' (Clausewitz 1976: 605), and argue

BOX 2.1 **Carl von Clausewitz**

Clausewitz's *On War* remains the most revered book on military strategy ever written and a standard text on contemporary reading lists for Security Studies students and military officer trainees, despite being written in the 1830s and never finished by the author. Clausewitz wrote the book whilst serving as the head of a Prussian military academy in Berlin. He had previously served as an officer in the Prussian army after joining as a cadet at the age of 12 and had seen action from a young age in the Napoleonic Wars. Clausewitz died in the cholera pandemic that swept Europe in 1831 before completing the book, but it was published posthumously by his widow in the following year.

As a result of this, *On War* contains a number of gaps and has frequently been misinterpreted. In particular, Clausewitz's insistence on seeing war as a facet of politics has often wrongly been understood as the glorification of war. Clausewitz shared Machiavelli's pessimism about human cynicism in politics but, as the quote which opens this chapter indicates, advocated war only when absolutely necessary and justifiable. The uncertainties inherent in battle, or the 'fog of war', make any decision to initiate conflict a gamble which should only be undertaken when the odds are stacked in your favour.

Over a hundred years after his death Clausewitz's rational approach saw him lauded by International Relations Realists as 'one of their own' but, such is his insight, other approaches have come to claim inspiration from his work. Wyn-Jones, a Critical Theorist critic of Realism, comments: 'I doubt very much that Clausewitz, with his speculative bent and his interest in Hegelian dialectics, would have ever made the grade in traditional security studies' (Wyn-Jones 1999: ch. 5).

that it should not be treated as an aberration but as a rational foreign policy option. This position is not, as it is sometimes painted, that of the warmonger. The glorification of warfare on the grounds of its usefulness for 'nation building', or even for humanity as a whole, by a twisted application of the Darwinian notion of the 'survival of the fittest', has permeated Fascism and virulent strains of nationalism but this is not Clausewitzian Realism. The conviction of the Realists is that war is a last resort but still very much a resort. According to this view, war is sometimes necessary and its occurrence cannot and should not be wished away. War, according to Betts, should be viewed as a 'rational instrument of policy rather than mindless murder' (Betts 1997: 8).

However, whilst Waltz buys into the human nature argument, the limitations of this explanation prompted him to additionally consider the higher levels of analysis. Looking at the historic pattern of warfare, it is quickly apparent that not all countries go to war with the same regularity, and some, like Switzerland, appear to be able to avoid becoming embroiled in armed conflicts for many centuries. The foreign policy choice of war may be rational but it is a choice not all governments take and it is evident that some states are more warlike than others. War, hence, is a political choice as well as a natural human inclination. In Waltz's third level of analysis he then tackled the point that the decision for governments on whether or not to go to war was influenced by wider international factors. The Realist assumption that the international political system of states is anarchic necessitates a readiness of governments to go to war if the national interest or a threat to the balance of power makes it necessary. Waltz thus pioneered the revamp of Realism into Neo-realism by adding greater consideration of structural explanations for war and peace alongside the human nature arguments.

Further differences of interpretation have emerged since Realism's 1940s–50s heyday, in response to both a changing world and the challenges that came to be posed by the re-emergence of Liberalism and arrival of other, rival theoretical frameworks. In particular, Realists came to differ as to whether the inevitability of conflict should be explained primarily by reference to levels 1 or 3 of Waltz's model. For *Offensive Realists*, like Mearsheimer, the anarchic system encourages selfish behaviour, but this is still an approach imbued with a deep pessimism and one which assumes the worst of power-seeking states pursuing hegemony (Mearsheimer 2001). Offensive Realists believe in the logic of the balance of power but are less convinced of its capacity to restrain power-hungry states than others within the broad school of thought. *Defensive Realists*, like Kenneth Waltz, accept that systemic factors have become more important than human nature in understanding conflict but they are less pessimistic about this change and believe powerful states are more inclined to settle for the status quo than push for hegemony (Waltz 1959). In other words, Defensive Realists see the state system as less anarchic than classic or Offensive Realists and are more positive about the potential offered by inter-state cooperation.

Liberal-Pluralists

Waltz's levels of analysis methodology also provides a useful means of comprehending alternative, Liberal and Marxist explanations for war. Liberal-Pluralists dispute the Realist proposition that war is an inevitable feature of international politics in any sort of world. The brutishness of human nature inherent in the Realist analysis is rejected and a more optimistic assessment made on the likelihood of war remaining a central feature of political life in the future. Just as many people lead blameless lives, so many states avoid violent conflicts and, though conflict is sometimes unavoidable for the preservation of justice in the world, it could be consigned to the history books given political change. To Liberals the lack of progress of humanity in curbing the resort to war is more about nurture than nature. It is socio-political rather than natural. In particular, at the state level democracies are considered to be more peaceful in their relations with other democracies and so democratization is welcomed.

At the international level the state system is viewed by Liberals as a further socio-political explanation for war. The arbitrary division of the world into competitive units has seen the populations of these states dragged into wars by aggressive self-serving governments, particularly non-democratic ones. This serves to exacerbate disputes beyond what is necessary or rational and leads to wars being prompted by misperception of an adversary and/or the likely gains to accrue from attacking them. If war were truly rational, every state which initiated conflict would win, which, of course, has not been the case. Hence, for Liberal-Pluralists, a cure exists to rid humanity of the cancer of war: the removal of its root cause through the erosion of state sovereignty. *Interdependence* and, to a greater extent, political integration serve to diminish war by revealing that the mutual gains inherent in cooperation outweigh the spoils of individual gain and reducing the likelihood of misperception causing unnecessary wars. The improbability of a new Franco-German confrontation, after three major wars in the course of a human lifespan, is the classic case used to uphold this view. Liberals also distance themselves from the Realist assumption of international anarchy by seeing international law, in the guise of collective security – the international community together keeping the peace – as representing a way in which military order can be maintained in international relations.

Marxists

Marxism, on questions of war as on most matters, focuses very much on the third level of analysis, but for economic reasons. Both human nature and state type are held to be largely irrelevant in the face of structural economic forces. The Marxist/Structuralist approach considers economic gain to be the underlying cause of most wars. Lenin famously argued that, contrary to most assumptions, the First World War was a war of imperialism, with the rival factions from Europe and the USA seeking to achieve mastery of each other's colonial possessions. In this view it was the inherent expansionist tendency of capitalism which prompted European imperial expansion and then US-led anti-Communist aggression and economic 'neo-imperialism' in the twentieth century. Drawing on the philosophy of Hegel, Marxists consider that history is determined by *dialectical* struggles, and the overthrow of capitalism by socialism would be the ultimate conclusion of such culture-clashes.

Contemporary neo-Marxists put particular emphasis on the influence of vested business interests – the military-industrial complex – in pushing states towards the use of force to secure economic gains. Wars can be a profitable exercise and it is in the interests of the armed forces, the arms industry and core importers like oil corporations that war remains a foreign policy option. As evidence that this proposition is not confined to the far left consider the words of US Republican President Eisenhower at the height of the Cold War:

> In the councils of government, we must guard against the acquisition of unwarranted influence, whether sought or unsought, by the military-industrial complex. The potential for the disastrous rise of misplaced power exists and will persist.
>
> (Eisenhower 1961)

Social Constructivists

Social Constructivism cannot be plotted onto the levels of analysis table as readily as the other approaches since it is an approach without the normative ideological roots of Realism, Liberalism or Marxism. Constructivists dislike assumptions and they cannot be said to have a 'default position' on human nature or state- or inter-state-level routes to peace. Social Constructivism has, though, contributed to the debate on the causes of war by bringing into focus questions of human agency and the importance of culture and ideas in understanding conflict. The greater subjectivity of the Constructivist approach lends itself to the contention that wars are often better explained by clashes of culture than abstract concepts such as power vacuums, the economic structure of the world or an absence of democracy. *Some* people are aggressive, but not all, and *some* states see the world as anarchic, but not all. Although generally less convinced by the certainties of the democratic peace theory, many Social Constructivists do share some common ground with Liberals in believing that war is not inevitable since governments can come to redefine their interests in favour of collective security and peace (Wendt 2003). Perhaps we can learn to stop fighting?

Prelude to the present military order

Two issues, very much global in their scope, dominated international relations in the latter part of the twentieth century: the Cold War and the process of decolonization. Both issues were largely resolved by the early 1990s, but their legacy lives on in many aspects of the contemporary global political system and in the conceptualization of their military security by states. The biggest Cold War alliance still exists, some Cold War tensions still persist, and the extraordinarily deadly means of prosecuting wars devised in this period continues to threaten the security of the whole world. Decolonization globalized the state system, transforming the make-up of that once exclusive club of sovereign states into the diverse membership that characterizes it today, whilst legitimizing independence struggles, many of which continue to resonate.

The Cold War

The term 'Cold War' entered popular contemporary parlance in the USA in 1946–7 to describe the tense hostility that had set in in relations with their recent wartime allies the USSR. The period of hostility and rivalry between the two coalitions led by these states, from the end of the Second World War in 1945 to 1990, was unlike any other phase of history. The two sides avoided outright military conflict with each other but fought out many *proxy wars*, whereby one side would fight an enemy sponsored by the other side (such as with the US war in Vietnam or the USSR's invasion of Afghanistan) or both sides would sponsor rivals in a conflict whilst cheering on from the sidelines (as for example with the Arab-Israeli dispute). Whilst this era cannot be said to be one of peace when it contained two of the bloodiest wars in history, in Korea and Vietnam, direct war between the major protagonists was avoided by the maintenance of a 'balance of terror', whereby both sides were deterred from such action by the massive scale of each other's military capabilities. The key variable that made this such a distinct phase of history was, of course, the advent of atomic/nuclear weapons, which served to make war something that threatened not only hostile states but the entire population of the Earth.

Why the wartime allies came to divide into two such antagonistic opponents so shortly after the Second World War is hotly disputed by historians of the period. Three broad schools of thought have emerged: the Traditionalists, the Revisionists and the Post-Revisionists. Traditionalists lay the blame for the Cold War with the USSR and argue that the confrontation occurred because, shortly after the ending of the Second World War, the USSR behaved in a manner which suggested they wanted to expand their influence over Europe and, at the same time, rebuffed American gestures of support and cooperation, such as the Marshall Plan of financial aid (Feis 1970; Schlesinger 1967). Revisionists take the opposite viewpoint, with writers such as the Kolkos and LaFeber pinning the blame for the Cold War on US aggression towards the USSR traceable back to the Bolshevik revolution (Kolko & Kolko 1972; LaFeber 1991). Post-Revisionists, though, emerged in the 1970s and 1980s with a different take on the causes of the Cold War. Writers such as John Lewis Gaddis, instead of blaming either side for initiating hostilities, take a more detached, Realist view which argues that both sides acted expansively in an inevitable process of filling the power vacuum that had been created in Europe (Gaddis 1997). The decline in power of Germany, France and the UK after the Second World War transformed the political landscape of the world, with two superpowers outside of the European heartland now ruling the roost. Those two superpowers, acting in accord with the logic of power politics, competed for the mastery of Europe, it is argued. The USSR did so in a traditional manner, by colonizing neighbouring countries in Central Europe. The USA did so in a more subtle manner, by linking themselves to the countries of Western and Southeastern Europe, militarily through NATO and economically through the Marshall Plan and other agreements. Hence, from this perspective, the Cold War was a classic balance of power struggle like many others throughout history, only this time conducted on a bilateral rather than multilateral basis.

Whichever perspective on the Cold War is taken, it is clear that American foreign policy underwent a profound shift in the late 1940s. The isolationist stance that had characterized US policy from the 1920s, entering the Second World War only after being attacked, was swept aside by a new approach to become known as the *Truman Doctrine*. President Harry Truman announced in 1947 that 'it must be the policy of The United States to support free peoples who are resisting subjugation by armed minorities or outside pressures'. The 'armed minorities' referred to were Marxist revolutionaries and the 'outside pressures' was code for the USSR. This represented a shift from the previous president Franklin Roosevelt (who died in office in 1945), who had been more tolerant of the USSR and consented to the principle of a Soviet sphere of influence in Central Europe at the Moscow Conference of 1944 (although he was not present at the meeting). American containment was put into practice with the signing of a series of bilateral and multilateral military alliances in the late 1940s and 1950s between the USA and countries of Asia and Europe located close to the USSR. The support for 'free peoples' heralded by Truman was put into

TABLE 2.3 Phases of the Cold War

First Cold War, 1945–69

1 Confrontation, 1945–62

The Cold War could be said to have begun with the declaration of the Truman Doctrine in 1947 but hostilities in US–USSR relations can be traced back to the closing stages of the Second World War and even before. In 1949 the USSR developed the atom bomb and NATO was formed, setting the parameters for two armed camps and a massive arms build-up. The Berlin blockade brought the two sides near to war that year when the USSR challenged the US–UK–French control of West Berlin. That year also saw China undergo Communist revolution and then, in the following year, fight with the North Koreans against the USA and her allies.

The Warsaw Pact was formed in 1955 by the USSR as an East European military alliance to rival NATO, and the USA and USSR came as close as they ever did to war in 1962 with the Cuban Missile Crisis when the USSR attempted to station warheads on the island.

2 Coexistence, 1963–9

The Cuban Missile Crisis was resolved with a deal whereby the USA removed missiles from Turkey in exchange for USSR not stationing weapons on Cuba. The very real possibility of nuclear war in 1962 prompted improved dialogue between the two superpowers. Arms control agreements were initiated and the logic of deterrence set in to US–Soviet relations with both sides recognizing the other's right to parity in military terms as a means of guaranteeing peace through the *balance of terror*. There was still military conflict in the Cold War, however, as evidenced by the US role in the Vietnam War from 1961 to 1975 supporting South Vietnam against Communist North Vietnam.

Détente, 1969–79

A major improvement in relations between the USA and USSR occurred after the accession of Nixon as US president. Extensive bilateral arms control deals were agreed and the 1975 Helsinki Accords saw the East and West blocs agree on various forms of political cooperation. The USA recognized Communist China for the first time in 1979. Some tensions remained, such as in the support for opposing sides in the Arab–Israeli disputes from 1973, but there was optimism that the Cold War might be coming to an end.

Second Cold War, 1979–90

1 Confrontation, 1979–85

The USSR's invasion of Afghanistan in 1979 ended détente. The USA did not consider this a tolerable incursion into a country in the Soviet sphere of influence and a period of renewed intense antagonism between East and West occurred. President Reagan increased military expenditure, abandoned arms control agreements and cut many economic links with what he termed 'the evil empire'.

2 End of the Cold War, 1985–90

Reagan's aggression succeeded in upping the ante to a point the USSR could not match, particularly with the 'Star Wars' Space Defence Initiative (SDI). Gorbachev came to power in the USSR in 1985 and, in order to save his country from economic ruin, embarked on a policy of rapprochement with the West, pulling out of Afghanistan and signalling a withdrawal from Central Europe. Gorbachev and US President Bush declared the Cold War to be over at the 1989 Malta Summit as Communist governments fell in the six countries of the Eastern Bloc. A 1990 Paris Treaty officially ended the forty-five-year power struggle.

practice in 1950 with the armed intervention by the USA and a number of allies in South Korea to aid their resistance struggle against invasion by Communist North Korea.

The Cold War went through distinct phases where hostility between East and West became more or less intense. Writers differ in the precise dating of these periods of thawing or freezing in Cold War relations but there is broad agreement on three main phases, summarized in Table 2.3.

Decolonization

At around the same time as the Cold War was coming to an end, another prolonged global struggle, erupting in periodic bursts of violence, was receiving its curtain call on the world stage. In 1990 Namibia finally achieved independence from a colonial power, South Africa, in the throes of democratic revolution. Although this was not the world's last colonial struggle, the end of the twenty-four-year armed campaign was important symbolically because it left the African continent free of European and European-settler rule. In 1945 there were only three independent states in Africa: South Africa (independent from the UK since 1910), Ethiopia (liberated from Italian rule in 1941) and Liberia (the only African state never to be colonized). Revolutions rarely happen in isolation and the process whereby Africa and large swathes of Asia threw off colonial rule can be viewed as a global phenomenon.

That this wave of decolonization (a previous wave had swept Latin America in the nineteenth century) should occur at the same time as the Cold War is not merely a quirk of history. The same balance of power shift which saw Western European powers fall behind the USA and USSR in the global pecking order and contributed to the Cold War, gave the colonies of France, the UK and other states the opportunity to turn the pre-1945 order on its head. This was most explicitly demonstrated in Vietnam, where anti-colonial war against France was directly succeeded by Communist war against a new external foe, the USA. In addition, Marxist ideology saw colonialism as a symptom of capitalism and hence the struggle against colonizers as something to be encouraged. This appeared to be confirmed in 1961 when Soviet President Khruschev announced that the USSR would support 'wars of national liberation' throughout the world. This perception of Soviet and Chinese influence prompted US involvement in Vietnam. In general, however, it was post-colonial power struggles, rather than the overthrow of European rule, which tended to be transformed into Cold War conflict. In Angola, the USSR, along with Cuba, gave backing to leftist guerrillas, whilst the USA supported the anti-Communist faction. That the Chinese should find themselves on the same side as the Americans in this conflict, however, gives some credence to the post-revisionist assessment of the Cold War as more of a plain power struggle than an ideological confrontation.

Indeed, decolonization was applauded not only by governments of the left. The USA used its position of mastery over the old powers of Europe to assert its moral support for the principle of self-rule for colonies. One of the few things the two new superpowers could agree upon in the late 1940s and early 1950s was that the age of colonialism was a part of the old European order which should be swept away. This was, of course, a somewhat hypocritical view given the USSR's recent acquisition of six satellite states in Central Europe and the USA's colonial rule of Puerto Rico and indirect control over South Korea, South Vietnam, Taiwan and the Philippines, but it was clear that the world had entered a new phase of international relations in 1945 in more ways than one.

A New World Order?

President George Bush (senior) is generally credited with having popularized contemporary usage of the term New World Order in a series of speeches in 1990 and 1991 to signify that the UN-backed and US-led allied force sent to Kuwait to drive out invading Iraqi forces was indicative of a very different world than that seen up until the end of the Cold War.

> What is at stake is more than one small country, it is a big idea – a new world order, where diverse nations are drawn together in common cause to achieve the universal aspirations of mankind: peace and security, freedom, and the rule of law.
>
> (Bush 1991)

Such optimism for a brighter future whilst basking in the afterglow of a triumphant victory is nothing new in international relations. The defeat of Napoleon Bonaparte in 1815 at Waterloo was achieved by a coalition of European powers, ending twelve years of conflict and marked by the Congress of Vienna which heralded a period of great power cooperation known as the 'Concert of Europe'. For a period of nearly forty years there was peace in Europe assisted by a loose system of diplomatic co-management of the continent between five countries: Britain, Prussia, Russia, Austria-Hungary and, novelly, their defeated but not estranged enemy France. The outbreak of the Crimean War of 1854, when Britain and France fought together with Turkey against Russia, effectively ended the Concert and Europe eschewed any attempt at collective policing until after the next epoch-making conflict, the First World War.

League of Nations

The 1919–20 Paris Peace Settlement following the First World War ushered in a new attempt to construct a better world order, led by the *Idealists*, most clearly articulated with the creation of the League of Nations. Idealist is a term that came to be applied to Liberal statesmen of the age, such as US President Woodrow Wilson, and academics, such as the UK's first professor of International Relations, Alfred Zimmern, who advocated that states should forgo the selfish pursuit of national interest and conduct their foreign affairs with a greater stress on international cooperation, morality and diplomatic openness. The world had been plunged into a war far more devastating than anything seen previously because states had aggressively pursued their own interests to the disregard of other states, bar those they had aligned themselves with in secretive military alliances. Hence the League of Nations sought to provide an arena whereby states could resolve disputes openly in conference or through the rulings of an international court (the Permanent Court of International Justice) and where protection for states could come from a global guarantee of collective security rather than through constructing covert military pacts.

Collective security is, in theory, a very old idea. Pierre Dubois, writing in the early fourteenth century, advocated the idea of the international community cooperating to keep the peace, and the liberal philosophers Kant and Bentham revived the notion, as an alternative to the balance of power, in the eighteenth and nineteenth centuries. The idea is also supported in the Holy Qur'an (49:9). Under this system acts of aggression prompt collective responses against the aggressors by the whole international community, rather than just by the attacked state and its allies or other states who consider their interests to be affected by the action. It was not until the League of Nations, though, that a system was put in place to make this idea a reality. The League enshrined collective security in its covenant, stating in Article 16 that a state waging war declared unjust by its member-states would be, in effect, waging war against the organization itself.

However, the League's peacekeeping mechanism failed and collective security was never activated. The outbreak of the Second World War was, of course, the clearest indication of this failure, but by this time the League had become an irrelevance anyway, having failed to act against blatant acts of aggression by its member-states on a number of occasions throughout the 1930s. In particular, the 1931 Japanese invasion of Manchuria, 1935 Italian invasion of Abyssinia (Ethiopia) and German military re-occupation of the Saar prompted some condemnations, but no military response. Soviet, German and Italian interventions in the 1936–9 Spanish Civil War were similarly ignored and although the USSR were expelled from the League in 1939 for the invasion of Finland, this was too little too late.

The League failed to implement collective security for two key reasons.

It did not represent the whole international community

The League of Nations was handicapped from the start by not being a truly global organization. The emerging superpower, the USA, never took up membership despite the fact that its President, Woodrow Wilson, had at the Paris Peace Settlement been its chief advocate. The USA, instead, retreated into its shell after the First World War, not to emerge until 1940 when the world had become a very different place. The other superpower in the making, the USSR, only joined the League in 1934, whilst Germany, Japan and Italy withdrew their memberships in annoyance at the token criticism they had received for their military adventurism. Collective security rests upon a genuinely collective commitment to upholding the peace and this is unlikely to be found if militarily powerful states are unwilling to contribute to this process or act against it.

Its decision-making procedure was unworkable

Shorn of any involvement by the USA and any real commitment to peace from Germany, Japan, Italy and the USSR, the League was left dominated by just two of the powerful states of the day, France and the UK. These two countries held permanent seats in the Council (as did the USSR during their membership) and represented the only serious military antidote to violations of the League's covenant. The French and British, however, having recently emerged from the bloodiest war in their histories and now embroiled in economic depression, did not have the stomach to become 'world policemen'. The two governments' policy towards aggression from other great powers was at the time one of 'appeasement' rather than confrontation, in the hope that granting some concessions to their rivals might be the best means of averting another catastrophic war. Hence the British and French governments went out of their way to ensure that condemnations of Japan for the horrific Manchurian invasion were not too severe, and that economic sanctions levied against Italy for the seemingly motiveless annexation of Abyssinia were cosmetic. The Council's voting system rested on unanimity which meant that Britain and France could always dictate the system, as could any of the other thirteen temporary member-states during their stay in the spotlight. Unanimity in an international organization, even amongst a sub-group of fifteen, is hard to find at the best of times and the 1930s was far from the best of times.

As with the Concert of Europe, the League of Nations ultimately collapsed amidst a new great power collision. Idealism came to be derided by a new generation of statesmen and scholars, the Realists, as being dangerously naïve and utopian. The Realists advocated a return to the order of the Concert of Europe on a global scale, with peace maintained by the great powers whilst respecting a balance of power between them. In this view the Crimean War had only occurred because Russia had upset the balance and the Concert should have been fully restored after they had been defeated. Balance had been noticeably lacking in international relations for the first half of the twentieth century, with the great powers generally divided into two armed camps and their expansions of power left unchecked. Idealism was not destroyed by the Realist backlash, however, and the construction of a new world order following the Second World War did not abandon its ideas so much as temper them with a heavy dose of Realism.

United Nations

The 1945–90 world order, in character, in many ways can be said to have been a hybrid of both the Concert and the League systems. The League of Nations was revamped in the guise of the United Nations and open diplomacy and international cooperation again encouraged. At the same time, however, a more Realist version of collective security was devised to be at the heart of the UN, with a 'concert' of five great powers entrusted to manage the system. The five great powers (the USA, UK, USSR, China and France) enjoyed the spoils of being on the winning side in the Second World War but they also learned the lesson of the Concert that was ignored by the League and sought to keep the vanquished on board in the new system. West Germany and Japan thus became key players in the new system (albeit economically rather than militarily) rather than dangerously ostracized. Japan had been on the winning side in the First World War but felt excluded by the other victors at the Paris Peace Settlement when the spoils were shared out, whilst Germany's harsh treatment is widely acknowledged as a factor behind the rise of Nazism.

The United Nations, in taking over the mantle of global peacekeeping from the League, did not abandon collective security, but sought to learn from its predecessor in devising a new more realistic and Realist system. The UN from the start set about ensuring that its membership was as universal as possible, in spite of a deep division in the international community from the global conflict just passing and the new one beginning to emerge. It maintained the idea of a fifteen-member sub-group to decide on peacekeeping strategy but was more explicit in granting privileges to the most powerful states. Unanimity was replaced with a voting system in which only five of the UN's Security Council would have the power to veto agreements. Those same five states would enjoy permanent membership of the Council, with the other ten members periodically elected from the rest of the UN membership and denied the power of veto.[1] These five states from the winning side in the Second World War were considered the great powers of the future and would, therefore, be essential in the implementation of collective security since there would be no standing UN army for such operations.

For the Security Council to act against threats to peace, whether to implement collective security or a lesser joint response, nine 'yes' votes are needed from the fifteen government representatives present at its venue in New York. Those nine affirmative votes, however, must include the assent of the 'permanent five'. Hence even fourteen against one would not be enough to secure agreement for an action if the 'one' is a permanent member. Those five countries, in effect, represent a sub-system within a sub-system, since their agreement is a precondition for action on behalf of the near-universal UN membership. Security Council members can elect to abstain rather than vote for or against a resolution which, for the permanent five, does not constitute a veto and would permit action if nine other votes are accrued. China chose this option in voting on the 1990 resolution triggering the Gulf War (Resolution 678) to distance itself from military action against Iraq but not be seen to block the will of the other Security Council members and the international community at large.

The Gulf War stands as one of only three occasions when collective security has been enacted. The first occasion was during the 'hottest' of the Cold War proxy conflicts, the Korean War. In 1950 the UN Security Council authorized international military action against North Korea for the invasion of South Korea. This first ever realization of a centuries-old Liberal dream was, however, very much a fluke event, never likely to be repeated during the Cold War. The Soviet Union and China did not use their vetoes to avert action against their Communist ally because neither of them were present in the Security Council when the vote was taken. Communist China had not been able to take up their seat in the UN, and with it their permanent place in the Security Council, because the USA had refused to grant diplomatic recognition to the new regime following the 1949 revolution. In protest at this the USSR boycotted a session of the Security Council allowing the USA to opportunistically push through a resolution that would otherwise certainly have been vetoed.

The USSR never repeated this form of protest and the Security Council remained paralysed until 1990 by the fact that the permanent five (including Communist China from 1979 after the normalization of relations with the USA) were unable to find unanimity to sanction any full military action against acts of aggression violating the UN Charter. The veto had been envisaged as a rare option of last resort for the permanent five, necessary to keep them on board for the maintenance of international peace, but became a routinely-used tactic to protect Cold War allies. In the first Cold War it was the USSR that made most use of the veto and in the second, when the changing UN membership began to deprive them of guaranteed support, it was the USA. This placed out of bounds any action against both countries' own military adventurism in Vietnam and Afghanistan or in response to the interventions of their 'client states' such as Israel (in the Lebanon) and Cuba (in Angola).

Collective security, covered by Chapter 7 of the UN Charter, is not the only peacekeeping option open to the Security Council and other, lesser, measures aiming to keep the peace were utilized during the Cold War. Chapter 6, which calls upon states to resolve disputes peacefully where possible, has been used as the basis for many Council resolutions sending in multilateral teams of UN monitoring troops to uphold ceasefire lines whilst diplomatic solutions are sought. Such UN forces were sent into Kashmir and Palestine in 1948 to assist in resolving the Arab-Israeli and Indo-Pakistani territorial disputes. The fact that both of these conflicts are still far from resolved today, though, gives an indication of the limitations to this UN peacekeeping strategy.

The realization that UN-assisted mediation was a limited means of restoring peace and that collective security was hamstrung by Cold War politics, prompted efforts outside of the Security Council in the 1950s to try another approach to peacekeeping. UN Secretary-General of the time, Dag Hammarskjöld, and the General Assembly, in which all UN members are represented equally, were central to this process. The 1950 'Uniting for Peace' General Assembly resolution, sponsored by the USA, aimed to pre-empt the inevitable presence of a veto-wielding USSR in a future scenario similar to the Korean War. Uniting for Peace gave the General Assembly a role in security issues, previously considered the exclusive domain of the Council. A special session of the Assembly could be called and be able to recommend international action in the absence of a Security Council agreement. There are no vetoes to be wielded at the General Assembly and every UN member is present so the required two-thirds majority for a resolution is far more likely than at the Security Council. Hammarskjöld put this new power into practice when he became a far more active Secretary-General than his predecessor on taking over the job in 1953. A UN Emergency Force was sent in to supervise the withdrawal of British, French and Israeli troops from Egypt during the 1956 Suez Crisis, despite the fact that the UK and France had prevented the Security Council authorizing any response to their invasion.

Hammarskjöld, as well as seeking to circumvent the Security Council, pioneered new approaches to peacekeeping beyond mediation. What Hammarskjöld referred to as 'preventive diplomacy' sought to initiate third party involvement in disputes before they became militarized, whilst what became known as 'peace enforcement' envisaged a more proactive deployment of UN peacekeeping forces than the manning of ceasefire lines. These ideas went beyond the 'pacific settlement of disputes' confines of Chapter 6 but were less contentious, and hence less likely to invoke a veto, than the collective security of Chapter 7. Hence Hammarskjöld referred to such measures as 'Chapter six and a half' of the Charter.

Chapter six-and-a-half peace enforcement was first clearly put into practice in 1960 when a brutal civil war in the Congo, following its independence from Belgium, prompted a rare display of solidarity between the Cold War protagonists on the Security Council. A UN force, made up of troops from a number of impartial countries, was sent in to the Congo not just to keep warring factions apart but to create the conditions for peace, using force where necessary. Some temporary calm was achieved by the UN intervention but optimism was punctured by the public decapitation of some Irish soldiers and the USSR's loss of appetite for such an extended UN role as the conflict unfolded. Hammarskjöld was killed in an aeroplane crash over the Congo in 1961 (prompting numerous conspiracy theories) and the idea of peace enforcement appeared to have died with him. The USA from the 1960s also became far less enthusiastic about finding ways to get around the problem of Security Council vetoes since it was an option they increasingly wished to utilize. Hence, UN forces that were dispatched to trouble spots over the next thirty years confined themselves more to forming 'thin blue lines' of largely inactive troops stationed between the protagonists.

Ultimately, the UN was hamstrung by the Cold War and 1990 saw reawakened hope for a genuine new world order rather than another false dawn since the leading protagonists of that conflict had, uniquely, ended on good terms and seeming to share a common vision for the future of the world.

Liberal perspectives on the New World Order

The end of the Cold War to many appeared to represent the ideological, economic and theoretical triumph of Liberalism since the core tenets of this political and economic philosophy all appeared to be likely to advance from the 1990s.

Democratization

The most profound suggestion of what the ending of the Cold War meant for international affairs and global security was the widely cited view of US academic Fukuyama that the West's victory marked the 'end of history' (Fukuyama 1992). Fukuyama reasoned that the ideological triumph of Liberalism over Communism was an ultimate victory that had set the world on a course for a new future, in which like-minded capitalist and democratic states conducted their relations in peace. This thesis reversed the Hegelian dialectic of Marxist theory and married it to the long-established Liberal principle that 'democracies don't go to war with each other'. Kant proposed this as far back as 1795 in his *magnum opus* 'Perpetual Peace' (Kant 1970) and it has been a consistent normative and empirical claim of Liberal-Pluralist International Relations scholars over the last half-century.

It is important to remember that the Cold War was more of a struggle between Communism and 'non-communism' than totalitarianism and democracy, as some-times characterized. The Western alliance were happy to prop up numerous dictatorships in the cause of deterring Communism, and the USA even assisted in snuffing out democracy in Chile (1973) and Guatemala (1954) when elections delivered leftist governments on their doorstep. The West's victory over the Soviet

Union and its 'allies' did, though, serve to accelerate the progress of democratization on both sides of the Iron Curtain. Although power politics can be seen to have played a significant part in 'breaking' the Soviet empire, the West's victory undoubtedly had an ideational dimension. The 1989 revolutions which swept through the six 'Eastern Bloc' Soviet satellite states, and effectively brought the Cold War to an end, occurred largely because ordinary Central/East Europeans wanted to live like West Europeans. The USSR's subsequent transformation has been less complete but all of its fifteen successor states have, at least partially, embraced capitalism and democracy. Western democracies have assisted many of the new states through the painful process of social, economic and political transition and, freed from Cold War constraints, their tolerance of intolerance has receded. The USA in the 1990s switched from the Truman Doctrine to the 'Clinton Doctrine' in which promoting the spread of democracy became an explicit foreign policy aim. NATO followed suit in insisting to the lengthy queue of prospective new members to its victors club, that only states with good democratic and human rights credentials would be allowed in. This had not been a precondition in earlier times when Greece, Turkey and Portugal had been recruited without such stipulations.

The proposition that democracies do not go to war with each other is well-supported empirically, so the fact that more and more states in the world have embraced democracy in recent years has given scope for optimism in the realization of Kant's vision. Kant, in fact, proposed that it was the trinity of democracy, trade and international cooperation that were the basis for a peaceful world, and these three factors are all more prominent today than at any point previously in history. Over two centuries after its promulgation, the Kantian peace proposition has been rigorously tested by Liberal-Pluralists for its applicability to the contemporary global political system. Russet and Oneal's 'Triangulating Peace', for example, drew on over a decade of statistical analysis, with each of these three corners of the 'peace triangle' examined in turn to show how they mutually reinforce each other over time in 'virtuous circles' (Russet & Oneal 2001). Democracies trade with each other more and form common organizations more, both of which are phenomena also demonstrably contributing to pacific relations. Democracies in dealing with other democracies more easily find non-military means to resolve inevitable clashes of interest that arise in their relations and increasingly realize that their interests are not served by violent confrontations. Democratic peace is a political theory with uncharacteristically solid empirical foundations if we consider that: '(e)stablished democracies fought no wars against each other during the entire twentieth century' (Russett & Starr 1996: 173). If we also consider that the number of democratic states in the world has generally increased over time, the future prospects for perpetual peace look good also. Both of these sets of figures are challengeable, but the overall trends they indicate present a strong case.

> [T]hrough careful statistical analysis, the chance that any two countries will get into a serious military dispute can be estimated if one knows what kinds of governments they have, how economically interdependent they are, and how well connected by a web of international organizations.
>
> (Russet & Oneal 2001: 9)

Just war

Another of the chief sources of optimism that marked the onset of the New World Order was that the ending of the Cold War might also bring to an end the era of total war, which so characterized the twentieth century. The Gulf War, as well as recapturing the seemingly lost dream of collective security, presented a revival of another old doctrine of international affairs thought consigned to history during the three world wars: just war. Just war doctrine dates back as far as the fourth century when Christian theologians, led by St Augustine, sought to move away from absolute pacifism and accommodate the idea that war might be morally acceptable in certain circumstances. In the seventeenth century the undisputed 'father of international law', Dutch jurist Hugo Grotius, then gave the doctrine a secular and legalistic footing amidst the backdrop of the Christian in-fighting of the Thirty Years War tearing Europe apart (Grotius 1853). Grotius set out to codify universally-applicable principles by which it could be judged that going to war was morally acceptable, *Jus ad bellum*, and accompanying principles for morally appraising the prosecution of a war, *Jus in bello*. The separate doctrines emphasize the key point that a war deemed just at the outset can become unjust if prosecuted in an immoral way. Precise interpretations of just war vary but, by the late twentieth century with writers such as Ramsey (1968) and Walzer (1978) re-packaging Grotius's work, the key principles of the twin doctrines could be distilled down to the following:

Jus ad bellum (justice in going to war)

(a) Must be waged by a sovereign authority.
(b) Must be a just cause for the war: self-defence or the enforcement of human rights.
(c) Peaceful means of resolving the dispute must have been exhausted.
(d) Must be likely to succeed.

Jus in bello (justice in the conduct of war)

(i) Means used should be proportionate to the wrong being rectified.
(ii) Unavoidable killing of non-combatants should be avoided.
(iii) Wounded troops and prisoners of war should not be killed.

Aspects of *Jus in bello* became codified in the laws of war, particularly in the Geneva and Hague Conventions, which evolved through the nineteenth and early twentieth centuries. *Jus ad bellum* during this period, however, tended not to amount to much more than principle (a) as the Westphalian notion of sovereignty crystallized into a form that legitimized whatever the state felt was necessary for its security or aggrandizement. Wars of colonial expansion presented perhaps the clearest departure from the notion of justice but justifications for such campaigns were still made on the basis that the vanquished peoples would benefit from being 'civilized'. Perhaps the most extreme articulation of this came from Gentili, who declared the genocidal Spanish campaign against native Americans in the sixteenth century to be a just war since the victims were cannibals (Gentili 1933).

The concept of total war in the twentieth century did most to set back the just war tradition. The idea that the whole of society were directly involved during war, rather than just the professional apparatus of government, had developed from the nineteenth century, with the growth of military conscription and state-promoted nationalism, but became fully realized in the era of the World Wars. From the perspective of any of its participants, the First World War exceeded any notion of proportionality and was entered into without much regard to diplomatic alternatives to fighting. The Second World War, from the perspective of the allied forces, satisfied the conditions of *Jus ad bellum* but possibly not principle (i) and most certainly not principle (ii) of *Jus in bello* if we consider the blanket bombings of German and Japanese cities.

The Cold War institutionalized this amoral necessity into everyday international politics. Nuclear deterrence rested on the notion that whole societies were legitimate military targets which, in itself, must negate any notion of proportionality as well as non-combatant discrimination. The rectification of what sort of wrong could justify the annihilation of the whole population of a country, or even the world?

The recession of such a scale of nuclear threat in the 1990s saw a concerted effort to recapture all aspects of the just war tradition in the Western-led wars of the New World Order. During the Gulf War the US-led coalition limited itself to the realization of UN-authorized aims and did not seek to topple the Iraqi regime, despite military and political pressure to do so. Saddam Hussein was forced out of Kuwait but not out of office. The war was also conducted along lines which sought to minimize civilian casualties through the use of 'smart' weaponry better able to target military and official state sites than in bombing campaigns of earlier eras. Similar sorts of campaigns were waged by NATO against Yugoslavia in 1999 and by the USA and UK against Afghanistan in 2001–2 and Iraq in 2003. The 1999 Kosovan War, in particular, marked a revival of morality in military conduct since it was in aim, principally, a humanitarian intervention.

Collective security and peacekeeping

As referred to earlier, the optimism generated by the end of the Cold War soon appeared to have some foundation when the two former chief protagonists were able to agree to sanction UN-sponsored military action against Iraq for the invasion of Kuwait in 1990. In reaching this agreement the world's premier powers were activating a long-cherished Liberal dream which had not only seemed impossible during the Cold War but had never in history been realized. After the shackles put on collective security by appeasement and then the Cold War, hopes were high for the UN to finally fulfil its ambitions in the 1990s. With the dark shadow of Cold War lifted there was optimism that the USA, Russia, China and other great military powers could free the UN Security Council from its Cold War straitjacket and cooperate to punish acts of aggression in a way not seen in the twentieth century or, to any real extent, at any previous time in history.

In addition, the UN sought to adapt to a changing world so that it could play a more meaningful role in conflict situations unlike the Iraqis' 'old-fashioned' invasion of a neighbouring state. Secretary-General Boutros Boutros-Ghali revived the spirit of Hammarskjöld in encouraging the General Assembly to support the implementation of 'Chapter 6 and a half' operations. The increased number of civil wars was making both Chapters 6 and 7 insufficient for the job and prompting the threat of Chinese and Russian vetoes, not in support of ideological brothers in arms but the principle of sovereignty. Boutros-Ghali revamped preventive diplomacy and peace enforcement in his 'Agenda for Peace' initiative, backed by the General Assembly in 1992 (Resolution 47/120), paving the way for the Security Council to sanction expansive operations in Bosnia-Herzegovina and Somalia in the early 1990s. Whilst these operations were hardly great successes – with NATO effectively taking over peacekeeping in the former and the latter left essentially unresolved – the principle that UN peace enforcement operations in civil war situations were legitimate was established and then later affirmed with the General Assembly giving unanimous support for the 'Responsibility to Protect' in 2005.

Collective security has not been enacted since its third implementation in the 2001 US-led Afghan War (though this was granted by the UN after the invasion in symbolic support). Peace enforcement, though, was given a new lease of life in 2011 when the Security Council sanctioned a military-backed 'no fly zone' over Libya to diminish the capacity of the Gaddafi regime to slaughter anti-government protesters rising up throughout the country, which ultimately led to his overthrow and assassination. NATO took on the enforcement role but in a more partial and expansive manner than the Russian, Chinese and many African governments found palatable, again illustrating the difficulties inherent in this approach to making peace. Nevertheless, the UN lives on and the world has not descended into another clash of the Titans. Great power interests continue to thwart collective security but this does not mean that the UN is an irrelevance. Hence, whilst the USA and Russia have often found themselves at loggerheads over the Syrian civil war since it erupted in 2011, UN Security Council cooperation has been enough to prevent them coming to blows with each other and provide a legal means to chemically disarm the Assad government after its apparent use of such weaponry against its own citizens.

In addition, the increased prominence of NATO and other regional peace-keeping solutions over recent years is not necessarily indicative of UN decline. In Bosnia and Libya NATO worked on behalf of the UN and this has been the case with the peacekeeping of other regional organizations like the African Union. Whilst the idea of the UN devolving some peacekeeping responsibilities to regional security organizations has only really been put into practice over the past twenty years, the notion of such an arrangement was around at the start of its history, but, like much of its potential, this was stymied by the Cold War. Chapter 8 of the UN Charter deals explicitly with 'Regional Arrangements'. Article 53(1) determines that: '[t]he Security Council shall, where appropriate, utilize such regional arrangements or agencies for enforcement action under its authority'.

Whilst its record is far from faultless, there is a case to be made that the world would be a lot less peaceful without the United Nations. Empirical studies support the notion that UN peacekeeping operations, often in conjunction with regional security organizations, have led to a reduction in conflict and that this has improved over time (Fortna 2008; Sambanis 2008; Hultman, Kathman & Shannon 2014).

> With zero PKO [peacekeeping operation] troops deployed, civil wars produce an average of almost 22 combat deaths per dyad-month. However, as the number of blue helmets deployed to a conflict zone increases, the predicted number of battle deaths drops precipitously. With a 10,000 troop deployment, casualty rates drop to approximately six combat deaths per month. This represents an approximately 73% reduction in battlefield violence, as the provision of 10,000 troops severely reduces the level of battle hostilities.
>
> (Hultman, Kathman & Shannon 2014: 747)

Realist perspectives on the New World Order

Realist caution against Liberal optimism that the passing into history of the Cold War would herald a new, uniquely pacific era of international relations could be considered borne out by certain military developments since 1990 which have not enhanced the military security of the world's states or people.

The persistence of Cold War disputes

In the 1990s, long before Putin's adventurism in Georgia, Ukraine and Syria, when Russo-Western relations were more cordial, serious questions could be asked as to whether the Cold War had actually ended. Many of the same points of contention that marked the 1945–90 era remained (and remain) unresolved. The Korean peninsula is still firmly frozen in the Cold War era, divided into two ideologically-defined states precisely as it was at the point of East-West stalemate after the war in 1953. Communist North Korea's relations with the West remain practically non-existent whilst it maintains political links with its war ally, China. North Korea's confirmation as a nuclear power in 2006 has seen this trouble spot become more dangerous than at any time since the 1950s. Relations between the USA, and most other Western states, and their second major Cold War foe, China, have remained frosty in the years since 1990. Economic cooperation has blossomed through mutual interest but diplomatic and military tensions remain. It is worth remembering that there was no official end to this dimension of the Cold War. No equivalent to the 1989 Malta Summit or 1990 Paris Treaty was signed by China and the US and a number of issues remain wholly unresolved. Most prominently, the status of Taiwan remains a source of tension and the island remains in a non-sovereign limbo, being claimed by China but still assured by the USA of its independence.

Whilst undoubtedly more cordial than during the Cold War and smoother than with those countries which have not abandoned Communism, US-Russian relations since the 1991 collapse of the USSR have also not been exactly harmonious. The Kosovan War of 1999 ended a period of rapprochement. The NATO victory was a bitter humiliation for Russia since to them it appeared to demonstrate Western contempt for their long-cherished foreign policy goal of 'pan-Slavism', in which East Europe was understood as part of their sphere of influence.[2] Russia secured a role in the peacekeeping process but, in a sign of how things had changed, were unable to maintain sole control of the airport they had captured since support troops were blocked from flying over the airspace of former allies Hungary or Romania due to Western pressure on *their* new allies. The encroachment of the US and their allies into their backyard was confirmed, in Russian eyes, when, in the same year as the Kosovan War, NATO expanded its membership to recruit three of their former Warsaw Pact allies: Poland, Hungary and the Czech Republic. The 2004 expansion took this a stage further by bringing into the fold three former members of the USSR itself, Latvia, Lithuania and Estonia. Far from exiting the stage after 1990, a Cold War alliance had not only played on but extended its role and subsumed part of the original object of their containment. NATO have repeatedly assured Russia that their containment is not its game anymore and, while expanding eastwards, gave them a guarantee that no east-facing missiles would be sited in the territories of the new member-states. The fact remained, however, that this was an alliance set up to counter Russian (Soviet) power and it was still there.

The Cold War 'hangover' offers a vindication of the post-revisionist view that the conflict was, in essence, just another balance of power struggle. The balance has tilted but elements of the struggle remain. Clark, in 2001, argued that the Cold War had not yet been fully resolved because the *process* of peacemaking (as opposed to an event such as the Malta Summit or Paris Treaty) had not been completed (Clark 2001: 6–11). The lack of a systematic attempt to mould a genuinely new world order in the 1990s can be explained in a number of ways, Clark posits. First, the fact that this was a cold rather than 'hot' war served as a disincentive to the protagonists to encourage a thaw. 'Since the Cold War was not a proper war it is fitting that it should be brought to an end by a peace that is not a proper peace' (Clark 2001: 4). Second, the Cold War was also an unusual war in that it was resolved through negotiation and a voluntary, rather than imposed, climb-down by one side. The fact that fruitful negotiations between warring parties preceded rather than proceeded the conflict served to make them appear superfluous later on. Third, even 'normal' multilateral wars are rarely ended at a stroke. Complete harmony is unlikely to succeed the hostility and certain unresolved issues are likely to live on. Clark makes a convincing case that there is often a certain 'time lag' following major multilateral conflict before real peace is achieved, but could it be that the Cold War will not so much fade away as metamorphosize into another global conflict?

This view was most notably articulated by the US Realist Huntington in his influential 'Clash of the Civilizations' thesis (Huntington 1993). Huntington contended that transnational cultural conflict was now where the logic of the security dilemma could best be applied, rather than inter-state rivalry. Major antagonism between democracy and Communism may be over, but there is no 'end of history' and the 'civilization' of Liberal democracy faces other challenges to its hegemony, particularly from the 'civilization' of Islam. The rise of anti-Western Islamic fundamentalism, Western-led wars in the Muslim states of Iraq and Afghanistan and the Islamophobic dimension of the Yugoslav wars seemed, to many, to bear out this prophecy.

From balance to an imbalance of power

The chief cause of Realist caution or fear for the New World Order was that it threatened a central tenet of their recipe for order, the balance of power. The unipolar world that emerged, according to orthodox Realist logic, should prove unsustainable and prompt other states to seek to topple the USA's pole position. This has not happened, of course, but the fear persists among some statesmen and Realist commentators that American preponderance is bound to breed resentment and be a source of general global instability. Kagan, an American academic with strong political connections to the State Department, has articulated the concern that a sole 'hyperpower' is reflexively drawn to an aggressive foreign policy.

> A man armed only with a knife may decide that a bear prowling the forest is a tolerable danger, because hunting it with a knife is riskier than lying low and hoping it never attacks. The same man armed with a rifle, however, will likely make a different calculation.
>
> (Kagan 2003: 2)

This scenario becomes problematic when the man takes to shooting at targets just in case they turn out to be a bear. These concerns came to greatest prominence in 2003 when the USA sidestepped both the UN and NATO in prosecuting another, far more contentious, war against Iraq. US preponderance is such that their hegemony looks unchallengeable but it has bred resentment in some parts of the world which threatens to puncture the idea of post-Cold War peace. In particular, there seems little doubt that Russian resentment at shifts in the balance of power since the early 1990s has been a factor in Putin flexing his muscles over the past decade in support of the 'near abroad' Russians in Georgia and Ukraine and his strategic ally in Syria.

Whilst it could be argued that persisting tensions between Moscow and Washington are hardly comparable to the Cold War standoff, there is a good case to be made that some conflicts have emerged or worsened *because of* rather than in spite of improved overall Russo-American relations. The rise since the 1990s of the phenomenon of 'failed states', where domestic sovereign control breaks down indefinitely, provides the clearest case of this. In some parts of the world superpower competition for influence was succeeded from the end of the 1980s by loss of interest. The fate of Afghanistan epitomized this with a 1980s proxy war transformed into an ignored 1990s civil war, only to be internationalized again in 2001 when superpower interest for non-Afghan reasons was re-ignited. War between Ethiopia and Eritrea and internal strife in Somalia and Sudan, although less explicitly post-Cold War conflicts, also bore the hallmarks of New World Order global indifference.

Democratic war?

Realist scepticism on the New World Order is also built upon a lack of conviction that democratization is the route to 'perpetual peace'. Whilst it may be true that democracies do not fight each other (though this is also disputed), they are just as prone to be embroiled in war as non-democracies and have a propensity to fight autocracies. The restraint shown by democracies in resolving disputes with states with similar political systems is frequently not exhibited in resolving disputes with non-democracies. Indeed evidence can be found to suggest that some democracies are predisposed towards violent resolutions of disputes when dealing with dictator-ships. Supportive cases include the 1956 Suez dispute, when France, Israel and the UK invaded Egypt, and the twenty-first-century US-led wars in Afghanistan and Iraq. Realists doubt that the spread of democracy is a guarantor of peace since national interests – not the political system of a rival – will determine decision-making on whether or not to go to war. In any case, democratization appears to have stalled in recent years, with many states – like Russia, Turkey and Venezuela – reverting to more authoritarian forms of government.

> Democracies may live at peace with democracies, but even if all states became democratic, the structure of international politics would remain anarchic. The structure of international politics is not transformed by changes internal to states, however widespread the changes may be. In the absence of an external authority, a state cannot be sure that today's friend will not be tomorrow's enemy.
>
> (Waltz 2000: 10)

The 'false promise' of international institutions and law

For Realists organizations and law offer a 'false promise' (Mearsheimer 1995) and serve to distract from the crucial route to order of balancing state power, best served by looser and more flexible alliances. Collective security still has a very limited history and coordinated military responses to aggression will only ever succeed when they also serve the national interests of great powers. The one clear-cut implementation of collective security in the 1990 Gulf War was highly atypical, coming at a time when the Soviet Union was on the verge of break-up and in sudden decline.

The track record of UN peacekeeping short of collective security is also not encouraging. As with its original trial in the Congo in 1960, peace enforcement operations have been marred by disappointment and controversy. In the 1990s the failure of UN troops to protect Bosnian Moslem citizens from Serb nationalist violence forced them, humiliatingly and symbolically, to hand over the mantle of peacekeeping to NATO. Before this in Somalia there were strong echoes of the Congo, when a US force sent in to bring stability and humanitarian relief to a complex civil war pulled out amidst accusations of having exacerbated the conflict and with televised images of their dead troops being dragged through the streets being beamed around the world.

Such images were still fresh in public and political minds when an even fiercer internal conflict in Rwanda erupted in 1994 and, this time, there was no intervention at all. When, five years later, violence erupted again in Yugoslavia it appeared as though the Security Council was still operating in the 'old world order' when Russian and Chinese vetoes proscribed collective security in spite of the obvious lesson from up the road in Bosnia that peace enforcement was not enough. Again NATO stepped in to fill the global void but this time with a full-scale and successful military operation. Although UN collective security was invoked for a third time, to legitimize the US war against Afghanistan in 2001–2, this was more of an act of symbolism since the world's most powerful state did not need military support to defeat one of the world's weakest. When the USA and UK then acted without either UN or NATO authorization in going to war with Iraq in 2003, collective security, and UN authority in general, appeared to be becoming, once again, a distant dream.

Limitations of just war

Realists acknowledge the value of just war principles as mutually-beneficial guidelines towards avoiding unnecessary conflict escalation but they both dispute and caution against the Liberal assertion that war has become more morally-driven: 'the just war tradition's concern with justice leads it to permit many more kinds of war than realism' (Morkevičus 2015: 11). As with much of humanitarian international law and custom, just war is a grey area in which inconsistent interpretation and application are inevitable. Owing to what Clausewitz called the 'friction' of war it is impossible to be entirely accurate in predicting the outcome of a military campaign or to fight a perfect battle free of mistakes.

Grey areas still remain in terms of deeming when a war is 'just'. Cynics have contended that the 'smart' bombing-led wars of recent years are as much a device for sanitizing war for domestic public consumption as showing compassion for civilians. Bombing from afar or via drones saves the lives of the bombers more than it does the civilians living near targeted sites. The New World Order wars have also raised questions of proportionality. Did NATO air strikes against Yugoslavia prompt Serb nationalists to step up the campaign against Kosovar Albanians, leading to more suffering than would have occurred if no military action had been taken? Did more Afghan citizens die (albeit accidentally) in US strikes than the 3,000 New York and Washington residents killed in the 2001 al-Qa'ida strikes which prompted the response? An even more problematic moral quantification emerged in 2003. Was the 2003 Iraq war justified on the basis that it pre-empted future threats from that country? This dilemma divided Western opinion from the start but, a few years into the conflict, few backers could be found.

The unravelling of arms control

The clearest manifestation of the dangers considered by many to be inherent in the breakdown of the Cold War bipolar balance of power has been the strain put on global arms control agreements by the new alignment. The balance of power has been explicitly recognized in multilateral treaties amongst the great military powers going back to the 1920s,[3] but was most institutionalized into the relations of the two Cold War nuclear superpowers, despite the level of hostility that existed between them. A combination of bilateral and multilateral arms control agreements involving much of the international community contributed to the bipolar 'balance of power' that marked the Cold War.

Deterrence, like arms control, was not new to the Cold War period but took on an added dimension to displays of 'gun boat diplomacy' in earlier ages, because of the sheer scale of the threat now being projected. Both superpowers had the capability to annihilate the other state and its people, necessitating the added ingredient of 'Mutually Assured Destruction' (MAD) to keep the balance. For both superpowers to be deterred from attacking each other they needed to know that initiating war would be futile since they, as well as their enemy, would face annihilation. For the logic of MAD to operate, both the USA and USSR needed to have a 'second strike capability', to be able to respond to any attack by the other. In other words, both sides needed to be in a position where they could not only obliterate the other in a first strike but also do so in response to the other side initiating hostilities. Hence, in spite of improved Soviet-US relations in the aftermath of the 1962 Cuban Missile Crisis and the gradual acceptance of military parity by both sides, the development of nuclear weapons and delivery systems accelerated until the end of the decade. By the 1970s, however, the Strategic Arms Limitation Talks (SALT) of 1972 and 1979 established the first meaningful bilateral arms control agreements, with ceilings placed on the production of a range of weaponry.

As well as maintaining an equilibrium between the superpowers, the balance of terror rested on keeping the balance bipolar (in terms of the two sides of the Cold War) since MAD logic would be lost in a multipolar system. Hence multilateral arms control agreements keeping the 'nuclear weapons club' an exclusive one formed an equally important dimension of Cold War military security diplomacy. By the signing of the 1968 Treaty on the Non-Proliferation of Nuclear Weapons (NPT), three other nuclear powers – the UK, France and China – had joined the club and agreed to the NPT's key rule constraining its members, like magicians in the 'Magic Circle', from revealing their secrets to outsiders. The same five states that made up the disharmonious concert of permanent members in the Security Council found it far easier to reach accord in nuclear diplomacy since, like magicians, they might be in competition with each other but could all lose out from openly showing how anyone could pull a rabbit out of their hat.

Whilst bilateral US-Russian arms control agreements have been maintained in the post-Cold War afterglow (albeit with a literal balance of warheads masking a reality of US supremacy due to superior quality and stocks held in storage), the multilateral regimes became strained by the new military power configurations of the 1990s. Non-proliferation had been one thing the five official nuclear powers could agree on during the Cold War, but now, their commitment began to waver. Chinese state officials, by now focusing their concerns on the Asian rather than global balance of power, are widely suspected of having assisted the Pakistani government in developing nuclear weapons to counter India's unofficial though well-known nuclear capability. Throughout the 1990s the nuclear club became far less exclusive. Pakistan and India openly tested their new weapons and, in doing so, the latter denounced the 'nuclear apartheid' of the NPT in privileging the 'big five' (Singh 1998). The break-up of the USSR saw some of its nuclear arsenal apparently go missing when a recount was taken after fifteen new states had succeeded the superpower, unleashing the nightmare scenario that some Soviet nuclear material could have got onto the global black market.

By the 1990s it was also apparent that Israel and North Korea, too, were nuclear powers and that Iraq and Iran were on the way to following suit. The NPT offers the incentive to non-nuclear states of aid for peaceful nuclear power production in exchange for not developing military uses for this resource. This, however, was not an incentive for India or Pakistan to sign up, and joining the nuclear club was widely greeted with jubilation amongst the peoples of the subcontinent. Not all

Western military strategists were alarmed at this particular breach of the magician's code. The cause for greater reflection in the recourse to nuclear rather than conventional weapons might bring some stability to Indo-Pakistani relations, many Realists reasoned. More worryingly for the old order was that North Korea and Iraq, who were signatories to the NPT, had managed to evade detection and gone down the road of developing the weapons unbeknown to the world. The Koreans trumpeted their achievement in an exercise of mini-compellence aimed at securing aid concessions from an alarmed West, while Iraq's progress was stumbled across by invaders during the Gulf War.

These developments showed up a central problem of the NPT, and of arms control in general, that of implementing and verifying agreements. Counting naval destroyers in the 1920s was relatively straightforward but modern weapons of mass destruction (WMD) are more easily kept out of sight, even in an age of satellite observation. The NPT limps on with some successes, such as South Africa's unilateral disarmament of 1991, but other contemporary multilateral regimes look increasingly irrelevant. The Comprehensive Test Ban Treaty (CTBT) (the successor to the 1963 Limited Test Ban Treaty) has yet to come into force since not all nuclear states (both military and non-military) have ratified – including the USA. Other non-nuclear WMD regimes are limited in their effectiveness. The Biological Weapons Convention came into force in 1975 but looks unlikely to ever achieve any effective verification since biological weapons are far harder to detect than the nuclear weapons which evaded detection in North Korea and Iraq. Chemical weaponry arms control dates back to the 1925 Geneva Protocol which, in the aftermath of its use in the First World War, prohibited the military application of poison gas. Today, international legal force is centred on the 1993 Chemical Weapons Convention which bans all forms of military chemical applications and commits ratifying countries who stockpile such weapons to destroy them. The regime does feature an inspection system, but has been patchily implemented by the key parties and main chemical weapons holders, the USA and Russia, and not ratified at all by the potential chemical weapons states of North Korea, Israel and Egypt.

For Realists the limitations of current arms control instruments illustrate that it is the balance of power, not law, that is needed to maintain order. Indeed, some Realists go as far as arguing that laws containing the proliferation of WMD are contrary to the natural order of the balance of power. Flying in the face of most politically-conservative opinion in the US, Waltz has reasoned that Iran should be allowed to arm itself with nuclear weapons – to allow a regional 'balance of terror' to emerge to keep a lid on conflict in the Middle East (Waltz 2012).

Marxist perspectives on post-Cold War military security

Like the Realists, Marxists do not consider that the political world changed for the better in any fundamental sense in 1990. From this perspective, before, during or since the Cold War, armed conflicts can be explained with reference to global capitalism and this is a system that has only strengthened since the demise of the Soviet Union. Klare, for example, sees US oil interests as having fashioned a long-term 'strategy of maximum extraction' in Washington which, as well as engineering regime change in Iraq, has incorporated the maintenance of strong ties with Saudi Arabia and the exertion of diplomatic pressure on Iran (Klare 2007: 82–4). This strategy long predates the New World Order. The 'Carter Doctrine', announced by the US president in 1980, made it plain that questions relating to the economic resources of distant states would enter into the calculations of the American national interest by stating that military action to secure oil imports and other economic interests was a possibility.

> An attempt by any outside force to gain control of the Persian Gulf region will be regarded as an assault on the vital interests of the United States of America, and such an assault will be repelled by any means necessary, including military force.
>
> (Carter 1980)

Carter's speech was intended as a re-statement of the Truman Doctrine and to signal an end to détente following the Soviet invasion of Afghanistan. However, whilst it might be expected that Soviet expansion would be poorly received by Washington, there was no obvious likelihood of this being a prelude to an attempted take-over of the Gulf and the doctrine struck many as a case of imperialistic opportunism. Engdahl posits that this strategy of asserting power over the oil fields of the Gulf actually predates both Bush and Carter and can be traced back to British policy before the First World War (Engdahl 2012). The wording of Carter's speech does, indeed, strongly resemble a 1903 British declaration by Foreign Secretary Lord Lansdowne that: 'we should regard the establishment of a naval base or of a fortified port in the Persian Gulf by any power as a very grave menace to British interests, and we should certainly resist it with all the means at our disposal'. In line with the 'Lansdowne Doctrine', the British and French secretly negotiated the Sykes-Picot agreement during the First World War under which they would essentially split the Middle East between them on the conclusion of the war and dissolution of the Turkish Ottoman Empire. The Russian allies of the British and French in the Triple Entente were also due to be part of this carve up but, ultimately, scuppered the plan when the Bolshevik revolution brought them out of the war and exposed the deal. This was a huge embarrassment to the British who, in working successfully with Arab forces against Turkey and Germany in the war, had appeared to have promised them independence. Anglo-French decline after the Great War and increased economic dependence on the US paved the way for the Americans to gradually succeed them as the guarantor of Western economic interests in the region. This was finally confirmed in 1956 when another secret plan for the Middle East hatched in Paris and London provided more embarrassment. The Suez Crisis unfolded after a secret Anglo-French invasion of Egypt occurred in order to safeguard economic interests deemed threatened by President Nasser's nationalization of the Suez Canal. The US disapproved of the old imperial venture and, using their economic leverage over the two countries, pulled the plug on it and sealed their position as the key power in the region.

Hence, for Marxists, an imperialist or business-led quest for mastery over resources explains war today as it did during and before the Cold War. The cast of lead actors on the world stage may change but the play remains the same and the production companies' profits keep rolling in.

Social Constructivist perspectives on the New World Order

As previously discussed, Social Constructivism's emergence is predicated on the belief that neither Realist, Liberal nor Marxist assumptions give us enough to explain how the world has evolved over the past few decades, and this very much applies to the post-Cold War military order. On the balance of power, Social Constructivists reason that there might be a strong case to be made that this did maintain order in previous phases of history but this is not sufficient reason to believe that a contemporary imbalance will lead to global disorder. Many of the states just down the military pecking order have no interest or desire to topple the USA since that country does not threaten them and they share many of its general aspirations for the world. Even those amongst that 'second tier' of military powers not as closely aligned to the USA as the UK, such as Russia, enjoy sufficiently strong ties to render war unthinkable. Ideological and territorial differences exist between China and the US but they pale into insignificance when set against the trading links and common economic interests that now link the two countries. In a more general sense, historical comparisons are fraught with problems. US military hegemony has prompted adventurism that alarms much of the world, such as in the 2003 war against Iraq, but this hardly compares to Napoleonic France or Hitlerian Germany. For Social Constructivists, 'things change' and, in particular, they reject the 'timeless wisdom' and cyclical historicism of Realism.

On the Liberal recipe for peace Social Constructivists tend to accept that democracies do not fight each other, but do not conclude from this that demo-cratization must be a route out of war, because democracy is a concept that can invoke force. Empirical evidence for democracies and partners in regional blocs not fighting each other is strong but, additionally, fighting over the idea/existence of democracy could be said to have been a factor in recent wars fought between democracies and undemocratic states such as in Iraq, Afghanistan and Yugoslavia. In particular, Social Constructivists have highlighted the phenomenon of 'warlike democracies' to demonstrate how ideas and perception undermine the logic of democratic peace theory. '(D)emocracies to a large degree create their enemies and their friends – 'them' and 'us' – by inferring either aggressive or defensive motives from the domestic structures of their counterparts' (Risse 1995: 19–20). Perhaps it is cultural affiliation rather than democracy that is the key to peace? Democratic peace proponents Oneal and Russett admit that two autocracies are more likely to have peaceful relations than one democracy and one autocracy (Oneal & Russett 1997: 283). Risse does, however, concede that democracies are overwhelmingly peaceful in their relations with other democracies. In a similar vein, Brock, Geis and Mueller posit a 'dyadic democratic peace theory' since 'democracies are peaceful *towards each other* but *in general* they are as war prone as any other regime type' (Brock, Geis & Mueller 2006: 3). Perpetual peace, then, might only become a reality when there are only 'us' and no 'them' in the world. This 'end of history', though, is not yet with us.

Similarly, whilst the Marxist notion that capitalism fuels warfare can easily be supported by certain case studies (such as with the importance of securing oil supplies in the 2003 Iraq war), suggesting that this is evidence of structural determinism is problematic if we consider the non-aggressive histories of capitalist countries like Sweden, Switzerland or Costa Rica, or armed disputes between socialist states such as the Sino-Soviet border conflict of 1969 or the implosion of Yugoslavia.

In a more general sense, war is often still considered a rational foreign policy choice for some governments but it is not a given that this choice will be taken by decision-makers, even if there are tangible gains to be had from them doing so. Germany and Japan have not risen again in a quest for military supremacy as much because their government and people have never wished to do so as because of their initial containment. The recognition that ideas and culture inform decision-making when it comes to the ultimate decision usually to face a government predates the full emergence of the Social Constructivists in the post-Cold War era. Mueller, in arguing for 'the obsolescence of major war' in the 1980s, demonstrated that the historical pattern of cyclical war between the great powers was not being maintained. The nuclear revolution was clearly a factor in this, making such wars irrational, but Mueller posited that an added (and related) dimension to this was a normative change towards seeing war as an unacceptable means of pursuing gain. Slavery had been a profitable venture for many states for a number of centuries but was eventually consigned to history (by most states) because compassion triumphed over economic gain (Mueller 1989). Hence there is some common ground between the Social Constructivists and the Liberals in acknowledging the possibility for progress through learning in international relations. In this view, whilst the track record of global collective security is not too encouraging, this should not lead us to view it as hopelessly utopian. Wendt, a Realist-leaning Constructivist, contends that China, the USA, Russia and any other great powers of the future are likely to accept restrictions on their war-making capacities in order to empower peacekeeping by a global supranational organization because this will make sense for them. A peaceful, orderly world suits the powerful, and the lessons of history will eventually be learned by them that this comes from evolving beyond anarchy (Wendt 2003).

An end to high politics?

Military threats to security have certainly not gone away in the years since the demise of East European Communism. However, although it persists in a number of forms, the Cold War's ultimate security threat of nuclear war has receded in scale and this has transformed defence policy in many states of the world. Korea remains stuck in the Cold War and the defence agendas of much of the global South have not been greatly affected, but military security policies have changed significantly in the states most affected by the Cold War, particularly in Europe and North America. In Central and Eastern Europe the former Communist states have either switched to the winning side or become preoccupied with new localized threats. The Western Cold War allies' response to the successful avoidance of that war has been to show a far

TABLE 2.4 Indicators of contemporary state military power

(a) Expenditure on defence (2015)

	State	Amount (US dollars)	Proportion of GDP (%)
1	USA	$611 billion	3.3
2	China	$215 billion (estimate)	1.9
3	Russia	$69.2 billion	5.3
4	Saudi Arabia	$63.7 billion (estimate)	10.0
5	India	$55.9 billion	2.5
6	France	$55.7 billion	2.3
7	UK	$48.3 billion	1.9
8	Japan	$46.1 billion	1.0
9	Germany	$41.1 billion	1.2
10	South Korea	$36.8 billion	2.7
World		$1.69 trillion	2.2

Source: SIPRI 2017.

(b) Size of full-time armed forces

	State	Number
1	China	2,333,000
2	USA	1,492,200
3	India	1,325,000
4	North Korea	1,190,000
5	Russia	845,000
6	Pakistan	643,800
7	South Korea	630,000
8	Iran	523,000
9	Algeria	520,000
10	Turkey	510,600

Source: IISS 2014.

(c) Size of nuclear arsenal

	State	No. of weapons
1	Russia	7,290
2	USA	7,000
3	France	300
4	China	260
5	UK	215
6	Pakistan	110–130
7	India	100–120
8	Israel	80
9	North Korea	10

Source: SIPRI 2016.

greater preparedness to get embroiled in new wars essentially of their choosing. These New World Order wars and lesser military incursions have been prompted not by imminent threats to 'national security' but more by justice and the maintenance of regional order. At least for part of the world, the idea that war is an option of last resort and all-subsuming of other concerns is eroding. For many states the resort to force is not being eliminated from foreign policy, it is becoming a more pragmatic, mainstream part of it, in line with Clausewitzian thinking.

From deterrence to the management of security?

As Rasmussen has persuasively argued, the changing nature of military threats has resulted in the means–ends rationality of traditional state security policy in some countries being gradually replaced by a 'reflexive rationality'. 'Risk is becoming the operative concept of Western security' (Rasmussen 2001: 285). Deterring or being ready to respond to massive military threats is no longer a sufficient basis for the construction of many states' defence policies. As the Cold War has receded into history, a more subtle strategy has been both necessary and possible for governments operating in relative peace. The management of security entails seeking to limit the risks likely to be encountered in the future as well as tackling imminent problems.

NATO's transformation since 1990 exemplifies this approach. As Forster and Wallace observe, 'NATO is becoming more of a European-wide security organization, less of an alliance' (Forster & Wallace 2001: 107). The enlargement of NATO, and its wider extension through the Partnership for Peace programme with non-members, has not been inspired by the organization's desire to become even more powerful, so much as the 'management of the future' and stabilizing East Europe (Rasmussen 2001: 289). NATO has also become increasingly involved in non-military security activities such as facilitating relief in cases of natural disasters (see Chapter 8). It is, indeed, increasingly doubtful whether NATO is much of a military alliance at all. The first and only time the organization's collective defence 'trigger clause', Article 5, was enacted was in 2001 in response to the September 11th al-Qa'ida strikes in the USA. This was purely a symbolic act of solidarity as the USA made it clear that the organization was not needed in the subsequent war in Afghanistan. When NATO could not agree on a collective response against Iraq in 2003 it was sidestepped by the USA and UK in much the same way as NATO had sidestepped the UN in the 1999 Kosovan War. The Kosovan War stands as the only military engagement by NATO, but the solidarity was, again, more symbolic and diplomatic than a case of military necessity. The USA, and their key ally in the informal 'alliance of English speaking nations', the UK, do not need NATO in a military security sense but the organization still serves their interests as a means of institutionalizing a wider *security community* in Europe.

The 'alliance of English speaking nations" (including Australia) invasion of Iraq itself represented a dramatic attempt at managing the future, risking the antagonism of some of their partners in the European security community, and their own casualties, in order to pre-empt bigger future risks from arising. Iraq did not present a 'clear and present danger' to any of the three invading states but it was reasoned by them that, if military action was avoided, the country *could* pose a major security threat through the development of weapons of mass destruction. The overthrow of

Saddam Hussein was also seen as a means to stabilize the Middle East and contribute long term to the mitigation of risks associated with anti-Western sentiment in the region. This, of course, is not how it has transpired, but that was the logic behind the intervention.

Not all states enjoy the luxury of being able to attempt to manage their and their people's security but it is an observable trend in some parts of the world. NATO, from the outset, sought to keep members like Greece and Turkey from fighting each other, but this became more pressing once the Cold War was over and such countries were stripped of a common enemy. The Organization for Security and Cooperation in Europe (OSCE) sought to build bridges between NATO and the Warsaw Pact states in the era of détente and looked, briefly, as if it might take on the mantle of keeping order in Europe at the end of the Cold War, before NATO revamped itself. The European Union was forged by the need to manage the future of Germany's relations with its European neighbours and its expansions have sought to stabilize the continent.

In Africa, the African Union and the Economic Organization of West African States (ECOWAS) have sought to fill the void of Northern indifference prompted by the end of the Cold War by enhancing regional stability through peacekeeping deployments in conjunction with the UN. MERCOSUR (Common Market of the South) in South America and ASEAN (Association of South East Asian Nations) in Asia, whilst strained economically by the divergent fortunes of their members, have both been fairly successful in building security communities amongst those countries.

Military conflict should no longer automatically be seen as 'high politics' and something resorted to when 'national security' is threatened. Humanitarian interventions and missions to maintain general order without 'national interests' being obviously at stake, such as in Kosovo or Libya, have become more common (see Chapter 5). Wars are increasingly fought for other, less fundamental foreign policy aims. This was most clearly illustrated by the 2003 Iraq war, prosecuted ostensibly on the war aim of better implementing an arms control agreement. The Iraq war also served to show how wars have become more 'routinized'. Despite months of diplomatic build-up to the conflict and in-depth media coverage, it was not clear when the war had actually started. Since the UK and USA had been bombing Iraq for twelve years, and attracting relatively little political interest in doing so, the boundaries between war and diplomacy were barely evident. Appetites for 'full-scale' war have lessened as a consequence of the disastrous Iraq invasion and more limited operations have become the norm and, perhaps, the future.

Other states have decided to spend the post-Cold War peace dividend on non-military concerns. Most European states' military expenditure has reduced, and at such a rate in countries like Belgium and Germany that concerns have been raised within NATO about a 'free rider' problem developing, with countries enjoying the security provided by collective defence without contributing much to it themselves. Iceland has not possessed its own armed forces either during or since the Cold War, allowing the US to simultaneously protect and utilize the island for its geo-political value, until choosing to leave in 2006. Costa Rica abandoned its armed forces after a civil war in 1949 (save for some state paramilitaries used for border controls and internal security) and has managed to remain an oasis of peace in an otherwise volatile region.

Other states have resorted to calling up private, freelance military forces in time of emergency rather than incur the costs of building up and constantly modernizing their own armed forces. Governments of failed, unstable or weak states, such as Sierra Leone, Ivory Coast, Angola and Papua New Guinea, have recruited from specially designed private military companies such as 'Sandline International' and 'Executive Outcomes' to help them deal with civil insurgencies. In addition, though, powerful states have also increasingly sought private solutions to military security problems. The USA recruited around 30,000 guards and analysts from fifty private security companies (PSCs) between 2004 and 2011 to assist their occupation in Iraq. This development opens up a legal minefield since private operatives fall outside of the confines of public international law, a problem that became apparent in Iraq with several accusations of excessive force levelled against PSCs who had been granted certain immunities from prosecution by the US government in order to carry out their duties.

There are few states in the world where the military security agenda is dominated by a major, imminent threat posed by another state's military forces. Maintaining internal order against the threat of insurgency and/or contributing to regional or global order or justice is more the order of the day.

Conclusions

The 'ending' of the Cold War has not changed the military security threats to the governments or peoples of many states, including those still affected by it (for example Korea or Cuba) or those for whom it was never the principal concern (for example India or Israel). However, the lifting of the over-arching threat posed by that conflict and the nature in which it (at least partially) ended have brought into question a number of long-held assumptions about the study and conduct of military security policy.

The three peace prescriptions of Kant, and his protégés like Russett, appear to have passed a number of trials but should not, however, be mistaken for panaceas. Kantian peace does appear to account for the demise of inter-state war but its logic does not explain the persistence of a number of civil wars. Democracy, trade and common political institutions have not deterred some French or British Islamic fundamentalists from pursuing conflict to achieve their aims. In addition, it is democracies, including those not predisposed to fight themselves, who do much to fuel conflicts in the undemocratic world through the lucrative trade in arms, usually justified on the national interest grounds of economic expediency. In noting this, however, neither can we conclude that Marxist economic determinism is the catch-all explanation it purports to be, even for explicitly imperial wars. In invading the Falkland Islands in 1982 the Argentine junta were seeking to acquire a British possession which had long been an economic burden to its colonial ruler. It was symbolism which prompted the invasion, and principle which prompted the campaign to recapture the islands.

After an initial upsurge in the number of military conflicts in the world on the passing into history of the Cold War, there is good evidence for the decline in resort to war. Conflict deaths (both inter-state and civil) fell from 164,000 per year in the

1980s to 92,000 in the 1990s and to 42,000 in the 2000s (World Bank 2011: 52; Uppsala/PRIO 2010; Petterson & Wallensteen 2015). Civil wars in Syria, Nigeria and Ukraine have reversed this general downward trend since the middle of the 2010s, but inter-state wars have become rare events and there is good reason to suppose that intergovernmental relations are slowly pacifying.

War waged by states has not disappeared but it has become less frequent and, at the same time, a more 'mainstream' political option for some. Other options for resolving disputes are increasingly open to governments but limited tactical military incursions are also an increasing option for some states. Clausewitz was right to say that war was a form of politics but this affirmation need not cause us to conclude that armed attacks are as inevitable as the differences of opinion that constitute politics. The New World Order is not all that 'new' or orderly but it is more peaceful than the orders preceding it and still offers hope for a more optimistic, pacifistic future.

 **Key points**

- The twin global issues of the Cold War and decolonization dominated the conduct of international relations in the latter half of the twentieth century and help explain the preoccupation of states today with externally-focused military security.
- The 'resolution' of the Cold War and decolonization in the early 1990s brought optimism that a 'New World Order' would usher in more peaceful inter-state relations and a greater commitment to globally-coordinated peacekeeping.
- Not all analysts shared the optimism generated by the apparent New World Order. The legacies of the Cold War and decolonization remain prominent and many Neo-realists contend that the disappearance of the Cold War balance of power brought with it new, and more de-stabilizing, military threats.
- Realists consider that war is an inevitable feature of international relations, contain-able by respect for the balance of power between states. Marxists consider war to be inevitable so long as the world remains predominantly capitalist. Liberal-Pluralists contend that the spread of democracy and interdependence, hastened in the post-Cold War world, offers hope for the eradication of inter-state war, which is becoming less common.

 Notes

1   The other ten Security Council members are elected for two years, by General Assembly vote subject to Security Council approval, on the basis of geographical quotas. Three are chosen from Africa, two from Asia, two from Latin America, one from East Europe and two from 'West Europe/others'.
2   Russian Pan-Slavism pre-dates the Cold War and can be seen as a common theme of Russian foreign policy dating back to the Tsarist era of the nineteenth century when support for Serb nationalism was demonstrated.
3   The 1922 Washington Conference bound the USA, UK, France, Japan and Italy to specific levels of naval power relative to each other.

Recommended reading

Clausewitz, C.V. (1976) *On War*, edited and translated by M. Howard & P. Paret, Princeton: Princeton University Press.

Fukuyama, F. (1992) *The End of History and the Last Man*, London: Hamish Hamilton.

Gaddis, J. (1997) *We Now Know – Rethinking Cold War History*, Oxford: Clarendon.

Goldstein, J. (2011) *Winning the War on War: The Decline of Armed Conflict Worldwide*, New York: Dutton.

Nye, J. & Welch, D. (2016) *Understanding Global Conflict and Cooperation: An Introduction to Theory and History*, 10th edn, London: Pearson.

Russett, B. & Oneal, J. (2001) *Triangulating Peace: Democracy, Interdependence and International Organisations*, New York: Norton.

Sorensen, G. (2016) *Rethinking the New World Order*, London: Palgrave.

Waltz, K. (1959) *Man, the State and War*, New York: Columbia University Press.

Walzer, M. (1978) *Just and Unjust Wars*, London: Allen Lane.

 Useful web links

- NATO: www.nato.int/

- Stockholm International Peace Research Institute (SIPRI): www.sipri.se/

- United Nations 'Peace and Security': www.un.org/en/sections/what-we-do/maintain-international-peace-and-security/index.html

Chapter 3

Threats to security from non-state actors

> *It is the war of every Muslim in every place, and the Islamic State is merely the spearhead in this war.*
>
> Abu Bakr Al-Baghdadi, ISIS leader, 2015

One man's terrorist . . .

'Terrorism' is, perhaps, the most contentious term in political science. Literally hundreds of definitions have been coined by scholars and practitioners of politics without any clear consensus on how best to articulate what is undoubtedly a significant phenomenon. As far back as 1983 Schmid listed 109 distinct definitions (Schmid 1983). In 2005 the 60th United Nations Summit made the most concerted effort to date to arrive at a universal legal definition but could not reach agreement. A report commissioned by the UK government in 2007 similarly concluded that, 'there is no single definition of terrorism that commands full international support' (Carlile 2007: 47). From 1983 the following definition has been used by the US State Department: 'premeditated, politically motivated violence perpetrated against noncombatant targets by subnational groups or clandestine agents usually intended to influence an audience' (USA 1983).[1] Curiously, this definition would not classify attacks by subnational groups against active but not in-battle US servicemen, such as the Hizbullah attack which killed over 200 in Lebanon in 1983, as terrorist strikes. The definition does, however, capture the essence of the phenomenon we have witnessed as a major issue of global security since the late 1960s, that of political violence waged by non-state actors. The 1968 hijacking of an aeroplane by the Popular Front for the Liberation of Palestine is often held to have initiated an era of regular conflict between states and non-state actors in Israel–Palestine and on many other fronts throughout the world. Non-state groups had, though, taken on states before 1968 and left their mark on history. Assassinations of state leaders have a long history and the First World War was sparked by the shooting of the prince of the Austro-Hungarian Empire by a Serb nationalist group. It was from the late 1960s, though, that unorthodox non-state military violence became more routine and increasingly targeted at a wider audience than selected, prominent individuals.

The term terrorism is, though, an unhelpful one to use in describing this phenomenon since it is so value-laden. Terrorism, clearly, is a pejorative word. It is a term bandied about in conflict situations in order to contrast one side's legitimate killing with another side's illegitimate killing. Most frequently this will be by state forces against non-state forces since, in international law, state violence can be legal whereas non-state violence never can. Clearly, though, 'terror' is something that can be inflicted upon people by governments as well as by non-state actors. The term terrorism, indeed, was first coined to describe the state-directed violence and intimidation of French citizens by the Jacobins in the early years of the French Republic after the 1789 revolution. Nazi genocide, Stalin's purges and the 'killing fields' of the Khmer Rouge are amongst the numerous subsequent and more extensive examples of this phenomenon. At the same time, violent non-state struggles often come to be seen by states and sections of global public opinion as legitimate, as was the case with the African National Congress's (ANC) democratic revolution in South Africa. Hence the oft-quoted maxim, 'one man's terrorist is another man's freedom fighter'.

Consider for a moment the US government's terrorism definition minus the clause 'subnational groups or clandestine agents'. The definition now describes perfectly the defence policy of most powerful states, and certainly the USA, in the 'total war' era of the twentieth century. The blanket bombing of civilians in the Second World War and the very essence of nuclear weapons strategy were/are based upon 'premeditated, politically motivated violence perpetrated against non-combatant targets' and are 'intended to influence an audience'. Even if we accept that state violence deliberately directed at civilians can be legitimate (such as the argument that the atomic strikes on Japan in 1945 ultimately saved lives by ending the Second World War), no one can suggest that the fear of nuclear annihilation is not terrifying. Even in this post-Cold War era, when non-combatant immunity has come back into fashion, nuclear deterrence as a concept still rests on the fear factor emanating from the extraordinarily destructive power of such weapons.

If we leave aside the nuclear threat, it is clear also that states will often deliberately kill civilians if they consider it necessary for their security interests. 'State terrorism' against foreign citizens can be direct, as in the random scud assaults on Israel by Iraq during the Gulf War in 1991, or indirect through the sponsorship of terrorist cells such as the anti-Western attacks believed to have been organized by Libya in the 1980s. State terrorism of this form is not solely the preserve of such brutal dictators as Saddam Hussein and Gaddafi, however. The 1985 French destruction of the ship *Rainbow Warrior*, used by the pressure group Greenpeace to protest against nuclear testing in the south Pacific, was evidence that democracies are not averse to killing civilians outside of a conventional war situation.

Hence the term terrorism is problematic since it seems to conflate two ideas: the deliberate terrorizing of civilians and force used by non-state actors. In the following analysis I will concentrate on the second of those two ideas and accept that terror can be inflicted upon people by their own government, by other governments and by other entities, non-state actors (state terror is considered in Chapter 5). Criminal groups can also, of course, terrify and kill people and this form of non-state actor is considered in Chapter 10. This chapter will focus on the form and severity of challenge to states and citizens posed by politically-motivated and violent non-state actors. 'Terrorism' by non-state actors is just one aspect of this. Of far greater prominence is the more conventional violence waged in civil wars, which now dominates the military security agenda.

Types of political non-state military groups

The most prominent contemporary armed political non-state actors are listed in Table 3.1. The prominence of the high-profile Islamist groups based in the Middle East and Afghanistan/Pakistan is predictable but, at the same time, the list is maybe more diverse than may be popularly imagined in the West, with three leftist groups

TABLE 3.1 Most prominent contemporary violent political non-state actors

(a) Terrorist groups ranked by recent annual deaths

	2014			2015	
1	Boko Haram	6,644	1	ISIS	6,141
2	ISIS	6,073	2	Boko Haram	5,478
3	Taliban	3,477	3	Taliban	4,502
4	Fulani Militants (Nigeria)	1,229	4	al-Qa'ida	1,620
5	Al-Shabaab	1,021	5	Al-Shabaab	819
Total		32,685	Total		28,328

Source: Institute for Economics and Peace 2016.

(b) Number of coordinated attacks, 2000–14

•	ISIS	757
•	Boko Haram	558
•	Taliban	444
•	al-Qa'ida in Iraq	400
•	Communist Party of India/Maoists	337
•	Al-Shabaab	244
•	Tehrik & Taliban Pakistan	175
•	FARC	165
•	New People's Army (Philippines)	119
•	Fulani Militants	104

Source: START 2015.

and three from sub-Saharan Africa among the ten most prolific of the twenty-first century. There is no doubting the prominence of the Middle East and Islamism in the current picture of non-state terrorism but it is also clear that geopolitics colours the perception of the phenomenon. Leftist insurgents in India or the Philippines in the post-Cold War era do not register very prominently on the global agenda (the FARC in Colombia do because of their link to the cocaine trade, as discussed in Chapter 10).

Nationalist

Secessionist

Historically, the most prevalent and successful form of political non-state violence has come from movements claiming to represent a nation using force to achieve independence for their people. Nations are socially constructed communities defined subjectively according to common characteristics that a given group feel distinguish them from other nations. Such characteristics vary from case to case but may or may not include language, religion or ethnicity. National self-determination, the belief that nations are entitled to sovereign statehood, has been a powerful force within international politics since the latter part of the nineteenth century. There has never been a precise match-up between nations and states in the world but the struggle to achieve this has continued on many fronts over the last 150 years as the world has retreated from an age of multi-national empire.

The belief that nations had a right to become nation-states and that it was in the interests of world peace that they achieve it, reached its high point at the 1919 Paris Peace Conference which broke up the Austro-Hungarian Hapsburg and Turkish Ottoman Empires. National self-determination is still a strongly held conviction of many people and statesmen today. As such it is the secessionist 'terrorists' who are most likely to be considered 'freedom fighters' or 'national liberation movements'. A number of contemporary states were founded by successful campaigns of non-governmental violence. As examples, Kenya and Algeria were ceded by the UK and France respectively after bloody struggles and, in an earlier age, the USA was born in such circumstances. Many present-day nationalist struggles against states have received large levels of international legitimization. The Palestinians and, to a lesser extent, the Kurds are cases in point. Violent secessionists represent a major security threat for the states from which they aim to secede but they rarely threaten other states, other than through fear of a copy-cat uprising in their own territory. Such groups do not challenge the Westphalian order[2] since many states consider them simply to be following in their own footsteps and even enhancing international security by moving the world closer to the ideal of the nineteenth-century *risorgimento* nationalists, such as Mazzini, who felt that if all nations became states there would be little left to fight about (Mazzini 1862).

Counter-secessionist

Nationalism can inspire some people to take up arms to secede but also inspire others to fight to prevent that secession. National self-determination is a messy business in the contemporary world where migration, inter-marriage and integration have made any neat political division of the world on national grounds far more complicated than in Mazzini's era. A secessionist's proposed nation-state will often include enclaves, or even geographically indistinct groupings, of other nationalities who favour the status quo and fear being severed from their present state. Hence Serb nationalists in Croatia and Bosnia-Herzegovina took up arms when those two states seceded from Serb-dominated Yugoslavia in 1991, and pro-British 'loyalist' violence in Northern Ireland emerged in the 1970s to counter Irish nationalist aspirations to unify the province with the Republic of Ireland.

Liberal

Nationalism is a broad political label and is sometimes also used to characterize movements that are not secessionist or counter-secessionist but popular uprisings seeking to radically change a country in the name of the people. Armed 'Liberal' struggles of this sort occurred in the revolutions of France in 1789, in South Africa in the apartheid era and in several Arab states in the 2011–12 revolts. The fact that very few would consider labelling these revolutionary movements as terrorist illustrates clearly the point that non-state force can achieve a high degree of international legitimacy.

Religious

The growth of religious fundamentalism over the last thirty years has seen a number of armed groups emerge which are inspired essentially by religious doctrine. Generally seen as a new wave of non-state violence, following the dominance of this form of conflict by nationalist and Marxist groups in the late 1960s and 1970s, armed religious fanatics, in fact, pre-date the 'age of terrorism' and can be traced back as far as biblical times.

Judaism

Probably the world's first organized campaign of violence by a non-state group against a government was waged by the Zealots of Israel against Roman rule. As such the Zealots and other similar Jewish insurgency groups could be understood as national liberationists, but a crucial motivation to their campaign was the religious conviction that the arrival of the Messiah would follow a period of mayhem. Hence Jewish doubters, as well as occupying Romans, were often victims of spontaneous acts of Zealot violence. Many centuries on, in Israel groups such as Kach and Kahane Chai have carried out acts of violence since the 1990s against Palestinians in the West Bank in a campaign of religiously-inspired Zionism (Jewish nationalist movement to establish a homeland and state).

Islam

Non-state violence in the name of Islam dates back to the Assassins of the seventh century whose murderous campaign is now immortalized in the English language.

The Assassins were Shi'a Muslims who stabbed to death prominent political and religious individuals who were felt to be resisting the advancement of their cause of the preservation of traditional Islamic values. Over a millennium later, political violence in the name of Islam returned to become a major feature of international politics. The 1979 Iranian Revolution, which overthrew a Western-oriented royal dynasty and put in its place a fundamentalist Shi'a regime, served as the catalyst for armed Islamist struggles, both Shi'a and Sunni (the two main sects), elsewhere in the Middle East and Africa. This modern wave of political Islam can actually be dated back as far as the 1920s and the anti-colonialist movement in Egypt which founded the Muslim Brotherhood, but was later inspired, radicalized and internationalized by the Iranian Revolution and the USSR's invasion of Afghanistan which occurred in the same year.

Post-revolutionary Iran gave active support to Shi'a groups such as Hizbullah seeking an Iranian-style revolution in Lebanon as well as resisting Israeli incursions into that country. Sunni revolutionaries, such as the Armed Islamic Group in Algeria and al-Gama'at al-Islmiyya in Egypt, were also inspired to seek the overthrow of governments they saw as immorally irreligious. Some Islamist groups took the fight beyond domestic revolution, rallying to the cause of Palestinian nationalist resistance to Israel and further to the USA and European countries seen as upholding Israel and meddling in the affairs of Islamic states. In this way Islamist violence has come to be seen as so much more of a security threat to Western democracies than other forms of non-state force. It tends to be more transnational in character and directly challenges notions of secularity and sovereignty which underpin the Westphalian order. In the aftermath of the September 11th 2001 strikes on the USA, Suleiman Abu Gaith, a spokesman of al Qa'ida mastermind Osama bin Laden stated:

> Every Muslim has to play his real and true role to uphold his religion and his action in fighting and jihad is a duty ... those youths who did what they did and destroyed America with their airplanes did a good deed. They have moved the battle into the heart of America. America must know that the battle will not leave its land. Go willing, until America leaves our land, until it stops supporting Israel, until it stops the blockade against Iraq.
>
> (Halliday 2002: 235)[3]

The challenge to citizenship and statehood posed by al-Qa'ida and its associates became acutely apparent in 2005 when it transpired that the suicide bombers who killed fifty-six London public transport passengers were fellow British citizens or 'home-grown terrorists'. ISIS-sponsored attacks on several European cities since then have followed this pattern, collapsing conventional notions of geopolitics.

Hindu

The Thugs, like the Assassins, attracted such fearsome notoriety that their name lives on centuries later as a noun in English and other languages. The Thugs (or Thugees) were a Hindu cult who killed, mainly by strangulation, an estimated one

BOX 3.1 **Abu Bakr al-Baghdadi**

In a clear illustration of radicalization by the Iraq War, this Iraqi religious scholar and member of the Muslim Brotherhood became active in resistance to the US invasion in 2003. Al-Baghdadi was imprisoned by the Americans in 2004 for his involvement in the Jaysh Ahl al-Sunnah wa al-Jamaah insurgent group but was seen as a low-level risk and served only a few months. However, in another classic model of radicalization, al-Baghdadi built up contacts with other radicals and groups in prison and, on release, rose up the ranks of a growing, disparate national insurgency. He assumed the leadership of ISIS on the death of its founder Abu Omar al-Baghdadi in 2010 and, in the following year, the role of the world's foremost Islamist terrorist after the assassination of al-Qa'ida's Osama bin Laden by US troops in Pakistan. Al-Baghdadi lavishly praised bin Laden on his death but, after a period of viewing al-Qa'ida as brothers in arms, ISIS split from the now fading group in 2014. Around the same time as this schism, ISIS felt emboldened to declare a caliphate from the land and oil fields they had conquered from the Iraqi and Syrian governments. Regularly reported to have suffered the same fate as bin Laden, al-Baghdadi has continued to defy a $25 million ransom placed on his head by Washington and find success in resisting the military might of both Moscow and Washington whilst recruiting and inspiring fighters from across the world to a strikingly brutal international campaign.

million people (mainly fellow Hindus), until they were eliminated by the British colonial rulers of India in the nineteenth century (Sleeman 1930). In general, Hinduism is noted as a religion of tolerance, and systematic religiously-inspired attacks on people of other faiths historically have been rare. Recent years, though, have seen a rise in Hindu fundamentalism and increased attacks on Moslems in India, encouraged by the radical 'Hindu nationalism' of the Hindutva movement. Over 2,000 Moslems were killed in a series of orchestrated massacres in Gujarat in February and March of 2002 (Human Rights Watch 2003). The chief minister of Gujarat state at that time, the Hindu nationalist Narendra Modi, was much criticized for his negligence over this but nevertheless went on to become Indian prime minister.

Christianity

Christian fundamentalism has long been blended with crude racism in US white supremacist groups such as Aryan Nations and the Ku Klux Klan, who continue to pose a domestic human security threat. In recent years the most prolific overtly-Christian violent non-state actor has been the Lord's Resistance Army (LRA).

The LRA, who are largely based in South Sudan, have been conducting a civil insurgency against the government of Uganda since the late 1980s aimed at the establishment of a theocratic state governed by the Bible's Ten Commandments. In doing so, the LRA have, however, violated most of the Ten Commandments themselves in a horrific campaign which has featured random murders, tortures, rapes and the enslavement of Ugandan children.

Buddhism

As a religion noted for its commitment to peaceful relations, Buddhism is less associated with aggressive fundamentalism then other major faiths but it is an indication of how far religious terrorists can bastardize the scriptures which inspire them that it too has spawned a radical, violent offshoot. The doomsday cult Aum Shinrikyo (Supreme Truth) was established in Japan in 1987 by its spiritual leader Shoko Asahara and developed an offshoot in Russia. In 1995, in an apparent step towards a take-over of the world, Aum members released the poisonous gas sarin in underground trains in Tokyo, killing twelve people and injuring over 5,000.

Marxist/Maoist

Prior to the rise of fundamentalist violence in the 1980s the biggest non-governmental security threat for most states came from armed leftist revolutionaries. As with religious violence, Marxist revolutionaries sometimes represented a threat beyond their country of origin in line with the internationalist doctrine they were fighting for. Many democratic states faced such threats in the late 1960s and 1970s. The Red Army Faction in West Germany, Red Brigade in Italy and Red Army in Japan were amongst the most prominent, becoming a primary security concern in their own countries and a source of international concern because of anti-capitalist actions taken throughout the world.

Leftist revolutionaries of this form are of less significance in the West today but have not gone away altogether, and groups in Turkey and Greece, in particular, have continued low-level campaigns. Leftist revolutionaries continue to have a high profile in some Latin American states, most notably in Colombia where the National Liberation Army (FARC) has long represented a direct challenge to the government, and with the Maoist Shining Path in Peru. Prominent groups also exist in the Philippines and India, whilst in Nepal the Maoists succeeded in assuming partial power in 2006.

As with other categories of political non-state violence, leftist terror did not emerge from nowhere in the 1960s and 1970s. Prior to the contemporary age of terrorism a range of small anarchist (essentially anti-capitalist) groups sent shock-waves around much of the industrializing world between 1880 and 1910 with a series of sporadic, high-profile assassinations that included the Russian Tsar (in 1881), French president (in 1894) and US president (in 1901).

Fascist/racist

Although an equally radical and aggressive ideology, Fascism has, historically, spawned fewer violent non-governmental groups than Marxism. This is because

Fascism is generally associated with the tightening of state authority and tends to be from 'above' rather than 'below'. In addition, of course, fascists tend to be foreigner-hating ultra-nationalists so where their actions have occurred they have, until recently, tended to be part of purely domestic campaigns. Some armed non-state far right groups emerged in the late 1960s and 1970s as counter-responses to Marxist revolutionaries. Ordine Nuovo (New Order) and a spin-off group, the Armed Revolutionary Nuclei (ARN), for example, carried out a number of attacks on civilians in Italy between 1969 and 1980.

In recent decades right-wing non-state violence has become much more racist than anti-Marxist. The Boeremag in South Africa have targeted black civilians in bombing campaigns; Russian National Unity have carried out a number of anti-semitic attacks; and less organized 'skinhead' violence has been a persistent threat to immigrant communities throughout Western Europe. These developments, though, tend not to be properly reflected in official statistics since many countries classify racist attacks as 'hate crimes' rather than terrorism. The fact that right-wing terror hence tends to be underrepresented was made graphically evident in 2011 when a lone gunman in Norway slayed seventy-seven professional and youth politicians he saw as epitomizing multi-culturalism. This sort of 'lone wolf' terrorism has also been increasingly evident amongst Islamic fundamentalist 'home-grown' activists.

Other ideologies

Eco-terrorists

An aggressively militant brand of 'deep green' ecologism has periodically emerged in Western Europe and North America from the 1970s. Animal liberationists have bombed laboratories known to carry out vivisection and occasional violent tactics have been launched against lumberjacks and building constructors. At a more systematic level, the Canadian-based group Sea Shepherd (a radical offshoot of Greenpeace) have invoked the fury of the Japanese government by carrying out a campaign of ramming and sinking whaling ships in the Pacific. The prominence of the Earth Liberation Front and Animal Liberation Front in the USA in the 2000s, in the eyes of the Federal Bureau of Investigation (FBI), saw eco-terrorism even eclipse far right anti-federalism to become that country's greatest domestic terrorist threat (Lewis 2005).

Single-issue groups

Other politically-motivated acts of violence can best be understood as a radicalization of cause groups, rather than part of any broader ideology or religion. Most prominent amongst such groups are anti-abortionists in the USA who have killed medics. In addition, anti-globalization demonstrations at the venues of global economic summits have occasionally turned violent. Such riots are frequently attributed to those bogeymen of yesteryear, the anarchists, but might, more rightly, also be considered an example of single-issue violence. Ironically, it is globalization which allows such groups to proliferate as the opportunities for international exposure, recruitment and tactical coordination for small-scale organizations are heightened through telecommunications advances.

The rise of political non-state violence

The rise of this form of conflict can largely be explained by the coming together of two factors. First, the tactics of terrorism allow the weak to take on the strong. This is not new and not only true of non-state actors. The term *guerrilla* warfare dates back to the Peninsular War early in the nineteenth century when irregular Spanish and Portuguese forces were able to achieve military successes against a far stronger French invading army. This phenomenon, though, can be dated back to ancient times, as illustrated in the previous section. Such a feat was repeated in the late twentieth century, in far more uneven contests, when Vietnamese and Afghan 'Davids' were able to defeat the American and Soviet 'Goliaths'. Soldiers indistinguishable from civilians make an elusive enemy and this is exacerbated when there is no clear link between them and their country.

A second factor behind the rise of 'the age of terrorism' is the advance of communications technology. For political non-state violence to be effective it needs an audience to communicate its message to and terrify into submission. The first indication of this use of a globalizing audience came with the nineteenth-century anarchist assassins whose acts gained the exposure of an emerging international media. The globalization of the media provides the 'oxygen of publicity' for putting into practice acts of political violence. The extensive and sophisticated use of the internet by al-Qa'ida and ISIS over the last decade provides the clearest example of this. Cheap and easily-available air travel has also served to facilitate international operations of violent non-state groups, both in terms of deployment and recruitment. Globalization has also assisted non-state groups in raising funds for their campaigns. This has particularly aided nationalist groups since 'ex-pat' communities in other countries are often keen to be remote revolutionaries, with a romanticized notion of their brethren's struggle. Irish republicanism greatly benefited from fundraising amongst US citizens of Irish descent, whilst Sikh nationalism in the 1980s was as much orchestrated by migrants in Canada as those residing in the territory seeking secession from India.

Globalization allied to increased state arms surpluses since the end of the Cold War has also contributed to disaffected non-state groups finding it easier to avail themselves of weapons with the proceeds of their fundraising activities. Non-state forces fighting proxy wars during the Cold War, such as the leftist UNITA in Angola or the anti-leftist Contras in Nicaragua, have suffered from losing state sponsorship, but other groups have been able to step up their campaigns. The flourishing global trade in arms can help sustain conflicts longer even than the political disagreements which triggered them. In some cases this has led to a blurring of the line distinguishing political from purely criminal violent organizations. 'Conflicts in a number of places (Colombia, Liberia, Tajikistan etc) have lost any of the ideological motivation they once possessed and instead have degenerated into conflicts among petty groups fighting to grab local resources' (Singer 2001: 196–7).

Political non-state violence has gradually become more and more globalized, but this is not entirely new. Armed Marxist and Marxist-leaning groups coordinated their actions in the 1970s, as exemplified by the 1975 kidnapping incident at an Organization of Petroleum Exporting Countries (OPEC) meeting in Vienna in which the unlikely trinity of the Popular Front for the Liberation of Palestine, Irish

TABLE 3.2 The top ten bloodiest single acts of non-state terrorist violence

	Place	Date	No. Killed	Action	Perpetrators
1	New York/Washington DC/Pennsylvania	Sept. 2001	2,993	Hijack of aeroplanes & suicide attacks on government & public buildings	al-Qa'ida
2	Badush, Iraq	July 2014	670	Bombing of prison killing Shia and releasing Sunni inmates	ISIS
3	Bedi, Nepal	March 2004	513	Massacre at police station and army barracks	Communist Party of Nepal
4	Sinjar, Iraq	Aug. 2014	500	Massacre and abduction of Yazidis	ISIS
5	Abadan, Iran	Aug. 1978	430	Arson of theatre	Islamist revolutionaries
6	Beslan, Russia	Sept. 2004	344	Hostages held at a school killed during siege	Chechen separatists
7	North Atlantic	June 1985	331	Bombing of Indian passenger plane	Sikh nationalists
8	Mumbai	March 1993	317	Series of bombings	Local Islamists
9	Gamboru, Nigeria	May 2014	315	Massacres and abductions of townspeople	Boko Haram
10	Palmyra, Iraq	July 2014	310	Attack and abductions of troops and gas-field workers	ISIS

Note: List excludes casualty figures from full-scale civil wars and counter-invasion insurgencies.

Source: Institute for Economics and Peace 2016.

Republican Army (IRA) and Red Army Faction were involved. 'Carlos the Jackal' played the role of the freelance transnational terrorist, linking together such leftist groups in this era, in much the same way as Osama bin Laden did for Islamic radicals in the 1990s and 2000s. The limitations of a balance of power approach to understanding global security politics are starkly exposed by the influence of such individuals and their networks. US diplomat Richard Holbrooke summed this up in saying of bin Laden: 'how is it that a man living in a cave can out-communicate the most skilful communications nation in the world?' (Cornwell 2002: 11).

The terror tactics of political non-state military groups are myriad and have evolved over time. The hijacking of aeroplanes ('skyjacking') was the tactic of choice in the late 1960s and early 1970s, the seizing of embassies was popular in the late 1970s and early 1980s, and the blowing up of mid-flight aeroplanes took centre stage in the late 1980s. Perennial favourite tactics include hostage taking, the assassination of prominent individuals and detonating bombs in government or public buildings. The September 11th 2001 strikes breathtakingly combined skyjacking and the destruction of public buildings with the added ingredient of suicide bombing in a single, unprecedented enterprise. Again, however, it is worth emphasizing that most non-state violence is far more 'mainstream' than such tactics and takes the form of sporadic guerrilla insurgency campaigns against state military forces. Table 3.3 lists the most bloody of such wars, excluding related civilian massacres, which are addressed in Chapter 5. It has become increasingly common for analysts of terrorism and non-state insurgencies to distinguish between 'old' and 'new' forms of the phenomena. Whilst old terrorism persists, many contemporary violent political non-state actors are small to the point of not being organizations at all and less explicit in their aims. Wilkinson, for example, suggests that only around a quarter of contemporary terror/insurgent groups have over a thousand members and increasingly are 'incorrigible rather than corrigible' (Wilkinson 2011: 7–20).

TABLE 3.3 The ten bloodiest civil wars in history

	War	Date	Deaths (battle + indirect)
1	Taiping revolution (China)	1850–1864	20 million
2	Russian civil war	1918–1921	8.8 million
3	Congo Free State	1886–1908	7.5 million
4	China (warlord/nationalist conflict)	1917–1937	4 million
5	2nd Congolese civil war	1998–2003	3.3 million
6	Chinese civil war	1945–1949	2.5 million
7	2nd Sudanese civil war	1983–1999	1.9 million
8	Ethiopian civil wars	1962–1992	1.4 million
9	Mexican revolution	1910–1920	1 million
10	Biafran revolt (Nigeria)	1967–1970	1 million

Source: White 2004.

Responses to political non-state violence

Table 3.4 attempts to distil the range of options open to governments seeking to counter the threat posed to them and their citizens by armed non-state political groups. Since the passing of the Cold War and the rise of global Islamist threats, government counter-terrorism strategies have become more multi-faceted and internationally-coordinated but, at the same time, more stringent.

TABLE 3.4 State counter-terrorist options

	Domestic	International
Political	'No deals' v. appeasement	Diplomacy – carrot & stick
Military	Covert operations	War/foreign policy change
Containment	Hardening targets	Intelligence sharing
Legal	Emergency legislation	UNSC & ICC
Educative	Change 'terrorists'/change society	Global discourse

Political

Domestic: 'no deals' versus appeasement

One option open to governments in facing up to the challenge of non-state violence is to come to some sort of accommodation with the group threatening to initiate or continue a campaign of violence. This may take the form of giving in to the demands made by terrorists in relation to a specific action, such as agreeing to free 'political prisoners' in exchange for the safe release of hostages. Governments have followed this course of action more frequently than is often appreciated as a simple means of avoiding bloodshed. Concessions are, of course, often kept quiet by governments since they do not want their citizens or other potential terrorists to see them as a 'soft touch'. The Japanese government, for example, secretly made a number of significant specific concessions to the Japanese Red Army in the 1970s including several prisoner releases. All governments, despite claims to the contrary, have 'given in to terrorism' from time to time in order to avert bloodshed. Though it is rarely officially admitted, it is known that several governments have paid Iraqi insurgent hostage-takers holding their nationals during the course of the conflict that has raged there since 2003.

In response to a longer-term campaign of non-state violence a government may come to see that the only way to achieve peace is through some sort of negotiated settlement with the organization, in much the same way as inter-state conflicts are often resolved. In fact, concessions are more probable in a state war with a non-state actor than in a war with another state since outright military defeat of the enemy is less likely. The IRA probably never consisted of more than 1,000 active servicemen but it could not be defeated by the armed forces of the UK since its members were not clearly distinguishable from ordinary citizens. Even the blanket bombing of Ireland, should such an extreme measure have been considered, could not have achieved victory for the UK since many IRA cells operated in London and elsewhere in England. Hence the UK government secretly initiated dialogue with the IRA in 1985, leading eventually to a compromised settlement which saw a former IRA activist take up a leading position within a power-sharing executive for Northern Ireland.

The Irish peace process represented a two-way compromise, with the IRA abandoning its armed struggle in exchange for a share of power, but non-state violence may succeed in winning a long-term campaign and force a capitulation of the government. The African National Congress (ANC) ultimately forced the white minority government of South Africa to stand down and accept a democratic revolution. In this case the government recognized that its position was hopeless and the capitulation represented the will of the people. In cases where armed groups represent a minority opinion, appeasement becomes more problematic from a democratic point of view. Neumann posits that negotiating with terrorists is the only way a democratic government can expect to end a conflict but nonetheless observes that the process needs to be more sophisticated than making sudden major concessions. Hence the Colombian government's outreach to leftist guerrillas in 1998, which included the surrendering of a huge tract of territory to the Revolutionary Armed Forces of Colombia (FARC) (which became known, unofficially, as 'Farcland'), empowered and emboldened the guerrillas, rather than bringing the conflict to an end. A much more gradual and phased process of incorporating armed rebels into the democratic process is required, as has been seen in Northern Ireland and has now emerged in Colombia (Neumann 2007).

Whereas appeasement may save lives in the short term, the possible downside of this approach, of course, is that it may give encouragement to other disavowed groups that violence pays dividends. The official approach of the US, Israeli and Russian governments, three of the main targets of much non-state violence over recent years, has been most characterized by the phrase 'no deals with terrorists'. President Putin has expressed this in unambiguous terms: 'Russia does not negotiate with terrorists, it destroys them' (Putin 2004). The basis of such a tough strategy is the belief that only by being seen not to back down can terrorism be deterred in the long term. The short-term result may be a loss of lives but the well-known military maxim that you may have to lose a battle in order to win the war holds sway.

Globalization, though, complicates this appeasement/no deals dilemma. For example, concessions made by the Indian government to Islamist militants who skyjacked a passenger plane in 1999 secured many Indian lives in the short term but came, possibly, with a bigger, global cost.

If any state deals with terrorists, it not only encourages stepped-up terrorism against its own interests but also creates problems for other nations. A classic case is India's ignominious surrender to the hijackers of flight IC-814. One freed terrorist hand-delivered by the foreign minister is the suspected financier of Mohammed Atta, the alleged ringleader in the September 11th terrorist strikes. Another released terrorist founded a group in Pakistan that has claimed responsibility for major Kashmir strikes.

(Chellaney 2001)

Evidence as to whether appeasement or zero tolerance is the most successful strategy for dealing with non-state violence is unclear. Walter Laqueur makes the case for zero tolerance in observing that, 'the more severe the repression, the less terrorism tends to occur' (Laqueur 1990: 207). Laqueur bases this assertion on observing the relative lack of non-state violence in authoritarian political systems compared to democratic ones, noting that 'terrorism in Spain gathered strength only after General Franco died' (ibid.). Particularly hardline counter-terrorist methods, attracting great international criticism, have since been deployed by authoritarian governments in successfully suppressing major insurgencies in 1990s Peru (leftists) and 2000s Sri Lanka (Tamil separatists). Hence supporting evidence can be found for Laqueur's argument but, at the same time, there is little likelihood of citizens of most democratic states accepting the idea of living in a police state of the order of Fujimori's Peru in order to deter terrorist threats. In addition, the zero tolerance stance of the governments of Israel, Russia and the USA has been accompanied by an increased level of non-state violence being perpetrated on their citizens over the last two decades.

The Americans and Israelis have taken a comparatively tough stance in their dealings with non-state forces, but the 'no deals' notion is really more rhetorical than real. Israel negotiated with terrorists in the run-up to the Oslo Accords in 1993 and is known to have authorized many Arab prisoner releases. The US-led 'war on terror' has actually included many 'non-war' dimensions such as authorizing prisoner exchange deals with ISIS. It appears, then, there is no simple answer to the question of whether or not governments should talk to terrorists or at least modify their behaviour in line with their demands.

International: diplomatic carrots and sticks

In cases of 'state-sponsored terrorism', conventional foreign policy tools aimed at pressuring governments believed to be funding or giving refuge to violent non-state organizations can be used. The Gaddafi regime in Libya, for example, in the 1990s appeared to cease backing anti-Western terror groups in response to the US, UK and other states utilizing, first, the diplomatic stick of isolation (through withdrawing diplomatic recognition) and then the carrot of restoring and enhancing political and trading links. However, one downside of the modern diplomatic trend of politicizing recognition (as opposed to the traditional Lauterpacht Doctrine of giving recognition to a regime that is in control whether you like it or not) is that the resulting pariah states are left free from diplomatic leverage. The fact that the Taliban regime in Afghanistan had never been recognized by the USA or any other Western state made it difficult to exercise political pressure on them to give up members of al-Qa'ida based in their territory in the wake of the 2001 attacks on the USA.

As a consequence of this lack of diplomatic leverage, one of the first actions of the US government following the September 11th 2001 strikes was to attempt to build a 'coalition against terror', recognizing that they would need the support not only of their traditional allies but of as many states as possible, in order to pursue a prolonged campaign against those responsible for this and other acts of anti-American terrorism. The diplomatic isolation of Afghanistan made the support of its neighbour Pakistan essential, particularly since it was one of only three states recognizing the Taliban government.[4] Pakistan could provide diplomatic leverage on a government it had helped bring to power as well as intelligence information on a country not well understood even by a superpower. Classic diplomatic bargaining was very much to the fore here, with Pakistan rewarded by the USA for turning its back on its ally, and risking the wrath of sections of its own population in doing so. Sanctions imposed in the wake of its testing of nuclear weapons in 1998 and the military coup which had brought its leader Musharraf to power were lifted and 'rewards' promised. The key regional powers, China and Russia, were also courted by the USA as were countries such as Syria, previously cited by the Americans as sponsors of terrorism, in an exercise of *realpolitik* designed to reduce the options open to an elusive transnational enemy.

That the world's only military superpower should need to coalition-build and horse-trade like this was testimony to the fact that the nature of military politics in a unipolar world is not necessarily distinct from previous eras of international relations, even if the sources of insecurity are far different than those encountered by the statesmen of yesteryear. Whilst the New World Order has proved a disappointment in many respects, countering Islamist terrorism is one issue of global military security that has consistently prompted significant cooperation among the UN 'permanent five' and other major powers. The state system itself is challenged by the rise of political actors who defy traditional norms of sovereignty, diplomacy and warfare, and so its members are increasingly rallying to its defence.

Containment

Domestic: hardening of targets

All governments faced by a substantial threat of non-state violence look to secure themselves and their citizens by containing such threats through the 'hardening' of potential terrorist targets. Security measures at most international airports were stepped up in the 1970s in response to the popularity of 'skyjackings' and this particular terror tactic became less frequent as a result. The September 11th (9/11) New York and Washington suicide pilots, of course, avoided encountering extensive security checks on international flights into the USA by hijacking passenger planes on internal flights, notable for much laxer security measures. Even in the wake of the 1995 Oklahoma bombing, by the US anti-federalist Timothy McVeigh, American notions of security remained externalized and moves to tighten checks on internal flights were resisted. By contrast, since the 1970s, airport security on internal flights in Israel has been as tight as it is for international flights. From 2001 US security for the first time began to be framed in a manner closer to that of Israel and other parts of the world in which threats from organized non-state violence are part of the political landscape.

Before 2001 the irritation and economic cost of slowing up the USA's dense network of internal flights was enough to outweigh the potential security cost in the minds of most Americans. Such costs and irritations are easily borne by people who perceive that they serve to enhance their personal security. Most Peruvians initially were happy to tolerate serious restrictions on their everyday lives in Fujimori's campaign against Shining Path and Tupac Amaru Revolutionary Movement (MRTA) in the 1990s. There is, however, a limit to what citizens of Western democracies will tolerate in the name of containing terrorism. Liberal opinion in the UK was hostile to suggestions by the Labour government in the wake of the 2001 attacks on the USA that identity cards be introduced for British citizens, so that state officials could keep a better track of the activities of foreign citizens. Indeed, the knee-jerk nature of such responses after acts of terror is evident in the fact that the UK government appeared to overlook the fact that the presence of such a scheme in the USA did not prevent the September 11th tragedy nor did it later deter the Madrid bombers in 2004. The subsequent rise of 'home-grown terrorism' has made this debate seem *passé*. Sensibly balancing the security and freedom of its citizens is perhaps the essence of democratic government in the twenty-first century.

International: intelligence sharing

Intelligence sharing on terrorism has increased since the 1990s both as a consequence of governments adapting to the changed geopolitical landscape and the re-deployment of existing Cold War cooperation. NATO did not concern itself greatly with non-state violence during the Cold War, but was jolted into action in this domain by the 9/11 strikes and in 2003 established the Terrorist Threat Intelligence Unit (later expanded to create the Intelligence Unit in 2011). Similarly, if less formally, the Five Eyes intelligence-sharing arrangement established by the 'Alliance of English Speaking Nations' of the USA, UK, Australia, New Zealand and Canada in 1947 to counter Communism is now primarily concerned with counter-terrorism. Elsewhere regional economic cooperation has come to spill over into intelligence sharing on political non-state violence, such as with the EU's Europol police-coordination unit, established initially to tackle narcotics movement across the Single Market (see Chapter 10), and the African Union's African Centre for the Study and Research on Terrorism.

In general, the end of the Cold War has improved intergovernmental solidarity and paved the way for a more systematic approach to tackling political non-state violence. The G7 cartel of the world's most economically powerful states became an unlikely focus for state cooperation against the menace of transnational military forces in the 1990s. The G7 together with Russia held a 'terrorism summit' in 1996 in Lyon, which sought to harmonize state approaches to the problem in order to avoid such groups exploiting policy differences. Issues addressed included collectively recognizing non-state violence as illegitimate, criminalizing fundraising for such groups, the need to avoid the appeasement of hostage takers, and tough sentencing for this sort of crime.

Legal measures

Domestic legal responses

The freedom versus security balancing act apparent in containing terrorism also faces governments when dealing legally with the suspected perpetrators of non-state violence (whether their own citizens or not, though most acutely when dealing with their own citizens). Many governments have responded to non-state security threats by introducing 'emergency legislation', which essentially suspends normal rights of citizenship for suspects from their own country or withdraws the rights normally enjoyed by non-citizens residing within their country. This has greatly increased since 2001, with Human Rights Watch estimating that 140 governments have followed the lead of the USA PATRIOT (Uniting and Strengthening America by Providing Appropriate Tools Required to Intercept and Obstruct Terrorism) Act, approved by Congress less than two months after 9/11 (HRW 2012). Amongst the sorts of legal measures enacted by governments in this respect are the following:

Proscribing membership of certain organizations

The act of being a member of an organization associated with acts of violence against the state, without necessarily being actively involved in such violence, has long been criminalized by governments. However, in democracies this strategy tends to lead to violent non-state organizations forming 'legitimate' political wings so that their spokespeople can continue to advance their cause without technically being associated with the violent organization. Examples of this include Sinn Fein, set up as the political arm of the IRA, and Herri Battasuna, the sister organization of violent Basque separatists ETA in the 1980s and 1990s.

The increased globalization of non-state political violence has led to the proscribed lists of terrorist organizations growing since 2001 to include groups with no track record of carrying out attacks in the country in which they are banned. New Zealand, for example, by 2012 had banned membership of some seventy-one groups despite having a recent history almost entirely devoid of terrorist incidents (HRW 2012). Whilst the notion of making it illegal to be a member of an organization committed to overthrowing the state is not especially surprising or controversial, the fear is that some governments have used this as a pretext for suppressing any sort of opposition groups, particularly if they are Islamic. For example, the Chinese government have proscribed membership of the East Turkestan Islamic Movement, and their counterparts in Delhi the Students Islamist Movement of India. India and China have had to face up to violent insurgencies in regions where these groups operate but human rights organizations contend that the proscribed groups are purely peaceful protesters (HRW 2012).

Internment

Emergency legislation enacted in the face of a terrorist campaign may also see the state grant itself the power to arrest suspects without having to resort to normal legal processes. Overturning legal principles dating back to the thirteenth century, the UK derogated from Article 5 of the European Convention on Human Rights shortly after the 9/11 attacks in order to be able to detain terrorist suspects for longer periods without charging them and with less evidence than ordinarily permitted.

Trial without jury

Concerns that jurors could be intimidated against finding members of major violent organizations guilty have prompted many governments to suspend the democratic norm of trial by jury for such trials. Most notoriously, the USA in 2007 began trying prisoners held at their naval base at Guantanamo Bay on the island of Cuba on suspicion of being al-Qa'ida or Taliban operatives, by military tribunal. Such was the international unease at this derogation from normal legal practice that even most of the USA's staunchest allies protested and demanded the release of their own nationals held in this way.

Sentencing

Governments also frequently act against political non-state violence by legislating for the perpetrators of such crimes to be subject to heavier sentencing by the courts than other violent criminals, in the hope of deterring such acts. The logic of deterrence, however, does not always work as well on armed revolutionaries as it does on armed criminals. High-profile imprisonment may serve to advance the cause of the terrorist/freedom fighter (as with Mandela) whilst a death sentence may turn a killer into a martyr and is, of course, hardly likely to deter a suicide bomber.

Restrictions on free expression

Governments have long been known to suspend another civil right of democratic citizens when dealing with advocates of political non-state violence, that of free speech and expression. France introduced such restrictions in the 1890s in response to the rise of anarchist attacks, but, again, this has risen in prominence in the contemporary era. Human Rights Watch suggest that fifty states, democratic and otherwise, have enacted laws curtailing free expression since 2001, including far-reaching encroachments on the freedom of the press in countries like Russia and Turkey (HRW 2012).

Surveillance

A central feature of the USA PATRIOT Act is the granting of greatly extended surveillance powers to law enforcement and intelligence agencies, and permitting the resultant 'wire taps' of suspected terrorist communications to be produced as evidence in court. Globally, 120 states have authorized increased surveillance powers, which have yielded some impressive results in terms of arrests and the foiling of attacks but have also eroded the privacy of millions of innocent citizens. More questionable, both on ethical and pragmatic grounds, has been the extension of police powers of 'stop and search' for potential terror suspects. Human Rights Watch estimate that well over half a million people in the UK were stopped and searched by police without normal levels of criminal suspicion between 2002 and 2011, resulting in not a single terrorist conviction (HRW 2012). This police power was revoked in 2011 on the basis of this demonstrable failure, but also through concern that the singling out of – principally – young Arab and Asian men in this way was likely to be counterproductive in tackling radicalization.

Global legal responses

It has taken a surprisingly long time for the Westphalian system as a collectivity to seek to rid itself of the systemic threat posed by non-state violence. The tendency for many states to empathize with nationalist struggles or see advantage in a rival state being weakened by civil strife stifled the development of international law and other collaborative arrangements for many years. UN Conventions outlawing skyjacking and hostage-taking were ratified in the 1960s and 1970s, but not until 1985 did Security Council and General Assembly Resolutions (579, 40/61) unite nearly all of the world in condemning all forms of non-state terrorism.[5] Additionally, states generally have been slower to develop extradition treaties for politically rather than criminally motivated aggressors and this is off-limits for the world's premier police cooperation organ Interpol. An important breakthrough, though, came with the 2004 Security Council Resolution 1566 which declared that terrorist tactics cannot be legitimate under any circumstances.

In 1993 the Security Council, under Resolution 864, imposed sanctions on a non-state actor for the first time and succeeded in bringing UNITA (National Union for the Total Independence of Angola) to the negotiating table through an arms embargo, travel ban and financial restrictions on the group's membership. The success of these measures prompted similar resolutions against al-Qa'ida members in the aftermath of the 2001 attacks on the USA. Resolution 1373 (2001) actually goes far beyond just targeting known terrorists and calls upon all states to criminalize the hosting and/or financing of all non-state military forces and share intelligence. A 1373 committee monitors this by producing reports on the record of states in complying with these requirements. Hence the aforementioned tightening of domestic legal measures against non-state political violence can be linked to the changed global environment.

Military

'Fight fire with fire' #1: covert domestic operations

Much non-state violence has taken the form of 'terrorism' because such strategies are not easily countered by states geared up to resist more conventional military operations. Hence, states faced with persistent non-state security threats have adapted their armed forces in accordance by creating special counter-terrorist units or by adapting existing special forces. The Israeli government authorized their intelligence agency Mossad to implement an operation named 'Wrath of God' as a direct response to the 1972 Munich Olympics massacre of Israeli athletes by the Palestinian nationalist group Black September. A Mossad unit were given the task of wiping out Black September and empowered to do so by whatever means necessary, even where this meant acting outside of international law by entering other states uninvited to carry out assassinations. This controversial strategy was vindicated in that Black September were effectively eliminated by September 1973, but the mistaken killing of an innocent waiter in Norway, unfortunate enough to look like a particular member of the target group, showed the ethical limitations of such an approach.

British counter-terrorism against Irish nationalist forces in the 1980s and early 1990s came to be led by the revival of the Special Air Service (SAS), set up during the Second World War as a crack unit to operate behind enemy lines. The SAS's success in killing a number of IRA personnel was a crucial factor in bringing the IRA and Sinn Fein to the negotiating table. Essentially a stalemate had been reached in the conflict, with both sides accepting that the outright defeat of the other was impossible. In the wake of the 9/11 strikes on the USA, many states reviewed their defence arrangements and such units became less 'special' and more of a standard security force. The defeat of the Tamil Tigers by Sri Lankan forces in 2009 was highly contentious in terms of the brutality used but also served to demonstrate that military victories against non-state insurgents were possible. For over twenty years conventional military action against the Tamils, including at one stage the use of troops from India, had failed to make the decisive breakthrough. However, from 2006, the deployment of small specially-trained Special Infantry Operations Teams behind the insurgent lines tipped the balance in favour of the government.

'Fight fire with fire' #2: international war

The 2001–2 Afghan War was the only 'full-scale' war to have been waged against a state because of an armed non-state actor within its territory but conventional international military responses at a lesser level have been used from time to time and have now become more regularized. The USA bombed Libya in 1986 in retaliation for its leadership's links with a number of incidents around the world which had targeted US servicemen. Similarly, in 1998 US air strikes targeted sites in Afghanistan and Sudan linked to al-Qa'ida in response to the bombing of their embassies in Kenya and Tanzania. Israel too has used military might to take on an elusive enemy. Controversial invasions of Lebanon in 1982, 1996 and 2006 sought to flush out the Palestinian Liberation Organization (PLO) and, in the latest incursion, Hizbullah bases in order secure their northern border. In a similar vein, Turkish actions against Kurdish separatists have included incursions into Iraq where the Kurdistan Workers' Party (PKK) and other related groups have long had strongholds. These limited military engagements have tended to be largely unsuccessful and, possibly, even counterproductive. The US strikes of 1998 hit an innocent target in Sudan, and the Israeli incursion of 1982 is best remembered for a massacre in a Palestinian refugee camp. Additionally, the greatest Libyan-backed anti-American atrocity (the Lockerbie aeroplane bombing) occurred two years after the 1986 Tripoli bombings, and the PLO and al-Qa'ida were not obviously deterred by the state actions targeting them.

Nevertheless, in the longer term, al-Qa'ida have been weakened and their principal Sunni Islamist successor ISIS pushed back by international military action, principally in the form of air support for governments and local insurgents who oppose them. At the same time as this form of intervention has consolidated, another 'war against terror' strategy has grown in prominence in the form of drone (unmanned combat aerial vehicle) strikes. Drones have proved attractive to the USA and other states as a means of delivering targeted strikes from afar without risking troop deployments. As with military counter-terrorism in general, this strategy has reaped some notable rewards but also much collateral damage and controversy. The military use of drones is new enough to be ambiguous in international law, and their use has stirred up such resentment in Pakistan, Yemen, Afghanistan and Syria that, again, this is a strategy which, ultimately, may act more as a recruiting sergeant for insurgents.

Traditional international military responses by the state can achieve some successes but only where the foe is closely linked with a government and a clear target can be aimed at, as was the case with the US war against Afghanistan in 2002. This campaign assisted the US 'war on terror' by removing a key support base for its principal enemy, al-Qa'ida, and killing a number of that organization's operatives, but, of course, it could never be as complete a victory as it would have been had the Afghan government itself been the direct enemy. Wars between states usually reach a definitive conclusion but wars against non-state actors rarely do. Non-state actors are unlikely to surrender since they can usually run away rather than face the music of a post-war settlement. Hence al-Qa'ida continued their campaign against the USA after 2002, depleted but not defeated, and its operatives still carrying the same grievances either in continuing with the group or joining others, like ISIS. The very notion of a war against al-Qa'ida's terror may even have been counterproductive since it elevated a loose protest movement to the sort of status previously reserved for great powers like Nazi Germany or the Soviet Union and inspired the likes of Boko Haram and ISIS. ISIS's dream of establishing a caliphate spanning Syria and Iraq will never come to pass because so much military might stands in the way. At the same time, though, no one seriously imagines that this military might can defeat the ideology of radical Islamism.

Invoking the language of national security in countering non-state violence is often not appropriate or helpful to the state. Horrific though 9/11 was it is worth remembering that the 'national security' threat posed by al-Qa'ida to the United States cannot possibly be compared to the Soviet Union during the Cold War or Japan in the early 1940s. Insurgencies can become matters of national security but 'new' global terrorism is invariably more of a human security matter not soluble by traditional security methods alone.

Non-state foes can be subdued for periods of time but, if the same grievances persist, others are likely to take up arms again for the cause. Indeed, the longer grievances fester the more they become socialized, and second- and third-generation 'freedom fighters' are no more likely to abandon their fathers' and grandfathers' cause than state citizens are to meekly submit to foreign invasion. Peace deals after long-term civil insurgencies tend to be particularly difficult since sections of the non-state force frequently become more absolutist in their stance. Hence in Northern Ireland, Israel/Palestine and the Basque country attempted settlements have split the nationalist movements and created hardline splinter groups. It is this limitation in the application of state power which prompted Paul Wilkinson famously to liken wars against non-state forces to 'fighting the hydra', the mythical beast that could respond to having its head cut off by growing another one (Wilkinson 1986).

Educative

Societal or terrorist change

In the same way that much state criminal policy has come to focus on tackling the 'causes of crime' as well as crimes in themselves, counter-terrorism is evolving towards the more subtle task of seeking to understand the grievances that motivate people to carry out such acts. The UK government's 'Prevent' strategy, launched in

2007, seeks to stop 'home-grown terrorism' partly by better understanding what societal explanations there might be for some of its citizens choosing to become suicide bombers, like the Islamic fundamentalists who killed fifty-two in London in 2005 and twenty-two in Manchester in 2017. Such exercises in 'anger management' are not about 'giving in to terrorism', as hardliners may complain, but are about the longer game of 'preventive diplomacy' through appreciating the underlying causes of such threats. This is an approach which, as discussed in the previous chapter, has become mainstream in inter-state military security politics and, as outlined in the following chapters, has emerged as a key strategy in countering most other security threats.

Global discourse

The task of understanding the grievances that prompt political non-state violence must also be the stuff of international politics. At the global level, equitable facilities to address grievances, such as a responsible UN Security Council with clear provision for dealing with civil conflict and the International Criminal Court, can perform a similar service if permitted to do so. Set against a functioning and just global polity, unjust non-state grievances, or grievances which persist in using unjust means, will more easily be identified as such and be able to be singled out for concerted global action of the sort traditionally reserved for unlawfully aggressive states. International recognition of educative solutions was evident at the United Nations' 2005 Madrid Summit. The summit was widely reported on as a failure for not securing an agreed definition of terrorism but, nevertheless, did get consensus on the key methods needed to diminish the phenomenon. Five pillars, or five 'D's, were identified and subsequently fleshed out in a Global Strategy Against Terrorism released in 2006.

> **D**issuade disaffected groups from choosing terrorism as a tactic to achieve their goals.
> **D**eny terrorists the means to carry out their attacks.
> **D**eter states from supporting terrorists.
> **D**evelop state capacity to prevent terrorism.
> **D**efend human rights in the struggle against terrorism.
>
> (UN General Assembly 2006 – emphasis added)

Conclusions: can political non-state violence be defeated?

The depressing truth is that there is no easy answer for dealing with non-state political violence and it probably can never be entirely defeated. That, though, is not to say that we cannot learn how to deal with insurgencies and non-state terror and minimize its impact. Cronin, drawing on extensive empirical evidence, suggests that there are six ways in which terrorist campaigns can come to an end:

* *'Decapitation'* – the terrorists are defeated, as appears to be the case with the Tamil Tigers in Sri Lanka.

- *Negotiations* – a two-way compromise ends the struggle, as with the UK–IRA peace settlement.
- *Success* – the 'terrorists' win, as with the ANC revolution in South Africa, many anti-colonial independence movements or the Maoists in Nepal.
- *Failure* – the terrorists implode due to a loss of support owing to public revulsion at tactics or a perceived loss of relevance. Many Marxist groups have declined in this way and al-Qa'ida may similarly fade away as they are superseded by other radicals.
- *Repression* – tough counter-terrorism subdues the terrorists without defeating them, as with the Russian suppression of Chechen insurgents.
- *Re-orientation* – the terrorism metamorphosizes into a full-scale insurgency or into criminal enterprises (such as 'narco-terrorism' in Latin America).

(Cronin 2009)

Cronin's analysis supports the notion that countering non-state political violence requires the careful blending of a range of the strategies previously outlined to fit the particular circumstances. Employing non-military, educative methods does not preclude the deployment of accompanying hardline counter-terrorist strategies, since it can give greater legitimacy to being tough on those who do resort to excessive means to highlight their grievances when there are other, peaceful avenues open to them. In this way the freedom fighter/terrorist dichotomy is more clearly resolved since, as Wilkinson memorably put it, 'one democracy's terrorist is another democracy's terrorist' (Wilkinson 2011: 207).

The unpalatable fact is that whilst grievances remain in the world, violence will always resurface. Acts of international terrorism by non-state actors are an unfortunate side-effect of a more open and closely-connected world. Short of closing all state borders and rolling back the democratization of the world and licensing the even greater threat of unrestrained state terrorism, non-state violence can never be comprehensively defeated. To admit this is not to say that nothing can be done about political non-state violence or that it is the fault of democracy and globalization. Grievances that prompt violence can be addressed, either through direct bargaining with the aggrieved or by the general evolution of a more just world. The same point made in the previous chapter with reference to inter-state war holds also for its sub-state variant. Since war is political, politics can resolve war (Halliday 2002: 58). Democracy and globalization can facilitate this. 'Terrorists' can become democrats and negotiate their position around a table rather than through force. Violent Irish nationalism was largely transformed into democratic Irish nationalism by giving the movement some legislative power in exchange for abandoning the use of military power. Begin, Makarios and Kenyatta made the transition from terrorist/freedom fighter to respectable and respected democratic politician in Israel, Cyprus and Kenya respectively.

Even though recent high-profile atrocities make this hard to appreciate, political non-state violence has generally declined in recent decades. The 2015 death toll of around 28,000 was a significant escalation of global terrorist deaths from the early years of the millennium. However, this is symptomatic not so much of a global trend as the persistence of a few chronic civil wars. The vast majority of these deaths are from five countries: Iraq, Nigeria, Afghanistan, Pakistan and Syria. These are all civil wars with strong international dimensions so distinguishing them from classic inter-state wars is artificial. Hence the recent rise does need to be understood in the context of the overall fall in war deaths discussed in the previous chapter. In addition, whilst 28,000 killings is horrendous and depressing this does represent a much lesser order of threat than any of the other issues addressed in this book.

Nevertheless, more can be done to overcome the barrier of sovereignty and improve counter-terrorism on the global stage. International cooperation has done much to lessen the recourse to military action by states and, given the opportunity, it can have the same effect for non-state actors. International law can directly target globally-operating groups and individuals through implementing effective travel bans and freezing their bank accounts in a way that state legislation or war cannot. The same increased interconnectedness of the modern world that has breathed life into political non-state violence can also help to suffocate it.

 ## Key points

- The term 'terrorism' is typically applied to non-state political violence but this is analytically unhelpful since states frequently terrorize their own and other states' citizens.
- Political non-state violence has been dominated by three types: nationalist, Marxist and religious.
- A range of tactics have been used by governments to combat threats of this kind, with no clear consensus on the most effective.
- Political non-state violence is now more common and persistent than state-to-state conflict, suggesting that greater recourse to negotiated solutions is required, however unpalatable this may be for governments.

 ## Notes

1 'Noncombatants' is taken to include off-duty or unarmed troops.
2 The sovereign state system: so named after the 1648 Treaty of Westphalia often seen as having initiated the concept of state sovereignty.
3 As published in the *Financial Times*, 10 October 2001.
4 The others were Saudi Arabia and the United Arab Emirates.
5 Cuba was the only state to vote against the General Assembly Resolution.

 ## Recommended reading

Cronin, A. (2009) *How Terrorism Ends*, Princeton: Princeton University Press.
Lutz, J. and Lutz, B. (2013) *Global Terrorism*, 3rd edn, Abingdon: Routledge.
Perspectives on Terrorism (journal): www.terrorismanalysts.com/pt/index.php/pot/index
Wilkinson, P. (2011) *Terrorism versus Democracy: The Liberal State Response*, Abingdon: Routledge.

Useful web links

- Global Counterterrorism Forum: www.thegctf.org/
- UN Counterterrorism: www.un.org/en/counterterrorism/
- University of Maryland Global Terrorism Database: www.start.umd.edu/gtd/

Chapter 4

Economic threats to security

We have the means; we have the capacity to wipe hunger and poverty from the face of the Earth in our lifetime. We need only the will.

President John F. Kennedy of the USA, World Food Congress, Washington DC, October 1963

Economic Insecurity

Economic insecurity can threaten both states and people. Governments can be economically weakened by the accidental or deliberate restriction of financial inflows or, internally, as a result of their citizens revolting against such changes. Internal economic pressures have long threatened national security. The French and Russian revolutions and many other notable insurgencies had at heart questions about 'who gets what', with powerful political systems delegitimized and toppled through their failure to ensure that their whole population was fed. National security, similarly, has long been threatened by deliberate acts of economic warfare in the form of sanctions or blockades or, less directly, through general commercial dominance or exploitation.

More starkly, though, poverty is a critical dimension of human security. 'Who gets what' is a particularly pertinent question to ask at the global level since there is demonstrably enough food in the world for all, but not everyone is getting their required share. Most challengingly for the conduct of international relations, the pursuit of national food security – by stockpiling and protecting what you have – ultimately serves to heighten this problem.

The concept of human security accommodates the consideration of a wide range of threats to life, of which poverty is undoubtedly the most significant. Poverty kills directly in huge numbers when people are unable to secure sufficient food to live because they lack the economic means to purchase or produce it, and this situation can arise in a number of ways. A famine can occur when an acute shortage of food is incurred across a broad swathe of people. More persistent is the continual threat posed to millions of people across the world by hunger due to economic circumstances. Additionally, people may be periodically exposed to life-threatening economic insecurity due to a sudden deterioration of economic circumstances resulting either from a recession or the imposition of trade sanctions for political reasons. Poverty is also an underlying cause of human death by other security threats. As Thomas states, 'the pursuit of human security must have at its core the satisfaction of basic material needs of all humankind. At the most basic level, food, shelter, education and health care are essential for the survival of human beings' (Thomas 2000: 7).

Satisfying the 'basic material needs of humankind' is not solely an economic task but it is, without doubt, principally achieved by the possession of money, personally and societally. Money is not the root of all of humanity's ills nor the sole cause of starvation and hunger. On the one hand, droughts and other natural phenomena can disrupt the food supply, and on the other, it is possible to feed yourself without buying the food. Money, however, can be used to secure yourself against natural hazards and insure you against fluctuations in the food supply caused either by natural or economic disruptions. In addition, self-sufficiency in food production, either for individuals or states, is an increasingly difficult means of achieving security. Money, so the saying goes, 'can't buy you love' but it can buy you a certain measure of that other of life's most precious commodities, security. Table 4.1 illustrates the point that the wealthy of the world live longer whilst the poor die young. There is

TABLE 4.1 The price of poverty – wealth and life expectancy

Ranking by GNP per capita, PPP*		Life expectancy	Ranking by HDI
TOP			
1	Qatar	(79.4)	33
2	Singapore	(80)	5
3	Kuwait	(76.5)	51
4	Liechtenstein	(81.1)	15
5	Norway	(81.1)	1
BOTTOM			
184	Niger	(61.9)	186
185	Burundi	(57.1)	177
186	Liberia	(61.2)	182
187	Democratic Republic of Congo	(59.1)	185
188	Central African Republic	(51.5)	187

* GNP is 'Gross National Product', the total earnings of all citizens of a country. This divided by the population of the country gives the GNP per capita. This figure is factored by PPP 'purchasing power parity', the relative worth of that country's money.

Source: UNDP 2016.

TABLE 4.2 Human development indicators

Top 10 by HDI		Top 10, HDI compared to GNP PPP		Bottom 10, HDI compared to GNP PPP		Bottom 10 by HDI	
1	Norway	1	Cuba (+48)	1	Eq. Guinea (-79)	179	Eritrea
2	Australia	2	Georgia (+38)	2	Kuwait (-48)	179	Sierra Leone
3	Switzerland	3	Ukraine (+34)	3	Gabon (-46)	181	Mozambique
4	Germany	4	Tonga (+33)	4	Botswana (-35)	181	South Sudan
5	Denmark	5	Kyrgyzstan (+32)	4	UAE (-35)	183	Guinea
5	Singapore	6	Moldova (+31)	6	Swaziland (-33)	184	Burundi
7	Netherlands	7	Tajikistan (+30)	7	Qatar (-32)	185	Burkina Faso
8	Ireland	8	Armenia (+28)	7	Turkmenistan (-32)	186	Chad
9	Iceland	9	Samoa (+27)	9	Iraq (-30)	187	Niger
10	Canada	10	Madagascar (+25)	9	South Africa (-30)	188	Central African Republic
10	USA						

Source: UNDP 2016.

not a precise correlation between wealth and life expectancy, but the match-up, particularly at the bottom of the scale, is still striking. The Central African Republic has the world's lowest GNP per capita and has also the third lowest average life expectancy. The world's poorest people are also, by and large, the world's most insecure.

There are, however, some anomalies which emerge from comparing income and life expectancy which demonstrate that there is more to security than money. Equatorial Guinea is continental Africa's richest country and ranked 56 in the world by GNP per capita but its citizens have a life expectancy of only 58, the fourteenth worst in the world. The country has acquired great export earnings from oil production but is, at the same time, beset with corruption, poor governance and civil turmoil. At the other end of the scale, the prominence of gun crime and lack of state health care provision in the US are factors in that country's citizens having an average life expectancy not in line with its wealth and below, for example, Cuba. The United Nations Development Programme (UNDP), to get over the limitations of judging development purely in economic terms, calculates a 'Human Development Index' (HDI) to rank a country's progress (see Table 4.2). This figure combines income, life expectancy and educational opportunities and attainment to give a more thorough picture of whether a state's wealth is being utilized to the benefit of its people. Hence states which, for various reasons, do not utilize their resources for the benefit of all of their people, like Equatorial Guinea or – higher up the scale – like Kuwait, are judged to be less developed than their GNP would suggest. Equally some countries, such as Cuba and Madagascar, under HDI can be understood as more developed than their income would suggest due to relatively good health and educational systems securing their citizens. At the same time, the most developed countries by HDI are rich but not necessarily the richest (see Table 4.2). Although there is more to it than money when it comes to achieving human security there is no doubt that it helps.

Famine

The most acute and immediate economic threat to human security comes in the form of famine, the worst of which in human history are listed in Table 4.3.

The information in Table 4.3 is highly approximated in a number of ways. First, famines are functionally related to other threats to human security such as disease, drought and flooding, which are considered elsewhere in this book. Floods and droughts wipe out crops and can cause famines, but they can also kill directly, whilst diseases are generally more virulent when infecting a malnourished population. Hence, determining the precise cause of death for people beset by such natural catastrophes is problematic and, as such, figures on famine fatalities are inexact. Second, even allowing for the blurring of the causal factors of death, disaster mortality statistics are notoriously unreliable. Governments tend to underestimate figures, whilst anti-government voices often exaggerate them for opposing political purposes. Most of the figures quoted in the table are contested and it is difficult to verify precise totals even with painstaking research. This problem is not solely one of authenticating historical records. Modern-day statistics also tend to be arrived at through educated

TABLE 4.3 The top ten famines in history

		Deaths	Principal cause
1	China 1958–62	30 million[a]	POLITICAL – forced urbanization and collectivization of agriculture
2	N. China 1876–8	12 million[b]	NATURAL – drought
3	Bengal 1770	10 million[c]	NATURAL – drought
4	C. India 1876–8	6 million[b]	NATURAL – drought
5	Ukraine 1932–3	5 million[d]	POLITICAL – harsh USSR quotas on Ukrainian grain collected centrally
6	N. Korea 1995–	2 million[e]	NATURAL – drought and floods
7	Bengal 1943–4	1.9 million[d]	POLITICAL – supply and price of rice negatively affected by Second World War
8	Rajputana, India 1869	1.5 million[f]	NATURAL – drought
=9	Orissa, India 1865–6	1 million[f]	NATURAL – drought in 1865 followed by floods in 1866
=9	India 1897	1 million[f]	NATURAL – drought
=9	Ireland 1845–7	1 million[g]	NATURAL – potato blight

Sources: a Becker 2000, b Davis, 2001, c Sen 1981, d Disaster Center 2003, e Natsios 1999, f Hazlitt 1973, g Ó Gráda 1999.

guesswork. The highly secretive North Korean government denied any problem of starvation for a number of years and have subsequently admitted to 'only' around 200,000 deaths due to this cause. Natsios's estimate of 2–3 million was largely derived from making extrapolations based on interviews with refugees (Natsios 1999). The true picture will probably never be known.

The causes of famine

A further abstraction in Table 4.3 comes from indicating the principal cause of each famine. Invariably there are a combination of factors which can explain such humanitarian disasters. As with the mortality figures, the causes of famines are frequently disputed by analysts and politicians. Most famines are the result of a combination of both natural and political factors, and disputes on causation centre on determining the relative weighting of the two contributory factors (hence, this section is included here rather than in the chapter on natural disasters). The famines in India and Ireland, for example, had natural causes but are generally considered to have been exacerbated by an ignorance of the local situation born of colonial/post-colonial rule. The North Korean famine had natural origins but was, undoubtedly, greatly worsened by the government's drive for economic self-sufficiency, which saw food imports reduced at the same time as the domestic food supply had dwindled.

The last two food crises declared as famines by the UN, in Somalia in 2011 and South Sudan in 2017, were linked to drought and underlying climate change but were mainly attributable to the food supply being distorted and abused as a result of civil conflict.

Marxist analysis argues that structural economic factors account for famines as much as the inadequate political responses of particular governments to crop failures. It is, indeed, striking that so many of the worst famines in history occurred in the late nineteenth century, an era of as then unparalleled global economic liberalization when the trade in foodstuffs greatly increased. Marx himself considered the famines of his era to be the product of capitalism, and his latter-day protégés, such as Davis, cite persuasive evidence that colonized or semi-colonized countries, like India and China, thrust into a global market economy, exported food to the developed world whilst their own nationals starved (Davis 2001: 27). The late nineteenth century, however, was also an era marked by extreme climatic conditions in Asia owing to an increased prevalence of the 'El Niño' effect. El Niño is a periodically occurring phenomenon whereby equatorial areas of the Pacific Ocean warm up causing atmospheric disturbances which can manifest themselves in periods of drought and flood, in place of the usual seasonal changes in weather. It appears that a combination of profound changes in both the natural and economic environments transpired to kill millions in Asia and elsewhere in the late nineteenth century. Those deaths should serve as a powerful warning from history of the need to temper contemporary economic globalization with political measures in order to be ready to deal with the rise of unexpected threats to economic security.

More problematic from a Marxist standpoint is that the clearest cases of man-made, political famine were the horrific twentieth-century disasters in Communist China and the USSR. The Chinese famine was influenced by the effects of excessive rainfall on harvests but there is little doubt that its principal cause was Mao Tse Tung's determination to pursue his 'Great Leap Forward' economic reform plan (which centred on forced collectivization), regardless of the human consequences. The Ukrainian famine did not have any obvious natural causes at all and appears to have been entirely political, deliberately engineered by Stalin to punish farmers of the region for their lack of enthusiasm for Soviet collectivization.

There are three fundamental explanations for any particular famine, related to the balance between the supply and demand for food:

1   A fall in the food supply.
2   An increase in the demand for food.
3   Disruptions to the normal distribution of food.

The third of these is most particularly influenced by politics and economics. As will be explored in the next section, if considered from a global perspective, all famines can be attributed to explanation 3 since there is demonstrably sufficient food in the world for all people to be adequately fed. We do not yet live by effective global governance, however, and all three explanations can variously be applied to the situation in states where famines are occurring. The food supply in countries can fall below the level sufficient to meet demand because of poor harvests, or the population can grow at a rate that the food supply is unable to match.

Increased demand due to overpopulation is a condition that has certainly affected most of the principal arenas of famine over the last century, such as in China and India where it has prompted domestic political action to curb the growth rate. A provocative argument from prominent American economists the Paddock brothers in the late 1960s went as far as to argue that India and other countries prone to famine had only themselves to blame and should be left to suffer for their own and everyone else's good. Overpopulation added to endemic poor government meant that, for some states, food aid was a waste of time and that they should be considered to form a 'can't be saved' group and ignored by the USA and other benefactors. 'Waste not the food on the "can't be saved" and the "walking wounded". Send it to those nations which, having it, can buttress their own resources, their own efforts, and fight through to survival' (Paddock and Paddock 1967: 229).

The economist Garret Hardin advanced a similar idea in formulating the analogy of lifeboats in an ocean to characterize states in a world where food supplies will eventually be used up in the face of population growth. Hardin's thesis argued for the application of 'lifeboat ethics' to combat this, which argued that international action to tackle famine was folly as wealthy countries would risk sinking their own 'lifeboats' in doing so. Better to let the overcrowded lifeboats of the Third World sink than ensuring that we all drown (Hardin 1996). Such apocalyptic views of the global security implications of overpopulation were common in the 1960s and 1970s and can be dated back as far as the eighteenth century and the works of Thomas Malthus (Malthus 1798). They are, though, rarer today since the central plank of the Malthusian and neo-Malthusian prediction, that world population will come to exceed world food supply, has not happened and does not look likely to do so, for the next few decades at least. The demand for food continues to increase in the less developed world and natural disasters continue to blight many of the same countries, creating food shortages, but most contemporary analysts of famine emphasize distributive factors in their explanations of particular cases. Modern governments can insure against future crop shortages by stockpiling reserves of food and protecting the price of agricultural products.

The leading writer in this approach to explaining famine is economist Amartya Sen (see Box 4.1). Sen expounds the 'entitlements approach' in which he argues that all individuals should by rights be able to expect to be protected from famine by their government, regardless of changes in food supply or population. In a convincing application of the democratic peace argument to economic rather than military security Sen draws on extensive evidence to propose that;

> no substantial famine has ever occurred in any independent and democratic country with a relatively free press . . .
> . . . Even the poorest democratic countries that have faced terrible droughts or floods or other natural disasters (such as India in 1973, or Zimbabwe and Botswana in the early 1980s) have been able to feed their people without experiencing a famine.
>
> (Sen 1999: 6–7)

BOX 4.1 **Amartya Sen**

The winner of the Nobel Prize for Economics in 1998, Sen is an Indian academic from Bengal who experienced the 1943–4 famine first-hand as a young boy. He was born on a university campus to Bangladeshi parents (his father was a Chemistry lecturer) and has graced most of the leading universities of the world in a glittering academic career. Sen has lectured in Economics at Cambridge, Oxford, the London School of Economics and Harvard, and his research has focused on the economic dimensions of poverty, famine and human

rights. As such Sen's work has found influence outside of the confines of Economics and he is revered in political science for his contribution to bringing a much neglected ethical dimension to the 'miserable science'.

Democratic governments are compelled to be responsive to the needs of ordinary people whose security is imperilled, whether directly or indirectly through the pressure of the media or other concerned citizens, in a way in which tyrannical dictators or neglectful colonialists are not. Democracy thus can save people as well as empower them. Food shortages will still occur from time to time but these can normally be planned for by governments and, when they cannot be dealt with, the international community can step in. Countless lives in North Korea would have been saved were it not for the fact that the state had virtually cut itself off from the rest of the world and external assistance had not been possible. Being part of the global economy would have saved the lives of many North Koreans. Being a democratic – or socially responsive – state within the global economy would have saved more still.

Global policy on famine relief

The principal instrument for coordinating famine relief at the global level is the UN's World Food Programme (WFP), a hybrid of the Food and Agricultural Organization (FAO) and World Health Organization (WHO). Created in 1963, initially as an ad hoc three-year project, the WFP has evolved into the 'food arm of the UN' (WFP 2002a: 1), with all of the characteristics of an IGO. Based (like the FAO) in Rome, with a permanent secretariat, the WFP is governed by an Executive Board who vote on where to allocate food aid from an annual budget of around $6 billion. Through the course of its working life this food aid has increasingly been targeted at countries suffering food shortages due to the effects of natural disasters or conflict rather than for general development purposes.

The stated aim of the WFP's work is 'eradicating hunger and poverty. The ultimate objective of food aid should be the elimination of the need for food aid'

(WFP 2002b: 1). In reality, though, the WFP is a global emergency service and the broad aim of achieving 'food security' – 'access of all peoples at all times to the food needed for an active and healthy life' (FAO/WHO 1992) – is a more profound goal beyond the reach of its budget and operations. This broader goal of food security, though, has made inroads on the global political agenda, as is discussed later in this chapter.

Hunger

Global political action, carried out intergovernmentally by the WFP and non-governmentally by pressure groups such as OXFAM, CAFOD and War on Want, has, in recent decades, succeeded in curtailing the escalation of famines, but such groups are quick to point out that these periodic disasters are merely the tip of the global hunger 'iceberg'. Far more people in today's world die of hunger through plain poverty rather than as a result of short-term regional imbalances between the supply and demand for food. The WFP claim that 795 million people in the world suffer from malnutrition and thousands of these die every day as a result of hunger and related ailments (WFP 2017).[1] Some consider this a conservative estimate but this death toll undoubtedly outstrips any other threats to human existence.

Why then does this relentless carnage persist in a world in which the food supply is sufficient to permit every person to consume enough to live a healthy life?

1 Failure of certain states to encourage modernization

The orthodox position on poverty argues that it can be eradicated by those countries affected pursuing economic development of the kind experienced by Northern states. This view advocates that less developed countries (LDCs) can best mimic Northern development by integrating themselves into the global economy to permit export-oriented industries to flourish and gain from the subsequent inward investment provided by multi-national corporations (MNCs). In this way the conditions for modernization can be created: wealth, democracy, education, state-welfarism and smaller families, all of which serve to alleviate poverty. The clearest articulation of this view came from the influential US economic historian Rostow with his 'Stages of Growth' thesis in the 1960s. Rostow analysed the process of development in the North and concluded that all states pass through five stages of progression towards 'take off' and an end stage of a wealthy consumer-driven society (Rostow 1960).

The failure of some LDCs to show any sign of such progression over the last fifty years has dented the rigour of Rostow's thesis but this orthodox position on development remains powerful in the discourse on international economic relations. The successful economic development of the newly industrialized countries (NICs), such as the 'Asian Tigers' of Taiwan, South Korea, Hong Kong and Singapore, after opening themselves up to foreign investment and developing export-oriented manufacturing industries, served to reinforce the notion that a global route out of poverty is available for those states stuck in pre-modernity.

2 *Structural violence*

In direct opposition to the orthodoxy, radical Marxist explanations for the persistence of poverty-induced hunger hold that it is, like famine, actually caused by the global economy. In the 1960s, Galtung, using language deliberately designed to 'securitize' the issue of global poverty, coined the phrase 'structural violence' to encapsulate the nature of this phenomenon:

> if people are starving when this is objectively avoidable, then violence is committed, regardless of whether there is a clear subject-action-object relation, as during a siege yesterday or no such clear relation, as in the way economic relations are organized today.
>
> (Galtung 1969: 170)

The conventional notion that economic development was a stage that all states would eventually reach if they underwent social and economic 'modernization' came to be challenged from the 1960s by Galtung and also by 'dependency theory' advocates led by Frank (Frank 1971). From this 'Structuralist' perspective, 'developing' states are nothing of the sort, they are dependent states, systematically and deliberately exploited by their wealthy counterparts. The global economic system requires underdeveloped states in order to feed the voracious capitalist appetite for more wealth in the developed world. Hence, building on evidence that some Latin American states' economic fortunes improved rather than worsened when their principal trading partners were distracted in the Second World War, Frank and others advanced the notion that the poor states of the world would be better off by cutting themselves off from the global North and concentrating on developing their own resources.

Wallerstein's 'World Systems Analysis' is a more sophisticated form of Structuralism which builds on the notion of a *core and periphery* inevitably occurring from the exploitative accumulation of wealth in dependent states (as expressed by Galtung and others) by applying this to the global level. In this view it is not so much the rich states of the world exploiting the poor states as a transnational wealthy class (including elites in less developed countries) exploiting a transnational class of the poor (including the poor in developed countries) (Wallerstein 1979). Hence for Structuralists only structural change – the overthrow of capitalism – can eradicate poverty.

3 *Ignorance*

A further explanation for the persistence of global poverty is that, in spite of the best efforts of pressure groups to highlight the phenomenon, governments and the general public of states wealthy enough to help are simply not sufficiently aware of the scale of the problem to 'find the will' called for in President Kennedy's speech over fifty years ago. Whilst famines have become less prominent over the last thirty years, partly due to international political and charitable responses, the underlying issue of basic hunger remains a persistent problem that is harder to highlight in the news media than through dramatic pictures of emaciated children amidst cracked earth and flies after a drought. '(B)ecause we view hunger in the background of life, the terrible toll does not enter our headlines, nor, for most of us, our concerns' (The Hunger Project 1985).

A reformist *Alter-Globalist* (as opposed to being pro or anti globalization/capitalism) does not accept that hunger is inevitable in a capitalist world economy but argues that global political failings are still culpable for the persistence of poverty. Alleviating hunger is possible without abandoning global capitalism by reforming international institutions and encouraging governments to act less selfishly in international trade. The 'Make Poverty History' campaign of the 2000s, for example, sought to increase public awareness of the daily death toll due to hunger and pressurize governments into structural political actions to alleviate this tragedy. Hence Alter-Globalists argue for a 'mixed economy' for the world in which more political intervention is required in some cases but, in other instances, the invisible hand of the free market should be allowed to do its work. In particular, the following defects in the global economy can be linked to the persistence of poverty and hunger.

Increased price volatility

Agricultural prices are traditionally more volatile than for most goods because of the simple economics of supply and demand. Whilst the demand for food will always be there – and probably rising – the supply of crops or meat is always subject to the vagaries of the weather. Fears of a bad harvest are deeply ingrained in the human psyche and partly explain the cautious and protective attitudes of governments and the public towards national agriculture, even in wealthy countries where food shortages are unlikely. In developing countries, where sudden price rises are more critical, intergovernmental coalitions such as the Group of 77 (G77) have, from the 1960s, called for the establishment of 'common funds' to stabilize the international price of food exports. The European Community, for example, introduced the STABEX mechanism – providing compensation for loss of earnings due to price drops in certain crops – as part of the 1975 Lomé Convention regulating its trading relations with African, Caribbean and Pacific former colonies.

STABEX was discontinued in 2000 in line with the expiry of Lomé (to be replaced by a less extensive FLEX system) and, in general, demands for Common Funds declined as food prices stabilized in the 1990s and early 2000s after a period of volatility in the 1970s and early 1980s. However, the major spike in prices that occurred between March 2007 and March 2008 saw the world average price of food soar by 56 per cent, with rises of 130 per cent in wheat and 74 per cent in rice (FAO 2008). Numerous factors were behind this, including supply-side problems such as particularly poor wheat harvests in Australia and Europe. On the demand side the economic growth of emerging markets, particularly in India and China, increased the market for milk, cereals and meat. A significant rise in the price of oil also had an impact on food prices because of the consequences of this for the cost of transportation. In addition, the speculative, short-term buying and selling of grain, in line with the unregulated bubble building up in the financial world at the time, also affected world prices. Several issues behind the global economic collapse of 2008 negatively affected food prices, but longer-term underlying factors explain the more general rise either side of the 2007–8 spike.

Environmental degradation of productive land

The well-documented environmental changes of desertification and deforestation have obvious dire consequences for the food supply, and the twin phenomena are both symptoms and causes of the wider threat to the world's productive capacity posed by climate change. Degraded land can rarely be reclaimed for agriculture, so the food security implications are obvious. In Haiti, for example, grain production is estimated to have halved between the 1960s and 1980s as a result of the progressive loss of fertile land (Brauch 2003). Degraded land also destroys natural habitats, which can have further knock-on human food security effects.

Like desertification – and indeed linked to it – deforestation refers to the progressive decline in the world's trees. Also like desertification it is a centuries-old phenomenon that is, to some extent, natural but has accelerated due to human exploitation, particularly in line with industrialization and the rise of industrial-scale agriculture. In the 2000s there was a net loss of 5.2 million hectares per year (equivalent to the size of Costa Rica)[2] (FAO 2011). Unsustainable agricultural practices, such as the growth in soy plantations, account for 80 per cent of this global total, with logging for timber, paper and fuel responsible for much of the rest (Kissinger, Herold & De Sy 2012: 5). Other contributory factors include the expansion of mining plants and urbanization. Forests supply much fruit and other key human foodstuffs and provide habitats for many animals useful for the human diet, as well as other creatures important to agriculture, such as pollinating bees.

Switching of production to non-food crops

A notable recent agricultural trend of switching from producing cereals and sugar to the profitable biofuel market has also served to shrink the world food supply. Amongst the most prominent biofuels are ethanol from sugar cane and biodiesel from grains. A World Bank paper has estimated that between 70 and 75 per cent of the rise in food prices between 2002 and 2008 was a consequence of the subsidization and tariff protection of the biofuel industries in the US and EU decreasing food production and bucking the market by squeezing out cheaper sources in Brazil and Africa (Mitchell 2008).

International sale of productive land

Also affecting the food supply in certain countries is the increasing phenomenon of 'land grab' whereby croplands in the global South are being sold off to Western or Chinese investors for a quick profit. This shrinks the global food supply, since such investors often switch production to biofuels, as well as creating more localized shortages and sources of political discontent. One estimate suggests that, in the 2000s, over 200 million hectares (eight times the size of the UK) was sold or leased externally (Anseeuw et al. 2011).

Agricultural trade distortion

Whilst global food production has increased since the rise of neo-Malthusian concerns that supply would be outstripped by demand in the late 1960s, the global trade in food is far from a free market and the Economic Liberal ideal of unlocking comparative advantage by allowing efficient producers to export as much as the rest of the world demands is notably absent. The agricultural industry in the global North has managed to remain largely exempt from the international trade liberalization of the last seventy years and, in many countries, enjoys heavy government subsidization and protection. This undermines the capacity of the global South countries – who tend to have a much higher proportion of their economy based on agriculture – to export their food produce to Northern markets. Over US$250 billion per year is spent in OECD countries to artificially prop up domestic farmers (*Economist* 2010), and the losses for developing countries resulting from this distortion of the free market are generally held to far exceed the sums given to them in foreign aid transfers. Developing countries have campaigned relentlessly for a liberalization of agricultural trade through the World Trade Organization since its inception in 1995 but, thus far, vested agribusiness interests in the global North have resisted this in as clear an illustration of 'beggar thy neighbour' protectionist economics as you can find.

Overfishing

Like agricultural production, fishing and fish consumption have accelerated with population growth and beyond, in line with consumption patterns over the past seventy years. The global market in 1950 was 19.3 million tonnes, but by 2009 this had risen to 163 million tonnes (FAO 2011: 4). However, unlike the Green Revolution in agriculture, human ingenuity has succeeded only in terms of learning how to catch more fish, not how to increase or maintain the supply. The FAO estimate that 57.4 per cent of fish stocks are now 'fully exploited' and 29.9 per cent 'over-exploited', meaning that less than 13 per cent are being sustainably harvested (FAO 2011).

Such a growth in fishing and fish depletion is due to the industrialization of the practice with the deployment of much bigger 'factory vessels', more indiscriminate harvesting of 'bycatch' and the rise of aquaculture (fish farming). The underlying problem is that fishing, politically, tends to be treated as an economic and social issue rather than a matter of conservation. Governments in domestic policy tend to focus on subsidizing the industry and in foreign policy tend to play 'beggar thy neighbour' in the face of a *collective goods problem*. Furthermore, in development policy, donor governments have generally promoted the modernization of LDC fishing industries in aid programmes. Globally it is estimated that $US35 billion per year is paid to the fishing industry, mostly encouraging modernization and paying fuel subsidies (UN 2017). In this way the classic development policy maxim of 'giving a man a fishing rod rather than the fish' is undermined since 'the man with the rod' is, in reality, often put out of business by the focus on industrialization in aid programmes. Overall, the global fishing industry actually runs at a loss of around $US5 billion per year, whilst if run in an optimal, sustainable manner it could deliver a $US45 billion profit (World Bank 2009).

Global policy on hunger

Despite being built upon US hegemony and a desire to uphold global capitalism against the threat of Communism, the new Liberal International Economic Order (LIEO) that emerged from the 1944 Bretton Woods Conference was not pure Economic Liberalism since international development policy was founded on the notion that interventions from global North states could and should stimulate economic growth in the South. The capitalist world had learned from the Great Depression of the 1930s that free markets do not always correct themselves when in a downturn, and Keynesian economics (named after the UK economist and politician John Maynard Keynes who was his country's head delegate at the Bretton Woods Conference) had become mainstream in domestic economic policy. Keynesian economics advocates government interventions and spending to combat unemployment and boost the demand for goods in order to kick-start a slumping economy. In line with this thinking, President Roosevelt had sought to regenerate the US economy in the 1930s by pumping money into the poorest areas of the country in his New Deal package (an approach not followed at the time in the UK). It was in this framework of thinking that the idea of a 'New Deal' for the capitalist world emerged in the mid-1940s with a US-led international drive to give foreign aid and developmental loans to the world's poorest countries and offering incentives for businesses to locate there in order to stimulate growth.

The very new political landscape at the end of the Second World War was where the idea of development in international politics took hold. Harry Truman first used the term 'underdevelopment' in his inaugural US presidential address of 1949. With Western Europe no longer the source of political power in the world, the one thing the two new superpowers could agree on was that the former colonies of Britain, France, The Netherlands and Portugal should be free to pursue their own destiny and given a helping hand to make their way in the world. Of course, Cold War *realpolitik* as well as empathy was at work and the US and USSR each saw the emergent 'Third World' as an arena in which they could secure strategic allies in the context of the unfolding ideological conflict. Many parts of Latin America, Asia and Africa hence became the focus of superpower competition, most prominently in Korea, Vietnam and Cuba.

Purer Economic Liberalism was revived in global economic discourse and practice in the 1980s and 1990s in the guise of the 'Washington Consensus' (so named to highlight the importance of the US government and the IMF, based also in Washington) after a period in the 1970s when the agenda of the New International Economic Order (NIEO), calling for protectionist measures to be specially permitted for developing countries, made some inroads as the 'Third World' asserted themselves. However, the debt crisis of the 1980s weakened the hand of the Third World and provided an opportunity for *monetarist* economic policies employed in the US and UK to be put into practice on the international political stage. Faced with the prospect of countries defaulting on their loan repayments, the emphasis of the World Bank and IMF in bailing out Third World countries in economic crisis shifted from lending more money to 'Structural Adjustment' policies of tying assistance to the enactment of measures to control inflation and promote economic growth more through private rather than state-led enterprises. Just as it was felt that poor citizens of the US and UK could best be helped by allowing them to help themselves by becoming less dependent on state benefits, saving their money and becoming more entrepreneurial, President Reagan and Prime Minister Thatcher felt poor states needed to keep their own finances in order and allow the invisible hand of market forces, rather than handouts, to fuel their development.

In addition, the end of the Cold War, although giving an opportunity for non-military issues to gain global attention, actually represented a setback for the Third World since there was no longer a First and Second World to play off each other. In the 1970s many African, Asian and Latin American countries had been able to compete for the attention of two superpowers who saw it as in their strategic interests to help them but, by the 1990s, this was no longer an option.

However, the twenty-first century has witnessed the emergence of a more reformist Alter-Globalist agenda, the Post-Washington Consensus, which, while still advocating economic development through modernization, acknowledges structural failings in the contemporary global economic system. The Economic Liberal tide, which had seen Reagan and Thatcher rise to power, ebbed away in the 1990s as evidence of the limitations of purely free market solutions to poverty became apparent. The Asian Tigers had followed a broadly orthodox script (albeit with a stronger role for government than many Economic Liberals would favour), but many global South countries found the prescription of opening up their economies to foreign competition a bitter medicine with no remedial effects. In Mozambique, for example, their once major cashew nut industry collapsed in the early 2000s when they were compelled to stop subsidizing the sector as a condition of World Bank loans. With more Keynesian, interventionist administrations coming into power in Washington and elsewhere, civil society criticism of Structural Adjustment became more prominent and, as a consequence, the World Bank came to listen to different voices and further re-oriented itself on a reformist and socially-conscious path: 'The overall goal of development is therefore to increase the economic, political and civil rights of all people across gender, ethnic groups, religion, races, regions and countries' (World Bank 1991: 31).

The seeming culmination of Economic Liberal globalization, with the launch of the World Trade Organization (WTO) in 1995 half a century after it was stillborn at the Bretton Woods Conference, has also helped re-invigorate the 'Third World'. The WTO, whilst undoubtedly dominated in its decision-making by the global North, has nevertheless given a prominent platform for the global South to project its voice, as it had previously been able to do in the 1970s NIEO era. Global civil society, with campaigns such as 'Make Poverty History', has also played its part in giving momentum to an agenda for reform. Hence some of the NIEO demands, having been largely ignored in the 1990s, have come back to the fore and, to some extent, been acted upon. The debts of some of the most hopelessly impoverished states have been written off or restructured and the IMF, and particularly the World Bank, have come to be more socially-conscious in their dealings with developing countries. The issue of opening up Northern agricultural markets to competition from the South has yet to be fully acted upon but is, at least, prominent in global economic negotiations.

In line with this Post-Washington Consensus, and in order to move international development policy beyond rhetoric and build a genuine consensus, a new global reformist agenda, the Millennium Development Goals (MDGs), was adopted by the

UN General Assembly in 2000. Importantly, unlike the NIEO, the MDGs were also adopted by the IMF, World Bank, Organization for Economic Cooperation and Development and G7 – institutions dominated by the global North and with more political muscle than the UN's talking shop. The eight broad goals of the MDGs were as follows:

- Reduce extreme poverty and hunger by half.
- Achieve universal primary education.
- Promote gender equality and empower women.
- Reduce child mortality by two-thirds.
- Reduce maternal mortality by three-quarters.
- Reverse the spread of HIV/AIDS, malaria and other diseases.
- Ensure environmental sustainability.
- Develop a Global Partnership for Development (fair trade and more aid).

As can be seen, the MDGs were far from a utopian wish-list and represented an attempt to set pragmatic and verifiable targets by which the international community could be judged (against a baseline of 1990). Progress towards meeting the MDGs by the target date of 2015 was mixed. The proportion of the world living on less than $1.25 fell significantly but hunger levels did not improve greatly, with the WFP estimating that the number of malnourished people in the world topped the 1 billion mark for the first time in 2009, significantly up on the 1990 level (WFP 2009). On unpicking these figures, a general trend for all the goals emerges. Asia, Latin America and North Africa did make significant progress, and met many of the targets on a regional basis, but sub-Saharan Africa was generally out of step with this improvement.

Concerns at the MDGs not being met and heightened anxieties over food security prompted by the post-2008 global economic downturn saw renewed efforts to continue on this reformist path and better enshrine the notion of a right to food. UN Secretary-General Ban Ki-moon established a High-Level Task Force on the Global Food Security Crisis in 2008 which, the following year, adopted a Comprehensive Framework for Action, a two-track strategy pledging food assistance to the most vulnerable in times of crisis as well as seeking to reduce vulnerability in the longer term. A desire to tackle global hunger at the high table of economic interests was also evident when the G8 ('Group of Eight' – the seven biggest economies plus Russia) adopted the L'Aqilla Food Security Initiative at its 2009 summit which (along with several other states and private donors) pledged US$20 billion for projects supporting food production in the global South over the next three years. In 2012, on the initiative's expiry, this was then followed up by a similar commitment under the 'New Alliance to Improve Food and Nutrition Security'. From 2013 the targets identified for taking governance beyond the 2015 deadline for the MDGs – the UN Sustainable Development Goals – then notably set several new challenges for the international community on deforestation, desertification, climate change and the over-subsidization of farming and fishing (see Box 11.3).

Hence, in spite of the persistence of hunger in over a tenth of the world's people, there has been significant normative progress on the notion that the international community has a 'responsibility to feed' as well as protect. The rise of a global discourse of a right to food – like a right to health (see Chapter 7) – is evident in civil society, looser grassroots activists, the United Nations and even the world's wealthiest countries, and may represent early evidence of a globalization of the entitlements thesis.

Depression

The creation of the present global economic system, at the Bretton Woods Conference in 1944, and its persistence and growth ever since, was/is inspired by the desire to safeguard national economic security. The USA, finding itself in the position of global hegemon in the wake of Europe's devastation during the Second World War, bore the burden of funding the new international financial institutions intended to stabilize the world's currencies and usher in free trade. To be sure, Washington took up the costly role of entrepreneur and manager of the new Liberal International Economic Order for some more conventional political motivations. Military security was seen as being enhanced by propping up the capitalist world against the potential spread of Communism, and it is customary for the world's premier economic power to promote free trade because, ultimately, they should enjoy the greatest spoils from the increased volume of world trade which follows. The British actively supported free trade in the nineteenth century for much the same reason.

In addition to these two motivations of economic gain and military security, however, the LIEO was moulded by the belief that building a system to support Economic Liberalism was a means of enhancing human security by tackling global poverty. In this way the LIEO differs from the nineteenth-century economic system, which was concerned only with free trade and did not have institutions intended to act as a safety net for states struggling with short- or long-term financial difficulties. The International Monetary Fund (IMF) was designed as an international source of liquidity for governments to borrow from when facing balance of payments difficulties, and the World Bank was created to facilitate development loans.

The Great Depression of the 1930s, in which thousands of people starved to death and/or others experienced abject poverty in both the developed and underdeveloped world, loomed large in the minds of the Bretton Woods negotiators and strengthened the resolve of capitalist states to move away from the protectionism of the first part of the twentieth century, seen as responsible for the economic meltdown (and, ultimately, the Second World War also). Clark describes the Great Depression, rather than either world war or ideological conflict, as 'the greatest formative event of twentieth century history' (Clark 2001: 28). The LIEO outlived the Cold War, even contributing to its termination through its success, and has widened (in terms of the states involved) and deepened (in terms of the extent of its political impact) in the years following, with the distant memories of the 1930s still lingering.

Since the 1930s and subsequent creation of the Bretton Woods system financial turbulence has recurred periodically and had profound effects on the economic security of a number of states and their populations. The oil crises of the 1970s were the economic making of a number of oil-producing countries, but their hiking up of the price of this crucial commodity prompted economic recession for much of the rest of the world. In 1997 the huge bubble that was East Asian economic growth burst, causing a loss of income for Japan and more serious hardship for some of the poorer countries affected. Despite the spread of financial contagion through East Asia and South America, the North American and European economies remained relatively unaffected and their fashion for allowing currencies to 'float', rather than be pegged to other currencies, and liberalizing capital markets (relaxing government rules on financial firms) persisted. After a decade of economic growth in Europe and North America, however, another sudden – and this time global – economic recession caused by financial turbulence threatened the remaining Bretton Woods edifice.

From 2008 a financial crisis spread through the world triggered by the collapse of the US housing market. Banks had been granting loans to people to buy houses much more readily than in the past and then selling on the money based on this debt to other financial companies to fund investments. These financial companies assumed these loans were 'secure' because mortgages have traditionally been viewed in this way (because the sum is seen as guaranteed by the fact that the banks have people's homes as collateral) and credit rating agencies in Wall Street and the City of London assured them that they were. House prices had been rising for several years, allowing this sort of lending to appear viable, but when this financial bubble inevitably burst, it became apparent that it was not. The loans were not traditional mortgages and were not secure because the banks had been increasingly lending to: (1) poor people unlikely to be able to make the repayments and (2) rich people who had bought property purely for investment purposes. Hence, when the poor borrowers started to default on repayments and rich borrowers responded to a fall in prices by simply handing over the house keys, the mortgage lenders were left owning property nowhere near the value of the sums of money they had lent. When it became obvious that banks had been lending sums far in excess of what they owned, businesses lost confidence in them and the whole financial system was plunged into chaos. Many major international banks collapsed, many others had to be bailed out with multi-trillion-dollar injections of government (i.e. taxpayers') money, and a slump in production occurred as businesses became starved of bank loans, creating a huge growth in unemployment. Across the world at least $US4 trillion was lost (to put this in context, global GDP or 'all the money in the world' at that time was around $US60 trillion) in the worst economic recession since the Great Depression of the 1930s.

The persistence of the recession undermined the position of the *Globalists* (or Economic Liberals) that this was a temporary setback; the bursting of another economic bubble after which the market would correct itself and allow the normal pattern of economic growth – which had dominated the past sixty years – to resume. For *Anti-Globalists* (or Marxists) the scale of the downturn provided damning evidence that capitalism is simply unsustainable as a global economic system. However, the Post-Washington Consensus has persisted and the *Alter-Globalist* view that the recession represented a political failing that could be rectified was, ultimately, strengthened. The prevailing opinion is that the fault for the recession lay in the failure of certain governments to properly control banks and the financial markets and the lack of robust international mechanisms to monitor financial flows.

By learning from the 2008 recession and putting reforms in place it is hoped that the global economy can be resurrected in a better, more regulated, form. Hence the IMF has been beefed up rather than slaughtered and the Bretton Woods system lives on, albeit with a wider cohort of economic giants, including the likes of China, India and Brazil, now calling the shots alongside the Western powers.

Many states were weakened by the 2008 recession, through a rise in indebtedness and political unrest, but both the global sovereign and economic systems have persisted. There has, though, been a considerable human security cost to the last decade of economic stagnation. A study by *The Lancet*, for example, estimated that 260,000 cancer deaths in the developed world could be attributed to poverty triggered by the recession (though not in states with universal health care) (Maruthappu et al. 2016). Economic insecurities, real or perceived, have also manifested themselves in heightened levels of discrimination and violence against migrants, ethnic minorities and women, as is addressed in the next chapter.

Economic statecraft

Whereas poverty can variously be attributed to natural disasters, domestic political disorder or global structural forces, the economic security of particular states and individuals also can be threatened systematically and deliberately by a state's (or grouping of states') foreign policy through various forms of economic statecraft. Davis and Gray argue that the use of blockades on food and other essentials from entering an enemy state in wartime constitutes a weapon of mass destruction, a term generally applied to nuclear, chemical or biological weapons (Baylis et al. 2002: 256–7). In instances such as the UK led blockade on Germany and its allies in the First World War the aim was to starve the government of war-making materials but also to starve the population of the target state into surrender, in line with the prevailing ethos of the time, that civilians were legitimate targets. In accordance with the retreat from *total war* and the revival of *just war* in recent years, the use of economic instruments of foreign policy has attempted to be more discriminating and to target governments and state structures rather than civilian populations. As with just military campaigns, however, the collateral damage associated with economic statecraft can still be considerable.

Economic instruments of foreign policy have grown in significance since the end of the Second World War and come in a range of forms, the severity of their likely impact related to the importance of the foreign policy aim they are intended to realize. Most sanctions do not have security implications and are used symbolically, such as in blocking the import of a particular good in a trade dispute. Additionally, in most cases the economic security of states and their peoples is only likely to be threatened by global economic action, depriving them of any legitimate trading partners. Unilateral sanctions imposed in the context of a diplomatic or economic dispute are usually symbolic since the target state can invariably find other trade partners. The collective international imposition of significant economic sanctions originated in the 1960s under the auspices of the UN Security Council, empowered by Article 41 of the UN Charter to act against threats to international peace and security. Cold War geopolitics limited this to resolutions forbidding trade with the racist regimes in Rhodesia and South Africa and it was not until the 1990s that Article 41 became widely utilized. The significance of Security Council-backed sanctions is that they become binding on all UN members, whether they individually support the measure or not. Bearing in mind the limited operation of collective security, UN sanctions represent the most significant example of global *supranational* policy seen to date.

The success of UN economic sanctions as a means of conducting coercive diplomacy is not easy to judge. The use of economic sanctions has increased greatly since the end of the Cold War but they are often controversial and, some feel, counterproductive. Criticisms levelled at the use of comprehensive economic sanctions are varied but, from a human security perspective, the most significant is the collateral damage that they can cause. In practice they have often proved to be a blunt instrument that tends to have more impact upon ordinary civilians in the target state than the government. These fears became most pronounced in the 1990s with evidence of starvation amongst Iraqis in the wake of long-standing UN sanctions. There is a good case to be made that these deprivations were more the fault of the Iraqi government than the UN sanctions but, either way, they led to thousands of deaths. Saddam Hussein's regime undoubtedly prioritized rearmament over famine relief in allocating expenditure from their shrinking budget and milked the suffering of their people in order to gain support for a lifting of the measures. However, wherever the fault ultimately lies, there is no doubt that thousands of Iraqis died as a result of economic hardship resulting from political action rather than any natural disaster. This illustrates another, related argument against economic sanctions: their success rests on the assumption that the target state government will act in a rational way, which dictators like Saddam Hussein may not.

The state security impact of sanctions is also debatable. The racist governments of Rhodesia and South Africa were overthrown but not until many years after economic action was taken. Iraq was forced out of Kuwait, but this was the result of military action rather than the initial sanctions imposed upon them. Saddam Hussein for many years defied UN demands for weapons inspectors to be allowed into the country until eventually facing military action again. The Yugoslav wars, also, ended more as a result of military and diplomatic interventions by the US than as a result of the economic measures imposed on the Milosevic regime by the international community.

Despite such reservations, the use of UN economic sanctions has increased in recent years and this trend looks set to continue. The popularity of sanctions principally lies in the fact that, when compared to military action, they are a cheap peacekeeping option, both economically and in terms of peacekeeper lives. They provide an option 'between words and war', allowing the Security Council to do more than merely condemn aggression where the will or need for collective military security is not present. In addition, despite the controversy surrounding economic measures against Iraq, the advent of 'smart sanctions' since the mid-1990s has served to counter the chief criticisms levelled at this political tool. Smart sanctions aim to be less blunt than comprehensive sanctions by focusing more specifically on the government and state officials of the target state.

All UN sanctions have now become more targeted and less comprehensive, both to increase their effectiveness and in an effort to avoid collateral damage.

The imposition of sanctions by the Security Council is followed up by the creation of a Sanctions Committee which utilizes expert opinion to consider the humanitarian effects of new economic measures, and their effects on third party states, and also seeks to oversee their effective implementation. Targeting individuals rather than the whole economy of a state by freezing bank accounts or imposing travel bans has proved effective in some sanctions regimes. In the 1990s an anti-democratic coup in Haiti was weakened in this way, and the Gaddafi regime in Libya was persuaded to cease sponsoring terrorism. Later, Iran were brought to the negotiating table over their nuclear programme by a range of targeted measures enacted from 2008. More targeted sanctions have helped alleviate some of the humanitarian side-effects, although in Iraq, even after the shift from blanket sanctions to the 'oil for food programme', hunger amongst the general population and evasion by MNCs remained major problems. The Iraqi case indicates that even the sharpest of instruments can be blunted when used against a stubborn and despotic leader.

Achieving global economic security

Very different prescriptions exist about how best to lessen the human security threat posed by economic want. The study of *International Political Economy* (IPE) conventionally has three main approaches which, as well as being paradigms for conceptualizing the economic world, can be understood as ideologies for enhancing economic security.

Marxists

Marxists (or Structuralists) consider the chief source of human insecurity, economic or otherwise, to be the global economy itself. Hence, as referred to earlier in the chapter, dependency theorists advocate that LDCs are best advised to concentrate on their own economies rather than integrate themselves more into an exploitative global trading system. From this perspective, global economic security can only be achieved by radical global change, with the LIEO making way for international socialism in which the inequalities inherent in the class structures that underpin capitalism are swept away.

Economic Liberals

Economic Liberals contend that more rather than less liberalization of the global economic order is needed for human security to be enhanced. The LIEO has allowed the people of the world to get richer by limiting the capacity of their governments to buck the market in claiming the money for themselves in tariffs. Free from meddling governments, international trade can increase in volume and serve the interest of humanity though the logic of 'comparative advantage'. Rather than having states pursue self-sufficiency, freer global trade allows countries or regions to produce what they are best suited to rather than 'a bit of everything'. Hence, in the logic of Economic Liberalism, more is produced and more is traded. The pioneer of this perspective was eighteenth-century Scottish economist Adam Smith, who greatly influenced British international policy in the following century (Smith 1776).

Some of Smith's contemporary protégés put the world's economic failings down to the LIEO not being sufficiently liberal and are concerned at recent shifts towards more socially-minded Keynesian liberalism in global bodies like the World Bank. Peter Bauer, an exponent of true global free market economics, once said of foreign aid that it is 'an excellent method for transferring money from poor people in rich countries to rich people in poor countries' (*Economist* 2002b). This view that taxed revenues and charity from the North tend to be squandered by elites in the South and produce dependency provides an interesting instance of the political right and left reaching the same conclusions about the world.

Mercantilists

Mercantilism, the economic sibling to political Realism, views the world through a lens in which the state is the referent object of security. This is mainly for the ontological reason that 'that is how it is', but also through the normative belief that people's lives and livelihoods are best safeguarded by the policies of their governments. At the extreme level Mercantilism has manifested itself in the foreign policy of *autarky*, whereby states have sought to enhance their power (and hence also their and their people's security) by foreign conquest to gain economic resources. In a more mainstream and contemporary form, what has been distinguished as 'Neo-Mercantilism' both sees and advocates the state putting their interest over that of the wider international community by promoting economic protectionism. Just as Realism has dominated foreign policy practice in military security, traditionally Mercantilism has guided governments in their international economic relations and continues to do so to a degree, even with the advance of free trade. The LIEO has advanced the logic of Smith further than at any point previously in history, but all states, including the liberal democracies, still have a reluctance to fully integrate themselves into the global marketplace, and the last decade of economic stagnation has boosted the allure of protectionism. In this view, one state's comparative advantage is another's disadvantage.

Conclusions

There is some compelling logic behind all three approaches to IPE when thinking about human security. The famines of the late nineteenth century bear testimony to the failings of laissez-faire economics at the global level. The persistence of hunger in a contemporary world of unprecedented wealth indicates that the system is still fundamentally flawed. The dependency theory solution of going alone, however, is no longer a serious option, such is the interconnectedness of the world today. Isolated, dogmatic and hungry, North Korea stands as a stark illustration of that. The Structuralist contention that global economic forces determine people's lives and deaths is no longer an argument aired only at Marxist rallies; it is demonstrably true and now part of mainstream thinking in IPE. The notion that North–South interactions in the global system are inherently exploitative does not, however, entirely stand up to scrutiny. Without doubt, the economic gap between the world's rich and poor continues to widen and many countries remain undeveloped and appear unlikely to develop in the foreseeable future. Many countries have achieved a degree of economic development, however, and nearly all have achieved human development. All states bar war-torn Syria and AIDS-ridden Swaziland saw their HDI scores increase between 1990 and 2015 (UNDP 2016). In addition, over 200 million people have been lifted out of hunger since 2009 in spite of a world with a growing population and stagnated economy.

There can be little doubt that liberalizing trade leads to more produce and wealth for the world collectively, but it is unsurprising that governments are reluctant to abandon Mercantilism given that there is a certain risk inherent in opening up your country in this way. The collective spoils of free trade are not likely to be distributed evenly and governments fear not getting their slice of the pie if it is a global free-for-all. Comparative advantage might make global economic sense but it might also represent governmental political suicide. Governments abandoning large swathes of their country's industrial or agricultural firms to allow more efficient foreign competitors in in their place, of course, risk courting huge unpopularity. This, however, does not indicate that protectionism is the best method of achieving human security, if seen from the global perspective. Agricultural and fishing protectionism in the global North keeps Northern farmers and food producers wealthy (and fishermen at least at work), but abandoning it would not imperil their lives. Lives in the global South, though, are threatened by the distorting effects of this protectionism. This illustrates clearly the failings of statecentricism in the pursuit of human security. Globalization, if driven purely by the economic interests of some states, can represent a threat to much of the world, but a more fully rounded form of globalization, with a social and political dimension, can do much to enhance human security.

 Key points

- Poverty is both a major direct threat to life, as a cause of famine and hunger, and a major indirect threat to life, since it heightens vulnerability to other threats.
- Famines usually have natural triggers but, ultimately, are man-made phenomena since they are sometimes politically motivated and nearly always politically avoidable.
- Famines are high-profile peaks of suffering dwarfed by the general, persistent threat of hunger.
- Hunger is avoidable since there is sufficient food in the world for all people but it remains a major problem due to global political failings which can, variably, be attributed to negligence or wilful exploitation in the global North or the failure to modernize in the global South.
- Life-threatening societal poverty may also occur as a result of economic recession or as a side-effect of sanctions targeting governments.
- Economic security from an Economic Liberal perspective is best achieved by more globalization, from a Mercantilist perspective by less globalization, and from a Marxist perspective by radical global change.

Notes

1   Malnutrition is defined by the WFP as a daily intake of below 1,800 calories; 2,100 is the recommended intake.
2   Whilst shocking, this does represent a reduction from an annual average net loss of 8.3 million hectares in the 1990s.

Recommended reading

Bergen, M. and Weber, M. (2014) *Rethinking the Third World: International Development and World Politics*, New York: Palgrave.
Galtung, J. (1969) 'Violence, Peace and Peace Research', *Journal of Peace Research*, 6(3): 167–91.
Paarlberg, R. (2013) *Food Politics: What Everyone Needs to Know*, Oxford: Oxford University Press.
Rostow, W. (1960) *The Stages of Economic Growth*, Cambridge: Cambridge University Press.
Sen, A. (1981) *Poverty and Famines: An Essay on Entitlement and Deprivation*, Oxford: Clarendon Press.

Useful web links

- Food and Agricultural Organization: www.fao.org/
- Sustainable Development Goals: www.undp.org/content/undp/en/home/sustainable-development-goals.html
- World Food Programme: www.wfp.org/

Chapter 5

Identity, society and insecurity

> *I love my country far too much to be a nationalist.*
>
> Source unknown

Security and society

The most obvious limitation of a statecentric national security approach emerges when governments become a direct source of their citizens' insecurity. Most of the millions of victims of the Hitler, Stalin, Pol Pot and myriad other tyrannical regimes throughout history were killed in the pursuit of national security, as those governments saw it. Individuals, by virtue of their identity, can in various ways come to be viewed as a threat to the national interest, or portrayed that way for political reasons by governments and/or dominant sectors of society. The notion of protecting human rights through legal, political and even military actions has evolved through recognition of this, but the paradox remains. In cases far less extreme than Nazi Germany, the Soviet Union or the Khmer Rouge, human rights and human security are frequently viewed as secondary to the pursuit of national security. As discussed in previous chapters, in many liberal democracies governments have demonstrated this through, for example, authorizing 'shoot to kill' counter-terrorist strategies or the blurring of the lines of just war principles in times of conflict. More commonly, in *all* states in the world – democratic or otherwise – human security has at times been imperilled by forms of violent societal discrimination which demonstrate the limitations of conventional domestic governance. The prevailing 'wisdom' that human rights, whilst important, can be trumped by national security is one of the most compelling arguments for collapsing the distinction and re-orienting political practice on the basis of human security.

Forms of violent discrimination

National identity

Virulent, violent nationalism – whether racist or xenophobic – has long rendered insecure people thought to threaten or live outside of the nation under consideration. Famously described by Benedict Anderson as 'imagined communities' (Anderson 1991), nations defy simple, objective definition yet have been for the last two hundred years the most significant referent object of security in international politics. What is taken to constitute a nation varies considerably from case to case. The 'we feeling' that distinguishes one's own nation from the rest of humanity is determined by various different factors. Ethnicity is closely linked to nationality in some states, such as Japan, but is less significant in countries with a tradition of multi-ethnic citizenship, such as France or the USA.

Where ethnicity is considered to define the nation, minority ethnic groups are not likely to be accommodated by or assimilated into the dominant, indigenous national group and risk becoming marginalized. At the lesser end of the scale this might be in the form of being denied the rights of citizenship in their country of residence, and in the extreme manifest itself in the horrors of genocide and 'ethnic cleansing'. 'Ethnic cleansing' entered the language in the 1990s to denote a policy less extreme than an outright attempt to annihilate a national group (genocide) but which aims to remove them from a given territory. The term was widely applied in relation to the Yugoslav war over the secession of Croatia and Bosnia-Herzegovina but was, in fact, a wholly inappropriate description. Croats, Serbs and Bosnian Muslims were/are not ethnically distinct since they are nearly all Slavs. National hatred seemed to appear from nowhere, with archaic historical and religious distinctions suddenly acquiring great significance. The deadly vagueness of national identity and its propensity towards promoting 'ethnocentricism', by stressing the difference between 'self' and 'other', became all too apparent to a horrified onlooking world.

Table 5.1 attempts to rank the worst genocides in history but it should be borne in mind that, due to difficulties in verifying wildly fluctuating figures, some historical massacres are probably denied their rightful place in this list. In addition, the distinction between genocide and war in the age of total war is not always clear-cut. However, since national identity is very much a phenomenon of modern history,[1] it is safe to assume that the desire to exterminate *the other* must also reside principally in the modern era. Pre-modern imperial conquests certainly claimed millions of lives but, in most cases, their aim was the conversion or subjugation of the conquered peoples rather than their annihilation. The Mongols were unusually savage in their ransacking of cities and so merit an inclusion, but the list excludes some notable long-term slaughters, such as the fate that befell African slaves and native Americans in the imperial era. It was in the twentieth century when ideas of nationhood began to be conflated with 'ethnic purity' in the extreme nationalism of Nazi Germany that 'genocide' entered the political lexicon and landscape (see Box 5.1).

The subjective nature of nationality heightens the importance of perception in this area of security politics. The perception that a minority nationality is a human security threat to the majority nationality, such as in the association of certain

TABLE. 5.1 The top ten ethnic/national genocides in history

	Victims	Perpetrators	Date	Numbers killed
1	Chinese	Mongols	1215–1279	18.8 million (i)
2	Slavs	Nazis, Germany	1940–1945	10.5 million (i)
3	Jews	Nazis, Germany	1933–1945	6 million (i, ii)
4	Persians	Mongols	1220–1222	6 million (i)
5	Nuer, Nuba & Dinka	Sudan	1983–present	1.9 million (ii)
6	Tibetans	China	1959–present	1.6 million (ii)
7	Germans	Poland	1945–1948	1.6 million (i)
8	Bengalis	Pakistan	1958–1987	1.5 million (i, ii)
9	Armenians	Turkey	1915–1917	1.5 million (ii)
10	Ibos	Nigeria	1966–1970	1 million (ii)

Sources: (i) Rummel 2003; (ii) Genocide Watch 2003.

BOX 5.1 Rafael Lemkin

Rafael Lemkin, an International Law lecturer at Yale University, both coined the term *genocide* and played a leading role in the formulation of the UN's 1948 'Genocide Convention'. Lemkin was a Polish Jew who fled Nazi persecution in 1939, moving initially to Sweden before then embarking on an academic and activist career in the United States. Lemkin's 1944 book *Axis Rule in Occupied Europe* was the first publication to use the term genocide which he defined as 'a coordinated plan of different actions aiming at the destruction of essential foundations of the life of national groups, with the aim of annihilating the groups completely' (Lemkin 1944: 79). The word, which combines the Greek *genos* (meaning race/family) with the Latin 'cide' (to kill), had particular resonance for him since forty-nine members of his family and six million of his fellow nationals had been murdered by what Churchill called the 'crime without a name'. Lemkin went on to play the leading role in the drafting of the UN convention on genocide and to participate as an adviser at the Nuremberg trials against Nazi war criminals. Something of a forgotten hero, Lemkin's grave at the Mount Hebron Cemetery, New York refers to him aptly as the 'Father of the Genocide Convention' (Korey 2001).

---

migrants or resident minorities with crime and terrorism, is a common trait. At a lesser level, and more commonly, the minority nationality may be perceived as a threat to the economic well-being or identity of the dominant group or their 'societal security' (Waever et al. 1993). Minority nationalities may even be perceived as threats to state security, as in the Nazi and neo-Nazi portrayal of Jews, formerly as Communists and latterly as part of a global conspiracy to control economic life.

Despite copious evidence to the contrary,[2] perceived threats to economic security and cultural norms have prompted a recent nationalistic surge in many Western states, which has manifested itself in a hardening of barriers and attitudes towards migrants. The death toll of refugees seeking to surmount ever more dangerous obstacles to crossing the Mediterranean to Europe from the Middle East serves to illustrate starkly this national/human security dichotomy. The illusory pursuit of national or societal security that lies behind the barbed-wire fences and barbed discourse of contemporary European immigration has produced mass human insecurity. Dehumanizing language typically refers to the movement of such people with verbs such as 'flows', 'floods' or 'swarms', and even governments mindful that migrants do not pose the sorts of threats posited in nationalistic media find themselves pandering to this populism for electoral gain. Indeed it can be argued that the whole discourse of migration, in terms of the relationship between the migrant and the state, is both inappropriate and archaic given the fluidity that characterizes much contemporary cross-border movement. Truong and Gasper, for example, contend that 'transnational mobility' gives better expression to the often temporary relocation of people in 'guestworker' arrangements (such as with many workers in the Arab Gulf states), free movement of EU citizens or student exchanges (Truong & Gasper 2011). Across much of the world it has become so common to find people residing outside of their country of citizenship – whether working, studying, visiting or fleeing turmoil – that the political conventions of the *social contract* and sovereignty have become concurrently less relevant or valid.

Religion

Religion as a basis for conflict or discriminatory violence is, of course, age-old. Religious identity predates national identity by many centuries and was the chief cause of wars and massacres within and between the rudimentary states of the pre-Westphalian era, aside from the age-old and perennial motive of straight territorial gain. The 1648 Treaty of Westphalia marked the end of a major religious conflict across much of Europe, the Thirty Years War between Catholicism and Protestantism, and also the end of an era of religious domination over the kingdoms of Europe. From 1648 the sovereignty of kingly states began to supersede the *supranationality* of the Pope, and the loyalty and identity of citizens shifted accordingly from their religion to their monarch and nation. In subsequent centuries the Westphalian system spread beyond Europe to the rest of the world, but nations have never entirely replaced religions as a social identity for which individuals are prepared to kill and be killed. In many cases national identity succeeded rather than superseded religious identity and provided a framework for pre-Westphalian conflicts of faith to persist in a sovereign, secular age. The Wars of the Reformation (which culminated in the Thirty Years War) were, essentially, still being fought in Northern Ireland in the 1990s, although by then this was very much about national self-determination rather than papal authority.

Since some nationalities are defined in religious terms, the presence of individuals of other religions is often portrayed as a threat to national cohesion and, hence, they can become the victims of state or societal repression. This was starkly illustrated by the phenomenon of so-called ethnic cleansing in Bosnia-Herzegovina in the 1990s. Slavic Serbs, Slavic Croats and Slavic Muslims, speaking the same language and having cohabited peacefully for decades, fought along religiously-determined battle lines in the middle of a secular state. The Bosnian Moslems, natives of the region whose ancestors had converted to Islam in the fifteenth century and who were no more religiously devout than the Catholic Croats or Orthodox Serbs, suddenly came to be seen as outsiders in their own country because of a *societal security* struggle between the other two nationalities. Serbian nationalism was reawakened by the break-up of the multi-national state they had dominated and rallied to its traditional cause of Islamophobia, fuelled by historic memories of their centuries of domination by the Ottoman Turks.

Whereas the break-up of Yugoslavia and the lower-level dispute over the status of Northern Ireland were really national conflicts with very deep religious roots rather than genuine clashes of faiths, there are numerous contemporary instances of blood being shed over insecurities rooted firmly in religion. Secular, Westphalian states today are still wary of the alternative lure religious identity may hold for their citizens. The radicalization (or politicization) of many religions in the last forty years has led to state and societal insecurity frequently being triggered by more 'real' challenges than the use of religion as a label of difference. Religious *fundamentalism* first came to the attention of the international community in 1979 when an absolute monarchy was transformed into Shi'a Moslem semi-*theocracy* in Iran. For Iranians, Shi'a Moslem clerics, who had always been their spiritual leaders, would now be their political leaders also. Revolutions in other countries have always made governments nervous of their own citizens following suit and, just like the French and Russian Revolutions in earlier eras, the Iranian revolt prompted copy-cat uprisings in other societies and pre-emptive strikes against this possibility by other governments. In Sunni Moslem states, such as Egypt, Algeria and Uzbekistan, the undisputed national religion, in fundamentalist form, came to be seen as a threat to the government, prompting civil war and societal fissures.

Where a radicalized religion is that of a minority group the insecurities of the dominant culture often lead to heightened persecution of 'the other'. Traditionally poor relations between Hindus and Moslem minorities in India have worsened over the last forty years, with Islamic fundamentalism prompting the rise of more militant strains of Hinduism. Western societal anxieties over migration have, in some cases, taken a more specific form than a more generalized distinction between self and other. The rise to prominence of populist nationalist movements in many Western European democracies over the past fifteen years and the election of President Trump in 2016 in the US called not for a general tightening of immigration, as traditionally favoured by far right politicians, but specifically for curbs on the entry of Moslem people.

Although many 'religious conflicts' are best understood as nationalist rather than theological struggles, religious issues can sometimes serve to inflame essentially national conflicts. Serb nationalist atrocities perpetrated on the Kosovar Albanians in the 1990s were partially explained by the sacred significance of Kosovo to the Serbian Orthodox church (who, themselves, were active in promoting Serb nationalism in the region leading up to Milosevic's campaign). Similarly, the Palestinian–Israeli dispute is especially complicated by the religious importance attached to Jerusalem by both sides (and indeed by Christianity), particularly in regard to the Temple Mount.[3] Hindu–Moslem and Hindu–Sikh tensions in India have periodically worsened following incidents relating to mosques and temples, respectively. The Tamil secessionist campaign in Sri Lanka, too, came to have a much greater religious dimension after their 1998 attack on the Temple of the Buddha's Tooth.

Gender

A further form of social identity which is frequently the basis of life-threatening discrimination is gender. A woman's gender, which encompasses her societal identity as well as biological sex, can often be a particular source of personal insecurity. Human security issues pertaining to women, such as domestic violence, have little chance of receiving attention in the traditional statist discourse of international relations since women tend to suffer a double discrimination. Women frequently suffer from being marginalized, first, in domestic politics (as a private, 'domestic' family matter) and, then, in international politics (as a private, domestic sovereign state matter).

In addition, female insecurity is often a particular by-product of religious or national/ethnic societal security concerns. Women are often constructed as the embodiment of national and/or religious culture and, as such, treated more harshly than men when they step outside of the culturally prescribed notion of a 'good woman' (Yuval-Davis 1997: 46). Hence adulterous women in some Islamic states are seen as a greater threat to cultural norms than their male equivalents and, as a result, are punished more severely, such as in 'honour killings' over adultery. Men too, in theory, are subject to the death penalty for this 'crime' but, in practice, are generally able to escape punishment or make a deal to save their lives. In this case, women, as a collective entity, are not being threatened, but individual women are subject to threats *because* of their gender. In addition, the pervading threat hanging over such women as a collective serves to deter them from voicing their fears and so highlighting their plight (Hansen 2000).

The insecurity of women can also be both heightened and obscured by the rise of military security threats to the state in which they live. Although wars continue (in the main) to be fought between men, the threat posed to women in such conflicts has risen greatly in recent history. Feminist IR writers have drawn attention to this as an antidote to the myth of war being fought by men on behalf of the women and children of their society or state. Those women and children have had to bear the brunt of the rise of the systematic targeting of civilians in war over the last century, make up the bulk of refugees and displaced persons resulting from war and have suffered the greatest deprivations due to states re-aligning their economies to the war effort.

In addition, the sexual abuse of women in wartime, although by no means a new phenomenon, has, in recent years, become more common without being fully appreciated. Tickner argues that 'rape is not just an accident of war but often a systematic military strategy' (Tickner 2001: 50). Rape has long been practised by invading military forces, to symbolize their power and the subjugation of the occupied peoples, but the scale of the attacks in recent ethnic conflicts does suggest something more orchestrated; 250,000 women are believed to have been raped in the Rwandan civil war of 1994 (Tickner 2001: 50) and at least 20,000 in the Bosnian War of 1991–5

(Pettman 1996: 52). Both of these wars were classic *societal security* conflicts where single countries were ravaged by internal national conflict. The demonizing of and the desire to humiliate 'the other', promoted by nationalists, directly or indirectly legitimized sexual savagery beyond the norm in military conflict. In the civil war that has raged in the Democratic Republic of Congo for six decades, the threat posed to women by systematic mass rape became even more acute due to the likelihood of contracting HIV/AIDS in the assaults. There can be no more stark an illustration of how women's insecurity is heightened by perceptions of national insecurity.

The most common threat to the lives of women arising from their sexual status, however, comes from a less obviously violent source than foreign soldiers or domestic abusers. Mary Anne Warren first coined the term 'gendercide' to highlight the scale of female-specific abortions and infanticide (Warren 1985). The general preference for male heirs in most societies is exacerbated in countries where overpopulation has prompted government measures to restrict the number of children per family. Though the scale of this phenomenon is uncertain, and the ethics of killing unborn infants unproblematic for many, it is clear that hundreds of thousands of female lives are not lived every year as a result. Baby girls in a number of countries are frequently murdered soon after birth, usually by starvation or wilful neglect when ill, whilst ultrasound scans of pregnant women also make sex-based abortions increasingly common. In China, where families with more than one child were for many years strongly 'discouraged', a sex imbalance of 118 males to every 100 females was evident by 2011. The Chinese government's alarm at the social effects of such an imbalance prompted them to restrict the availability of ultrasound scans, meaning that infanticide became the best explanation for the sex disparity. Similarly, the 2011 census in India, where government policy combating overpopulation also encourages single offspring, revealed that the country had 7.1 million fewer girls under the age of 7 than boys, mainly due to sex-specific abortions. Worldwide, it is estimated that 117 million women are not alive as a consequence of this phenomenon (UNFPA 2012). The fact that an individual's sex and gender can be the source of their insecurity cannot be seen more clearly than in them being fatally discriminated against before even being able to live their life.

During a woman's lifetime, sex-based domestic violence remains a significant threat. It has been estimated that 38 per cent of women in the world who are murdered are killed by male partners and that 30 per cent of all women in intimate relationships with men have been violently attacked by them (WHO 2016c). The inaccuracy of the conventional externalizing of security threats is never more apparent than in this instance, where the threat comes not only from within the individual's own country but from within their own, immediate family.

It is important to note, however, that the victims of 'gendercide' are not always women. In both inter-state and intra-state war the systematic culling of men 'of fighting age' amongst enemy non-combatants has long been a military tactic. The mass killing of potential soldiers was a feature of the early German campaign in the USSR in the Second World War and was evident in the Serb massacres of Kosovar Albanians in the run-up to and duration of the 1999 Kosovan War (Jones 2000). Additionally, it is males who form the bulk of war casualties, as they do of criminal murders and industrial accidents. It is a paradox of human life that it is far safer to be born a boy but grow up as a woman.

Sexual orientation

Aside from nationality, ethnicity, religion and gender, a further form of identity subject to life-threatening discrimination is homosexuality and other minority sexual orientations. Many people have been killed and continue to be killed purely on the grounds that they practise consensual sexual activities with other people of the same sex. Homosexuals were targeted alongside minority ethnic groups and the disabled in the Nazi holocaust and many thousands were sent to death camps.[4] Nazi discrimination represented an extreme manifestation of state prejudice against homosexuality evident in nearly all countries at the time (far less frequently against lesbianism) and still apparent in many states today. Domestic legal restrictions on homosexuality have greatly lessened in most of the developed world over recent decades but in 2016 there were still seventy-four states legally prohibiting same-sex relationships, including nine which retained the death penalty for homosexuality (Afghanistan, Iran, Mauritania, Pakistan, Qatar, Sudan, Saudi Arabia, UAE and Yemen[5]). In many of these states illegality is a technicality which does not necessarily lead to prosecution, but several Iranians have been hanged in recent years for consensual, adult homosexual acts (*Independent* 2016).

Even where homosexuality is not a capital crime being gay can cost you your life. Violent political non-state groups, of various shades, have targeted homosexuals and other sexual minorities in campaigns in a number of countries. Right-wing death squads have murdered homosexuals in Colombia, as have the left-wing MRTA in Peru (Narrain 2001). In some states the government may be complicit in such attacks, even if they are not directly responsible. President Mugabe's remark in 1995 that homosexuals were 'less than human' undoubtedly contributed to the subsequent proliferation of attacks on gay Zimbabweans in the course of the internal conflict raging in the country. Even in some countries were homosexual rights are firmly entrenched, societal 'gay bashing' remains a significant problem. The murder of fifty people in a gay nightclub in Orlando in the USA in 2016 by a lone fanatic made this starkly apparent.

Disability

Disabled people, too, were amongst the array of 'undesirable' minority groups targeted in the Nazis' reign of terror in Germany. An estimated 200,000 mentally ill or physically disabled people were killed between 1939 and 1945 under the 'T-4' programme in Germany and the occupied territories (Burleigh 1994). The policy was presented as 'euthanasia' but the practice of deliberate starvation and the administering of lethal injections were far from the contemporary notion of consensual 'mercy killings'. The T-4 programme represented an escalation of the war against the disabled, which had previously concentrated on sterilizing rather than killing those with physical or mental impairments. Between 1934 and 1937 around 225,000 of Germany's disabled population were made incapable of reproducing new disabled (or, indeed, able-bodied) people (Kevles 1995: 117).

This initial Nazi strategy of ridding their country of the disabled was, however, largely uncontroversial. Many other states at the time were introducing similar, if less extensive, schemes as the 'science' of eugenics gained popularity. Eugenics is the science of 'improving' humanity by restricting reproduction of those deemed imperfect. The USA had sterilized 36,000 disabled people by 1941 (Kevles 1995: 116) and eugenics programmes had been introduced in Sweden, Denmark, Finland and in one Swiss canton between 1929 and 1939 (Kevles 1995: 115). 'Democratic Eugenics' (Drouard 1998: 174) continued in some of the Nordic states until the 1970s. The ethical tide has ebbed away from eugenics in most democracies, but the sterilization of the disabled persists in many contemporary states. In 2013 and 2015 the Australian government were admonished by the UN Committee on the Rights of Persons with Disabilities and then the UN Human Rights Council for permitting the sterilization of disabled girls and women without their consent.

As with other forms of discrimination, though, a general improvement in disabled rights should not blind us to a continued human security threat resulting from societal attitudes. Even in countries in which the disabled are legally well-protected social discrimination can take extreme forms, such as in Japan in 2016 when nineteen patients in a care home were murdered by a lone fanatic – Uematsu – as part of a planned personal slaughter of the weak.

Politicide

Strikingly absent from the UN definition of genocide (see Table 5.3) is the mass, systematic killing of political and/or social opponents by radical governments or non-governmental forces. Since the targets of such action are not necessarily national, ethnic or religious minorities, the distinct category of *politicide* is necessary for a complete understanding of the phenomenon of societal massacres. The omission of politicide from the UN Genocide Convention is the result of the predictable opposition of the USSR in the late 1940s to classifying their extermination of opponents and undesirables alongside that of the Nazis. As Table 5.2 indicates, the USSR regime represented at the UN drafting of the Convention on Genocide can claim the dubious distinction of being history's most brutal ever. Rummel estimates that some 62 million political and social opponents were killed during the three-quarter-century

TABLE 5.2 The top ten politicides in history

	Perpetrators	Victims	Date	Numbers killed
1	Stalinist USSR	class enemies, dissidents	1928–1953	49.5 million (i)
2	Maoist China	class enemies	1949–1976	35 million (i, ii)
3	Nationalist China	Communists, other opponents	1927–1949	10.2 million (i)
4	Chinese Communist opposition	nationalists	1927–1949	3.5 million (i)
5	Khmer Rouge	class enemies	1975–1979	2 million (i, ii)
6	North Korea	class enemies	1949–present	2 million (i)
7	North Vietnam	class enemies	1954–1975	1 million (i, ii)
8	Ethiopia	class enemies	1974–1979	750,000 (i)
9	Lenin's USSR	class enemies, dissidents	1917–1922	750,000 (i)
10	Indonesia	Communists	1965	500,000 (ii)

Sources: (i) Rummel 2003; (ii) Genocide Watch 2003.

lifespan of the USSR, and the Stalin era, alone, can lay claim to having been the largest single cause of human mortality bar the Black Death. Rummel observes that the average Soviet citizen was more at risk of being killed by their own government than the average smoker is from lung cancer (Rummel 2003: table 1.3).

Politicide was very much a twentieth-century phenomenon owing to the polarization of political ideologies in this period. Ruthless leaders have long slaughtered opponents away from the battlefield in order to buttress their power or through the paranoia that autocracy frequently brings, but, in the last century, this blended with ideological zeal in a deadly cocktail. As Table 5.3 indicates, major politicides have invariably been carried out either by or against Communists/Marxists of various shades. The limitations of conventional approaches to Security Studies, which hold that significant threats come only from other states and that the Cold War was a period of peace, are surely exposed by the unparalleled human suffering resulting from twentieth-century politicide.

Securing the individual – the global politics of human rights

The notion of governments taking politico-legal steps to protect individuals other than their own nationals/citizens is a relatively recent one in international affairs and still a long way from being firmly established in international law.

Empowering the individual – international human rights law

Table 5.3 charts the progress of international human rights law over the last two centuries. Developments have tended to occur amidst the optimism of reconstruction following major international conflicts, dating back to the end of the Napoleonic Wars in Europe. The unparalleled human suffering associated with the Second World War predictably provided the most significant catalyst.

Genocide

Though the word did not exist at the time, the first systematic international political response to an act of genocide occurred during the First World War when a declaration was made by the allied powers of France, Russia and Great Britain about the Turkish massacres of Armenians. The 1915 declaration stated that the allied powers would hold the Ottoman government responsible for the various atrocities going on as well as the murderous mobs directly responsible. The allies, however, were only partly true to their word on the termination of the war. Under the terms of the Treaty of Sevres, Turkey was obliged to bring to justice those responsible for the massacres. Some Turks were prosecuted internally and Great Britain even took the step of holding some of the suspects themselves, incarcerating them in Maltese jails before returning them to Turkey in 1921. The 'Young Turk' revolution of 1922, however, brought about a reconciliation between the allied powers and the new secular Turkish republic and a new treaty (the Lausanne Treaty) in 1923 absolved the new government of responsibility for pursuing crimes committed in the Ottoman era (Schabas 2000: 14–22).

TABLE 5.3 Key developments in human rights law

1815	Congress of Vienna	The 'Concert of Europe' powers agreed to end the slave trade.
1864	1st Geneva Convention	First of series of conventions giving legal protection to wounded or surrendered individual combatants in war and to non-combatants.
1890	Brussels Convention on Slavery	Outlawed the slave trade.
1901	International Labour Office workplace standards	Origins of notion of universal workers' rights. Not highly influential but paved the way for the creation of the International Labour Organization in 1919 as part of the League of Nations system.
1919	League of Nations Minorities Section created	The League did not develop a systematic human rights regime but made guaranteeing the rights of national minorities a condition of membership for some states and condemned state discrimination against minorities in the PCIJ Minority Schools in Albania 1935 case and other Advisory Opinions.
1926	Slavery Convention	Made slavery itself (in addition to slave trading) illegal.
1946	United Nations Commission on Human Rights established	Authorized by Article 68 of the UN Charter, the Commission worked on wording a Declaration. A full-time Commissioner of Human Rights was initiated by the 1993 Vienna Convention.
1948	Universal Declaration of Human Rights	Declaration adopted by the UN General Assembly establishing a Bill of Rights for the world comprising thirty short articles of mainly civil and political rights.
1948	Convention on the Prevention and Punishment of Genocide	The convention proscribed acts which aim to 'destroy in whole or in part a national, ethnic, racial or religious group'. This legislation was reinforced by a 1951 ICJ declaration that genocide is a crime in customary international law (i.e. binding on all states regardless of whether they ratified the convention).
1951	Refugee Convention	Makes it illegal for a receiving state to deport a refugee to a country where they are likely to be persecuted.
1966	Covenants on (i) Economic, Social & Cultural Rights and (ii) Civil & Political Rights	The legal machinery to implement the Universal Declaration came in two instruments. ESCR lists entitlements individuals can expect *from* their states (such as work and education). CPR lists individual freedoms *against* the state (such as free speech).
1969	Convention on the Elimination of All Forms of Racial Discrimination	Outlaws racial or national discrimination and holds the states accountable for societal violations. A CERD Committee monitors implementation and can investigate individual complaints.

Continued

TABLE 5.3 continued

1981	Convention on the Elimination of All Forms of Discrimination Against Women	A Bill of Rights for the women of the world outlawing violent and social state discrimination.
1984	Convention Against Torture	Followed up Article 5 of the UN Declaration to criminalize state torture under any circumstances.
1989	Convention on the Rights of the Child	Declares that 'the best interests of the child' should be respected in legal actions (e.g. in decisions on imprisoning or deporting their parents).
1990	Convention on Rights of All Migrant Workers and Members of Their Families	Protection of economic migrants from exploitation.
2006	Convention on the Rights of Persons With Disability	Protection of disabled people from economic exploitation or social discrimination.

In 1951 the International Court of Justice declared that, since the 1948 convention was so widely ratified, genocide came into the category of 'customary international law', making it a crime anywhere in the world. This means that genocide can be understood as a rare case of public international law functioning as 'proper' law. Countries which have not ratified the convention are not excluded from its jurisdictional reach[6] and there is a duty on all states which have ratified to prosecute those guilty of the crime where they can. The precedent for the universal jurisdiction of the Genocide Convention was established by the 1962 Eichmann case when Israeli secret agents kidnapped the former Nazi general and tried him in Israel for anti-Jewish genocide.[7] Twenty years later the USA agreed to Israel's request for another suspected mass-murderer, Demjanjuk, to be extradited for trial. Additionally, Canada and Australia had trials in the 1990s against naturalized citizens for participation in Second World War atrocities against Jews, in which the accused were acquitted but the principle of universal jurisdiction confirmed.[8] The revival of both genocide and international morality in the 1990s gave fresh impetus to the principle of enforcing the 1948 convention and saw, amongst others, successful cases brought in Germany and Belgium for 'crimes against humanity' committed in Bosnia and Rwanda.

Racial discrimination

For ethnically-based abuses short of genocide (i.e. not systematically seeking to eliminate a whole group) the Convention on the Elimination of All Forms of Racial Discrimination (CERD) came into force in 1969 outlawing racial or national discrimination and holding the ratifying states accountable for societal as well as governmental violations. Since it is near universally and unreservedly ratified, CERD is significant enough to amount to 'an international law against systemic racism' (Robertson 2000: 94). Many liberal democracies have followed the lead of CERD in framing domestic race relations laws and criminalizing the incitement of racial hatred. For example, Greece's new constitution on democratizing in 1975 was framed partly in reference to CERD. The CERD regime also permits individuals to take up cases against governments. Set against this, however, countries with the most serious ethnic tensions have systematically failed to report to the CERD Committee which implements the regime.

Torture

The 1984 Convention against Torture followed up Article 5 of the UN Declaration to criminalize state torture under any circumstances (including the theoretical 'ticking bomb' scenario – where an apprehended terrorist refuses to reveal the whereabouts of an explosive device primed to imminently inflict mass casualties – frequently offered as a defence of such tactics). The Torture Convention is considered part of customary international law but has seen its rules bent even by Western liberal democracies. The US government's approval for 'torture lite' techniques such as sleep deprivation and 'water boarding' (simulated drowning) at its Guantanamo Bay military camp on the island of Cuba holding prisoners of the Iraq and Afghan wars was a clear case of this.

Refugees and migrants

The 1951 Geneva Refugee Convention continued with the League of Nations' refugee regime by declaring it illegal for a receiving state to deport a person fleeing persecution to a country where they are likely to be imperilled. The convention at the time was largely seen as a 'mopping up' operation for living victims of Nazi oppression, in the same way that the League's regime was aimed at re-settling people uprooted by the Russian civil war, but it has become much more than that. By 1967 it was clear that long-running conflicts, such as in Palestine and the Congo, were making refugees far more than a temporary phenomenon and a protocol to the convention removed geographical and time limits from its scope and effectively universalized and made permanent its core provisions. By 2015, 142 states were covered by both the convention and the protocol.

In recent years, however, the permanence and universality of the Refugee Convention have started to come into question. Countries have always differed in how readily they will grant asylum to a refugee, but some governments have begun to question whether they should continue to be bound to give refuge at all. This is largely the result of the unforeseen rise in refugee numbers. In 2015 there were an estimated 21.3 million refugees and asylum seekers in the world, up from around 3 million in the early 1970s[9] (UNHCR 2017). The increased prevalence and persistence of civil wars is a major factor behind this. People in many democratic countries have pressured their governments for action to curb the numbers of asylum seekers through the belief that many are really economic migrants using political unrest in their countries as a pretext for moving. As a result of this, many governments – such as in Australia and the UK – have made the process of applying for asylum more rigorous and even resorted to incarcerating asylum seekers until their applications have been processed. In 2016 the Danish prime minister, Rasmussen, called for the obligation to grant asylum to be repealed, openly voicing a view previously whispered by several other Western governments and potentially opening the door to a human rights regression previously unheralded in international law.

Women

The 1981 Convention on the Elimination of All Forms of Discrimination Against Women (CEDAW) is, on the face of it, impressively universal, having amassed some 189 ratifications by 2016. Robertson, however, argues that CEDAW is far less influential than its close relation CERD, owing to the number and nature of reservations to its provisions lodged by the ratifying parties (Robertson 2000: 94). The most frequently derogated-from articles are 5 and 16 which deal with, respectively, the role of women in relation to customs/culture and the family. Since these two factors are those that most threaten the security of women, this is a serious limitation on the convention's effectiveness. Hence the sex discrimination inherent in certain aspects of Sharia law as applied in some Islamic states is out of the reach of the convention. It should be added, however, that many Western European states have ratified with reservations and that the USA has not ratified at all (see Table 5.4).

Despite this, the 1981 convention is not a paper tiger and it has made a contribution to protecting the rights of women. The Committee on the Elimination of Discrimination Against Women (CEDAW Committee), set up by the convention, is at the heart of an international regime which, at least to a limited extent, empowers individual women in a number of countries with rights not adequately covered in the twin Human Rights covenants. An optional protocol to CEDAW was adopted in 1999 and by 2016 had been ratified by 108 states, giving the CEDAW Committee the power to pursue cases brought by individual women in those states. CEDAW has, on occasion, been cited in defence of women in domestic legal cases, and the constitution of Brazil was amended to bring it into line with its provisions (IFUW 1999). The 1993 UN Declaration on the Elimination of Violence Against Women and the 'Platform for Action' agreed at the 1995 Beijing Conference deepened the range of global norms concerning women's rights, but these instruments lack the legal force of the CEDAW regime, limited though that is. As illustrated earlier, violence and wider discrimination based on sex remain endemic in much of the world and much remains to be done to properly secure women.

The disabled

Around 700 million people, or one-tenth of the world's population, are restricted by mental, physical or sensory impairment but, until recently, were not specifically covered in international human rights legislation. In 1987 discussions in the General Assembly over a convention on the human rights of the disabled were postponed when a number of states' delegates indicated that they considered the disabled to already be adequately covered in existing human rights legislation (O'Reilly 2003). Disabled rights have advanced significantly in most countries over recent decades but the fact that 80 per cent of the world's disabled people live in LDCs, where the means of facilitating their involvement in social and economic life may be absent even if the will is present, serves to heighten their vulnerability. An umbrella pressure group network, the International Disability Alliance, was at the forefront of the campaign to plug this gap and establish a UN convention for the disabled. A strong campaign persuaded the General Assembly to set up an ad hoc committee to draft a Convention on the Rights of Persons With Disabilities, which was then adopted unanimously by the Assembly in 2006, entered into force in 2008 and, by 2016, had amassed 171 parties. The articles of the convention, in general, look to ensure a better quality of life for the disabled through fuller participation in society, with economic and social rights such as entitlements to employment and education, accompanied by civil liberties such as reproductive rights.

Abuses not specifically covered by global human rights regimes

Homosexuals

Even more clearly than with women's rights, the difficulties of overcoming cultural differences in establishing global standards are apparent when considering the rights of homosexuals and other minority sexualities. The UN has been unable to reach a consensus to give the same status to sexual freedom as religious or political freedom in international human rights law. The right to have same-sex relationships is not covered in the UN Declaration or covenants and the extermination of people on grounds of their sexual practices is not included in the 1948 Genocide Convention. However, some tentative steps in the direction of securing global human security for homosexuals have been taken. In 1991 Amnesty International began including within their category of 'prisoners of conscience' (those whose release they demand) homosexuals imprisoned for private consensual sexual activity. The European Court of Human Rights have interpreted Article 8 of the European Convention on Human Rights, which upholds 'Respect for Private and Family Life', to include gay rights. As a result of this, homosexuality was decriminalized in Northern Ireland (1981), the Republic of Ireland (1988) and Cyprus (1993). The UN Human Rights Committee similarly ended the criminal prosecution of homosexuals in Tasmania, Australia with a ruling in the 1994 Toonen case. The Human Rights Committee does not have official judicial powers but was asked for its opinion on this case by the Federal Government of Australia before repealing the Tasmanian law. Despite such developments, the state-sanctioned incarceration, and even execution, of people for private, consensual acts persists in many parts of the contemporary world. Persecution on these grounds is still persistent enough in the liberal, democratic world to ensure that enthusiasm for extending the reach of global protection to individuals for this particular form of discrimination has not, as yet, been sufficient to overcome the usual barriers of sovereignty.

Politicide

The 1999 Pinochet case, when the British government rejected a Spanish prosecutor's request to extradite the former Chilean president who was visiting the UK, proved to be a key test case for the status of politicide in international law. UK courts would not accept the Spanish grounds of genocide as a basis for handing over the former tyrant since his crimes were targeted against leftist opponents rather than a national

TABLE 5.4 Ratification rate for key human rights instruments

	Civil & political	Economic & social	Refugees	Race	Women	Children	Migrants	Disabled	ICC	Overall (%)
Brazil	✓	✓	✓	✓	✓	✓	✗	✓	✓	89
France	✓	✓	✓	✓	✓	✓	✗	✓	✓	89
Germany	✓	✓	✓	✓	✓	✓	✗	✓	✓	89
Japan	✓	✓	✓	✓	✓	✓	✗	✓	✓	89
S. Africa	✓	✓	✓	✓	✓	✓	✗	✓	✓	89
UK	✓	✓	✓	✓	✓	✓	✗	✓	✓	89
Russia	✓	✓	✓	✓	✓	✓	✗	✓	✗	78
China	✗	✓	✓	✓	✓	✓	✗	✓	✗	67
India	✓	✓	✗	✓	✓	✓	✗	✓	✗	67
Iran	✓	✓	✓	✓	✗	✓	✗	✓	✗	67
S. Arabia	✗	✗	✗	✓	✓	✓	✗	✓	✗	44
USA	✓	✗	✗	✓	✗	✗	✗	✗	✗	22

Note: Genocide and torture conventions are not included since they constitute customary international law.

or religious minority (Robertson 2000: 229). However, although the Pinochet case outcome disappointed human rights activists, it was still a significant step forward for global policy. Pinochet was released and allowed to return to Chile due to ill health but the UK law courts made it clear that his crimes did amount to 'crimes against humanity' against which sovereignty was no defence. The International Criminal Court (ICC) which has the authority to act on crimes against humanity, has at least the capacity to end the anomaly of this most heinous and widespread of crimes being overlooked in international human rights law.

Implementing human rights

Codifying law is only part of the process of developing human rights. Implementing international law is always a more difficult task than with domestic law because of the barrier presented by the notion of sovereignty, and this is especially so when law is focused on individuals, traditionally considered the preserve of governments and domestic courts.

United Nations

There are UN mechanisms for implementing human rights but they have been uneven in their impact. The UN Commission on Human Rights' record on encouraging the implementation of the Declaration and covenants it crafted was, according to the esteemed human rights lawyer Geoffrey Robertson, 'woeful' (Robertson 2000: 45). The Commission, restrained by intergovernmental politicking, failed even to condemn the horrific politicides/genocides in Cambodia and Uganda in the late 1970s. In Uganda dictator Idi Amin had massacred political opponents and expelled thousands of ethnic minorities from his country. In Cambodia Pol Pot's reign of terror had seen up to a million of his own citizens slaughtered for the ideological mission of returning his country to 'year zero'. The Commission was beefed up in the 1990s, with the appointment of a full-time Commissioner at its head, but still lacked any enforcement powers beyond 'naming and shaming'.

In order to enhance implementation, the General Assembly in 2006 approved the creation of a new body to take over from the Commission, the Human Rights Council (HRC). The HRC meets three times per year (the Commission met only once per year) and comprises representatives of forty-seven states elected by the General Assembly. Concerns that the voting procedure would continue the trend established under the Commission of electing members from countries with poor rights records and that its actions might be politicized were cited by Israel for their non-involvement in the organ. Human rights pressure groups have criticized the election of states such as Saudi Arabia to the HRC, but signs of ethical decision-making could be seen in the failure of Russia to secure a seat in 2016 (although, of course, this could equally be explained by Western-led power politics). Ultimately the HRC still can do no more than name and shame, but a systematic process of reviewing all members' implementation records has been quite effective in this regard given the soft-power incentives for avoiding criticisms.

Also contributing to the implementation of human rights standards are committees established with some of the covenants and conventions that have entered into force. The Human Rights Committee was set up to monitor the implementation of the Covenant on Civil and Political Rights. The committee has been criticized by some human rights analysts for its limited impact (Robertson 2000) but has, on occasion, been able to engineer changes in state law, such as on homosexuality in Australia in the aforementioned Toonen case.

The Committee on the Elimination of Racial Discrimination (CERD) and the Committee on the Elimination of Discrimination Against Women (CEDAW Committee) have the capacity to take up individual cases for states that permit this. CEDAW has on occasion been cited in defence of women in domestic legal cases. Within the children's rights regime a UN Committee on the Rights of the Child examines parties' progress in implementing the convention and has made some progress in embarrassing some governments into implementing legal changes, such as separating juvenile from adult war criminal suspects detained in Rwanda. The HRC and implementing committees have had some successes in informing legal cases but these instances are few and far-between and, of course, the countries concerned are not the ones where the most serious human rights violations are occurring, which are invariably – though not exclusively – undemocratic states.

Civil society

Pressure groups have played a big role in facilitating the implementation of international law on human rights by forming a key partnership with the United Nations. Amnesty International, which has grown from a one-man campaign, launched by British journalist Peter Benenson in 1961, to a multi-million-pound operation with over 2 million members in over 150 countries, work on highlighting non-compliance with the UN Covenant on Civil and Political Rights and have a particular focus on judicial rights (e.g. fair trials). As well as helping implement existing legislation, Amnesty have taken the lead in promoting the development of new law to be taken on by the UN, such as with the Torture Convention. The USA-based group Human Rights Watch, whilst also working in conjunction with the UN, have focused on facilitating the implementation of the Helsinki Accords, established during the Cold War to improve human rights in the context of East–West relations, and most of their activities serve to highlight violations of free expression. Over 200 other pressure groups perform similar functions in the world today, mainly in the area of civil and political rights.

National courts

Since genocide, torture and 'crimes against humanity' are part of customary international law some national courts have come to assume the right to pass verdicts on crimes committed on individuals other than their own citizens. In the 1990s new impetus was given to the politics of human rights by the ending of the Cold War but the world also witnessed the spectre of genocide revived in Rwanda and Yugoslavia. This prompted successful cases brought in Germany and Belgium for such crimes committed in Bosnia and Rwanda.[10] In addition, the 1999 Pinochet case in the UK was a test case in international human rights law, not only in confirming a right to arrest suspects of crimes against humanity but also setting a precedent that diplomatic immunity (Pinochet claimed this as a former president and 'life Senator') was no protection against such crimes.

A setback to the development of this method of implementing global human rights came with a 2002 verdict by the UN's court, the International Court of Justice, which ruled that Belgium was not entitled to try a government minister of the Congo, Ndombasi, for his role in a massacre of Tutsis in Kinshasa.[11] Belgian authorities were instructed that they had no right to strip Ndombasi of diplomatic protection, even in view of the gravity of the offences of which he was being accused. This development was to the relief of some in the Belgian government who had become alarmed at the likely diplomatic fallout from their country vainly seeking to bring a long list of recent tyrants to justice in Brussels. The ICJ verdict brought dismay to human rights activists for setting back the cause of universality in human rights law but, ultimately, the case may help strengthen the arguments in favour of global justice. The prospect of dozens of states around the world simultaneously pursuing various individuals in the name of international law could also be said to demonstrate the necessity of a global judiciary less vulnerable to criticisms of partisanship and more likely to be able to meet success in pursuing individuals traditionally protected by sovereignty. The International Criminal Court (ICC), considered in the next section, could yet fulfil this function in spite of some teething troubles.

Global courts

The idea of an international court to try individuals, alongside the International Court of Justice dealing with state-to-state conflicts, was around at the birth of the United Nations but, like many other global aspirations, was frozen in time by the Cold War. An international criminal court had earlier been proposed during the time of the League of Nations in relation to a stillborn 1937 convention dealing with terrorism. An early draft of the Genocide Convention floated the idea of a court to enforce its provisions but this was soon shelved as too radical a notion to put to the bifurcating international community (Schabas 2001: 8). Instead Article VI of the convention provides for justice to be dispensed either in the courts of the country where the crimes occurred or else in a specially-convened international tribunal. This was the case with the Nuremberg and Tokyo trials, which prosecuted Nazi and Japanese war criminals in the 1940s, and the ad hoc tribunals established by the Security Council to try individuals for genocide and war crimes in Yugoslavia and Rwanda in the 1990s.

The idea of the ICC did not perish during the Cold War years and, when the opportunity then presented itself at the close of the 1980s, the UN's International Law Commission (ILC), a body responsible for promoting the codification of international law, revived the plan. In 1992 the General Assembly gave the go ahead to the ILC to draft a blueprint for the ICC, paving the way for the 1998 Rome Conference, at which the statute for the court was agreed upon and opened for signature. By 2002 the statute had received enough ratifications to enter into force and the court was born. Only seven states opposed the court at the Rome Conference (the USA, Israel, China, Iraq, Sudan, Yemen and Libya) and by 2016 it had 124 parties. The US declined to ratify the Rome Convention that underpins the ICC largely on the grounds that it would be unconstitutional to permit a US citizen to be tried outside of the US legal system for an alleged US-based crime and that, as the world's only superpower, they would be more likely to have cases brought against them than other states.

How influential the ICC can become remains to be seen but it could eventually give real meaning to international human rights law by exercising the sort of supranational authority witnessed only sporadically and selectively to date. A key difference between the ICC and previous ad hoc human rights courts is that it does not have to get approval to act from the 'Big 5' in the UN Security Council and so is less vulnerable to criticisms of partiality to the Great Powers and of only ever being an arbiter of 'victor's justice'. In 2005, a significant boost to the credibility of the court was given by an agreement by the UN Security Council to refer to it the Darfur (Sudan) genocide case despite the initial hostility of the USA to involving a body it does not support and the fact that Sudan was not a party. In time, the court could also potentially widen the grounds upon which it can launch a prosecution beyond the current remit of genocide, war crimes and crimes against humanity since Article 10 of its treaty refers to the evolution of its statutes in line with customary international law.

However, the progressive deepening evolution of the ICC is far from inevitable and cracks have appeared over the court's track record of trying several African dictators but taking no action over the Iraq War (for which the UK government could, in theory, be prosecuted). Burundi withdrew in 2016 citing anti-African bias and the destabilizing effect of prosecuting state leaders. Burundi, initially, appeared to be joined in this exodus by South Africa and Gambia and potentially others, with the African Union having expressed continent-wide dismay at the court's record. Around the same time Philippine President Duterte also suggested that they might secede and Russia withdrew their signature from the ICC statute (though they had never ratified). There is good reason to be concerned at the neo-imperialist focus on Africa whilst ignoring Western 'war crimes' but, equally, it is worth noting that these critical governments have all taken a markedly authoritarian turn in recent years and have plenty to hide from justice, whilst the African Union's primary interest is in state stability rather than human rights. The fact that some governments take any opportunity to criticize human rights instruments is precisely the reason that they are needed.

Regional courts

European Convention on Human Rights

The regime centred on the Council of Europe, an older and wider body than the European Union, is undoubtedly the most extensive international human rights system in the world. The regime was established in 1950 and now covers forty-seven states (essentially all of Europe – including Turkey and Russia – bar Belarus, the continent's last fully-fledged dictatorship). Individual petition by citizens is the main channel for taking up cases, although some cases taken up by one government against another have also occurred.

The convention originally sought to implement the UN Declaration in Western Europe but has evolved into something much more extensive than anything within the UN system. The European Court of Human Rights (ECHR) has gradually assumed the right to be 'creative' in interpreting the articles of the convention thereby allowing it to pass verdicts – binding on all government parties – that go well beyond the most blatant forms of human rights abuses. The ECHR, for example, have interpreted Article 8 of the European Convention on Human Rights, which upholds 'Respect for Private and Family Life', originally intended to give protection against forced sterilizations, to include gay rights and so greatly advance this.

Organization of American States (OAS)

The OAS's Declaration on the Rights and Duties of Man actually pre-dates the UN Declaration (by seven months) but the western hemisphere's human rights regime lags well behind its European counterpart. There is a similar institutional set-up with an Inter-American Convention Commission to take up cases from individuals as well as states, and a court, but the system has had very little influence. Gross human rights violations in most of its twenty-six parties throughout much of its history have undermined the regime's credibility, as has the non-participation in the court of its two potentially most influential members: Canada and the United States.

Africa

The AU's African Charter on Human and People's Rights (Banjul Charter) of 1981 established a court by a 1998 protocol which came into being in 2004. By 2017 the African Court on Human and People's Rights had thirty parties and, whilst its work had been quite limited, it had managed to get Burkina Faso to reopen a closed investigation into a journalist murdered in 1998. Elsewhere in Africa the Economic

TABLE 5.5 Regional human rights regimes

Regime	Year began	Membership	Political impact
European Convention	1953	Most of Europe	Commission and Court able to make supranational verdicts. Individual petition possible
Banjul Charter	1981	Most of Africa	Commission promotes human rights but there is no implementing body
Inter-American Convention	1978	North & South America	Commission and Court but has little influence
Arab Commission	1968	Arab states of Middle East	No Convention developed. Speaks out on Arab rights in Israel
The Commonwealth	1931	Former British colonies	Has suspended membership and imposed political sanctions on member states for human rights abuses

Community of West African States (ECOWAS) has a Court of Justice which, though not ostensibly a human rights judiciary, has built up case law in this area. In particular, in 2008 this court passed a landmark verdict against the government of Niger for failing to protect a girl from being sold into slavery.[12]

Foreign policy

The 1990s saw something of a rise in 'ethical foreign policy' with countries declaring that human rights would be allowed to enter the calculations of foreign policy objectives long dominated by the geopolitics of Cold War. In the UK Robin Cook was explicit in stating this on becoming foreign minister of the Labour government in 1997 and, in the US, the 'Clinton Doctrine' emerged with greater emphasis on the diplomatic encouragement of democracy and human rights than seen since the Wilson government of the 1920s. In fact, however, the starting point of this development can be traced back to the détente era of the Cold War in the 1970s when it appeared that the conflict was coming to an end with a significant thaw in East–West relations. The Helsinki Accords of 1975 was the high point of détente, a wide-ranging diplomatic/human rights treaty which saw the West agree not to interfere in the affairs of the Eastern Bloc in exchange for the Soviets improving human rights in their empire. A notable reduction of political persecution in the USSR did occur after this and also in the West since the US was now vulnerable to charges of hypocrisy if it persisted in propping up oppressive military dictatorships who took an anti-Communist line. An ethical foreign policy is always a hostage to fortune, however, and numerous claims of hypocrisy have been levelled at the US, UK and other countries when lurches back to following the 'national interest' have occurred.

On a more consistent level, human rights have been clearly stated as an objective of Dutch and Norwegian foreign policy since the early 1970s. Norway and the Netherlands together with Sweden and Canada came to be known as the 'like-minded countries' for their generous foreign aid budgets and particularly for linking this to the human rights record of recipient countries. The governments of Norway and Canada have subsequently played the lead roles in launching the Human Security Network, an alliance which advocates the development of global policies focused on the human interest, whether or not these happen to coincide with state interests. Cynics have suggested that this sort of strategy is just a tactical move by less powerful governments to raise their diplomatic profile through populism and that it is easier to take the moral high ground when you can more easily avoid the tough politics of the 'low ground'. IR human rights specialist Jack Donnelly, for example, comments that 'small states rarely have to choose between human rights and other foreign policy goals' (Donnelly 2007: 135). The US and UK have used such arguments in defending something of a return to Cold War *realpolitik* in controversial actions taken in the 'war against terror' since 2001 (see Chapter 3).

Fighting for the rights of others – humanitarian intervention

Wars prompted by the abuse of another country's citizens are a relatively recent historical development and still shrouded in controversy. Declaring war against a country for the mistreatment of one's own nationals resident there is far more solidly established in international law. Perhaps the most liberal interpretation ever of this doctrine came in 1850 when the UK threatened Greece with war for a Greek mob's attack on the home of Don Pacifico who was part-Gibraltarian and hence a British subject.

Table 5.6 presents a chronology of military interventions which have purported to have been inspired, at least partially, by the motivation of relieving the suffering of nationals distinct from the interveners. Differentiating between a humanitarian military action and one motivated by more traditional spurs of gain, self-defence or ideology is nearly always a difficult judgement. In all of the listed cases one or more of these more familiar reasons to take up arms have been claimed by some observers to be the real cause of war.

The legal basis for humanitarian intervention is a moot point and it has come in and out of fashion in international affairs over recent centuries. Grotius, in the seventeenth century, considered rescuing imperilled non-nationals to come into the category of just war, but it was not until the Concert of Europe era in the nineteenth century that the concept began to be put into practice. Humanitarian intervention, along with just war in general, fell out of favour amidst the amoral Realism of twentieth-century state practice, but rose to prominence again in the 'New World Order' that was heralded by the demise of the Cold War in 1990. Robertson provides a striking illustration of this by contrasting the UK government's enthusiasm for the 1991 'Safe Havens' action in Iraq and the 1999 Kosovan War with a Foreign Office assertion in 1986 that: 'contemporary legal opinion comes down against the existence of a right of humanitarian intervention' (Robertson 2000: 401[13]).

Despite more frequent recourse to it in recent years, humanitarian intervention remains a highly contentious concept in international relations since it challenges that fundamental underpinning of the Westphalian system, state sovereignty. International law is unclear on the issue. The UN Charter appears both to proscribe and prescribe the practice. Articles 2.4 and 2.7 uphold the importance of sovereignty and the convention of non-interference in another state's affairs but Chapter VII suggests that extreme humanitarian abuses can constitute a 'threat to peace', legitimizing intervention. The universal acknowledgement of the Responsibility to Protect by UN members in 2005 did, though, offer some clarity that humanitarian interventions were legal.

The main concern with humanitarian interventions can be summarized as follows:

Abuse of the concept

One man's humanitarian intervention is always another man's imperialist or balance-of-power-inspired venture. All of the interventions listed in Table 5.6 were opposed by some states, unconvinced by the moral assuagements of the intervener. In all cases other motivations for intervention can easily be found. The Tanzanian and Vietnamese interventions of the late 1970s overthrew two of the vilest governments in history but were widely condemned in the democratic world, assuming the missions to be driven by power (in the former) and both power and ideology (in

TABLE 5.6 Notable 'humanitarian interventions' in history

Intervention	Interveners	Humanitarian spur
Greece (Ottoman Empire) 1827	France, UK & Russia	Turkish massacre of Greeks
Lebanon (Ottoman Empire) 1860	France	Massacre of Christians by Druze
Serbia, Montenegro, Bosnia-Herzegovina, Romania & Bulgaria (Ottoman Empire) 1877–8	Russia	Massacres of Bulgarians by Turkish partisans
Cuba (Spanish Empire) 1898	USA	Atrocities against Cubans by Spanish colonialists
Macedonia (Ottoman Empire) 1905	Bulgaria, Greece & Serbia	Oppression of Christians by Turks and nationalist violence
Congo 1960–4	(1) Belgium, (2) UN, (3) Belgium & USA	Civil war and massacres following independence (from Belgium)
Dominican Republic 1965	USA	Protect foreign citizens from new military dictatorship
East Pakistan 1971	India	Pakistani genocide against breakaway region (Bangladesh)
Zaire 1978	France & Belgium	Massacres of civilians by anti-government guerrillas
Cambodia 1978	Vietnam	'Autogenocide' of various sections of own people by Khmer Rouge government
Uganda 1979	Tanzania	Expulsions, massacres and human rights abuses against ethnic minorities and opponents
Central African Republic 1979	France	Overthrow of Bohasia government responsible for massacres of civilians

Grenada 1983	USA and Organization of East Caribbean States	Protect foreign citizens after military coup
Panama 1989	USA	Protect foreign citizens in civil unrest
Liberia 1990–7	(1) Nigeria, (2) ECOWAS	Restore order amidst civil war
Iraq 1991	UN	Protect Kurds in north and 'Marsh Arabs' in south from government massacres
Yugoslavia 1992	UN	Protect Bosnian Muslims from Serb massacres
Somalia 1992–3	UN	Restore order amidst civil war
Haiti 1994–7	UN	Restore democracy and order following military coup
Sierra Leone 1997	ECOWAS	Restore order amidst civil war
Kosovo (Yugoslavia) 1999	NATO	Protect Kosovar Albanians from Serb massacres
East Timor (Indonesia) 1999	INTERFET* (Australia, UK, Thailand, Philippines & others)	Maintain order in transition to independence
Libya 2011	NATO (on behalf of UN)	Protect anti-government protesters from massacre

* International Force East Timor. Also involved were: Brazil, Canada, Denmark, Egypt, Fiji, France, Germany, Ireland, Italy, Jordan, Kenya, Malaysia, New Zealand, Norway, Portugal, the Republic of Korea, Singapore and the United States.

the latter). It was notable that NATO's 1999 action in Yugoslavia, ultimately, was 'sold' to the general public of the intervening countries more on the grounds of maintaining European order than as averting humanitarian catastrophe. Some measure of self-interest, alongside compassion for others, appeared to be necessary to justify going to war.

Inconsistency in application of the concept

The various European interventions in the Ottoman Empire which set the precedent for applying Grotian morality in international affairs also helped to undermine the concept of humanitarian intervention and increase cynicism about it as a workable doctrine. Although abuses did occur under the Ottomans they were no more despotic rulers than some of the interveners and it is hard to escape the conclusion that the interventions really represented clashes of the civilizations, with Europeans rallying to the cause of Christians under the yoke of Moslem rule.[14] More recently, the willingness of the UN and NATO to act in defence of anti-government protesters in Libya in 2011 stood in stark contrast to the lack of response to similar crackdowns on protesters elsewhere in Yemen, Bahrain and Syria that same year. Libyan oil and the Libyan leader Gaddafi's previous sponsorship of anti-Western terrorism made it easier to get international agreement than for the other Arab despots. Equally, humanitarian intervention is always more likely to be considered an option where the target state is not going to be too tough a military opponent. Power politics dictates that Chinese abuses in Tibet or Russian aggression in Chechnya were/are never likely to be awarded the same response as Serb or Iraqi atrocities. Selective justice undermines the principle of humanitarian intervention, many claim.

Cultural relativism

A core argument against humanitarian intervention is that rights and cultures vary so significantly from state to state that judging a country as being a danger to its own citizens is likely to be prejudicial. Such judgements are likely to be made by the dominant power of the day and so, in effect, represent a hegemonic imposition of a particular ideology. Nearly all (if not all) states have seriously violated their citizens' rights at some time. Following from this, would it follow that an invasion of just about any country by any other country could be legitimized?

May worsen the situation

Additionally, even where a clear case of tyranny can be established, there is the concern that intervention may not be the answer to the problem in that it can only inflame the situation. Can the use of violence be an appropriate response to the use of violence? Many critics contended that NATO's action in defence of the Kosovar Albanians led to an escalation of the Serb campaign against them. Whilst few Kosovans today would support this, the de-stabilization of Libya since 2011 does lend itself well to this contention.

Counter-arguments

It is clear that humanitarian intervention can probably never be a perfect method for combatting tyranny. Inconsistent application of the principle is inevitable given that it might not be practical to intervene in some cases since the target state may fight back and lead to more bloodshed than might have been the case if no action had been taken. However, does this mean that no action should ever be taken and the world should sit on its hands whilst avoidable slaughters are being carried out? Should the *realism* of doing something to avert catastrophe when it is clearly achievable be subsumed by the *Realism* of doing nothing unless the interests of the intervener are at stake? If an individual walking through a city witnesses two assaults, one by a large armed man and another by a small unarmed man, is it better to be morally consistent and walk past both incidents? The just war principle of avoiding conflict escalation can be applied to humanitarian intervention to give a working doctrine which, if not perfect, is surely better than doing nothing.

Universalism versus cultural relativism

As previously referred to in considering the case of humanitarian intervention, the chief moral objection to the universal application of human rights is the position commonly known as cultural relativism. This position argues that the world's cultural diversity makes any attempt to apply rights universally, at best, difficult and, at worst, an immoral imposition of dominant cultural traits. President Jiang Zemin of China articulated this view on a state visit to the USA in 1997 in defending his government from criticisms on its human rights record: 'The theory of relativity worked out by Mr Einstein, which is in the domain of natural science, I believe can be applied in the political field. Democracy and human rights are relative concepts and not absolute' (Kaiser 1997).

Zemin's statement in support of cultural relativism came fifty years after the first major articulation of this viewpoint in international politics in the run-up to the 1948 Universal Declaration of Human Rights. Concerns at the notion of a global bill of rights riding roughshod over the minority cultures of the world prompted leading anthropologists, including Melville Herskovits and Ruth Benedict, to petition the UN Commission for Human Rights.

> Standards and values are relative to the culture from which they derive so that any attempt to formulate postulates that grow out of the beliefs or moral codes of one culture must to that extent detract from the applicability of any Declaration of Human Rights to mankind as a whole.
>
> (American Anthropologist Association 1947: 542)

In Benedict's view, and that of most traditional anthropologists, the notion of what is morally right can only equate to what is customary within a given society (Benedict 1934). Hence the notion of rights pertaining to all humankind is not 'natural'. Rights are the rules of mutual give and take which develop over time within a society in order for it to function peacefully and survive. Rights are, in effect, implicit agreements arrived at within societies. The American Anthropological Association (AAA), as a counter to criticisms from human rights activists that they and their discipline were immoral, issued a declaration in 1999 giving qualified support for UN human rights legislation. The AAA now argue that human rights are 'an evolving concept' and that they have come to see global policy as a way of campaigning to preserve human cultural difference (AAA 1999). Anthropology as a discipline, however, continues to be very influenced by the positivist epistemological belief that value judgements over cultures other than one's own are an imposition of those values.

In contemporary philosophy a leading exponent of relativism is Gilbert Harman, whose writings may have influenced Zemin since he argues the case that scientific relativity ought to inform our understanding of morality: '(T)here is no single true morality. There are many different moral frameworks, none of which is more correct than the others' (Harman 1996: 8). Cultural relativism comes in various strengths. The strongest position is to reject any notion of universal human rights, but the more moderate form asserts that the rights of the collective should temper the prescription of individual liberty.[15] There is a flavour of moderate relativism in the Banjul Charter's emphasis on the rights of 'peoples', alongside individual rights. 'They [peoples] shall freely determine their political status and shall pursue their economic and social development according to the policy they have freely chosen (Article 20).'

Neither the Banjul Charter nor an anthropologically-enriched UN regime, though, have had to stand the course of practical implementation. Simultaneously upholding both individual and collective rights is highly problematic. Rwandan Hutus as a collective freely chose to slaughter 800,000 individual Tutsis for their own social, political and economic development. Existing universalist human rights for sure did not save the Tutsis, but this was due to lack of will to implement existing legislation. Prioritizing collective cultural rights and state sovereignty over those of individuals would not only fail to stop genocide but even offer a defence of it.

The 1948 Universal Declaration of Human Rights was written and signed up to at a time when the membership of the UN was far from universal. Much of Africa and Asia was still under the colonial yoke and hence not represented among the independent states making up the General Assembly. The declaration does reflect Western liberal philosophy in its focus on protecting the individual from the tyranny of the state and resembles in particular the US and French constitutions. The cultural imposition argument, however, is overstated. No state voted against the Declaration and most of the abstainers were later brought on board. Although Saudi Arabia objected to the notion of religious freedom, other Islamic states such as Syria, Iran and Pakistan did not. The USSR and its East European allies objected to the lack of emphasis in the Declaration given to economic and social rights but this was rectified in the development of the twin covenants that later followed. The twin covenants stand as a broad legal instrument empowering individuals both with rights against states and with entitlements from states going beyond many Western bills of rights.

A fundamental weakness with relativist arguments in regard to human rights is that they presuppose that societies or cultures can secure the rights of their individual constituents endogenously. However, nations as social entities are rarely, if ever, directly represented in the political world. Multi-nationalism, whether arrived at through migration or historical accident (such as in the partitioning of Africa), is the norm in the modern state system. If the states of the world mirrored its distinct 'cultures', ethical/cultural relativism might stand as a realistic alternative to universalism in protecting human rights. In the real world, however, how are the rights of cultural minorities within states to be fully safeguarded? The fact that national or religious minorities or women are frequently imperilled rather than protected by states cannot be questioned. The homogeneous 'traditional' culture advanced by relativists is rarely found in the countries to which it is attributed and complaints of the inappropriateness of 'Western' human rights are usually made by tyrannical regimes trying to justify repressive policies in the name of 'nation building'. Women, the disabled, homosexuals and people linked by any other form of collective identity stand little chance of having their 'cultural differences' respected when they overlap with far more influential 'cultures'. Entrusting states to be the arbiters of human rights frequently leads to the imposition of dominant cultural norms on minority cultures in precisely the fashion that relativism purports to prevent. Rhoda Howard has referred to this as 'cultural absolutism', as a counter to the relativist claim that human rights are a form of absolutism (Howard 1995).

Even if a more optimistic view of the relationship between governments and individuals than that encouraged by recent history is taken, states still offer a limited guarantee of future human security since their own position is far from secure. The lifespan of many states over the last century has been much the same as that of their citizens. The economic rights afforded to its people by the USSR and its allies, such as employment, disappeared with the fall of Communism as quickly as the civil and political rights of Latvians, Estonians and Lithuanians had been snuffed out by their annexation by the USSR.

It can further be argued that relativism in regard to ethics and rights is not only unhelpful but ontologically flawed. The temptation to want to protect the weak from the strong in international affairs is obvious, but think for a moment about the implications of applying cultural relativism in other situations. If cultural relativism should apply at the global level should it not also be applied at the domestic level to recognize the impunity of criminal culture from the imposition of state values? If it is wrong to apply values universally then why is it not also wrong to apply cultural relativism universally? If all cultural moralities are equally valid, does this mean that contradictory moral opinions can both be valid?

The (strong) relativists' answer to the final of these three questions is to adopt the position of 'methodological relativism' or 'truth relativism' and suggest that the idea of validity has no bearing in ethics, or indeed in any social scientific context. This position, associated in Sociology with Bloor (1976) and in Philosophy with Davson-Galle (1998), posits that moral judgements have no rational basis and are, in effect, no more than matters of taste. This position, however, can lead only to a nihilistic abandonment of reason and the tolerance of intolerance. Abandoning reason and any notion of right and wrong in ethics is not only unhelpful in terms of giving the green light to genocide and any other form of human abuse, it can also be argued to be logically flawed. Proving truths in a social context is more difficult than in natural science, but some philosophical methods have been advanced to show that moral judgements can be rationalized. Apel, for example, demonstrates that people necessarily accept certain fundamental ethical norms as binding in the process of making everyday communication possible. In any form of communication the idea of truth and lies must implicitly be accepted by someone communicating or communication would have no meaning (Apel 1990). The strict observance of truth relativism would mean that you could not participate in any discussion on ethics. Those philosophers, anthropologists and others who deny the universality of rights do so by making arguments grounded in reason. Zemin in upholding the relativity of human rights on his 1996 visit to the USA did so by justifying China's different interpretation of the concept from that favoured in the West. In a world in which transnational communication is ever more prominent and cultures increasingly intersect, surely the notion of relativism unravels.

It is right to be concerned about ideologies that oppress other cultural values, whether blatantly through nationalist hatred or more subtly through economic domination, but this itself is a moral judgement. You cannot properly respect another culture if you cannot also criticize another culture. Instead of reducing ethnocentricism, relativism in this way can actually encourage its proliferation by reinforcing in all cultures the sanctity of their own values. The moral isolationism promoted by such an approach has been the basis of the various forms of societal discrimination which have so blighted recent history, and which global human society must at least try to eradicate.

Human rights and human security

As in other areas of law and politics, human security has often come to be viewed as superfluous or a distraction from the important business of human rights.

> States that do not protect their citizens from want, crime, torture, discrimination or gender-based violence when these abuses are considered human rights violations are no more likely to protect their citizens when those same abuses are considered violations of their citizens' securities.
>
> (Howard-Hassmann 2012: 100)

However, the very fact that, despite their significant advance over the past seventy years, human rights in much of the world continue to be treated as secondary to the pursuit of national security is testament to the fact that the discourse of rights is not enough to secure individuals. It *is* semantic to advocate human security but semantics are important in politics. The whole discourse of national security and national interest has evolved in order to seek to justify the unjustifiable. The discourse of human rights has also evolved but has come to struggle in the face of the bogeymen of the Islamist terrorist and the criminal immigrant. As with many issues, the word 'security' is associated by many human rights lawyers with 'national security' and instinctively viewed suspiciously as the antithesis of rights. This, though, is not human security and human security does not threaten human rights. Whilst human rights are widely held to be trumped by national security in conventional political practice, human security is an alternative to the latter rather than the former. Human security is not a distraction from human rights but a means of reinforcing their sanctity. The anti-globalist retreat to nationalism evident in the UK exit from the EU, the election of Trump in the USA and the authoritarian turn of countries like Turkey and Venezuela makes the case for encouraging a fundamental evolution away from statecentricism ever more apparent.

 Key points

- The security of individual people is frequently threatened by their own governments and other groups in their society because of their social identity.
- The chief forms of social identity subject to life-threatening discrimination are nationality, religion, sex, sexual orientation, disability and ideology.
- Global political action to protect individuals against discrimination on national or religious grounds has evolved significantly since 1945 but has been patchily implemented. Global policy relating to discrimination on the grounds of the other forms of social identity is far more limited.
- Sovereignty and the belief that rights are culture-bound, and hence not appropriate for global policy, remain significant obstacles to the further development of global policy in this area.

Notes

1   It is generally accepted that national identity evolved from the late eighteenth century when ordinary people, through greater communication, began to be more aware of people from other countries and were hence able to perceive of their own societies as having certain distinguishing characteristics.

2   See for example: OECD (2014); IMF (2016).

3   Ironically, as the site of Abraham's offer to sacrifice his son to God, Temple Mount unites the three great monotheistic faiths. It is also, however, the site of Solomon's temple in Judaism and of Mohammed's ascent to heaven in Islam (marked by the Dome of the Rock Mosque).

4   The numbers killed are unclear. See Grau (1995) for a detailed account of this, often neglected, episode in history.

5   In addition parts of Iraq, Nigeria, Somalia and Syria also had the death penalty for homosexuality.

6   In 2016 there were still forty-six UN member-states that had not ratified the Genocide Convention. Amongst this number were several who had joined the UN only since 1990 and may be expected, in time, to ratify. Included amongst the others, though, were a number of states against whom over the last fifty years charges of genocide could have been levelled, such as Somalia and Indonesia. A more curious non-ratifying state is Japan.

7   Attorney General of Israel v. Eichmann, 36 International Law Report 277.

8   Regina v. Finta (1994), Supreme Court of Canada, 24 March. Polyukhovich v. Common-wealth (1991), 172 C.L.R. 501 (Australia).

9   This includes 5.2 million Palestinian refugees not under the mandate of UNHCR.

10   Public Prosecutor v. Djajic, No. 20/96 (Sup. Ct. Bavaria, 23 May 1997).

11   Democratic Republic of the Congo v. Belgium, ICJ verdict, 14 February 2002, General List no. 121.

12   Hadijatou Mani Koraou v. Niger (2008).

13   UK Government (1986) Foreign Policy Document No. 148, British Yearbook of International
      Law 56, Section 2, para. 22.
14   Individuals rallied to these causes, such as the English poet Byron who died in Greece
      preparing to fight in their independence struggle.
15   Frankena uses the term 'meta-ethical relativism' for the stronger version (Frankena 1988).
      Some contemporary anthropologists now distinguish between cultural and ethical relativism;
      the former being purely descriptive whereas the latter is normative (Rosaldo 2000).

Recommended reading

Donnelly, J. (2012) *International Human Rights*, 4th edn, Cambridge, MA: Westview.

Robertson, G. (2012) *Crimes Against Humanity: The Struggle for Global Justice*, 4th edn, London:
      Penguin.

Schabas, W. (2009) *Genocide in International Law: The Crime of Crimes*, 2nd edn, Cambridge:
      Cambridge University Press.

Tickner, A. (2001) *Gendering World Politics: Issues and Approaches in the Post-Cold War Era*, New
      York: Columbia University Press.

Useful web links

- Amnesty International: www.amnesty.org/

- Genocidewatch: www.genocidewatch.org/

- International Criminal Court: www.icccpi.int/php/show.php?id=home&l=EN

- Rummel, R., 'Freedom, Democracy, Peace; Power, Democide and War':
  www.hawaii.edu/powerkills/welcome.html

Chapter 6

Environmental threats to security

> *The air we breathe is not the property of any one nation – we share it. The big oceans are not divided by national frontiers – they are our common property. What is asked of us is not to relinquish our national sovereignty but to use it to further the common good. It is to abide by certain agreed international rules in order to safeguard our common property, to leave something for us and future generations to share.*
>
> Olof Palme, Stockholm Conference, 1972

Introduction

Security threats emanating from the 'environment' present humanity with three key political dilemmas:

1. The threats are usually less clear-cut and direct than the other types of threat considered in this study. The threat posed by issues like climate change and ozone depletion may be profound but they are, in the main, still perceived as longer-term creeping emergencies rather than imminent disasters and attacks.
2. Countering the threats is usually costly and requires a significant compromising of economic interests.
3. The threats often can only be countered by globally-coordinated political action.

Most domestic political systems have evolved to a position where the first and second of these dilemmas can be overcome. Civil society advocacy and government learning have gradually led to more long-termist policies being developed mitigating threats to both human and non-human state residents. Environmental policies in

Western Europe and North America have, since the 1960s, seen economic interests compromised to limit uncertain threats posed to human health and to wildlife. Over recent years, most of the world, to differing extents, has followed suit. The third dilemma is, of course, beyond governments acting in isolation but is slowly coming to be addressed by an evolving global *epistemic community* and polity. Global civil

---

BOX 6.1 **The polluter's dilemma**

In a fictional scenario, suppose that four states share a common sea and for many decades have deposited waste materials in the sea without political restriction. However, pollution levels in the sea have now reached levels that are affecting fish stocks and tourism on the coast, prompting the four governments to convene a conference to discuss the possibility of a coordinated response.

The costs of pollution to each state's income and the costs of enacting restrictions on pollution (by enforcing new regulations on ship owners) are represented below.

State	Cost of Pollution	Cost of Curbing Pollution
A	$2 million per year	$1 million
B	$2 million per year	$3 million
C	$4 million per year	$13 million
D	$6 million per year	$11 million

What policy is in the best interest of each state?

For State A the decision is clear. Curbing pollution makes economic sense, with a net benefit arising within a year of action. For State B, also, a net benefit is likely soon enough for this to make political sense. Such gains are, however, contingent on *all* states enacting the reforms, so States A and B must also rely on States C and D following suit. For these two states, and particularly State C, the costs of curbing pollution outweigh the costs incurred for several years and possibly beyond the lifespan of their governments' terms in office. Although there is a gain to be made in the long term, the decision is more difficult because, as well as imposing short-term and unpopular costs, there is the nagging fear that acting on this might not even work since another state may not also implement the cuts. States A and B also share this dilemma – the polluter's dilemma – since, although their cost-benefit analyses are more straightforward, their fear of States C or D not acting is higher. Any one of the states may conclude that it is worth carrying on polluting and enjoy the benefits of an overall reduction in pollution through relying on the others to enact cuts – the *free-rider problem*.

Ultimately, coordinated action is in the interests of all, but short-termism and a lack of trust in other states make it difficult to guarantee that states will choose this option – *the collective goods problem*. This problem recurs regularly in international environmental politics.

---

society and scientific communities are simultaneously pushing governments to rethink the first and second dilemmas and provide the means for achieving the third. Central to this process is the slow but inexorable realization by governments that environmental threats are 'real' and the apparent 'national interest' of resisting economic compromise may not always serve their citizens' interests. Political dilemmas can always be resolved when this is understood. The three dilemmas presented here are not, in fact, unique to environmental politics. For most states very similar compromises have been made in the name of military security, since – as explored in Chapter 2 – military threats are usually not immediate and require great expense and international diplomatic cooperation to deter. Global, rather than state, political action is necessary for the enhancement of human security in all of the issues considered in this study but it is most crucial in the realm of environmental security. This is encapsulated in the 'polluter's dilemma', a variation of the popular 'prisoner's dilemma' game theory metaphor (see Box 6.1).

The notion and practice of treating the threats and dilemmas posed by environmental change as matters of security have evolved over the last half-century but remain contentious in two dimensions. On the one hand there is a traditional Realist view that non-military issues do not warrant such treatment and, on the other, an ecological view that these concerns should not be militarized. Securitization, of course, need not mean militarization, but the human security (freedom from want variation) rationale that the annual millions of deaths from pollution and potential global Armageddon from climate change or ozone depletion are enough to merit emergency treatment, has suffered by being in the shadow of these two camps.

The rise of environmental issues in global politics

The politicization and globalization of the environment

Global environmental politics is a relatively 'new' dimension of international relations and of politics in general, but that is not to say that problems of environmental change are in any way new. The extinction of certain species of animals due to human reck- lessness (for example the dodo) and the diminution of woodland areas through overexploitation are centuries-old phenomena. The origins of international policy on environmental change can be traced back as far as 1889 and an international convention to prevent the spread of the disease *phylloxera* in grapes, which was threatening the European wine industry. This and other agreements such as the 1902 Convention on the Protection of Birds Useful to Agriculture (the first inter- national instrument on animal conservation) were, however, motivated by economic rather than environmental concerns. In other words they were *anthropocentric* rather than ecocentric. During the twentieth century conservation policies evolved in several European and North American states and internationally (on whaling) but these were principally concerned with conserving nature in order to sustain hunting so were not matters of security, be it of states, humans or other life forms.

The 1960s saw a significant rise in prominence of environmental issues in North America and Western Europe, and the emergence of environmental politics, beyond purely economic concerns, on the international political agenda. A major

---

BOX 6.2 Rachel Carson

Rachel Carson, correctly, is widely feted as having launched environmentalism as a political ideology in the early 1960s with her hugely influential magnum opus *Silent Spring*. The title of the book forewarns of a future world without the songs of birds and is best remembered for highlighting the harmful effects of DDT on wildlife. The book also, however, pioneered awareness of the human health repercussions associated with the use of DDT and other chemicals.

Born in Pennsylvania in 1907, Carson became a marine biologist in an age when women scientists were extremely rare. Her determination to succeed against the odds saw her publish *Silent Spring* in 1962 despite a long-standing fight with cancer and attempts to block its publication by a hostile chemical industry. The book had been serialized in the *New Yorker* magazine prior to its release and caused such interest that chemical companies began fearing a consumer backlash against their products and mounted vitriolic attacks on the scientific authenticity of the work. These attacks failed to prevent the book becoming a major success commercially and politically, both in the USA and across the developed world. Carson succumbed to cancer just two years after the release of the book; a disease the causes of which she had done so much to increase the understanding of. She was at least able to witness before her death the beginning of legislation being passed to curb the use of polluting chemicals and the birth of a new political era.

---

factor in this was the publication of Rachel Carson's hugely influential pollution polemic *Silent Spring* in 1962. *Silent Spring* most notably highlighted the effects of the insecticide dichloro-diphenyl-trichloroethane (DDT) on wild animals, vegetation and rivers, and quickly influenced US insecticide policy on *ecocentric* grounds. DDT came to be restricted even though it was increasing agricultural profits. The book also, however, considered the implications for human health of indiscriminate insecticide use and this aspect began the process of forcing environmental change onto the global political agenda and securitizing some of the many issues in this area (see Box 6.2). In the wake of *Silent Spring* new political concerns began to be voiced, such as with the effects of *acid rain* (rainwater polluted by industrial emissions), and older issues, such as oil pollution by tankers, were given far more prominence.[1]

Heightened concern over the human health effects of pollution and other forms of environmental change at the global level was confirmed by the UN convening the 1972 Conference on the Human Environment (UNCHE) at Stockholm. The conference was boycotted by the USSR and its Eastern Bloc allies but attended by representatives of 113 states. The Stockholm Conference did not directly produce a new body of international law but it had a catalytic effect in identifying some key

principles which challenged the conventions of state sovereignty and put environmental change permanently on the agenda of international politics. 'Principle 21'
confirmed that states retained full sovereign authority over resources located in their
own territory but charged them with the responsibility to exploit them with regard
to the effect of this on the environment of other states ('the polluter pays principle').
The parties to the conference also agreed to acknowledge the concept of a 'common
heritage of mankind' whereby resources located outside of territorial borders (such
as minerals on the deep seabed) should be considered as belonging to the international community collectively, rather than being subject to a 'finders keepers/losers
weepers' approach to their ownership. Stockholm did have a direct institutional
legacy with the creation of the United Nations Environment Programme (UNEP),
permanently placing the policy area on the international stage. Overall, the conference's most significant legacy was in putting environmental questions firmly on
the political agenda by prompting many governments to create new ministers and
departments of the environment and greatly deepening and widening a global network
of environmental pressure groups.

The securitization of the environment

The two major geopolitical shifts that affected the world in the 1970s, and then at
the end of the 1980s, served to bring the environment into widened security purview.
For many, a link between resource depletion and military power politics calculations
began to become apparent in the economic downturn of the 1970s and then become
firmly established after the conclusion of the Cold War.

The economic downturn that accompanied the oil crises of the 1970s shook
international relations practically and academically. The US and Western economies
had thrived under the Bretton Woods monetary system centred on Washington
through the 1950s and 1960s, but it all came unstuck in the 1970s. This era of US
hegemony came to an abrupt halt amidst the global economic recession of 1971–4.
The sudden rise in oil prices, instigated by the Organization of Petroleum Exporting
Countries (OPEC) taking advantage of having secured political control of this crucial
commodity from multi-national corporations (MNCs), allied to the spiralling costs
of the Vietnam War, led to the US budget deficit (amount of debt acquired through
borrowing) getting so large that bondholders and other governments began to lose
faith in the dollar continuing to hold its value in relation to gold. With the US having
passed their peak in oil production and recognizing that a post-hegemonic future
lay ahead in the global economy, the 'Carter Doctrine', announced by the US president
in 1980, made it plain that questions relating to the economic resources of distant
states would enter into the calculations of the American national interest by stating
that military action to secure oil imports and other economic interests was a possibility. A preparedness to fight to secure international economic interests had, of
course, been evident long before 1980. Securing access to resources was a key
rationale behind the autarky of economic nationalism that marked the first half of
the twentieth century and the imperialism that had marked much of the millennium.
The rise to high politics of oil pricing in the 1970s, though, prompted greater scrutiny
of the importance of threats to the supply of key economic resources to states.

The securitization of energy became allied to the rise in neo-Malthusian concerns that global overpopulation could drain the world's resources that had gathered momentum in the late 1960s Political Ecology movement (see Chapter 4), and greater recognition that resources could be threatened by environmental degradation as well as through political action. Paul Ehrlich's influential *Population Bomb*, for example, used dramatic language and metaphors in the cause of securitizing overpopulation. '[W]e can no longer afford merely to treat the symptoms of the cancer of population growth: the cancer itself must be cut out.' 'The battle to feed all of humanity is over' (Ehrlich 1968: xi).

It was not until the 1990s, though, when the agenda of international politics was allowed to broaden, that environmental degradation as a potential state security threat began to take prominence in academia and mould the thinking of some foreign policy makers. Economic statecraft had been revived as an instrument of foreign policy by the oil crises (a second crisis occurred in 1979 triggered by the Iranian Revolution), but it was not until the strategic constraints of the Cold War had been lifted that a full manifestation of the Carter Doctrine was put into practice with the US-led action against Iraq in the Gulf War. A just war and long-awaited display of collective security the liberation of Kuwait may well have been, but few would dispute that securing oil supplies was a key additional motivation for the allied forces' action.

Sustainable development

Prior to the securitization of environmental change in the 1990s UNEP, civil society and epistemic communities acted to globalize the issue area after the upsurge in interest in resource depletion in the 1970s had subsided. Again fuelled by the oil crisis, Third World governments came to assert themselves on the international stage, as discussed in Chapter 4. A right to develop free from neo-imperialist meddling did not sit easily with essentially being told to curb population growth and restrain industrial production by the global North. The vast majority of environmental problems are related in some way to the processes of economic development and growth, which have dominated how governments frame their policies both domestically and in the global marketplace. Industrialization and urbanization, the classic ingredients of development, put increased strain on a country's resources, whilst changing its pattern of land use and altering nature's own 'balance of power'. Increased industrial and agricultural production invariably brings more pollution as well as more raw materials, food and wealth. The fundamental paradox of how to reconcile economic security with environmental concerns was apparent at Stockholm in 1972 but shelved through the desire to demonstrate solidarity, but, by the 1980s, it could no longer be ignored. By then it had become clear that global environmental policy was being stymied because, although the developed world was coming to terms (albeit partially) with the need to embrace a 'limits to growth' approach, LDCs would not compromise economic security since the stakes were so much higher. As Indian president Indira Gandhi announced at Stockholm in 1972, the world should not forget that 'poverty is the worst pollution'.

In an effort to get around this problem, the UN General Assembly in 1987 set up a World Commission on Environment and Development, chaired by Norwegian politician Brundtland (see Box 7.1). The 'Brundtland Commission' produced a report entitled 'Our Common Future', which identified *sustainable development* as the solution to the economic–environmental paradox, and this soon became the guiding ethos for future global environmental policy. Sustainable development sought to win the backing of LDCs for environmental policy by reassuring them that this would not compromise their political priority of achieving economic development. The global North would have to take the lead in implementing costly anti-pollution measures and recognize that the South would need more time to follow suit. To the South this was only fair since the North was responsible for most global pollution and had been able to develop without constraints being put on their industrialization. To many in the North this was the only way to win support from LDCs – who would eventually come to be major global polluters also – for action on tackling ozone depletion and climate change.

Sustainable development is less pessimistic than the 'limits to growth' thesis, which dominated environmental policy thinking in the 1970s, in that it does not consider economic growth to be anathema to avoiding pollution and the depletion of the Earth's resources. Economic growth, even for wealthy states, is fine so long as it is at a level that can be sustained in the long run and does not come at the cost of degrading the environment. Hence sustainable development tries to speak the language of the 'rational actor' by calling upon governments to be more long-termist in their economic policy. Rapid economic growth today may enrich the present generation but risk impoverishing or endangering future generations if resources are not utilized in a sustainable and responsible manner. Sustainable development is also, however, less optimistic about the future than the approach to the Earth and its resources adopted by a number of thinkers and statesmen. The non-arrival of a demographic doomsday of the sort forecast by Malthus back in the eighteenth century or by the 'neo-Malthusians' in the 1960s prompted some 'Cornucopians' to suggest that economic growth need not be restrained at all since technological progress and human ingenuity can be relied upon to surmount future problems. Lomberg's 2001 work *The Sceptical Environmentalist*, for example, attracted great interest (and great derision from ecologists) for questioning whether implementing international policy on global warming made any rational sense. Lomberg did not deny that global warming was a human-caused problem, but suggested that it was not as significant a threat as it had been painted and that the expenditure allocated to tackling the problem would be better spent on addressing global poverty (Lomberg 2001). Cornucopians and neo-Malthusian 'limits to growth' advocates are still prominent positions in the dialogue on global environmental policy, but sustainable development, holding the middle ground, has become the principal guiding ethos of the international regimes that have emerged in the last twenty years.

The Brundlandt Report prompted the UN General Assembly in 1989 to approve a twenty-year follow-up conference to Stockholm to flesh out the concept of sustainable development. As the title indicates, the 1992 UN Conference on the Environment and Development (UNCED), held in Rio de Janeiro, recognized the need to couple together the two issue areas and was a much larger and more diverse gathering than in 1972; 170 states were represented, most at some stage by their heads of government, and some 1,400 pressure groups were also present at the myriad formal and informal meetings that characterized the conference. In contrast, at Stockholm, twenty years earlier, only two heads of government and 134 pressure groups had attended. Although decision-making authority was reserved for government delegates, the pressure groups at Rio played a pivotal role in organizing the event and in the extensive lobbying of the decision-makers.

Among twenty-seven general principles agreed to in the 'Rio Declaration' at the summit were two particularly important breakthroughs. Principle 7 identified the 'common but differentiated responsibilities' of developed and less-developed states in environmental protection, a key aspect of the sustainable development concept. The global South were part of the process but the North would have to take the lead and incur most of the initial costs. Principle 15 acknowledged the legitimacy of the 'precautionary principle' in developing environmental policy. This strengthens the meaning of sustainable development by proposing that a lack of absolute scientific certainty over the harmful side-effects of some form of economic activity widely believed to be environmentally damaging should not be used as an excuse to continue with it. This was an important agreement because issues of environmental change tend to be complex and subject to some level of scientific disagreement. In the face of this, excuses can readily be found for ignoring environmental demands, and the case for continuing to favour unhindered economic growth strategies appears stronger.

Like Stockholm, the Rio Summit did not create international law at a stroke but, unlike Stockholm, it did explicitly set the signatory governments on a legislatory path. 'Agenda 21' of UNCED set out a programme of action for implementing sustainable development across a range of environmental issues. Issues debated in recent years but not yet subject to conventions, such as climate change, deforestation, desertification, biodiversity and hazardous waste management, were formally given approval for action. A Commission for Sustainable Development was established to regularly review progress towards establishing and implementing the conventions that were to follow. In addition, a crucial tenet of sustainable development was realized in the creation of a fund subsidized by developed countries from which LDCs could draw, the Global Environmental Facility.

Whilst progress has been slow, sustainable development has succeeded in building a consensus on the need to tackle issues of environmental change at the global level. Although national economic interests continue to present a barrier to confronting the 'inconvenient truths' posed by environmental change, global discourse and policy have evolved. The acceptance of a target of restricting global warming to a 1.5–2°C rise at the 2015 Paris UN Climate Change Conference by rich, poor and fossil-fuel-exporting states made this apparent, as did the universal adoption of the Sustainable Development Goals to guide global policy until 2030.

Environmental securitization in theory

Whilst it was the post-Cold War optimism of the early 1990s that encouraged the 'securitization' of environmental problems, such an approach was being articulated as far back as the early 1970s on the basis of resource depletion. The Liberal arch critic of Realism, Richard Falk, in *This Endangered Planet*, articulated that: 'We need to revamp our entire concept of "national security" and "economic growth" if we are to solve the problems of environmental decay' (Falk 1971: 185). In a similar vein, the Sprouts' *Toward a Politics of the Planet Earth* trumpeted the need for IR to focus on global as opposed to national security because of the scale of threat posed by resource scarcity and overpopulation (Sprout & Sprout 1971). Going back further still, Osborn in 1948 opined that resource scarcity could be a cause of war nearly half a century before this notion came to be popularized: 'one of the principal causes of the aggressive attitudes of individual nations and of much of the present discord among groups of nations is traceable to diminishing productive land and to increasing population pressures' (Osborn 1948: 200–1). Written before the Cold War had fully set in place, this highlights just how that conflict came to dominate the security agenda in the second half of the twentieth century.

State securitization

Towards the end of the Cold War such environmental security thinking began to permeate the political mainstream and even find the ear of a superpower. An influential article by US diplomat Jessica Mathews for the conservative journal *Foreign Affairs* highlighted the need for states to give proper concern to the newly-apparent threats posed by environmental problems. Mathews, a former member of the US government's National Security Council, followed the line of reasoning of Osborn, Falk and the Sprouts but in a more state-centred, Realist analysis. In addition to calling for greater consideration in foreign policy of the effects of resource depletion on the political stability of poorer states, Mathews argued that environmental problems with global ramifications, such as ozone depletion, climate change and deforestation, should become issues of state security concern because they were the underlying cause of regional instability (Mathews 1989). Though less heralded, four years earlier legendary US diplomat George Kennan, in the same journal, had argued that the world faced 'two unprecedented and supreme dangers', which were nuclear war and 'the devastating effect of modern industrialization and overpopulation on the world's natural resources' (Kennan 1985: 216).

From these seeds sown by Kennan and Mathews in the 1980s a new strand of IR enquiry emerged in the post-Cold War New World Order era, positing that heightened competition for resources would increasingly be a cause of war, particularly in LDCs. Canadian academic Homer-Dixon and US journalist Kaplan were at the forefront of this area of study (Homer-Dixon 1994; Kaplan 1994). 'Environmental scarcities are already contributing to violent conflicts in many parts of the world. These conflicts are probably the early signs of an upsurge of violence in the coming decades that will be induced or aggravated by scarcity' (Homer-Dixon 1994: 6). Around the same time that the Homer-Dixon/Kaplan thesis was emerging, increased competition for that most precious of all resources, water, heralded a similar and significant 'water wars' literature highlighting how arid regions, such as the Middle East, could increasingly see access to water used as a weapon (Starr 1991; Bullock & Adel 1993).

Many others have come to link scarcity with war, and a subsequent strand of the resource war literature has emerged specifically in relation to climate change. Dupont and Pearman, for example, posit that a warming world has increased the likelihood of conflict in five key ways: resource scarcity, land being rendered uninhabitable due to either water scarcity or inundation, the effects of disasters and disease, greater refugee movements and an increased scramble for remaining resource sources (Dupont & Pearman 2006). In an empirical study by Columbia University, similar in style to the Homer-Dixon research, it was found that countries affected by the El Niño–Southern Oscillation extreme weather phenomenon between 1950 and 2005 were twice as likely to experience major civil or international conflict (i.e. those with at least twenty-five fatalities) as those not. Cases in point highlighted in the study included the fact that El Niño struck Peru in 1982, in the same year as the Shining Path insurgency took off, and that civil wars in Sudan had flared up in parallel with the emergence of extreme weather conditions. The study concluded that 'when crops fail people may take up a gun simply to make a living' (Hsiang, Meng & Cane 2011).

Human securitization

Going beyond the 'widened security' Realism of securitizing environmental issues where national interests are seen to be invoked are Critical and Human Security approaches focusing on the manifold threats environmental change poses to people. The clearest case of how environmental change can become an issue of human security is in the threat posed by climate change. The Earth's average temperature has risen consistently over the last century and it is now almost universally accepted that this is more than a natural development and likely to accelerate if not responded to. The central cause of global warming is an exacerbation of the natural phenomenon of the 'Greenhouse effect', due to increased industrial emissions. Increased releases of carbon dioxide and methane over the years, principally through the burning of fossil fuels, have served to exaggerate the natural tendency of the atmosphere to trap a certain amount of infrared sunlight after it is reflected from the Earth's surface. The implications of this are various but include increased desertification, a raising of sea levels due to the polar ice caps melting, more extreme weather events and the spread of a range of tropical diseases all carrying significant threats to human life in various forms (see Table 6.1). The World Health Organization suggest that

TABLE 6.1 Ten major security threats posed by global warming

- More frequent and lengthy heatwaves
- More frequent droughts
- Coastal flooding due to sea level rises
- Reduced crop yields due to reduced rainfall
- Spread of tropical diseases north and south
- Increased rate of water-borne diseases in flooded areas
- Ocean acidification due to carbon dioxide affecting fish stocks
- More frequent and stronger riverine flooding in wet seasons due to glaciers melting/reduced water supply in dry season
- Increased incidences of wildfires
- More frequent and stronger windstorms

TABLE 6.2 Annual deaths due to pollution

1	Household air pollution (smoke)	4.3 million
2	Outdoor air pollution (ambient particulate matter)	3 million
3	Lead poisoning	0.67 million
4	Water/sanitation pollution	0.34 million
5	Ozone	0.15 million
6	Residential radon exposure	0.1 million

Sources: Lim et al. 2012; WHO 2016d.

around 150,000 deaths a year since the early 1970s can be attributed to the gradual rise in temperatures across the world (McMichael et al. 2004). The human cost of ozone depletion by the accumulation of chloro-fluoro-carbons in the upper atmosphere – in exacerbating the threat posed by cataracts and skin cancer – also became apparent towards the close of the Cold War and was key to propelling environmental change much higher up the international political agenda than seen before and, probably, since. Aside from these globally-threatening forms of pollution, more general contamination by smog, smoke and long-range contamination of the air and water by pollutants claims over 8 million lives a year (see Table 6.2).

Environmental securitization in practice

As discussed elsewhere in this book, designating an issue as a matter of security is not just a theoretical question but carries 'real world' significance. The traditional, Realist way of framing security presupposes that military matters (and certain economic issues for Neo-Realists) are security issues and as such must be prioritized by governments above other 'low politics' issues, important though these might be. Human needs and ecocentric concerns cannot be addressed unless the country is secure in the first place is the logic informing this stance. Whilst traditional 'narrow' Realism is undoubtedly apparent in real world IR, some securitization of environmental issues has been evident in the corridors of power mirroring the academic dialectic previously discussed.

National environmental securitization

Whilst it was the lifting of the Cold War shadow that permitted some securitization of the environment, such concerns were periodically aired in international diplomacy in the 1970s and 1980s. Although the 1972 Stockholm Conference did not securitize environmental change and put it at the top of an international political agenda still, in spite of détente, dominated by the Cold War and impending global recession, some 'high politics' was witnessed at the event. Most notably, Swedish prime minister Olof Palme used the event to denounce the use of herbicides in war as 'ecocide'. Palme made no explicit reference to the recent American use of the infamous jungle defoliant *Agent Orange* in the Vietnam War, but the implied criticism caused grave offence to the Nixon administration, who responded by withdrawing the US ambassador from Stockholm. Full diplomatic relations between the two countries were suspended for over a year.

A less predictable environmental champion than Sweden was the Soviet Union who, despite absenting themselves from the Stockholm Conference, chose to play the 'green card' on occasion during the Cold War. In the mid-1970s the Soviets were able to exploit the backlash against the US over *Agent Orange* and become the unlikely pioneer of international legislation proscribing deliberate environmental destruction in warfare (the 1976 Environmental Modification Treaty (ENMOD) and Geneva Conventions Protocol I of 1977). A decade later, a changing Soviet Union under Gorbachev used environmental cooperation in the Arctic as an olive branch as part of his strategy of accommodation with the West, most notably in his Murmansk address of 1987 (Gorbachev 1987). In the new Western-oriented Russia that emerged after the end of the Cold War and the exit of Gorbachev, Moscow, rhetorically at least, appeared to become a full convert to the cause of securitizing the environment. In 1994 the government Commission on Environmental Security adopted a declaration stating that:

> Environmental security is the protection of the natural environment and vital interests of citizens, society, the state from internal and external impacts, adverse processes and trends in development that threaten human health, biodiversity and sustainable functioning of ecosystems, and survival of humankind. Environmental security is an integral part of Russia's national security.
>
> (Russia 1996: 55)

More predictable converts to making the environment the stuff of high politics have emerged in North America and northern Europe. The resource wars literature was particularly influential on the Clinton administration in the early 1990s, convincing them that environmental degradation represented a potential source of military insecurity. Homer-Dixon is known to have been invited to brief Vice President Al Gore and the State Department on several occasions (Floyd 2010: 75–6). In 1993 a new government position in the Defense Department was created with the Deputy Under Secretary for Environmental Security, and the Environmental Task Force was set up as part of Washington's intelligence network. The following year the securitization of the environment was made explicit in the National Security Strategy: 'an emerging class of transnational environmental issues are increasingly affecting international stability and consequently present new challenges to U.S. strategy . . .' (USA 1994: 1).

In 2007 Foreign Minister Margaret Beckett used the UK's presidency of the UN Security Council to push through, with some resistance from other members, the first discussion on an overtly environmental topic in reasoning that climate change carried implications that 'reach to the very heart of the security agenda' (Beckett 2007). A major influence on this stance was the Stern Report of the previous year, compiled by a British economist on behalf of the UK government, which provided an economic security rationale for prioritizing action on climate change.

Stern calculated the cost of non-action on climate change as amounting to at the very least 5 per cent of global GDP for ever more. Set against this, the cost of effective action to curb climate change would amount to around 1 per cent of global GDP per year (Stern 2006). In 2008, following up on the Security Council initiative, climate change was referred to in the UK's inaugural National Security Strategy and, a year later, a new role of Climate and Energy Security Envoy was created. The Netherlands' 2006 Foreign Policy Agenda also specifically acknowledges the role that environmental degradation plays in threatening global security. The Dutch additionally, though, go beyond national security widening in declaring that one of the eight goals of this policy is 'to protect and improve the environment' (Netherlands 2006).

The ecocentric turn of making the environment the referent object of security, evident in Dutch foreign policy, has also been advanced in a different political form in recent years outside of the Western world as part of the 'new left' wave in Latin America from the late 2000s. The critical stance on Western capitalism and focus on indigenous people that mark this political movement have found expression in the empowerment of nature. In 2008 Ecuador's new constitution declared that nature had the 'right to exist, persist, maintain and regenerate its vital cycles, structure, functions and its processes in evolution' and mandated the government to take 'precaution and restriction measures in all the activities that can lead to the extinction of species, the destruction of the ecosystems or the permanent alteration of the natural cycles' (Ecuador 2008). Whilst many countries have cited environmental protection in their constitutions none have done so in such unambiguously ecocentric terms. This 'rights of nature' approach has also been followed by the Morales government in Bolivia where the 'Law of Mother Earth' has defended the right of nature 'to not be affected by mega-infrastructure and development projects that affect the balance of ecosystems and the local inhabitant communities' (Bolivia 2011). For both countries this idea of environmental rights has come from the twin impact of indigenous people's empowerment and a legacy of environmental pollution. The rights of long-marginalized indigenous Americans (of which Morales is one) have become an important domestic political concern, aided by greater international discourse on this realm of politics promoted within the UN system by the Trustee Council, the Working Group on Indigenous Populations, the Human Rights Council and the International Labour Organization. In addition, the long-standing problem of pollution from oil in Ecuador and tin in Bolivia has heightened environmental concerns beyond the level witnessed in most developing countries.

Some states have even securitized the environment in the most explicit and traditional way by sending in the troops to tackle ecological disasters. In 2009 Bangladesh deployed armed forces to lead the national response to the cyclone *Aila*. More significantly, Brazil established the National Environmental Security Force to combat deforestation in 2012, employing a combination of armed forces and police to tackle the huge problem of illegal logging in the Amazonian rainforest.

Whilst it could be argued that none of the aforementioned political announcements or initiatives really make environmental change the number one diplomatic priority, it is clearly the priority for some states most affected by climate change. For low-lying island states the prospect of a rise in the level of the oceans is a human and state security threat of the utmost gravity.

> We want the islands of Tuvalu, our nation, to exist permanently forever and not to be submerged underwater merely due to the selfishness and greed of the industrialised world.
>
> Saufatu Sopoanga, Prime Minister of Tuvalu, at the 2002 World Summit on Sustainable Development (Sopoanga 2002)

Governments of these states have sought to emphasize the urgency of international action in diplomatic forums and in media-friendly stunts such as the holding of a cabinet meeting of the Maldives government underwater in 2009. However, realistic as to the likelihood of their pleas being acted upon, the governments of the Maldives, Tuvalu, Nauru and Kiribati have already made plans to shift their entire populations to other locations.

Intergovernmental environmental securitization

In the politics of intergovernmental organizations we can again see the notion of securitizing the environment begin to emerge in the early 1970s before properly flourishing in the aftermath of the Cold War. Swedish prime minister Olof Palme was, again, pivotal in securitizing the environment at the United Nations. At the UN Commission on Disarmament and Security in 1982 Palme called on member-states to move beyond considering collective security and embrace 'common security', bringing into focus threats emanating from overpopulation, environmental degradation and resource scarcity (Palme 1982). Two years earlier Palme was part of the Independent Commission on International Development Issues, which gave rhetorical support for securitizing the environment, stating that: 'few threats to peace and survival of the human community are greater than those posed by the prospects of cumulative and irreversible degradation of the biosphere on which human life depends' (ICIDI 1980).

In the 1980s the onset of the second Cold War limited the advance of this environmental security agenda, but the mantle was picked up again in the revival of multilateralism from the 1990s, and has found expression within the UN system. In 2009, following the Security Council discussion of climate change two years earlier, the UN General Assembly took up this theme with a resolution on 'Climate Change and its Possible Security Implications' calling on all UN agencies to prioritize climate change, drafted by the government of low-lying Nauru and unanimously adopted (A64/350). Perhaps, though, the clearest illustration of the environment becoming the stuff of widened security comes from its embrace by the Cold Warriors of NATO:

> Based on a broad definition of security that recognizes the importance of political, economic, social and environmental factors, NATO is addressing security challenges emanating from the environment. This includes extreme weather conditions, depletion of natural resources, pollution and so on – factors that can ultimately lead to disasters, regional tensions and violence.
>
> (NATO 2013)

Human Security approaches, highlighting the necessity of tackling vulnerability to environmental problems, have also been strongly advocated within the UN system by recent Secretary-Generals, the Human Security Unit of the Office for the Coordination of Humanitarian Affairs within the Secretariat and, most notably, the UN Development Programme (UNDP). As with state practice, though, environmental securitization by IGOs tends to mean different things to different actors.

Evaluating environmental securitization

The question of whether environmental problems merit the politically significant label of 'security' is a complex one and highly contested. On the one hand, the complexity and uneven human impact of environmental issues lead to disputes about the scale of threat they pose or an attitude of denial in the face of 'inconvenient truths' often geographically or chronologically distant. On the other hand, there is a lack of consensus as to what 'security' actually means. For some, unable to break free of a militarized and statecentric view of IR forged in the three global wars of the twentieth century, environmental challenges can only be considered the stuff of security if they can be seen to cause wars or threaten the sovereign apparatus of states. For others, receptive to ontological and epistemological challenges to the conventions of IR that emerged following the end of the Cold War, environmental threats can and should be securitized by abandoning the preoccupation with the state and the military and facing up to a different nature of threat. A third perspective agrees with the second in terms of the scale of threat posed by environmental problems but resists securitization through concerns that this risks invoking inappropriate, militaristic 'national security' responses.

Deudney cites three key arguments for not extending the reach of Security Studies to incorporate environmental issues:

1   It is analytically misleading to think of environmental degradation as a national security threat, because the traditional focus of national security – interstate violence – has little in common with either environmental problems or solutions.
2   The effort to harness the emotive power of nationalism to help mobilize environmental awareness and action may prove counterproductive by undermining globalist political stability.
3   Environmental degradation is not very likely to cause interstate wars.

(Deudney 1990: 461)

Point 3 is a direct rebuttal of the Homer-Dixon-led approach of coupling certain environmental issues with military security, which is certainly open to challenge. Despite its influence on the thinking of the US government and others, the approach of framing environmental scarcity as a military security matter has not been without its critics. The empirical evidence linking environmental degradation and political conflict is, by Homer-Dixon's own admission, not straightforward, prompting scepticism as to whether other variables are the real causes of conflicts in situations where environmental scarcity can be demonstrated. The assumption that changes in the balance between resources and people create political problems is viewed as flawed logic by resource war sceptics. Critics have reasoned that it is easy to link droughts in Sudan to the Darfur crisis and other civil conflicts in the country but such events are unfortunate facts of life in the Sahel and the responsibility for the bloodshed lies squarely with the Janjaweed insurgents and the Sudanese government for giving a green light to their murderous campaigns (Brown & McLeman 2009: 297). History also can provide plenty of evidence of environmental disasters and extreme weather conditions *not* prompting conflict. The devastating dustbowls that struck the US Great Plains in the 1930s did not trigger conflict (Brown & McLeman 2009: 296). Neither was conflict a consequence of the 2010 earthquake in the far more politically volatile state of Haiti, in spite of the widespread assumption that it would be. Australia has been as much affected by El Niño as Sudan or Peru but has not been struck by civil war, for obvious economic and political reasons. The cited cases could suggest a correlation between conflict and underdevelopment and a lack of democracy, more than environmental scarcity.

Deudney's second point rightly implies that global problems require global responses rather than relying on individual state calculations of rationality, a standard challenge presented by environmental problems to the traditional statist national interest-based model of how foreign policies should be constructed. For human security advocates, though, the weakness in Deudney's argument comes from a statist bias in another way. Nationalism is, indeed, an inappropriate political ideology to tackle most environmental problems, but who has ever proposed this as a solution to climate change or pollution? Deudney, in common with most traditionalists, conflates 'security' with 'something that requires a military response by the state' rather than seeing it as a condition which relates to people's lives and which can be acted upon at various political levels. 'Both violence and environmental degradation may kill people and may reduce human well-being, but not all threats to life and property are threats to security' (Deudney 1990: 463). This represents an explicit admission that 'security' can have no meaning other than as a synonym for 'military defence against other states'.

For human security advocates the scale of threats to people posed by environmental change is so far removed from the way in which issues are conventionally ordered on the political agenda by states that International Relations theory and international political practice need to find ways of accommodating them, or cease to be connected in any meaningful way with human behaviour and needs. Eight million people a year already die from pollution and this is set to get much worse. War and terrorism set against this represent much lesser threats (around 170,000 deaths per year). Most of these deaths by pollution can be avoided by political action, therefore if steps are not taken to avoid them a political failing has occurred. Are people indirectly killed by a known problem not insecure?

However, another concern with securitizing the environment is the lack of consensus and subsequent confusion over what this actually means. De Wilde points out that there is a fundamental problem in very different ideas coming to be conflated in the environmental security literature: (a) the environment as the referent object to be secured by urgent human action; (b) human civilization as the referent object to be secured against environmental change (De Wilde 2008: 598–9). This argument has validity since securitization does mean different things to different thinkers, governments and international organizations. Civilizational security can and has been invoked on occasion but risks accusations of exaggeration, particularly in light of the hysteria prompted by overpopulation concerns in the late 1960s. Securing the environment against human harm can be understood as the fundament of political ecology and, as such, could be accused of just giving a new and unnecessary label for ecocentric policy. However, whilst it has been criticized for its vagueness and comes in different strengths, human security does have a clear referent object – the human. Given the transboundary and global nature of environmental problems the human is also a more clear-cut reference point for security than the state in this issue area. 'Territorial security, for delimited groups may once have been fundamental to achieving "the good life", but it now seems more likely that the security of the global environment (incorporating localities) is the basic condition for human security' (Dyer 2000: 449).

Human security is still somewhat problematic from an ecological perspective since this is, by definition, an anthropocentric rather than ecocentric way of framing problems. However so long as human security is understood in the context of us being part of a global biosphere, the safeguarding of which enhances both human and non-human interests, this need not be a problem. Dalby argues that the key to safeguarding human security in issues such as climate change and resource depletion is to cease framing such problems in the context of 'environmental threats'. Dalby defines security in terms of a referent object which is the global totality: 'the assurance of relatively undisturbed ecological systems in all parts of the biosphere' (Dalby 2002: 106). Thinking in such ecological terms means that social and economic transformations are not treated as distinct from atmospheric or biological developments in terms of their consequences. Human security can then be incorporated into this logic of ecological security. 'When people do not have enough options to avoid or adapt to environmental change such that their needs, rights and values are likely to be undermined, then they can be said to be environmentally insecure' (Mathew et al. 2010: 18).

Appreciating that human phenomena like urbanization or increasing consumption have effects in the natural world with implications for human security can improve the management of threats. Security threats can be more subtle than the rapid emergence of a hole in the ozone layer, and the solutions more complex than switching from the use of CFCs to replacement chemicals. A better appreciation of this complexity could help alleviate these difficulties before they become imminent crises. The traditional practices of international relations, though, are much better suited to responding to crises rather than tackling long-term, underlying causes of these sources of insecurity.

A further consequence of this residual Realism still permeating real world international politics is that securitizing the environment for many still invokes a perception of militarization which, apart from some utility for deploying armed forces in the aftermath of a natural disaster, offers no solutions whilst presenting further problems. National securitization may be welcomed in terms of getting governments on board and giving environmental issues the spotlight they often deserve, but old habits die hard and this does tend to frame the issues in Realist terms. The discourse of environmental change in venues of intergovernmental 'high politics' invariably becomes reduced down to the resource wars thesis or the apparent threat posed by a rise in environmental migration. Environmental degradation is deemed important because it might be a cause of war and instability rather than because it *is* a threat to life in itself. The UK UN delegation in 2007 cited the following security implications of climate change: border disputes due to the melting of ice sheets and rising sea levels; increased migration with 'the potential for instability and conflict'; conflict over energy supplies; conflict due to scarcity; conflict due to poverty; and conflicts related to extreme weather events (UNSC 2007). Hence the UK advocacy of action on climate change at the UN Security Council was as Realist as the Chinese and South African resistance to this. Compassion for the fate of peoples most affected in arid, low-lying or polar regions doubtless played a part in the thinking of Beckett, Blair and the Labour government, but a clear self-interest was considered apparent and British permanent membership of the Security Council provided a good opportunity to attempt a 'tactical securitization' of the issue. The Chinese and South Africans, in disputing this securitization move, were not rejecting the notion that climate change was an important concern, but calculating that it was not in their national interests to debate this in the Security Council.

The playing of the national security card over climate change by some countries is instinctively treated with suspicion by others because of what national security is understood to stand for in the discourse of international relations all have been engaged in over the past century. It invokes a militarization of politics with an aggressive interference in the affairs of others or a defensive retreat behind strengthened armed borders, neither of which are relevant for the multi-dimensional threats posed by climate change. The rhetoric of climate change securitization has done little to dispel this notion. The debates in the Security Council, the foreign policy statements of the US, UK and others, plus the academic arguments of the likes of Homer-Dixon have highlighted national security threats of failed states, resources conflict and mass migration. However, tightening up borders to deter environmental migrants is directly contradictory to the human interest, and the solution of armed humanitarian interventions in response to lawlessness deployed in other contexts is unlikely to be either welcomed or useful.

The misgivings of the Chinese and South Africans over debating climate change in the Security Council doubtless have something to do with their determination not to have to compromise their economic development, but there is some merit in the argument that it is an issue better tackled elsewhere. In theory it is appropriate that climate change be debated at the high table of global high politics, but the problem with this in practice is that the UN Security Council has always been an arena of great power *realpolitik*. It is the arena where Soviet and US Cold War adventurism was ignored and, in the present age, where violations of international law by countries like Israel and Syria are still ignored because of their continued sponsorship by Washington and Moscow.

The militarization of environmental issues is not only unwarranted but, possibly, inaccurate. Environmental change may even be a source of peace rather than conflict. Contrary to many assumptions, there is no real evidence of transboundary environmental problems or greater resource scarcity prompting war and, indeed, the environment can be 'used' in the context of peace-building. Gorbachev's initial westward olive branches were to propose environmental cooperation in the Arctic and on tackling pollution. In a more concrete example of peace-building in 1998, the Peru–Ecuador Cordillera de Condor 'Peace Park' was consciously established by both governments to dampen the long-running border dispute between the Andean neighbours by designating a contested mountainous region as a zone of conservation (Conca & Dabelko 2002).

An additional problem with securitization is that it fuels accusations of scare-mongering and exaggeration from vested interests seeking to downplay environmental problems. The overpopulation hyperbole of the late 1960s and subsequent expansion of the food supply through technological innovation in the Green Revolution fed the dangerous climate change scepticism which stifles requisite urgent international action today. Concentrating on highly speculative and unproven links between environmental change and war, rather than rigorously researched and already evident negative consequences of climate change, pollution or deforestation, does not help in overcoming such accusations.

Conclusions

The consideration of environmental issues as matters of security has gathered momentum academically and politically, but remains highly contested. This is not only a consequence of environmental issues being given different levels of priority by different ideological perspectives, but also a question of appropriateness. Those resisting securitization are not only the environmental sceptics but also environmentalists alarmed at the apparent coupling of the issue area with the politics of national interest and militarism.

Where the military assumption can be overcome, the national securitization of the environment can still tend to lead to inappropriate solutions. Technological quick fixes, reactive responses after a crisis and headline-grabbing stunts are often more politically attractive than the slow, unspectacular politics of tackling underlying causes of vulnerability. Low-key, gradual, technical solutions, however, are usually what are needed to address insecurities arising from environmental change. It was the careful, prolonged work of transnational scientists and civil society actors rather than grand government gestures that achieved the international political successes seen in combating ozone depletion, based on the Montreal Protocol of the 1985 Vienna Convention, which UNEP claim has averted 1.5 million cases of skin cancer and 130 million cataracts (UNEP 2012). Put in these terms this is environmental policy clearly in the cause of human security, but putting limits on industrial emissions is not what most people think of as the politics of security. The problem of securitizing the environment is, as Prins and Stamp memorably put it, 'you can't shoot an ozone hole' (Prins & Stamp 1991: 12).

Key points

- Issues of environmental change have often been framed as (widened) national security concerns – both academically and governmentally – through fears of resource depletion triggering conflicts, but this thesis is disputed.
- Issues of environmental change are also often framed as human security concerns, because of the considerable death toll attributable to pollution, but this is contentious,

both to traditional security theorists and to some ecologists fearful that the 'label of security' will prompt inappropriate political responses.

 Note

1   The 1967 *Torrey Canyon* disaster, when an oil tanker was wrecked and spilled its load off the coast of the Scilly Isles, UK, was particularly influential in stimulating awareness of and an international political response to oil pollution.

 Recommended reading

Dalby, S. (2009) *Security and Environmental Change*, Cambridge: Polity.
Floyd, R. & Mathew, R. (2013) *Environmental Security: Approaches and Issues*, London and New York: Routledge.
Hough, P. (2014) *Environmental Security: An Introduction*, London and New York: Routledge.
Mathew, R., Barnett, J., McDonald, B., O'Brien, K. & Dabelko, G. (eds) (2010) *Global Environmental Change and Human Security*, Boston: MIT Press.

 Useful web links

- United Nations Environment Programme: www.unep.org/
- United Nations University Institute for Environment and Human Security: https://ehs.unu.edu

Chapter 7

Health threats to security

> *A ruined planet cannot sustain human lives in good health. A healthy planet and healthy people are two sides of the same coin*
>
> Margaret Chan, World Health Organization
> Executive Director, 8 December 2015

The globalization of ill health

Disease has long been the biggest threat of all to humanity and, despite the advances of medical science, looks set to continue to be for the foreseeable future. The Black Death of the fourteenth century claimed more lives than any military conflict before or since, whilst the great influenza epidemic of 1918–20 killed far more than the Great War that it closely followed. As far back as the sixth century, the 'Plague of Justinian', which started in Constantinople and then spread throughout the Mediterranean, was a classic 'national security' issue since it precipitated the fall of the Byzantine Roman Empire (McNeill 1989: 101–6). Today, AIDS (Acquired Immune Deficiency Syndrome) represents a far greater threat to life than armed conflict for most sub-Saharan Africans and for many millions more in all of the inhabited continents of the world. In addition, the threats posed by diseases tend to be transnational and as such represent a security challenge not easily countered by a human race artificially subdivided into independent, though not impervious, units.

As with famines and hunger, however, major epidemics and pandemics (international epidemics) of diseases represent only dramatic periodic escalations of an underlying and persistent threat. Tables 7.1 and 7.2 give an indication of the scale of this threat, the greatest challenge of all to human security. By the end of the 1970s there was optimism that humanity's war against disease was being won.

TABLE 7.1 The ten deadliest disease epidemics and pandemics of all time

	Epidemic/pandemic	Location	Date	Death toll
1	Black Death	World	1347–1351	75 million
2	AIDS	World	1981–	35 million
3	Influenza	World	1918–1920	21.64 million
4	Plague	India	1896–1948	12 million
5	Typhus	Eastern Europe	1914–1915	3 million
6	'Plague of Justinian'	Eastern Mediterranean	541–590	'millions'
=7	Cholera	World	1846–1860	'millions'
=7	Cholera	Europe	1826–1837	'millions'
=7	Cholera	World	1893–1894	'millions'
10	Smallpox	Mexico	1530–1545	up to 1 million

Sources: Ash 2001: 31; WHO 2017: www.who.int/gho/hiv/en/

Disease is an enemy which can probably never be entirely defeated, but in the three decades which followed the Second World War, a growing belief emerged that scientific and medical advances could eliminate many infections and at least contain the others. The attack was led by the use of synthetic (organic) insecticides, following the 1939 discovery of dichloro-diphenyl-trichloroethane (DDT), and its use against disease-carrying insects such as mosquitoes and tsetse-flies. The defence against disease was strengthened by significant medical advances which discovered and refined antibiotics, such as long-acting penicillin, which could directly attack the microbes themselves or immunize whole vulnerable populations against threatening diseases. Coordinating this joint strategy was a new global body set up as part of the United Nations, the World Health Organization (WHO).

A WHO led-immunization campaign entirely eradicated smallpox in 1978, saving around two million lives a year, whilst the use of DDT in WHO-led operations quickly curbed the annual death toll attributable to malaria to a similar degree without actually eradicating the disease. In line with these and many other successes, the WHO optimistically declared in 1977 that victory against disease was in sight in setting the target of 'Health for All by the Year 2000'. By the end of the century, however, the WHO's hope that it could shift its main focus to Primary Health Care (ensuring all people have access to health care, clean water and sanitation) had been overtaken by events with the revival of apparently dormant illnesses and the arrival of new, even more virulent diseases.

Although human history is replete with peaks and troughs of disease, a number of factors particular to the contemporary world can be offered as partial explanations for the globalization of disease and other illnesses over the last four decades.

Increased travel and migration

History shows that epidemics and pandemics of diseases have tended to occur when previously isolated human populations mix. The Roman Empire was beset by periodic plagues of previously-unknown magnitude, new diseases entered Europe from Asia

TABLE 7.2 The ten most significant global communicable, maternal and nutritional diseases

	Disease	Cause	Main areas affected	Annual deaths (m)
1	Lower respiratory	Influenza and pneumonia viruses, passed by coughing and sneezing	Global but most deadly in LDCs	2.7
2	Neonatal	Complications for babies in birth	LDCs, particularly sub-Saharan Africa	2.2
3	Diarrhoeal	Diseases carried by water-borne viruses, bacteria and parasites (e.g. cholera, dysentery, E coli)	LDCs, particularly sub-Saharan Africa	1.3
4	AIDS	Virus transmitted by bodily fluids	Global but principally sub-Saharan Africa	1.2
5	Tuberculosis	Bacterial infection transmitted by coughs and sneezes	LDCs, principally Africa & South-East Asia	1.1
6	Malaria	Parasites transmitted by mosquito	The 'Tropics'	0.7
7	Nutrition	Malnutrition disorders such as iodine or iron deficiency	LDCs, particularly sub-Saharan Africa	0.4
8	Meningitis	Bacterial infection of brain and spine	Across middle of Africa	0.4
9	Maternal	Infections and complications for the mother in childbirth	LDCs, particularly sub-Saharan Africa	0.3
10	Intestinal	Contaminated water, e.g. typhoid	S. Asia & S. Africa	0.2
Total				11.3

Source: Figures from *Lancet* 2016.

in the wake of Marco Polo's establishment of links in the thirteenth century, and diseases left Europe for the Americas with Columbus and his successors from the late fifteenth century (Pirages & Runci 2000: 176–80). Human groups over time can evolve immunities to certain strains of disease which when encountered by humans who have evolved (genetically) from other geographical areas can be deadly. The prevalence of holiday ailments, often erroneously blamed on foreign food, bears testimony to the fact that this phenomenon persists. Ever-greater levels of contact between people ultimately could diminish the deadliest impacts of this by making human immunities more similar but, in the meantime, contemporary global social change is a root of the problem rather than the cure.

The much more frequent movement of people around the globe also serves to transport diseases dangerous to all to new parts of the world in ever-greater quantities. Aeroplanes and international shipping are well established hosts for the spread of dangerous pathogens, carried either directly by the tourists or on insect or rodent vectors. For example, in 2016 there were eighteen recorded outbreaks of measles worldwide of which fifteen were carried by people travelling (principally from Asia) and the other three were recorded in migrants and refugees (Berger 2017). Immigrants will, of course, tend to be 'vetted' for alien diseases by state authorities before admission into the country, but this is neither feasible nor politically acceptable for tourists and other visitors entering or, particularly, for citizens returning from abroad.

Increased trade

As with travel, the link between trade and the spread of disease is well-established. The Black Death arrived in Europe directly via goods imported from the Orient and, although trading standards have evolved greatly since that time, the rapid proliferation of trade links in recent years has opened up more potential routes for diseases to spread. In particular, the globalization of food production has been accompanied by the globalization of food-borne illnesses. In 2011, for example, over forty people were killed by a sudden outbreak of *Escherichia coli* (E coli) in Germany. Despite the high levels of bureaucracy that characterize the European Union's Common Agricultural Policy, scientists could not be sure where the vegetables infected by the bacterium originated, whilst politicians in Germany, Spain and elsewhere pointed the blame at each other. Outbreaks of disease occurring in food production could, in the past, be reliably dealt with by imposing a quarantine around the event and culling all potential carriers within. However, this is no longer a guaranteed solution since the proceeding stages of production and the consumers come from increasingly far afield.

Displaced persons

Just as more frequent voluntary movements of people have increased outbreaks of diseases, so too have more frequent enforced movements, as a consequence of natural or human disaster. People fleeing countries beset by war or famine will be far more likely to be carrying diseases and also more vulnerable to contracting them. Recipient countries, though, may be able to help refugees and prevent the further spread of disease. At much greater risk are peoples coerced into moves to other parts of their own state rather than abroad, who technically are not refugees but 'internally displaced persons (IDPs)'. Such people are less likely to receive assistance, either domestic or international, and tend to be forced to settle in overcrowded and unhygienic locations. For example, the displacement of around 1.6 million in Borno State, Nigeria, resulting from the Boko Harem insurgency, has led to a series of deadly outbreaks of cholera and polio since 2014.

Insect and microbe resistance

A major factor behind the counter-attacks of bacteria against humanity in the war against disease since the 1970s referred to earlier has been the increased redundancy of human weaponry. The globalization of the human strategy of mass vaccinations and chemical pest control has had the side-effect of globalizing resistance. Both pathogens and the pests by which they are transmitted have increasingly developed immunities to the pesticides and antibiotic drugs used against them. Many insects and rodents have become resistant to insecticides and rodenticides used against them over the last seventy years, with diseases like malaria resurging from near elimination as a result. Similarly, many antibiotics have become increasingly ineffective in treating illnesses they once could be relied upon to combat. That most renowned panacea penicillin, for example, can no longer be guaranteed to treat gonorrhea or pneumonia. Additionally, resistance requires increased innovation in antibiotic development, increasing the costs of treatment and exacerbating the vulnerability of people in the world's poorest states. The problem has escalated in recent years, prompting the head of the WHO to refer to this as a 'global crisis' and 'slow motion tsunami' (Chan 2016). For both pesticides and antibiotics, overuse has been a part cause of increased target resistance, and more cautious application is now understood as the best strategy against an enemy more ingenious than imagined in the 1950s and 1960s. That period of the conflict between man and disease looks ever more like a victorious phase in a protracted war.

Urbanization

The trend for population growth in urban areas at the expense of rural areas has been witnessed since industrialization began in Europe in the eighteenth century but has become particularly prominent in the global South over recent decades. This has had profound implications for the spread of disease in two dimensions:

1   Overcrowding in megacities has led to many people living in squalor, providing the conditions for diseases associated with poor sanitation to emerge and for other diseases to be more readily transmitted amongst a large population. Examples of this include dysentery and cholera, chiefly spread by unsanitary food and water.
2   Urban encroachment on traditionally distinct rural areas can cause diseases associated with the rural environment to contaminate the urban population. In addition, entirely new human ailments are believed to have emerged as a result of greater contact with other animal species allowing for the cross-species

transmission of 'zoonotic' diseases. This cross-species transmission can work in both ways. Greater human encroachment into woodland areas, for example, has led to an upsurge in the transmission of *Lyme* disease in Europe and North America, carried by parasitic ticks on deer. In Japan there has been a sharp rise in cases of *alveolar echinococcosis* (AE) which is carried by larvae on wild dogs, packs of which are now established in a number of cities. Overall three-quarters of all human diseases are zoonotic (Mackenstedt, Jenkins & Romig 2015).

Development projects

Human-driven changes to the environment other than urbanization can also upset the equilibrium in a given ecosystem and cause a resurgence of certain diseases. Large dam projects in Africa, for example, have been known to have contributed to the proliferation of water-breeding disease vectors such as mosquitoes and water snails, causing the spread of Rift Valley Fever and schistomiasis (National Intelligence Council 2000).

Technological advances

A further but inverted link between economic development and disease can be seen in the spread of certain diseases associated specifically with technologically-advanced societies. There can be no doubt that modern medicine saves more lives than it claims, but the death toll attributable to it is still considerable. Around 37,000 people a year across the European Union die of nosocomial infections (hospital-acquired) such as *Staphylococcus aureas* (the bacterium causing 'Toxic Shock Syndrome'), associated with modern invasive medical procedures and over-reliance on antibiotics (ECDC 2017).

Global environmental change

Even if a small number continue to question whether global warming is natural or man-made, it is beyond dispute that average temperatures on Earth have risen over recent decades and this has had and will continue to have a considerable bearing on the spread of certain diseases. Tropical diseases, associated with insect vectors native to equatorial areas, are becoming increasingly common in areas with traditionally more temperate climes. The warmer the weather the more readily mosquitoes breed and bite, and malaria and other diseases have recently become a health threat in countries outside of the insects' usual habitat. The USA, for example, has been hit by West Nile virus as far north as New York every summer since 1999 and, in 2012, an epidemic claimed 286 lives in Texas (Murray et al. 2013). A record number of cases of the bacterial lung infection *legionnaires' disease* in the UK in 2006 led the Health Protection Agency to claim that the country had suffered its first casualties from infectious disease due to global warming (Laurance 2006). The WHO estimate that air pollution accounts for 5 per cent of the annual global deaths from heart disease and climate change is responsible for 3 per cent of malaria and diarrhoea fatalities (Hughes et al. 2011: 93).

Failed and failing states

As with the growth of other causes of human insecurity, the increased number of politically chaotic states, associated with the contemporary age, has exacerbated the dangers posed by disease. Political upheaval in sub-Saharan African states such as Sudan, Somalia and the Democratic Republic of Congo has contributed to poverty and the limited development of public health and sanitation provision. Even in states less anarchic and less naturally prone to disease epidemics than sub-Saharan Africa, health threats to security have emerged in line with political upheaval. One of the side-effects of Russia's difficult process of political, social and economic transition since the fall of Communist rule in 1991 has been the rise of vaccine-preventable diseases like tuberculosis and diphtheria, largely attributed to poverty and cuts in health expenditure. Failed states also, of course, encourage migration and the global spread of disease in addition to localized epidemics.

Global market forces

Economic globalization has some negative implications for human health beyond the side-effects of creating a single market for food. The trade, tourism and general reputational costs are such that governments have been known to downplay or deny disease outbreaks. A study has suggested that President Mbeki's policy of denial over HIV/AIDS in South Africa may have cost a third of a million of his citizens their lives (Chigwedere et al. 2008).

Cultural globalization

The diffusion of disease around the world is not entirely a one-way process of transmission from South to North. Globalization has also seen certain non-communicable 'lifestyle illnesses', associated with mass-consumption societies of the global North, head southwards as people in LDCs adopt some of the unhealthy practices associated with modernization. The consumption of high-fat and high-sugar foods, for example, has led to previously minor health problems such as obesity, heart disease and diabetes becoming more prominent in many LDCs and even in the societies on the margins of highly developed states. For example, a rise in rates of obesity and diabetes amongst indigenous peoples of the Arctic has resulted from the nutrition transition to Western consumption patterns. The mechanization of travel and decline in hunting in some communities have also added to the obesity problem as the Arctic lifestyle has become less active (Sharma 2010). Globally, cases of diabetes rose from 108 million in 1980 to 422 million in 2014 (with nearly all of this increase in Type 2 of the disease, closely associated with sugar consumption and obesity), with the Middle East most acutely affected (WHO 2016a). Tobacco smoking has also become more common in a number of LDCs (encouraged by Northern MNCs faced with a declining market at home), leading to a rise in lung cancer. Native Alaskans are nearly nine times more likely to die of alcohol-related health problems than the average US citizen (Seale, Shellenberger & Spence 2006). Overall it is pertinent to remember that non-communicable ailments far outstrip communicable diseases and account for 71 per cent of all deaths in the world (*Lancet* 2016) (see Table 7.3).

TABLE 7.3 The ten deadliest non-communicable diseases in the world

	Disease	Contributory factors	Areas particularly affected	Annual deaths (m)
1	Cardiovascular (heart attack or disease, stroke)	Poor diet, obesity	E. Europe & C. Asia	17.9
2	Cancers: lung 1.7; colon 0.8; stomach 0.8; liver 0.8	Tobacco smoking, poor diet	E. Europe and N. America	8.8
3	Respiratory, e.g. bronchitis	Tobacco smoking, pollution	S. and E. Asia	3.8
4	Neurological, e.g. Alzheimer's	Poverty, depression	N. America and N. Europe	2.3
5	Diabetes mellitus	Poor diet – excessive sugar	S. Pacific islands	1.5
6	Cirrhosis (liver)	Alcohol	C. Asia & Africa	1.3
7	Kidney diseases	Diabetes and high blood pressure	Latin America and Middle East	1.2
8	Digestive, e.g. peptic ulcers	Poor diet, alcohol consumption	S. Asia and C. Africa	1.2
9	Congenital abnormalities	Lack of pre-natal diagnosis	Africa and Middle East	0.6
10	Mental/substance use	Depression	E. Europe and S. Africa	0.3
Total				39.8

Source: Figures from *Lancet* 2016.

TABLE 7.4 Ten highest national suicide rates, 2012 (deaths per 100,000)

1	South Korea	36.8
2	Guyana	34.8
3	Lithuania	33.5
4	Sri Lanka	29.2
5	Surinam	28.3
6	Hungary	25.4
7	Kazakhstan	24.2
8	Japan	23.1
9	Russia	22.3
10	Latvia, Belarus	21.8

Source: WHO 2016b.

Not captured in this figure of 71 per cent is an additional annual death toll of over 800,000 attributable to life-threatening mental illness. As highlighted in Chapter 1, more people elect to end their own lives than are killed by others. In young adults (15–29 year olds) suicide is the second biggest cause of death and the proportion is significantly higher among men (WHO 2016b). This rate has actually fallen in recent years (9 per cent drop between 2000 and 2012) as governments with higher rates have become aware of this and developed policies to address the phenomenon, such as decriminalizing suicide, increasing the understanding of depression and making access to methods – such as firearms and toxic chemicals – more difficult. In Guyana, for example, it has become apparent that the country's extraordinary suicide rate (see Table 7.4) is linked to the easy availability of deadly pesticides and the widespread stigmatization of mental ill health. Hence in 2013 the WHO undertook to address this global problem by launching an Action Plan, highlighting good practice from national strategies and aiming to lower the rate by 10 per cent by 2020 (alongside a similar non-communicable disease Action Plan).

The development of global health policy

The transnational threat posed by infectious disease outbreaks has long been apparent to statesmen and participants in international commerce but counter-measures were slow to develop owing to an absence of any real epidemiological understanding of contagious diseases not spread directly by human to human (such as leprosy). The first systematic political measures to contain the international spread of disease can be dated back to fourteenth-century Venice and the origins of imposing a 'quarantine' on people arriving from certain countries. Ships which had come from or visited ports known to be afflicted with the Black Death were required by law to wait anchored at sea for thirty days, before being allowed to land if no evidence of the plague was apparent. This procedure was referred to as 'trentina' from the Latin for thirty and when, in the next century, the time scale was extended to forty days it became known as 'quarantine' from the Latin for forty days.

Other European states adopted similar quarantine measures over the next three centuries but coordinated international action to combat the spread of disease was not attempted until the mid-nineteenth century, when the unprecedented growth in international trade and birth of Liberal internationalism prompted the 'Concert' powers to respond. From 1851 a series of International Sanitary Conferences were held but, in an era when barriers to free trade and navigation were anathema to the great naval and commercial powers, they failed to produce a convention to harmonize quarantine practices for cholera, plague and yellow fever. A breakthrough, however, occurred in 1892 at the seventh International Sanitation Conference when a convention for cholera was agreed upon by most of the European maritime powers, followed by another dealing with the age-old threat of the plague ten years later. These conventions were merged into a single International Sanitary Convention in 1903 and the seeds of today's global health polity were sown with the emergence of the International Sanitary Bureau in the USA (later to become the Pan American Health Organization, now the World Health Organization's arm for the Americas) and the intensification of talks for a global IGO for public health. In 1907, L'Office Internationale d'Hygiene Publique (OIHP) was agreed upon, with a Parisian headquarters, a permanent staff and a decision-making body made up of (eventually) representatives of over fifty governments and colonial administrations. The OIHP sought to disseminate medical information as well as codifying quarantine agreements and expanding the scope of the International Sanitary Convention.

The OIHP continued to function despite the creation of a new global health organization as part of the League of Nations system established after the First World War. The Health Organization of the League of Nations (HOLN) was established amidst the carnage of typhus, cholera and influenza epidemics which dwarfed even the horrors of the world's greatest ever military conflict. The OIHP continued to have authority over the International Sanitary Conventions (which were expanded by conventions for smallpox and typhus in 1926 and for aerial transport in 1935) whilst the HOLN focused on advising countries on containing the spread of epidemics through specialist commissions of experts.

The HOLN's role decreased sharply at the outset of the Second World War as the whole League project crumbled in the face of a pronounced failure of collective military security. The League's well-documented peacekeeping failings, however, detract from the fact that the HOLN (and other specialized agencies) had proved highly successful. The HOLN had succeeded in containing the spread of typhus from East Europe in the first year of its operation in 1921, and fostered the development of an international *epistemic community* of health specialists who, undoubtedly, contributed greatly to the rapid improvement in human health standards throughout the world in the twentieth century.

During the Second World War a new international body was set up to offer humanitarian assistance to countries on the cessation of fighting. The United Nations Relief and Rehabilitation Administration (UNRRA) started operations ahead of the rest of the planned United Nations system set to replace the League of Nations at the full conclusion of the war. From 1944 to 1946 UNRRA supplied food and equipment to countries where fighting had stopped and in many cases this came to be accompanied by medical personnel and drugs for countries racked with disease.

A 1946 cholera outbreak in China, for example, was brought under control by the supply of an effective vaccine from the USA. UNRRA also assumed control from the OIHP (which continued to exist until officially absorbed by the World Health Organization) for administering the International Sanitary Conventions.

UNRRA, however, was only ever intended to be a temporary programme and it was wound up in 1946 when its work was considered to be complete. The 1945 San Francisco Conference which founded the United Nations system did not envisage a successor to the HOLN but a resolution of the first UN General Assembly in 1946 paved the way for the creation of the World Health Organization.

World Health Organization

A WHO Interim Commission came into operation in 1946 prior to the establishment of the WHO proper in 1948 and had a notable success in controlling a 1947 cholera epidemic in Egypt. The organization was from the start marked by an independent streak and it was agreed that the term 'United Nations' should not feature in its official title and that it would have a far more decentralized structure than any other UN specialized agency. The decision to devolve a great deal of the work of the WHO to six regions (Africa, the Americas, Europe, Eastern Mediterranean, South-East Asia and Western Pacific[1]) was partly a practical decision as it facilitated the continuation of the world's oldest health IGO as the American arm of the new global body.

Centrally, the work of the WHO is directed by an annual World Health Assembly (WHA), held in Geneva, in which delegates of its 194 member governments vote on budgetary matters and overall policy. The WHA elect a geographically-balanced thirty-four-member Executive Board to oversee the implementation of WHO policy. The Executive Board members are intended to be public health specialists rather than government delegates although there are also six Regional Committees which are made up of health ministers. The WHO Director-General is elected by the WHA, on the recommendation of the Executive Board, and serves a five-year term at the Geneva headquarters supported by 30 per cent of the WHO's 8,000-strong secretariat. A further 30 per cent of the secretariat serve the regions whilst the remaining 40 per cent are spread throughout the world in field programmes or as resident advisers to government (WHO 2012b). The WHO is financed by two distinct budgets. The regular budget, made up of assessed governments' contributions, finances the central institutions. In addition, extrabudgetary funds are made up of voluntary additional contributions from government, other UN agencies (particularly the World Bank) and private sources. These extrabudgetary funds can be targeted at specific programmes at the donor's request. The American information technology tycoon Bill Gates, for example, has made contributions to campaigns on guinea worm disease eradication and HIV research.

The undoubted high point of the WHO's history was the global eradication of smallpox, declared in 1978 after a vast immunization campaign. This momentous effort, which had to overcome obstacles such as a cultural reluctance to accept injections in some parts of India, saw many millions of people vaccinated and around two million lives a year saved. Other successes include greatly reducing the impact of *onchoceriasis* (river blindness) through pesticide sprayings of the larvae of the *simulium* black fly and the development of the drug *Ivermectin* and bringing *yaws* and *poliomyelitis* close to eradication through antibiotic and vaccination campaigns.

Fuelled by the breakthrough inventions of penicillin and DDT in the 1940s, global health security appeared to be a realizable dream for the WHO, but many of the battles in this major war have not been won. In 1955 a global eradication programme for malaria was launched, the largest of its kind in public health history. The use of DDT around human dwellings in the late 1950s and 1960s rapidly killed all mosquitoes that came into contact with it, and virtually eliminated the disease in all areas in which it was used. An illustration of DDT's success in eliminating malaria comes from comparing the numbers of infections before and after its extensive use in Sardinia, Italy. There were 78,000 cases of malaria on the island in 1942 prior to the use of DDT, compared with only nine in 1951, after several years of treatment with the insecticide (McEwen & Stephenson 1979: 23). Replacement insecticides did not match the success of DDT in its early years, and malaria resurged in Africa, South-East Asia and South America. In Ceylon (now Sri Lanka), where DDT had reduced the annual number of malaria outbreaks to seventeen by 1963, its withdrawal prompted a resurgence of the disease to greater levels than ever, reaching an estimated two million cases in 1970 (Hicks 1992). By the 1990s malaria was claiming around 1.5 million lives a year worldwide, with the disease gaining resistance to drugs such as chloroquine and mefloquine, in addition to the *anopholes* mosquito's increased resistance to DDT and other insecticides. In 1998 the WHO, abandoning all aspirations to eradicate the disease, instead launched the far more conservative 'Roll Back Malaria' campaign focusing on improving access to treatment in Africa and increasing the use of insecticide-laden nets to deter rather than eliminate the mosquitoes (WHO 2002a). This more pragmatic strategy has reaped rewards, with a 60 per cent fall in the global malaria death rate between 2000 and 2015 (WHO 2015a). Eradicating malaria, though, is no longer considered realistic by most experts.

In spite of its achievements, the WHO, along with other specialized agencies under the UN umbrella, became the target of criticism in the 1980s and 1990s for being over-bureaucratic and inefficient. The free market philosophy of US and UK premiers Reagan and Thatcher sought to challenge what they considered to be complacency in global public bodies in the same way as they had done for state bureaucracies in the USA and UK. The clearest manifestation of this challenge came with the withdrawal of those two countries from the United Nations Educational Scientific and Cultural Organization (UNESCO) in 1984 and the withholding of a proportion of the US regular budgetary contributions to UN agencies from 1985. In response, the election of the highly respected Dr Gro Harlem Brundtland (see Box 7.1) in 1998 heralded a reform of the structure of the WHO, still widely considered necessary in spite of the ebbing of Reaganite ideology and the existence of more internationalist governments in London and Washington at that time. In an exercise reminiscent of the overhauling of welfare systems in most developed states, Brundtand's measures were taken to streamline bureaucratic procedures and incorporate greater financial accountability aided by the utilization of private managerial expertise and greater levels of transparency.

The WHO has also been subject to criticism from an opposing coalition to the Reaganite free marketeers, made up of some medical professionals, humanitarian

NGOs and functionalists (proponents of greater internationalization led by specialist organizations), concerned that the organization had lost its political influence and been relegated to a purely technical advisory role. The history of the WHO can be characterized by periodic shifts in overall strategy towards achieving the aim, specified in its charter, of the 'attainment by all peoples of the highest possible level of health'. The strategy of the WHO in its early years was 'vertical' in that the emphasis of its work was on targeting specific diseases for eradication campaigns. At this stage the role of the WHO was essentially non-political since its approach of applying technical fixes to problems was universally accepted as effective and appropriate. However, once it became evident that insect and microbe resistance to antibiotics and pesticides made combating the spread of disease more complicated than had at first been anticipated, 'horizontal' strategies for achieving global health security came to be advocated in opposition to the 'vertical' orthodoxy, and the whole issue area became politicized. Horizontal strategies favour tackling underlying problems that exacerbate the effects of disease as the best means of advancing global health, and this became characteristic of WHO activities from the mid-1970s and found expression in the 'Health For All' strategy.

The horizontal approach to global health has met resistance from some states because technical quick-fixes remain popular in spite of some notable setbacks. As seen in other global issue areas, disasters trigger responses from the international community better than 'routine' suffering, and tackling epidemics head-on remains an instinctive response. The extrabudgetary funds allocated to the WHO, which finance the disease-specific programmes, have grown since the late 1970s whilst the regular budget has been frozen. This has had the effect of counteracting the horizontal ethos expounded by the World Health Assembly and Executive Board and, in the minds of some, has served to undermine pursuit of global health security. Garrett contends that the international community's emphasis on HIV/AIDS has actually worsened the overall health of many countries particularly blighted with the infection because HIV medics are often segregated from other health workers and money has drained out of public health budgets.

> Guinea-Bissau has plenty of donated ARV [HIV anti-retroviral drug] supplies for its people, but the drugs are cooking in a hot dockside warehouse because the country lacks doctors to distribute them.
>
> (Garrett 2007)

This separation occurs because of the stigma associated with the disease and the preference of international donors for working through NGOs, and is exacerbated by the brain drain of global South medics to the North.

Hence, entering the twenty-first century, the WHO found itself criticized on two fronts and its overall direction caught between that advocated by vertical 'eradicationists' (Godlee 1995) and horizontal proponents of containment. Brundt-land's stewardship saw the WHO become more open and cost-efficient, to the satisfaction of the USA and other major donor states, but it has not been afraid to court corporate displeasure. This was evident in the revamping of the anti-tobacco campaign, which in 2005 culminated in the entry into force of the Framework Convention on Tobacco Control, against much corporate opposition. It was also evident in a campaign in support of the 'essential drugs' programme which spawned two significant legal victories in 2001. Several US American pharmaceutical firms and the US government were persuaded to drop legal challenges preventing South African and Brazilian firms from marketing cheaper versions of generic HIV drugs. In both instances the legal cases had sought to uphold WTO Trade Related

---

BOX 7.1 Gro Harlem Brundtland

Few individuals can have had the influence over such a range of international political issues as three-times Norwegian prime minister Gro Harlem Brundtland. The daughter of a doctor-turned-politician, in the early 1970s Brundtland followed in her father's footsteps by swapping the physician's coat for a political career. A socialist, though married to a conservative politician, she quickly entered government as environmental minister from 1974 to 1979.

A decade later, Brundtland's credentials as an environmentalist saw her appointed as chair of the UN-sponsored World Commission on the Environment and Development (WCED), charged with the task of advancing global environmental policy. The commission helped forge the concept of sustainable development, which became the guiding ethos of future global policy, finding expression at the landmark 1992 UN Conference on the Environment and Development (UNCED) at Rio de Janeiro. Sustainable development not only put the environment firmly on the international political map but re-vamped thinking and policy on global poverty. In recognition of her contribution to this, Brundtland was awarded the Third World Foundation Prize in 1988.

Brundtland's role in the WCED coincided with her second stint as Norwegian head of government, heading the most female cabinet in history, having been the country's first woman prime minister in her first stint. After a third spell as premier in the 1990s, she returned to her roots in public health in becoming elected as Secretary-General of the WHO in 1998. A popular leader, she did much to restore the vibrancy and credibility of a position and organization that had been much criticized under her predecessor, and oversaw an unprecedented global fundraising effort to help fight disease.

Since leaving the WHO in 2003 Brundtland has brought her wide-ranging skills to The Elders: an NGO founded by Nelson Mandela comprising leading ex-statespeople seeking solutions to global problems. In 2011 she was an intended target of the racist terrorist Brevik's murder spree in Norway but, thankfully, had left before he arrived.

Intellectual Property Rights (TRIPS). A global public outcry over the cases prompted the backdown and marked a significant victory in this particular recurring clash between competing international laws satisfying the sometimes rival values of wealth maximization and human security.

The WHO's twin funding mechanism may cause confusion and attract criticism from two directions, but it does allow the organization to continue to attract public and private monies for high-profile campaigns, whilst persisting with a more socially-oriented functionalist political direction driven by the organization itself. Hence the *British Medical Journal* in a 2002 editorial declared its qualified support for the twin-track approach: 'both [horizontal and vertical programmes] are needed. Vertical programmes will be unsustainable without well functioning healthcare systems, but vertical programmes on, for example, immunization can achieve a great deal rapidly' (Smith 2002: 55).

Global public and private partnerships

The bureaucratic centralization of WHO introduced by Brundtland was accompanied by the partial outsourcing of some of its vertical operations into Global Public and Private Partnerships (GPPPs) (Buse & Walt 2000). Enterprises such as the Global Programme to Eliminate Filiarisis (GPEF), Guinea Worm Eradication Programme and (the largest of all) the Global Fund to Fight AIDS, Tuberculosis and Malaria have brought in substantial extrabudgetary funds, whilst retaining links with the WHO as one of a number of 'partner' institutions. This represented a trend throughout the UN system from the 1990s in an effort to bring in funds and revitalize the specialized agencies. Public health has been the most prominent of the issues affected owing to the centrality of the private chemical manufacturing industry to any immunization or pest control scheme. The rise of corporate social responsibility has seen much-needed cash injections into public health programmes, but concerns have been expressed that this could be detrimental to the horizontal public service ethos and work of the WHO. Some fear that the independence of the WHO could be compromised by the need to satisfy sponsors and that its overall strategy might become more diluted and/or fragmented (Buse & Walt 2000: 705). Corporations involved, at least partially, for public relations purposes may be keen to focus resources on projects likely to succeed, rather than those that are most deserving, and be more hesitant to tackle more stigmatizing diseases such as sexually transmitted diseases (Walt & Buse 2000; Oxfam 2002; London School of Hygiene & Tropical Medicine 2002).

The governance of the GPPPs, however, is not as skewed in the direction of donors and corporations as might be imagined and efforts have been made to achieve a balance of stakeholders on the governing boards, in a manner similar to that employed on WHO programmes and Expert Groups. The Executive Board for the Global Fund to Fight AIDS, Tuberculosis and Malaria comprises twenty voting members. Fifteen are government ministers (eight from donor states and seven from across the global South), three are pressure group representatives (one from the North, one from the South and one a person with HIV, TB or malaria), one is a representative from the Gates Foundation (as the major private sponsor) and one is a representative of the salient private sector (Global Fund 2016). The board acts on the advice of a Technical Review Panel made up of experts selected from individual applicants chosen by the Executive Board according to geographical and gender quotas. Hence, whilst many medics have reservations about GPPPs, Brugha and Walt, writing in the *British Medical Journal*, accepted that: 'It is only through a global fund that this kind of concerted global action between major corporate and public sector players can be achieved' (Brugha & Walt 2001: 154). That business is driven by profit and that market forces are not always compatible with the public good is obvious and something to be safeguarded against in politics, but, if the public good can be served by uniting actors with disparate reasons for achieving a similar goal, then socially-conscious politicians should not instinctively dismiss such alliances. More money on global health should be welcomed but there is a need to ensure that the public good is not compromised and the bigger picture is appreciated.

> Instead of setting a hodge podge of targets aimed at fighting single diseases, the world community should focus on achieving two basic goals: increased maternal survival and increased overall life expectancy.
>
> (Garrett 2007)

Other UN agencies and programmes contributing to global health

UNAIDS

UNAIDS was set up as a programme of the WHO in 1986 in response to the spread of the new disease, along similar lines to its other disease-fighting arms. In 1996, however, UNAIDS became a UN programme in its own right co-sponsored by ten UN agencies and programmes including the WHO, World Bank and UNESCO. This reflected the scale of the threat posed by AIDS, necessitating a response beyond the means of the WHO, but also, according to some, a lack of faith in the WHO to lead such a venture (Godlee 1994: 1494–5). UNAIDS is based in Geneva with a secretariat of over 800, divided between the headquarters and various country offices. It was the first UN organ to include pressure group representatives in its executive, although voting rights in the Programme Coordinating Board are restricted to the twenty-two government representatives, elected by the UN's Economic and Social Council (ECOSOC) according to geographical quotas. The ten co-sponsors also have permanent representation on the board without voting rights and many of their field workers carry out UNAIDS work in developing countries. UNAIDS' annual budget grew from a modest $60 million in 2001–2 to stabilize at $485 million from 2014 (UNAIDS 2016) and it has been widely lauded for its fundraising activities. Global health 'Horizontalists', though, have sometimes been critical of UNAIDS for not considering underlying problems in countries most affected by the disease, such as the criminalizing of homosexuality or neglect in helping drug users, and have advocated handing responsibility for leading international policy back to the WHO (England 2008; Das & Samarakera 2008).

World Bank

The World Bank from the outset was intended to play a role in promoting public health in LDCs through its Health, Nutrition and Population division (HNP), although it was not until 1970 that it granted a loan via this arm of its organization (Abbasi 1999). By the 1990s, however, the HNP was outstripping the WHO in its outlay on projects (Stott 1999). The 1993 World Development Report 'Investing in Health' heralded this new direction for the World Bank, inspired both by a desire to be more compassionate in its development projects and the pragmatic logic that economic growth is more likely in a healthy population. Despite this, by virtue of its nature, the World Bank's role is vertical rather than horizontal since its funds are targeted at specific countries rather than global health needs in general.

UNICEF

UNICEF was established by the General Assembly in 1947 before the creation of the WHO with the aim of providing emergency food and health care to children affected by the Second World War. It became a permanent agency in 1953, based in New York with eight regional offices around the world. UNICEF is widely seen as having shifted over its lifespan from a horizontal approach to global health, in line with the WHO, to a more selective, vertical strategy (Werner 2001; Koivusalo & Ollila 1997: 209). From standing shoulder to shoulder with the WHO at Alma Ata in 1978 when the 'Health for All' crusade was launched, by the mid-1990s UNICEF had moved closer to the World Bank in focusing on the implementation of specific projects rather than the gradualist advancement of Primary Health Care. Werner considers this not to be a shift in ideology by the organization but, rather, the effect of UNICEF being a voluntary fund and so constrained by the preference of its donors for programmes of vaccinations and drug administrations over education and structural improvement (Werner 2001). A key factor in the rise to prominence of UNICEF and particularly the World Bank has been that their point of contact with governments is through finance rather than health ministries, which are usually more politically powerful (Koivusalo & Ollila 1997: 207–8; Abbasi 1999; Godlee 1994: 1405).

The state securitization of health

The WHO Constitution states that 'the health of all peoples is fundamental to the attainment of peace and security' (preamble). Hence it was recognized in the early days of the United Nations that military stability and the security of states, the chief aims of the overall UN system, rested on more than the blend of collective security and concert power politics that made up the Security Council. This reflected a lingering of some of the spirit of Idealism soon to be diluted by the Cold War. Though the WHO proceeded to carry out some remarkable public health work during the Cold War years, greatly enhancing human security, this state security dimension to health was largely forgotten until the Idealist renaissance that came with the passing of that conflict in the 1990s.

The WHO Secretary-General Nakajima took steps to re-establish the state security–world health link and revive state interest in the organization's work in a 1997 article and series of speeches (Nakajima 1997). A further development came in 2000 when the UN Security Council adopted a resolution in response to the threat to the international community posed by AIDS. The resolution called upon the UN agencies to increase collaboration and was modest in its assessment that the 'HIV/AIDS pandemic, if unchecked, *may* pose a threat to stability and security' (United Nations Security Council 2000: 2, emphasis added). Whilst this was a remarkable understatement in the face of a scourge killing millions of people and economically undermining many states, it was still significant in that it marked the first occasion that a health issue was debated at the high table of *realpolitik*.

Hence this 'securitization' of AIDS was, like the securitization of the environment in mainstream politics, a case of considering the implications of this threat for military security rather than the general security of individual people. The term *microbialpolitik* was coined by Fidler to describe this phenomenon (Fidler 1999). The 2000 Security Council Resolution refers to the dangers posed by UN peacekeepers being infected with HIV, whilst the US State Department interest focused on the potential for disease to 'exacerbate social and political instability in key countries in which the United States has significant interests' (National Intelligence Council 2000: 2). Southern Africa is most frequently cited in this context. In Zambia three government ministers died of AIDS in the 1990s and, at the turn of the century, it was estimated that half of the police and armed forces were HIV-positive (Price-Smith 2001: 14). In particular, the threat of diseases being deliberately unleashed in acts of warfare has, since the 2001 domestic anthrax attacks in the USA, elevated questions on the availability of antidotes and the preparedness of emergency forces for combating epidemics to matters of high politics ('biodefense'). A 2003 article by Prescott in the avowedly 'traditional' security journal *Survival* argued for greater Northern aid for Southern health problems and applauded the greater international cooperation of medics in the wake of the SARS outbreak as it augured well for preparing for a bio-terrorism attack (Prescott 2003). Horrific though the spectre of biological warfare is, it is pertinent to remember that only a handful of people have ever died in this manner whereas millions every year perish as a result of diseases which, although naturally occurring, are nonetheless preventable by human endeavour.

The state securitization of health has had some positive benefits for enhancing human security. The USA was better able to deal with recurrences of West Nile virus in 2002, which had been an annual summer event since 1999, because of a strengthening of information links between hospitals motivated by fear of biological terrorism (*Economist* 2002c). In addition, essentially self-motivated policy can contribute to the global common good. President Bush (Jr), as clear an exponent of the 'national' interest as you could find, in his 2003 'State of the Union' address announced a major increase in the US contribution to the global campaign against AIDS, malaria and tuberculosis. Political stability in Africa and tackling a US problem at source may have been the chief aim of this initiative, but human security was additionally enhanced as a result. Further illustrating that traditional securitization can also be effective in establishing a precedent for giving health concerns greater international political priority, a 2014 UNSC response to the Ebola pandemic (Res. 2177) was notably different from the 2000 AIDS resolution in dispatching a public health mission to West Africa without any military rationale.

The human securitization of health

The impact that infectious disease epidemics can have on their own or another state's power capabilities is certainly something governments should factor in to their foreign policy decision-making, but the security most threatened by disease is that of ordinary people rather than states. The inappropriateness of the high politics–low politics distinction in international relations is most clearly apparent when considering health issues. Recognition of this can be dated back to the 1940s, when the discipline of International Relations was still in its infancy. David Mitrany took on the mantle of internationalism from Kant, Bentham and the Idealist statesmen of the 1920s and 1930s and developed the theory of functionalism, prescribing and predicting a future post-Westphalian world order in which people's needs would be met by functional INGOs rather than by states. Functionalism is both normative and descriptive. Mitrany considered the growth of functional international organizations (organizations with a specific function such as the OIHP) in the late nineteenth and early twentieth century to have been a boon to ordinary people's lives and something around which to build a new, better post-war world. The international system of states was alien to the needs of people since it artificially divided humanity into competitive units which overemphasized the 'high politics' of securing the state through military means at the expense of health and welfare. Hence Mitrany and the Functionalists advocated the growth of functional international organizations run not by government delegates but by internationalists specializing in the particular function concerned. The belief was not that this would happen overnight but that gradually and inexorably people would come to see that their interests were better served by such organizations and switch their loyalties away from their own states and nationalities. Thus a world revolution would occur quietly and slowly by a process referred to as 'spillover', as the functions of government transferred to a more appropriate polity which would emerge over time. Crucially, Functionalism very much advocates revolution from below and opposes world or regional federalism since this would be the creation of political institutions by politicians rather than their natural evolution, and thus risk replicating the illogical high–low politics distinction. Functionalism favours a farewell to states rather than their amalgamation into larger ones (Mitrany 1975).

The WHO is an intergovernmental rather than a true non-governmental functional organization, as Mitrany would have favoured, but it has developed an independent and global perspective from its epistemic community of experts and serving medics. It has frequently been criticized by both Functionalists and intergovernmentalists for not being fully in either of these camps, but its track record in the provision of the global good of public health is unprecedented in human history. It is inconceivable that the charitable cooperation of governments could have achieved the eradication of smallpox and so saved the lives of two million people a year. The logistics of mounting a genuinely global vaccination campaign, which had to overcome political and cultural obstacles to the intervention of foreign doctors, could only be dealt with by a body representing the whole world, rather than a powerful sub-set of it. In spite of its setbacks, the WHO has presided over a period of unprecedented improvements in human health. Life expectancies in the global South have improved markedly despite the fact that these countries continue to bear the brunt of health problems. World life expectancy (at birth) during the lifespan of the WHO has increased from 46.5 to 71.8. Whilst some of this can be attributed to economic growth, the greatest improvements have occurred in the global South (particularly Asia) and public health interventions are the major explanation for longer life. In a major study to evaluate the reasons for reduced mortality in the twentieth century, Preston estimated that, contrary to popular assumption, economic development accounted for only 15–20 per cent of the global improvement in life expectancy between the 1930s and the 1960s. Overwhelmingly this improvement was attributable to better public and professional knowledge with regard to disease prevention and cure (Preston 1975). Subsequent studies by the World Bank (1993) and World Health Organization (1999b) have corroborated this finding.

The globalization of health security

In common with the other areas of global security, globalization is for health a two-edged sword. It brings with it new threats and challenges but also new opportunities for better coping with threats both old and new. Although the opportunities for diseases to diffuse throughout humankind are greater than ever before, the means of mobilizing resistance to this are also greater than ever and can only get stronger. The widening and deepening of politics characteristic of the modern global condition offers a number of possibilities which can enhance the health security of all people and, in particular, those most insecure in the global South.

The use of information technology to advance the global dispersion of medical knowledge

Over recent years there have been major advances in the use of computer and communications technology to advance the knowledge of and means to contain and control the spread of disease. The WHO launched the HINARI Programme for Access to Health Research in 2002 in an effort to offset the perennial criticism that the fruits of globalization are rarely enjoyed globally. To improve medical knowledge in LDCs, in line with its horizontal strategy, the WHO has promoted free or low-cost internet access to thousands of online medical journals and helped make available cheap software for improving medical delivery systems. Private information systems, such as ProMED and TravelMED, perform similar services but the WHO's global reach and public orientation give their network greater significance and scope for future development.

The use of information technology to strengthen global policy

IT advances have also served to strengthen the capacity of the WHO to detect and respond to disease outbreaks at the global level. Despite concerns over the dilution of its political leadership in global health, the WHO, with its near universal membership and undoubted epistemic leadership, has been able to put itself at the forefront of this development, giving greater authority to existing global rules on disease notification and opening the way for the development of further ones. An Outbreak Verification System was initiated in 1997, to improve upon the previous system of relying on official state notifications to the WHO of significant disease outbreaks. As mentioned earlier, some governments can be coy about releasing such information whilst some might lack the capacity to do so effectively. Part of this system is the Global Public Health Intelligence Network (GPHIN), which routinely scans media sources for epidemiological information and passes it on to the WHO to verify and inform relevant authorities in an early warning system. The significance of this development is shown in the finding that of all initial reports gathered under the system in the first two years of its operation 71 per cent came from unofficial (generally media) sources rather than official ones (Grein et al. 2000: 100).

The Global Outbreak and Alert Response Network (GOARN) in 2000 further developed this capability by globalizing and coordinating various regional and disease-specific surveillance networks into a single 'network of networks'. GOARN has also worked on pooling the resources of participating states and organizations so that international teams of experts can be quickly assembled and dispatched to outbreak scenes. Hence, in 2003, the notoriously secretive Chinese government was quickly forced into coming clean after initially attempting to downplay the outbreak of severe acute respiratory syndrome (SARS). China is estimated to have lost $1,000 billion due to the SARS outbreak of 2003 but, when the second wave of the disease struck the following year, the government reported it immediately and fired the officials deemed responsible for covering up the facts in the original outbreak (Upton 2004: 76). David Heymann, head of the WHO's communicable diseases operations, has even gone so far as to suggest that, '[h]ad this system been in place in the early 1980s, AIDS might never have become a global epidemic on the scale we see today' (Heymann 2001: 12). In line with such developments, the keystone of WHO policy, the International Health Regulations (IHRs), which require governments to give international notification of epidemics, entered into force in 2007. The IHRs, which can be dated back to the International Sanitary Conventions at the dawn of global health policy, aim to extend notification obligations beyond the long-standing requirements for cholera, plague and yellow fever to all threatening diseases.

The strengthening of global civil society

Many pressure groups, such as OXFAM and Save the Children, have a long history of highlighting the plight of disease victims but recent years have seen a significant deepening of NGO activity in this field. A new breed of pressure groups have come to use advanced communications technology to assist medics in LDCs. The US-based group SatelLife, for example, make use of satellites to link medics in LDCs to their developed world counterparts. TEPHINET (Training Programs in Epidemiology and Public Health Interventions Network) was set up in 1997 and disperses help on a not-for-profit basis. The medical profession itself also increasingly lobbies at the global level. MedAct is a group comprising health professionals which campaigns for governments to give greater consideration to the health impact of their policies in areas such as military security and economic development. This is a more overtly political stance than the traditional neutrality of groups such as the Red Cross, seeking to provide relief to human suffering in crisis situations. The radicalization of pressure groups, in public health and in international relations in general, is epitomized by the work of the group Médecins Sans Frontières (MSF) (Doctors Without Borders). MSF consciously choose to ignore the constraints of sovereignty in their operations, sending in medical teams to countries without being specifically requested to enter by the government and making overtly political statements on the right of individual people to receive medical attention: a global 'right to life'. The UN–NGO symbiosis, best known in the global politics of the environment and human rights, is also evident in health. Public health pressure groups enjoy a healthy relationship with the WHO and have been extensively consulted and utilized in initiatives such as GOARN.

Greater public scrutiny of business

As with the 'greening' of petrochemical firms witnessed in the politics of the environment, greater consumer awareness has prompted MNCs operating in the developing world to improve their public image. The cynic can point to tax breaks often open to MNCs who make charitable contributions and to the advertising pay-offs of apparent philanthropism, but the fact remains that businesses are donating significant sums to public health in the developing world and contributing to a global good. At the same time, blatantly cynical activities by MNCs which undermine public health are increasingly likely to be highlighted by pressure groups and be used to damage their image in the eyes of ever more enlightened consumers. The backtrack of the pharmaceutical firms and US government over the patenting of HIV drugs in Brazil and South Africa, referred to earlier, provides a clear instance of this.

Democratization and more socially responsive government

The logic of Sen's 'entitlements thesis' (discussed in Chapter 4), that famines are less likely under democratic conditions, holds also for public health in general. Citizens empowered with the vote are unlikely to tolerate governments negligent in securing their health. The Indian state of Kerala has been highlighted by Sen and others as a case study of human development in the face of economic adversity. The state government of Kerala in the 1970s introduced a major reform package of social security provision and land redistribution in the face of significant political protest. Despite insignificant economic growth in the state, Keralan citizens' lives improved remarkably over the next two decades, including a major advance in life expectancy. Sen's advocacy of a 'support-led' approach to development does not simply equate democratic political systems with better health since he emphasizes how countries like China and Cuba have achieved better health for their people than wealthier, democratic states by having well-funded public health and education systems (Dreze & Sen 1991: 221–6). Marxist/Maoist governments generally have an instinctive, ideological commitment to public health which does not need to be prompted by society (the Keralan government was also leftist). Thus it is the globalization of socially-responsive government rather than simply democratization that has contributed to improved standards of public health.

The globalization of the public service ethos

The injection of private money into global health programmes has brought with it fears that policy could be transformed from the 'Health for All', social security approach expounded by the WHO to a more uneven charitable approach. Similar fears were expressed when developed democracies began undergoing a 'welfare backlash' from the mid-1970s when the cost of state support began to spiral due to ageing populations and higher levels of unemployment. Countries of Western Europe and North America responded, to varying degrees, by incorporating private solutions to public health in what has been described as a 'welfare mix' (Rose & Shiratori 1986). However, the wholesale dismantling of welfare state provision has not happened in any country, despite economic and political arguments favouring this, partly because public opinion considers state health provision a right and partly because public health practitioners have powerfully resisted this. Similarly, medics and scientists operating at the global level provide a powerful lobby in favour of maintaining the WHO's horizontal strategy. The epistemic community for global public health is an influential one since its opinions are generally seen as informed and clearly inspired by the provision of a public good rather than any sectional interest. The standing of the WHO was evident in 2003 during the SARS outbreak when governments and the general public interpreted their recommendations not to travel to the affected cities of Beijing and Toronto as authoritative 'bans' (much to the annoyance of the Chinese and Canadian governments), and they again became the source of global authority when the H1N1 influenza ('swine flu') pandemic caused panic in 2009. The growth of new NGOs, internationally-oriented doctors and the persistence of the WHO have together helped formulate a culture in the politics of global health in which the dominant discourse is based on a right to health for all, even though this is proving harder to achieve than imagined in the 1970s.

The WHO has recently found itself the focus of widespread criticism for its performance in the face of recent pandemics. They were widely accused of over-reaction to the 2009–10 swine flu outbreak and then of failing to act quickly enough in response to the 2014–16 Ebola pandemic. In mitigation it is worth noting that somewhere between 151,700 and 575,400 died in the swine flu pandemic which is hardly a trivial matter. Similarly, it is a myth that the WHO sat on its hands while Ebola raged though West Africa. One hundred and thirteen experts were dispatched early on after the outbreak by an organization hampered by 13 per cent cuts to its budget imposed by member-states and by private companies ignoring its advice and restricting trade and travel to the region (Kamradt-Scott 2016). In addition, local failings provided extra hurdles to the WHO, with the government of Guinea falsely claiming that they had the disease under control and criticizing their Liberian counterparts for asking for assistance. In addition, much of the press in Liberia were also critical of their government and argued that the disease was a hoax cooked up by Western pharmaceutical companies. In essence, whilst the WHO unfairly shouldered the blame for widespread public health failings, this reaction, in fact, was indicative of a widespread recognition of their centrality in global health politics. Appreciation of the WHO from the global general public remains high on both a pragmatic level, spurred by personal security fears, and on an empathetic level, due to greater awareness of the suffering of others.

Conclusions

Whilst the global nature of health and its centrality in life and politics are barely contestable, the question of securitizing such concerns remains divisive. As with addressing poverty or environmental change, many within civil society instinctively recoil at the idea of securitizing health. The head of MSF, Andre Perache, for example, has argued that this approach 'risks distorting priorities and moving resources away from other more pressing health needs' (Horton 2017: 892). In contrast, Heymann from the WHO contends that 'global health security is a tool of foreign policy and we should be glad of that. Global health security strengthens public health. It mobilizes financial and technical resources. And it saves lives in all countries by preventing epidemic diseases' (Horton 2017: 892).

There is good reason to worry about populism and state interest distorting the advance of public health but, ultimately, the two are not opposing goals. Aside from the human security logic of acting on global public health issues, a simple widened security state-utilitarian logic also supports action. Benatar, Daar and Singer argue that:

> it is both desirable and necessary to develop a global mindset in health ethics, we also suggest that this change need not be based merely on altruism, but could be founded on long-term self interest. For example, it has been shown by mathematical modelling for hepatitis B that resources needed to prevent one carrier in the United Kingdom could prevent 4,000 carriers in Bangladesh, of whom, statistically, four might be expected to migrate to the UK. Thus it would be four times more cost-effective for the UK to sponsor a vaccination programme against hepatitis B in Bangladesh than to introduce its own universal vaccination programme.
>
> (Benatar, Daar and Singer 2003: 133)[2]

 Key points

- Increased human movements and societal changes, associated with contemporary globalization, have heightened the cross-border threat posed by both transmittable and non-transmittable illnesses.
- Technical solutions to combat diseases were successful from the 1940s to the 1970s, most notably in the eradication of smallpox by the WHO, but increased resistance to drugs and pesticides has prompted a resurgence of some diseases like malaria.
- This setback prompted the WHO to advocate a more 'horizontal' approach to global public health in which alleviating the underlying causes of vulnerability to disease is stressed. At the same time the 'vertical' approach of seeking to eradicate diseases continues to be pursued by the WHO in alliance with private donors.
- The traditional state security implications of diseases like AIDS have attracted greater governmental interest in global public health policy.

- Globalization may be a cause of global health problems but it also offers opportunities for enhancing global health security through the harnessing of transnational information flows to disseminate medical knowledge and by empowering the WHO to coordinate policy.

Notes

1   Some of the regions are only loosely geographical; 'Eastern Mediterranean' comprises most of the Arab world, Iran, Afghanistan and Pakistan; South-East Asia includes India and North Korea; Australia and New Zealand are linked to much of East Asia in the 'Western Pacific region'.
2   This estimate is based upon N. Gay & W. Edmunds (1998) 'Developed Countries Should Pay for Hepatitis B Vaccine in Developing Countries', *British Medical Journal*, 316: 1457.

Recommended reading

Elbe, S. (2010) *Security and Global Health: Toward the Medicalization of Insecurity*, Cambridge: Polity Press.

Lee, K. and McInnes, C. (2016) *Framing Global Health Governance*, London: Routledge.

Pirages, D. & Runci, P. (2011) 'Ecological Interdependence and the Spread of Infectious Disease', in Cusimano, M. (ed.) *Beyond Sovereignty: Issues for a Global Agenda*, 4th edn, Boston: Wadsworth, Cengage: 264–81.

Rushton, S. & Youde, J. (2015) *Routledge Handbook of Global Health Security*, London: Routledge.

Useful web links

- Global Fund to Fight AIDS, Tuberculosis and Malaria: www.theglobalfund.org/en/
- UNAIDS: www.unaids.org/
- World Health Organization: www.who.int/en/

Chapter 8

Natural threats to security

> *We cannot stop the forces of nature, but we can and must prevent them from causing major social and economic disasters.*
>
> Kofi Annan, UN Secretary-General, 1999 (Annan 1999)

Natural disasters

A major source of insecurity for much of the world's population is rooted in the natural, non-living world, from physical phenomena originating in the Earth's interior, its atmosphere and even from beyond our planet. The phrase 'Acts of God' encapsulates the notion of human helplessness in the face of such dangers which are out of our control, but the truth is that natural disasters are as much socio-political as geological or meteorological phenomena. '[A] disaster is the intersection of two opposing forces: those processes generating vulnerability on one side, and physical exposure to a hazard on the other' (Blaikie et al. 1994: 22). It is socio-political factors that make people vulnerable to hazardous natural events. The fact that people live, whether through their own choice, ignorance or compulsion, in places known to be prone to disaster is one such factor. Another is the capacity and/or willingness of governing authorities to take steps to mitigate the potential human cost of events known to be likely to occur.

Table 8.1 illustrates not only the horrific scale of human casualties that can accrue from natural disasters but also the importance of the socio-political component in such events. The Huang Ho and other Chinese rivers are more prone to dramatically bursting their banks than most of the world's waterways, but this has been well known in China for centuries. Overpopulation, poor government and the human propensity to risk residing in such hazardous places for the benefits of farming on the fertile soils deposited by the flooding are major contributors to the shocking death toll that has accumulated over time. The annual death toll by natural disaster is more variable than the other issues considered in this book but, in terms of sudden deadly impact, events like the 2010 earthquake in Haiti and the 2004 tsunami in South Asia – which both claimed well over 200,000 lives – far outstrip any recent wars or insurgencies.

Historically, floods and earthquakes have presented the greatest natural hazards to human life but, in the 1990s, windstorms claimed more lives. These three categories of disaster have continued to account for thousands of deaths per year in the twenty-first century, as Table 8.2 illustrates. Statistics since the turn of the millennium, however, differ from previous eras since three particular events, the 2003 and 2010 heatwaves in Western Europe and Russia and the 2004 Indian Ocean tsunami, were far and away the most calamitous incidents of their kind in history and have elevated the position of these phenomena to higher than ever before.

TABLE 8.1 The ten worst natural disasters in history

	Place	Date	Type	Fatalities
1	Huang Ho River, China	1931	flood	3.7 million (i, ii)
2	China	1959	flood	2 million (i, ii)
3	Upper Egypt & Syria	1201	earthquake	1.1 million (iv)
4	Huang Ho River, China	1887	flood	900,000 (iii)
5	Shaanxi, Shanxi & Henan, China	1556	earthquake	830,000 (iii)
6	Huang Ho River, China	1938	flood	500,000 (ii)
7	China	1939	flood	500,000 (i, ii)
8	Bangladesh	1970	cyclone	300,000 (i, ii)
9	Tang-shan, China	1976	earthquake	242,000 (i)
10	Indian Ocean	2004	tsunami	227,000 (i)

Sources: (i) CRED 2011; (ii) Disaster Center 2003; (iii) Castello-Cortes & Feldman 1996; (iv) NGDC 2003.

TABLE 8.2 Average annual death toll by types of natural disaster, 1996–2015

1	Earthquakes	24,920
2	Tsunamis	12,507
3	Windstorms	11,956
4	Extreme temperatures	8,293
5	Floods	7,503
6	Droughts	1,115
7	Avalanches/landslides	902
8	Wildfires	74
9	Volcanic eruptions	36

Source: CRED 2016.

Earthquakes

Earthquakes, more clearly than any natural hazard, demonstrate the centrality of the social component in the onset of a disaster. Though the scale of seismic shocks in the Earth's crust cannot be entirely predicted, the places where such shocks occur are well established. Seismic activity is most pronounced on the margins of the Earth's tectonic plates, such as along the San Andreas Fault Line, which marks the point at which the Pacific plate meets the North American plate. The threat to humanity posed by earthquakes is almost entirely due to the secondary effects of seismic waves destroying the human infrastructure built in such susceptible areas rather than the event in itself. The following secondary effects are particularly dangerous:

1   *Surface faulting*: Direct death by earthquake is rare but possible if someone is killed by a fall into a fault line, which has been widened or moved by seismic waves. More commonly, though still a relatively minor form of earthquake-related fatality, people can be killed by buildings being dislodged in this way.

2   *Ground motion*: Of far greater significance than faulting is the shaking effects of seismic waves on the Earth's surface. A combination of the waves' amplitude, frequency and duration will determine how much ground motion they create. This is generally most pronounced near the earthquake's *epicentre* (the point on the surface directly above the source of the seismic wave, the *focus*). Ground motion in itself is not especially hazardous but the effects it has on the human environment can be devastating.

   (i)   *Falling buildings*: The most common cause of death during an earthquake is as a result of the collapse of dwellings or other constructions. Recent history's most calamitous earthquakes, in Tang-shan, China in 1976 and Haiti in 2010, each killed nearly a quarter of a million people in this way. In both cases most of the city's buildings were destroyed during the principal earthquake and many of those that survived were then toppled by the aftershocks that followed. Hence, the design and location of buildings in earthquake-prone areas is a critical factor in the scale of security threat they represent. In some cities in locations vulnerable to earthquakes, such as Tokyo and San Francisco, the security threat to citizens is significantly diminished by the implementation of regulations requiring particular safety-conscious engineering techniques (such as using steel-reinforced concrete) in the construction of buildings.

   (ii) *Fire*: The structural damage caused by earthquakes can prove lethal in ways other than crushing victims with masonry or causing them to fall to their deaths. A common knock-on effect is the spread of fire through a town hit by an earth tremor. Most of the casualties of the famous earthquakes that hit San Francisco in 1906 and Tokyo in 1923 were killed in fires instigated by damage to cookers and heating equipment. In Tokyo fire swept through wooden dwellings specifically designed to avoid the sorts of casualties associated with the fall of stone buildings.

   (iii) *Liquefaction*: Deaths may also result from earthquakes when geological conditions permit ground water to seep to the surface due to seismic disturbance in a process known as *liquefaction*. This can result in major land subsidence or flooding. It is in this way that many of the victims of the 1985 Mexico City earthquake perished.

(iv) *Landslides*: Earthquakes can also pose a hazard by prompting the fall of stones or soil from a hillside overlooking a town.

Tsunamis

The Japanese word 'tsunami' (meaning literally 'harbour wave') is the correct term for what are sometimes erroneously referred to as 'tidal waves'. These giant sea waves are not produced by tides but by seismic activity such as volcanic eruptions and, particularly, earthquakes (hence they are sometimes classified as a facet of earthquake disasters). Tsunamis generally have a wave-length of between 100 and 150 kilometres (around 100 times the size of an ordinary sea wave) and can travel hundreds of kilometres at speeds ranging between 640 and 960 km/h. On the high seas, however, they can be very difficult to detect since their height may be no more than a metre (Whittow 1984: 554). By far the most devastating tsunami in history occurred in December 2004 in the Indian Ocean, triggered by earthquakes along the margins of the Indian and Eurasian tectonic plates near Aceh, Indonesia and the Andaman Islands of India. Over 220,000 people were killed as a result of rapid coastal flooding in Indonesia, Sri Lanka, India, Thailand, Malaysia, the Maldives and Somalia (CRED 2011).

Though historically they are comparatively rare, tsunamis appear to have become more common and deadly in recent years. In 2011 the most powerful earthquake ever recorded to have struck Japan (9.0 on the Richter scale) triggered a tsunami that swept vast waves over towns along the north-east coast of the country, leaving 28,050 people dead and many thousands more homeless (CRED 2011). The Japanese authorities were well prepared for an earthquake – even of this intensity – but less so for the consequent tsunami.

Windstorms

Cyclones

Known variously as hurricanes (in North America) or typhoons (in East Asia), cyclones are storm systems based on an area of low atmospheric pressure in tropical climes. Storm-force winds circulate around the calm 'eye' of the weather system (anti-clockwise in the northern hemisphere, clockwise in the south) accompanied usually by torrential rains. The most devastating consequence of a cyclone is coastal flooding caused by a *storm surge*, when winds create huge sea waves. It was in this way that upwards of 300,000 people were killed around the Ganges delta in Bangladesh in 1970. Deadly wind damage and riverine flooding can also result from cyclones.

Tornadoes

Like cyclones, tornadoes are storms which rotate around an eye of very low atmospheric pressure. However, in contrast, they tend to be narrower and faster and generally originate inland rather than at sea. The world's most deadly tornado occurred again in Bangladesh when 1,300 people were killed around the town of Saturia in 1989 (Castello-Cortes & Feldman 1996: 27). Owing to their narrow, funnel-like shape, the destruction caused by tornadoes tends to be quite localized, although they move across the surface in a somewhat unpredictable manner. Damage by tornadoes tends to be of three forms:

1   *High winds*: Extremely strong winds associated with tornadoes can cause significant damage to buildings, either directly or through the propelling of debris.
2   *Updraught*: The circulatory winds and low pressure vortex can cause large objects and even people to be 'sucked up' the tornado funnel and deposited up to several kilometres away.
3   *Effect of low pressure*: The extremely low air pressure in the eye of the tornado is the most hazardous element of the phenomenon. Buildings caught in the eye are prone to explode because of the resultant difference in pressure inside and outside of the walls.

Sandstorms

Sand and dust carried by windstorms can also present serious threats. Desertification has increased the frequency of this in recent decades and sandstorms now present a regular menace across the Sahara, Middle East and China. The misery of residents in war-torn Homs in Syria, for example, was compounded in 2015 by a sandstorm which claimed at least a dozen lives.

Floods

Floods, historically, are far and away the biggest security threat to humanity from the non-living world. Although overtaken by windstorms in recent years, most of these fatalities were also the result of flooding triggered by the effect of cyclones. Floods often occur as secondary effects of other natural phenomena but can present a direct hazard to human life in a number of ways.

Flash floods occur when heavy rainfall exceeds the capacity of the ground to absorb the water and causes a rapid, widespread deluge. Nearly 2,000 people were killed in north-western Pakistan in this way in 2010 (CRED 2011). *Riverine floods* occur when precipitation causes a river to burst its banks. This is the most dangerous type of flooding since it is relatively common and rivers frequently run through densely populated areas. The Huang Ho river system in China can lay claim to being the most hazardous natural feature on Earth having claimed millions of lives over the centuries. Additional flooding hazards can occur when an excessive inflow from rivers as a result of snow melt causes lakes or seas to flood.

Drowning, obviously, is the major means by which floods can kill but this can happen in a number of ways. People may simply be engulfed by rising waters, become trapped in buildings or cars or caught in river sediment deposited by the waters. Collapsing buildings and trees form an additional significant hazard and structural damage may also lead to deaths by electrocution and even, with grim irony, fires. Hypothermia and water-borne diseases are also often associated with flooding. Flooding, though, only represents a hazard when it is not predictable. The regular, seasonal flooding of rivers can not only be managed but utilized for its human benefits since silt deposits from rivers bursting their banks provide fertile soils. It is instructive that, in spite of the devastation flooding has brought to the region, the Bengali language includes a word for flood with a positive connotation. Of the two most used terms, *barsha* refers to the usual and beneficial floods, whilst the word *bona* is reserved for more infrequent and destructive deluges.

Avalanches/landslides

Sudden mass movements of snow and ice down a mountainside, known as avalanches, can kill by directly smothering people in a valley or, more commonly, by destroying buildings. 'Wet' snow avalanches, which tend to occur in spring when mountain snows begin to melt, tend to be the most destructive. The biggest ever avalanche disaster occurred in Peru in 1970 when nearly all of the 20,000 inhabitants of Yungay were killed when an earthquake triggered a wet 'slab avalanche' of ice and glacial rock to fall down the side of the country's highest mountain, Nevado Huascaran. Airborne powder-snow avalanches are less hazardous but can also kill as they are frequently preceded by avalanche winds which can cause houses to explode as a result of rapid changes in air pressure (Whittow 1984: 45).

Landslides are a common knock-on effect of other geothermal and meteorological phenomena and are sometimes man-made, but can occur independently by the natural process of gravity acting on soil and rock accumulated on a hillside. Typically, rainwater is the catalyst for this process. A period of torrential rainfall in northern China in 2010, for example, prompted mudslides in Gansu which led to 1,765 fatalities (CRED 2011).

Extreme temperatures

Both 'hot waves' and 'cold waves' can kill. The deadliest recorded heatwaves hit Western Europe in 2003 and Russia in 2010, both claiming over 50,000 lives (CRED 2011). Dramatic short-term rises in temperature can kill through heatstroke, and cold waves can kill directly by hypothermia or frostbite, but most casualties are more long-term and subtle. Most cold-wave deaths are caused indirectly as a result of power lines freezing or heavy snow crushing dwellings. Most heatwave deaths are a result of an exacerbation of existing illnesses in the old and infirm. Unpredictability is the key danger in these events. The 38°C temperatures that Moscow and other Russian cities experienced in August 2010 would not have killed in other parts of the world but there they were unprecedented and unprepared for.

Droughts

Prolonged periods of unseasonable hot weather can also, of course, be deadly by drying soils and shrinking the water supply. The principal human security cost from these droughts is famine, although, as discussed in Chapter 4, this is very much a political matter since stockpiling food and water is a reasonably straightforward matter.

Wildfires

Wildfires are prominent in woodland regions with an arid climate and strong winds. Droughts and hot winds can dry vegetation which may then be ignited by lightning or other forces causing fires which spread to other trees or shrubs carried by the wind. The USA and Australia are particularly prone to wildfire in the summer. The worst ever disaster occurred in 1871 in the US states of Wisconsin and Michigan, when around 1,500 people perished (Smith 2001: 248). Australian bushfires of 1974–5 burned around 15 per cent of the whole country (ibid.) and, in 2009, claimed 180 lives (CRED 2011).

It is debatable, however, whether wildfires should be considered natural disasters at all since most of them, ultimately, are man-made, resulting from the negligent management of forests or the accidental spread of fire from discarded cigarettes or camping activities. A US study found that, over the past forty years, the principal spur for forest fires has changed from lightning to humans, with 97 per cent of Californian blazes started by people (Balch et al. 2017). Indeed, it has become increasingly apparent in recent years that many wildfires are not only not natural but are not accidents either. Many of the aforementioned wildfires in California are known to have occurred as a result of arson, for insurance scams or other criminal motives. There was a public outcry in Australia in 2002 when it transpired that the 2001–2 'Black Christmas' fires that devastated large areas of New South Wales were deliberately started by a number of youths and young adults for no clear motive. The human aspect, whether deliberate or accidental, has become more significant with the increased encroachment of settlements into wooded areas, and wildfires are becoming more common and even a regular phenomenon in certain places.

Volcanic eruptions

The threats to human life from volcanic activity come in many, diverse forms:

1   *Lava flows*: The most familiar threatening image of volcanicity is the sight of molten lava flowing down the hillside. Today, though, lava flows represent a minor threat to life since they are generally sufficiently slow and well enough observed to permit the evacuation of nearby settlements.
2   *Pyroclastic flows*: More deadly than lava flows are the movements of mixtures of volcanic gases and debris that can be formed on the side of a volcano. The Roman city of Pompeii, famously, was destroyed in this way and the highest death toll by volcanicity in the twentieth century was similarly accounted for when 29,000 people were killed near Mount Pelee on Martinique in 1902.
3   *Lahars (volcanic mudflows)*: Volcanic debris mixed with water can also form a deadly agent, principally since this moves further and more quickly than lava or pyroclastic flows. The 1985 Nevada del Ruiz eruption in Colombia killed 23,000 people in this way when a relatively small eruption produced pyroclastic flows which mixed with snow at the summit and flowed many kilometres down the valley, engulfing the town of Armero.
4   *Tephra*: Various solid objects can be spat out at high speed during a volcanic explosion. Chunks of molten lava chilling in the air to form 'volcanic bombs',

volcanic glass and ash may be showered onto residential areas. Eruptions of Mount Pinatubo in the Philippines in 1991 killed over 200 people principally as a result of tephra collapsing the roofs of houses in nearby settlements. Tephra may also create knock-on disasters by downing aeroplanes, instigating lightning and damaging infrastructure and crops. A famine occurred following the 1815 Tambora eruption in Indonesia, the largest and most deadly volcanic eruption in history, killing 82,000 people in addition to the 10,000 direct deaths from tephra and pyroclastic flows (University of North Dakota 2002).

5   *Poisonous gases*: Many toxic chemicals can be emitted by volcanic eruptions, including carbon dioxide, carbon monoxide, sulphur dioxide, hydrogen sulphide and gaseous forms of hydrochloric and sulphuric acid. It is even possible for poisonous gases to be released from a volcano without any eruption. In Cameroon in 1986 1,700 people were killed by a cloud of carbon dioxide released from Lake Nyos, a crater on a dormant volcano (a *caldera*). The gas had seeped out of underground magma into the lake and was then released into the atmosphere owing to some sort of disturbance to the water (Coch 1995: 97).

Space invaders – natural threats to security from other worlds

Although they have yet to greatly impact human society, natural phenomena emanating from beyond the Earth must also be seen to represent a security threat. 'An asteroid of size 1km or more hitting our world at the minimum possible velocity (11km/s – the escape velocity of the Earth) would release at least as much energy as 100,000 one-megaton hydrogen bombs' (Kitchin 2001: 54). Asteroids are minor planets within our solar system which vary in size from a diameter of around a thousand kilometres to less than one kilometre. Most lie between the orbits of Mars and Jupiter, but some, the 'Earth Crossing Asteroids' (ECAs), can cross this planet's orbit of the Sun. The ECAs together with comets and meteoroids (debris from asteroids or comets) which pass close to the Earth are collectively referred to as 'Near Earth Objects' (NEOs). The possibility of one of these celestial objects striking the Earth, and the likely effects, has been the subject of increasing speculation in recent years and some measures have been taken to improve the capacity to predict if such a collision could occur and initiate thinking on how it could be avoided. The 'Torino Scale' has been devised to rationalize the likelihood of asteroid collision (Peiser 2001) (see Table 8.3).

There are no validated records of human deaths due to NEO collisions but there is evidence that such events have occurred. Meteoroids regularly enter the Earth's atmosphere (what are referred to as *meteors*), where most burn up and disappear, but some survive long enough to strike the surface (*meteorites*) or explode close to the surface (*bolides*). Evidence that comets can collide with planets was provided in 1994 when *Shoemaker-Levy 9* was observed crashing into Jupiter. The 'Cretaceous/Tertiary Impact', caused by either a comet or an asteroid, 65 million years ago created the 250-km-wide Chicxulub crater in the Gulf of Mexico and is widely held as responsible for the extinction of the dinosaurs and various other life forms. A bolide is believed to be responsible for the 1908 phenomenon around the River Tunguska in Siberia when over a thousand square kilometres of uninhabited forest was flattened. In 2013 clear proof that meteoroids pose a human threat was

TABLE 8.3 The Torino Scale

0	Events having no likely consequence	collision will not happen
1	Events meriting careful monitoring	collision is extremely unlikely
2 3 4	Events meriting concern	collision is very unlikely 1% chance of localized destruction 1% chance of regional destruction
5 6 7	Threatening events	significant threat of regional devastation significant threat of global catastrophe extremely significant threat of global catastrophe
8 9 10	Certain collisions	localized destruction (occur every 50–1,000 years) regional destruction (occur every 1,000–100,000 years) capable of causing global climate catastrophe (occur less than once per 100,000 years)

Note: This scale was devised by Professor Richard Binzel.

provided elsewhere in Russia when a filmed bolide in Chelyabinsk caused hundreds of injuries.

Surveillance of the night sky for early detection of NEOs has increased since the launch of the Spaceguard initiative by NASA in the early 1990s and its subsequent link-up with other national schemes as part of the UN-authorised International Asteroid Warning Network. What could be done if an NEO was set for collision with the Earth remains to be established, however. Military solutions have figured prominently in discussions. The possibility of destroying an NEO by nuclear strike has been aired regularly, particularly in the USA, the state most likely to be able to attempt such an action. Nuclear deterrence is always a divisive security measure, however, and a less dramatic strategy of deflecting an NEO off course by crashing an unmanned spacecraft into it is now more commonly suggested.

The rise of human vulnerability to nature

Natural disasters are, of course, as old as humanity. Even older, if the risk posed to other animals from natural events, such as the fate that befell the dinosaurs, is considered. Although the overall historical trend has been downwards since the 1930s, the frequency and deadliness of natural disasters have increased since the early 1990s. A number of factors have contributed to this:

Poverty

Between 1996 and 2015 the death rate per disaster was five times higher in low-income than in high-income states (CRED 2016). Clearly money can buy some degree of security from natural disasters. More particularly it is the sort of well-evolved legal environment associated with economic development that brings security to people. 'It is not an "Act of God" that no more than 10 per cent of the multi-storey structures in Indian cities are built according to earthquake resistant norms' (Wisner 2000). Striking evidence of this was provided in 2010 when two major earthquakes struck the Americas. A month after the Haiti disaster devastated the western hemisphere's poorest country, comparatively wealthy Chile was rocked by a earthquake that was 500 times as powerful but claimed only 500 lives.

Bankoff, however, cautions that shifting the focus for dealing with natural disasters from technical responses to tackling underlying vulnerability carries a danger of conflating securing those at risk with modernization and traditional notions of economic development. Designating large proportions of the population of the global South as 'vulnerable' reinforces the notion that such people can only be 'saved' by technical assistance from the North (Bankoff 2001). Some aspects of economic globalization have served to make LDC populations more vulnerable at the same time as furthering their economic development. Prioritizing economic growth over safety has sometimes served to make LDC populations more vulnerable at the same time as advancing their 'development' by encouraging them to live in overcrowded cities. Additionally, the 2005 New Orleans floods in the wake of Hurricane Katrina demonstrated that inadequate governance and social exclusion can render sections of the population of wealthy, developed countries insecure. The devastation caused by the 2011 Japan tsunami and 2010 New Zealand earthquake also served as reminders that development, democracy and experience do not guarantee human security.

Better information

There is a case to be made that one key factor behind the recent rise in natural disasters is simply that more are being reported in the world's media. The ever extending lenses of the global media and concerted efforts of a developing global epistemic community continue to bring more events than ever before into focus. The annual number of recorded natural disasters in the world was consistently in double figures in the 1970s and 1980s but has been in triple figures since 1990 (Swiss Re 2012).

Population growth

Since 'if people are not involved there is no disaster' (Loretti 2000), the more people there are in the world the increased likelihood there is of a natural hazard having human security consequences and becoming a natural disaster. As significant population growth in the world is now largely confined to the global South, where disaster mitigation policy tends to be as underdeveloped as the economy, ever greater numbers of people are being exposed to natural hazards.

Urbanization

The burgeoning population of the global South in the main manifests itself in the growth of major cities. Around half of these new *megacities* which have emerged are located in areas prone to seismic or storm activity. Most of the quarter of a million people who perished as a result of the Haiti earthquake in 2010 were residents of shanty towns clinging to the hillsides that surround the capital, Port au Prince. Whilst not anywhere near the scale as in the global South, even in the world's wealthiest countries a correlation between urbanization and natural disasters can be seen. The increased regularity of flooding in many towns and cities is now known to be linked to the concreting and tarmacking over of grassland as homes encroach into the countryside. In 2015, when at least sixteen people were killed in floods on the Côte d'Azur in France, local authorities blamed the unprecedented deluge on the disappearance of natural escapes for the rainwater owing to building work (Lichfield 2015).

Land degradation

As in the previous illustration, natural disasters can be triggered or exacerbated by a lack of natural defences. Hence, changes in land use can have disastrous side-effects. For example, the loss of traditional vegetation on river banks can increase the likelihood of flooding, and on hillsides can make land slips more likely (UNEP 2002: ch. 3, p. 10).

Refugees

Increased flows of refugees and internally displaced people over recent years have contributed to the increase in number and deadliness of natural disasters. Desperate and increasingly unwelcomed people are likely to settle in insecure places. Many amongst the largest contemporary refugee movements, from Afghanistan, Iraq and Syria, have settled in earthquake-vulnerable regions of Turkey and Pakistan and been prominent amongst the victims of recent disasters.

Climate change

Natural hazards can be understood to occur for rational, natural reasons. Tropical cyclones, for example, can be viewed as 'safety valves' which dissipate the build-up of excessive heat in the ocean or atmosphere (Ingleton 1999). The progressive warming of the planet, then, can be correlated to the increased prominence of windstorms over recent decades. The 2003 and 2010 European heatwaves provided even clearer evidence of a correlation between global warming and natural disasters.

Global economic forces

In the same way that new health and environmental threats can be linked to social change prompted by global economic forces promoting modernization, so too can those from natural hazards. Changes to the human–environmental equilibrium can prompt natural disasters or make people more susceptible to 'regular' hazards. In addition, the traditional relationship between people and natural phenomena may be weakened by globalization. Societal coping mechanisms can develop over time in areas prone to extreme meteorological or geothermal events and these might be undermined by profound socio-economic changes related to modernization and development. For example, flooding in Central America and South-East Asia is believed to have worsened due to the construction of dams and roads through tropical forests (Hiller & Nightingale 2013).

Well-meaning outside interventions can sometimes even prove unhelpful. Traditional tactics for dealing with flooding in Bangladesh, which include building portable houses, burying precious possessions and responding to certain behaviour patterns in animals associated with an imminent cyclone, have tended to be overlooked by outside agencies. A report on NGO activity in Bangladesh found that well-equipped relief agencies were sometimes less prepared for a flood than the local population, with serious consequences since they had assumed control of response operations (Matin & Taher 2000). Civil society has learned from this to be more inclusive, such as in appreciating that local people can be aware of smells, sounds and animal behaviour that are a precursor to a river flood. However, governments seeking to employ technical solutions often continue to think they know best and ignore such inputs (McGilvray & Gamburd 2010; Dewan 2015).

In thinking about natural disasters, then, 'vulnerable' should not simply be conflated with 'undeveloped' or 'poor', even though there is clearly some correlation. Various factors, natural and social and local and global, combine to render certain individuals vulnerable to natural hazards. From a 'horizontal' perspective, the strategies most effective for securing vulnerable people from the risks presented by natural hazards come from reducing their vulnerability through societal learning and empowerment. The less vulnerable of the world can assist in this with emergency assistance and technical applications to tame the effects of natural hazards, but also by tackling their own contribution to exacerbating the effects of such hazards. Progress on the former has, to date, been much more impressive than the latter.

Preparing for the unexpected – the global politics of natural disaster management

The horizontal versus vertical approaches debate seen in combating global disease resurfaces in the global politics of natural disasters.

Traditional security responses

Natural disasters present a straightforward basis for governments to widen state security since armed forces can easily be utilized for relief operations. In India a specialist military unit, the National Disaster Response Force, was set up in 2005 and has been engaged regularly since in leading rescues and relief operations during floods, cyclones and also building collapses. The post-Cold War 'peace dividend' in Europe has seen armies increasingly engaged in this non-military function, as is most clearly illustrated by the increased prominence of NATO in this sphere of activity.

In a classic instance of traditional security widening, part of the post-Cold War restructuring of NATO saw, in 1998, the establishment of a unit at its Brussels headquarters to utilize military resources to protect citizens from natural rather than military threats. The Euro-Atlantic Disaster Response Coordination Centre (EADRCC) is a tiny cog in the NATO machine but its creation epitomized not only a widening of its notion of security but also the widening of its sphere of operations beyond the defence of NATO member-states. The EADRCC is, in fact, coordinated by the Euro-Atlantic Partnership Council (EAPC), in which the twenty-eight NATO states are linked to twenty-two non-NATO partner states, and emerged from a proposal by one of those partners, Russia. NATO has had a role in disaster relief dating back to 1953 when North Sea floods prompted the initiation of a 'Policy on Cooperation for Disaster Assistance in Peacetime', but the EADRCC has enhanced this significantly.

A Euro-Atlantic Disaster Response Unit (EADRU), comprising both military and civilian experts from the EAPC countries, has been dispatched by the EADRCC to many prominent recent disasters within the EAPC area, such as to the USA for Hurricane Katrina and most notably outside of this area to Pakistan in 2005 when the government requested help with earthquake relief operations. Coordination with the UN is aided by deploying EADRCC staff at its Office for the Coordination of Humanitarian Affairs (OCHA). The success of this NATO operation has prompted the emergence of a similar regional international mechanism for the Association of South East Asian Nations (ASEAN), the Agreement on Disaster Management and Emergency Response (AADMER), which entered into force in 2009.

Disasters can sometimes inspire acts of security cooperation and conciliation which are at odds with diplomatic hostility. The 'disaster diplomacy' warming of relations between Greece and Turkey after earthquakes ravaged both countries in 1999 is a classic case of two governments and societies overcoming cultural and political differences when faced with a common foe. At one level this was a case of basic human empathy at the societal level triumphing over *realpolitik* and then being reciprocated, but Ker-Lindsay demonstrates that the case is more revealing than that. The level of cooperation between the two governments, which surprised the rest of the world, was a result of an agreement reached at a meeting of foreign ministers a few months before the earthquake (Ker-Lindsay 2000). Turkish foreign minister Cem and his Greek counterpart Papandreou had met principally to discuss the regional military security implications of the crisis unfolding at that time in Kosovo. Sharing a common concern about the possible spread of conflict to other parts of the Balkans and the flow of refugees from Yugoslavia which was already happening, the two traditional foes engaged in uncharacteristically cordial dialogue. One dimension of this, barely noticed at the time, was to offer reciprocal help in the instance of a deadly earthquake striking either country. Relations between the two governments remain somewhat frosty on certain issues but have certainly continued to be better than for many years prior to 1999 and societal contact has increased since the disasters. This represents a clear case of spillover and the partial establishment of a *security community*, with sectoral cooperation promoting wider cooperation between governments and bringing people closer together through realizing their common interests. A similar scenario was witnessed in 2001 when the destruction wreaked by earthquakes in India prompted offers of relief from Pakistan and the first contact between the two countries' leaders for two years. Such occurrences may assist in improving relations but security communities require more systematic levels of cooperation and information-sharing to be able to develop.

As with other non-military issues, though, the national security framing of natural disaster threats can lead to inappropriate solutions. In 2010–11 a cholera epidemic occurred amongst Haitians who had been re-housed by UN troops after the earthquake, due to the installation of inadequate sanitary systems in the new dwellings, which, ultimately, resulted in over 10,000 deaths. A SIPRI study of troop deployments in the aftermath of disasters found that such operations have the advantage of being able to quickly mobilize large numbers of people but, on the debit side, tend to be expensive and poorly coordinated with humanitarian agencies (SIPRI 2008).

The rise of horizontal policy

Proponents of a horizontal approach have become more prominent in recent years, challenging traditional assumptions that the best way to minimize human suffering from 'Acts of God' is through the refinement and better application of technological solutions or post-disaster troop deployments (a vertical approach). It has long been apparent in domestic politics that security from disaster comes from the 'long game' of reducing vulnerability. Penning health and safety legislation rather than sending in the troops is what secures people from natural hazards. An added factor behind the disparity in death toll between the 2010 earthquakes in Haiti and Chile, referred to earlier, is the democratization of the latter set against the political instability of the former. Stringent national building safety codes had evolved though a period of democratic stability in Chile, and the Bachelet government responded rapidly and efficiently to the disaster (Smith & Flores 2010). There is good evidence that democratic citizenship provides some measure of security from natural disaster. Civil society in Turkey was jolted into life by the 1999 earthquakes and a major pressure group campaign critical of the government and existing legislation of a kind not seen before emerged. Consequently a crisis centre was created by the government and responses to a second earthquake that year were much more efficient (Smith & Flores 2010).

The appliance of science, indisputably, is vitally important in developing strategies to predict when disasters are likely to occur, lessen their human impact when they do occur and assist in the process of recovery from damages that accrue. 'Horizontalists', however, contend that securing people from the effects of natural disasters is as much a social as a technical task. Security for people threatened by natural hazards cannot be achieved by tackling the physical causes of their risk if social factors making them vulnerable are not addressed. 'In many cases nature's contribution to "natural" disasters is simply to expose the effects of deeper, structural causes' (IFRC 2001: introduction).

The International Decade for Natural Disaster Reduction (IDNDR)

The 1990s were designated as the International Decade for Natural Disaster Reduction by UN General Assembly Resolution 46/182 in 1989, following the recommendation of a specially commissioned ad hoc group of experts. The decade inspired unprecedented levels of international cooperation in this policy area and the formation or deepening of numerous epistemic communities for particular disaster forms. The decade also, however, witnessed an upsurge in the number of fatalities from natural disasters, which served to illustrate that transnational scientific cooperation, though welcome, was not enough.

The IDNDR approach was largely technical and vertical. A number of sectoral initiatives were launched such as the Global Fire Monitoring Centre, Tsunami Inundation Modelling Exchange Programme and Tropical Cyclone Programme which improved transnational early warning capacities. A number of pilot studies were also activated during the decade by coordinating the work of existing international organizations such as UNEP, WHO and the World Meteorological Organization (WMO) who collaborated in trial runs for a Heat/Health Warning System to better anticipate extreme weather.

The 'horizontalist' Britton says of the decade:

> There is little doubt that IDNDR was effective in encouraging nations to focus attention on the threat posed by natural hazards and in creating an environment wherein greater international collaboration was fostered. Nevertheless, the fundamental task of reducing societal consequences of disaster reduction remained.
>
> (Britton 2001: 45)

The Secretariat of the IDNDR itself admitted: 'The application of science and technology was recognized as being essential for reducing the risk of natural disasters, but in the early years of the decade, it became evident that this was not sufficient by itself' (Jeggle 1999: 24).

The International Strategy for Disaster Reduction (ISDR)

To continue the work undertaken under the IDNDR, a successor UN body was established in 1999 and launched in 2000. The ISDR was adopted at the 1999 IDNDR Programme Forum and then ratified by both the UN General Assembly (54/219, 22 December 1999) and ECOSOC (E/1999/63, 30 July 1999). The ISDR has a small secretariat based in Geneva under the authority of the Under-Secretary-General for Humanitarian Affairs, and a policy-making body, the Inter-Agency Task Force on Disaster Reduction (IATF/DR), chaired by the same person.

The ISDR declare that their overriding aim is: 'To enable all societies to become resilient to the effects of natural hazards and related technological and environmental disasters, in order to reduce human, economic and social losses' (ISDR 2002a: 1). This aim is to be achieved in four ways: (1) stimulating public awareness; (2) obtaining the commitment of public authorities; (3) promoting interdisciplinary cooperation; and (4) fostering greater scientific knowledge (ISDR 2002a: 2).

The ISDR has incorporated more horizontal, mitigation-based approaches in its overall strategy than during the IDNDR. 'Vulnerability to disasters should be considered in a broad context encompassing specific human, social/cultural, economic, environmental and political dimensions, that relate to inequalities, gender relations and ethical and racial divisions' (ISDR 2002b: 21).

In a similar manner to that seen in the politics of health, the horizontal approach to securing people against natural hazards has come to prominence through its promotion by *epistemic communities* and operates alongside higher-profile vertical strategies. The ISDR maintains research on technical solutions to particular forms of hazard but has a far more holistic approach than that seen during the IDNDR. UN agencies have also shifted the emphasis towards a more horizontal strategy. From 2001 the UNDP began work on the first World Vulnerability Report, an annual index to aid disaster mitigation based on identifying where the world's most vulnerable populations, from a socio-economic perspective, are located. Whilst it might be expected that the UNDP would approach the problem of natural hazards from a socio-economic perspective, a more surprising convert is the World Bank, who have moved well beyond lending money just for post-disaster reconstruction. The Disaster Management Facility (DMF) established in 1998 aims to improve state preparedness

---

BOX 8.1 Paddy Ashdown

The UK Liberal politician Paddy Ashdown was commissioned by the British government to lead a review of international disaster relief operations in 2011. After a distinguished military career, Ashdown entered politics and served as leader of the Liberal Party between 1988 and 1999. He subsequently has worked in a variety of diplomatic roles with the UN, most notably serving as High Representative for Bosnia and Herzegovina between 2002 and 2006.

Ashdown's Humanitarian Emergency Response Review considered that 'the UN is the only legitimate authority that can lead but is often too weak and slow to do so', and proposed the following key factors to be given greater emphasis in its work on disasters:

- **Resilience** – invest in infrastructure to avoid disasters occurring.
- **Leadership** – the UN should invest in 'leadership cadre'.
- **Innovation** – more thought is needed on how best to respond to disasters. For example money may be more effective than blankets or food.
- **Accountability** – recipients of relief aid must be consulted so that social issues, such as vulnerability and gender, can be accounted for.
- **Partnership** – relief should be multilateral and involve NGOs.
- **'Humanitarian space'** – there is a need to think about the political context of a disaster – e.g. work with 'neutral' NGOs where states are not welcome, be prepared to get UN support for military support where this is necessary.

(Ashdown 2011)

through insurance and better public education (Arnold & Merrick 2001). In the sphere of global civil society the Global Disaster Information Network was launched in 1998 linking experts from academia, industry, IGOs, pressure groups and governments with the express purpose of providing information to potential victims rather than money to victims after the event.

In 2006 the Central Emergency Response Fund (CERF) was established after a resolution of the UN General Assembly (60/124), to manage the dispersal of emergency aid (for war and disease as well as disasters). Despite this, there is still a notable unevenness in international disaster aid donations. In 2010 eight times as much was spent on each earthquake-affected Haitian as on each flood-affected Pakistani (Ferris & Petz 2011: 23).

Additionally, international responses to disasters still tend to be after the event rather than pre-emptive. This is not only less effective but also often wasteful. In 2006 the government of Mozambique requested £2 million of emergency aid which would have been sufficient for them to prepare against imminent floods but, shorn of tragic images to project to the world, no supply of funds was forthcoming. When the subsequent floods duly arrived, the international community dug deep, but too late, to find £60 million (Ashdown 2011). Hence there remains dissatisfaction with the capacity of the 'international community' to respond to disasters, as illustrated in Box 8.1.

However, the epistemic consensus on a horizontal approach has made inroads in international political practice. The Sendai Framework for Disaster Risk Reduction agreed at the Third UN Conference on Disaster Risk Reduction in 2015 sets out seven targets for the ISDR to lead efforts towards achieving by 2030: (1) Reduce mortality; (2) Reduce numbers affected; (3) Reduce economic losses; (4) Reduce damage; (5) Increase national risk reduction strategies; (6) Support LDCs; (7) Increase early warning systems. Accompanying these aims are four 'priorities for action', which are more explicitly horizontal in their approach: (1) Understand risk; (2) Strengthen risk management; (3) Invest in risk reduction and recovery; (4) Enhance preparation and 'build better' recovery (ISDR 2017).

Conclusions

As with the global politics of health, the horizontal approach to securing the lives of those most prone to natural disasters has steadily gained credibility in epistemic communities and in the global polity, but struggles to win the hearts and minds of governments and the general public of countries moved to help those people. Despite efforts at improving global management, humanitarian aid still tends to be after the event rather than pre-emptive. The long game of promoting education, economic development and local empowerment is simply less 'sexy' than sending in relief workers and raising charitable donations. 'It is hard to gain votes by pointing out that a disaster *did not* happen' (Christopolos, Mitchell & Liljelund 2001: 195). In 2013 Chancellor Merkel toured parts of Germany affected by flooding mindful of the political capital in recent German history from acts of 'disaster statesmanship'. When Gerhard Schroeder regained the chancellorship at the 2002 German elections it was widely felt that his crisis management during recent devastating floods secured victory in a tight election. To put it another way, Schroeder won *because* German flood defences failed. Had they succeeded he would have been denied the opportunity to don his waders and demonstrate compassion and leadership in the media spotlight.

The 2004 Indian Ocean tsunami and 2010 Haiti earthquake prompted impressive global relief operations but also demonstrated how unnecessarily insecure large swathes of humanity are in the current world. Global governance, driven by human security rather than sporadic bouts of human compassion, could have saved most of the tsunami victims: specifically through the implementation of an early warning system of the kind operated in the wealthier Pacific rim and, more generally, through the appreciation of the way in which vulnerability turns natural hazards into human tragedies. Additionally, the very fact that such calamitous tragedies would not register on the 'seismographs' of narrow (and some wider) security scholars serves as a reminder as to the irrelevance of such approaches to the discipline.

Inter-state competition and sovereignty have little to offer when it comes to dealing with natural disasters, other than the occasional deployment of troops to help after the event. Sharing security information in this context carries no risks and can only serve to make states more secure. As with other issues, 'securitization' by widening rather than deepening can lead to a misallocation of resources. The concern that the 'war on terror' may be hampering governments in dealing with other threats to their citizens became apparent in 2005 with the US administration's response to the New Orleans disaster. The first batch of relief supplies sent to the area by the Federal Emergency Management Agency (FEMA) was made up of materials intended for dealing with the aftermath of a chemical terrorist strike.

Natural disasters are global problems in both a natural geographic and human sense and state borders are irrelevant in both regards. The natural dimensions can better be countered by a pooling of human efforts and ingenuity and the socio-economic dimensions of vulnerability can better be addressed by global action. Global problems require global solutions and natural disasters are doubly global problems.

 **Key points**

- Natural disasters are socio-political phenomena since it is human vulnerability to natural hazards, rather than the hazards themselves, which chiefly accounts for the security threat they pose.
- Earthquakes represent the biggest contemporary 'natural' human security threat, followed by tsunamis, which are usually triggered by earthquakes.
- Human vulnerability to natural hazards has increased in recent years due principally to population growth and movement in the global South.
- Global policy to mitigate the effects of natural disasters has traditionally been dominated by technical fixes, such as increasing predictive capacity, but recently has begun also to address the underlying socio-political issue of human vulnerability to hazards.

Recommended reading

Blaikie, P., Cannon, T., Davis, I. and Wisner, B. (2005) *At Risk: Natural Hazards, People's Vulnerability, and Disasters*, London and New York: Routledge.

Coppola, D. (2015) *Introduction to International Disaster Management*, 3rd edn, Oxford: Butterworth-Heinemann.

Hannigan, J. (2012) *Disasters Without Borders: The International Politics of Natural Disasters*, Cambridge: Polity.

Hobson, C., Bacon, P. and Cameron, R. (2014) *Human Security and Natural Disasters*, London: Routledge.

Smith, K. and Petley, D. (2013) *Environmental Hazards: Assessing Risk and Reducing Disaster*, 6th edn, London and New York: Routledge.

 Useful web links

- Centre for Research on the Epidemiology of Disasters (CRED): www.cred.be/
- International Asteroid Warning Network: http://iawn.net/
- NATO 'Euro-Atlantic Disaster Relief Coordination Centre': www.nato.int/eadrcc/home.htm
- United Nations International Strategy for Disaster Reduction: www.unisdr.org/

Chapter 9

Accidental threats to security

> *If the daily global casualty rate at work would be concentrated in one place, it would be all over the first pages of the world's newspapers.*
>
> Karl Tapiola (ILO 2005)

Accidents will happen? The nature and form of man-made accidents

Of all of the issues considered in this volume, (entirely) man-made accidents, in their various forms, are least frequently thought of, and hence acted upon, as matters of security. However, unnatural structural or mechanical failings represent a major risk to human life throughout the world and it is a risk that has grown over time and looks likely to continue to do so. The absence of explicitly threatening causal factors, be they non-human or human with 'malice aforethought', has led to accidents being, to a certain extent, accepted as 'one of those things' and safety from them not becoming securitized in the same way as other causes of harm. Most accidents, though, are avoidable and rooted in contemporary human societal practices that are becoming more widespread throughout the world. As such, 'technological' and 'traditional' accidents are actually no more unavoidable than other social systemic problems like war and crime. In particular, accidents have underlying socio-economic causes inextricably linked to the global politico-economic system. As for all the issues of global security, with accidents the not so fickle finger of fate points in familiar directions: towards the poor and the weak. Africans are three times more likely to die in road accidents than Europeans even though they are far less likely to own a car (WHO 2017).

TABLE 9.1 The world's worst ever transport disasters

	Place	Date	Type	No. killed
1	Philippines	1987	Ferry crash (Dona Paz)	4,000 (ii)
2	Salang Tunnel, Afghanistan	1982	Fire in road tunnel	2,000 (i)
3	Haiti	1993	Ferry sunk (Neptune)	1,800 (i, ii)
3	Mississippi, USA	1865	Steamship exploded (Sultana)	1,800 (iii)
5	North Atlantic	1912	Ship sunk by iceberg (Titanic)	1,500 (ii)
6	Senegal	2002	Ferry sunk (Joola)	1,200 (ii)
7	Japan	1954	Ferry (Toya Maru)	1,172 (i, ii)
8	Egypt	2006	Ferry sunk (al-Salam)	1,028 (ii)
9	Canada	1914	Ship sunk (Empress of Ireland)	1,014 (ii)
10	New York, USA	1904	Ship fire (General Slocum)	1,000 (ii)

Sources: (i) Ash 2001; (ii) CRED 2011; (iii) Potter 1992.

Transport accidents

Major transport disasters have politicized safety issues over the last one hundred years with domestic security measures frequently enacted by governments after the event. Many states re-wrote maritime safety legislation after the infamous *Titanic* disaster exposed weaknesses in the provision of lifeboats and other procedures and this also provided the spur for the first international policy. This 'closing the stable door after the horse has bolted' approach was witnessed following a number of the disasters listed in Table 9.1.

However, just as the iceberg that sank the *Titanic* revealed but a tiny fraction of its full dangerous form to the doomed ship, the chief risk to life posed by travelling is largely unappreciated. As illustrated in Chapter 1, road traffic accidents claim well over a million lives per year worldwide, the biggest cause of all deaths apart from disease, and it is a figure that continues to rise. Such deaths occur so regularly and so universally that they tend not to attract the sort of attention given to sporadic ferry, rail or air crashes and have for some time been almost uncontroversial. Short argues that the scale and predictability of this toll has served to distort the meaning of the word 'accident'. These are not accidents in the traditional sense of being unforeseen events since we expect them and also know that it is the poor who bear the brunt of the carnage (Short 2012: 143–4). The vested interests of the oil industry, car manufacturers and motorists blind us to this hugely clumsy 'elephant in the room'.

This complacency has, to some extent, begun to change in the global North in recent years as data, showing significant disparities in deaths between countries, has proved that the toll can be reduced through governmental action. Hence the French government in 2003 initiated a campaign focused on better enforcement of existing speeding restrictions which saw an immediate 20 per cent cut in annual deaths (WHO 2004b). Similarly, road deaths in New York in the 2000s were lower than when counting began in the 1920s, and have halved in Sweden since 2000 (*Economist* 2014). Invariably where domestic safety standards are relatively lax, deaths on the road are relatively high. Sometimes, as in the case of France, cultural factors associated with risk and motor travel can explain laxer standards but, usually, the most secure motorists drive on roads regulated by the most stringent legislation in the most developed and wealthy states.

Domestic political action on accidents has tended to be more stringent, however, for public rather than private transport. The greater bursts of killing in train, aeroplane or ferry crashes tend to be more newsworthy and heighten both public anxiety and a governmental sense of responsibility. Again, however, insuring against such events is a cost much more likely to be absorbed in countries developed enough to sacrifice some profit for safety. The prominence of ferry disasters in the global South in Table 9.1 bears this out. Packing more bodies on a ferry pushes up the profits but also the danger level. It is a similar story with air travel. Global deaths in the 2000s have halved from what they were in the 1970s but much of the remaining toll is attributable to flights with older aircraft in the global South (ICAO 2011; Aviation Safety Network 2017).

Structural accidents

Like transport accidents, disasters due to structural failure have occurred for as long as construction has been part of human life but have become far more common and dangerous in the industrialized age. Improved safety standards for public buildings in most countries have seen deaths reduced from a high point in the latter half of the nineteenth and first half of the twentieth century. However, accidents of this form cannot be eliminated altogether in a modern world characterized by crowded urban living and working. It is instructive to note that the Great Fire of London in 1666, which destroyed most of the city, claimed only an estimated five or six lives since escaping low burning buildings was straightforward. Urbanization is today most pronounced in the countries of the global South where safety standards are usually as underdeveloped as the economy, and it is here where the chief threats lie.

TABLE 9.2 The world's worst structural accidents

	Place	Date	Type	No. killed
1	Mecca, Saudi Arabia	2015	Stampede	2,411 (iv)
2	Santiago, Chile	1863	Fire in a church	2,000 (iii)
3	Chungking, China	1949	Spread of dockside fire	1,700 (i, ii)
4	Canton, China	1845	Theatre fire	1,670 (i)
5	Hakodate, Japan	1934	Urban fire caused by chimney collapse	1,500 (i, ii)
6	Mecca, Saudi Arabia	1990	Collapse of pedestrian tunnel	1,426 (ii)
7	Baghdad	2005	Bridge collapse due to stampede	1,199 (ii)
8	Shanghai	1871	Theatre fire	900 (i)
9	Vienna	1881	Theatre fire	850 (i)
10	St Petersburg	1836	Fire at circus	800 (i)

Sources: (i) Ash 2001; (ii) CRED 2011; (iii) Smith 2001: 319; (iv) AP 2015.

Note: Excludes structural disasters instigated by natural phenomena.

As with natural disasters, though, economic development is no panacea, as is evidenced from seeing wealthy Saudi Arabia at the top of Table 9.2. In 2015 during the Hajj over 2,000 chiefly foreign pilgrims died in a stampede at Mina near Mecca when a bottleneck was created by huge numbers of people arriving from different directions onto a particular street. This was not the first major disaster to occur during the Hajj. Over 1,400 perished due to the collapse of a tunnel in 1990 and there have been several other incidents before and since this. Over 400 of the pilgrims killed in 2015 were Iranian, which served to further sour relations between Riyadh and Tehran already strained by the Syrian and Yemeni civil wars and a general Sunni–Shi'a 'cold war'. The Iranian government blamed the 2015 and previous disasters on poor Saudi event management born of complacency, with their pilgrimage coordinator Said Ohadi stating, 'it is not God's will, it is man's incompetence', and Ayatollah Al Khameni going further and declaring that 'they murdered them' (BBC 2016).

Industrial accidents

Most clearly associated with modern living is industrialization, which is itself associated with far more hazardous forms of employment and production than pre-industrial economic activity. Table 9.3 illustrates that, like structural disasters, major industrial disasters can be prevented. Most of the disasters listed occurred in countries in the early stages of industrialization and economic development.

TABLE 9.3 The world's worst industrial disasters

	Place	Date	Type	No. killed
1	Bhopal, India	1984	Chemical leak	17,500
2	Hineiko, China	1942	Mining disaster (explosion)	1,549
3	Dhaka, Bangladesh	2013	Collapse of block of factories	1,129
4	Courrières, France	1906	Mining disaster (explosion)	1,099
5	Jesse, Nigeria	1998	Oil pipeline fire	1,082
6	Chelyabinsk, USSR	1989	Gas pipeline explosion	607
7	Oppau, Germany	1921	Chemical plant explosion	600
8	Texas, USA	1947	Ship carrying fertilizer exploded in port	561
9	Cubatao, Brazil	1984	Petroleum plant fire	508
10	Lagunillas, Venezuela	1939	Oil refinery fire	500

Source: Centre for Research on the Epidemiology of Disasters (CRED) 2017, www.cred.be/.

Notes: Excludes disasters instigated by natural phenomena, military strikes, or military accidents. Lightning strikes caused explosions of arsenals in Rhodes, Greece in 1856 and in Brescia, Italy in 1769 claiming around 4,000 and 3,000 lives respectively (Ash 2001: 215). Dambursts are also excluded. Notable examples of military accidents include: the explosion at an ammunition dump in Lucknow, China in 1935 which killed 2,000; the explosion of the ammunition ship Mont Blanc after collision near Halifax, Canada in 1917 which killed 1,963; and the explosion of ammunition trucks in Cali, Colombia in 1956 which killed 2,700 (CRED 2011).

Chemical

The world's worst ever industrial accident occurred at Bhopal, India on 3 December 1984. During the production of the pesticide *Carbaryl* the plant, run by the US-based MNC *Union Carbide*, accidentally released 40 tonnes of the highly-toxic chemical methyl-isocyanate (MIC) used in the production process. Between 15,000 and 20,000 people living near the plant were killed and around 500,000 other people have since suffered from a range of long-term health effects and birth defects (*Encyclopedia Britannica* 2015). As an intermediate chemical (rather than the end product), MIC did not feature on the world's foremost safety inventory of the time, UNEP's International Register of Potentially Toxic Chemicals, and Indian authorities were unaware that it was being stored. Consequently, medics had no clear understanding of how to treat survivors. Investigations also proved that safety standards on the plant were weak and that previous fatal accidents had occurred.

According to Dudley, at a 1986 'Chemistry After Bhopal' conference organized by the chemical industry a spokesman likened the disaster to the sinking of the *Titanic* (Dudley 1987: x). In the same way that the world's most infamous transport disaster prompted an evaluation of safety standards but not the abolition of passenger sea travel, industrial chemical production should not be restricted on the back of one major disaster, it was claimed. Whether Bhopal was a freakish one-off, however, is disputed. The disaster prompted a rise in pressure group activity and academic research into chemical safety in the developing world which suggested a reversal of the *Titanic* analogy was more appropriate. Bhopal, rather, represented the tip of the iceberg with many less visible disasters lying submerged from public and political view. Twenty years on from Bhopal the International Labour Organization (ILO) suggested that the Indian government had reported 231 work-related fatal accidents when the true figure was nearer 40,000 (ILO 2005).

Nuclear

The two most significant nuclear accidents of the twentieth century occurred in the two superpowers of that age whose unprecedented levels of international political influence were built on that very power source. In 1979 at the Three Mile Island nuclear power plant in Pennsylvania a technical malfunction caused a release of radioactive gas from one of the reactors. There were no confirmed casualties from this accident but it attracted huge publicity which was seized upon by anti-nuclear protesters, and the US nuclear industry began to scale down as a consequence. The 1986 Chernobyl disaster in the former USSR was the worst ever nuclear power plant disaster and, in line with the added 'fear factor' associated with this form of energy production, stands as history's most notorious industrial disaster to date. Lax safety standards are generally held as the key reason for an explosion and fire which destroyed one of the plant's four power reactors and released huge amounts of solid and gaseous radioactive material into the surrounding area. Thirty-two plant and emergency staff were killed in the immediate aftermath of the explosion and, in the following weeks, some of the radioactive material was deposited over a large swathe of northern Europe prompting an unknown number of long-term deaths. In 2011 nuclear safety was again put in the spotlight with the Fukushima Daiichi nuclear power station disaster, prompted by the devastating tsunami that struck Japan. Three workers were killed and thousands of residents moved out of the region and, whilst levels of public radiation exposure were officially reported as not being dangerous, many fear that significant longer-term health defects are yet to emerge.

Structural

The second worst industrial disaster in history, in 2013, was a work-related structural failure rather than a case of pollution. Over a thousand clothing workers, from several firms, perished in the Savar building collapse in Dhaka, Bangladesh. It transpired that extra storeys had been added to the building and workers had been told to continue operating there despite engineers expressing safety concerns at this extension.

As with transport disasters and most human security threats, however, large-scale and/or high-profile disasters like at Dhaka, Bhopal and Chernobyl represent only a small, highly visible, fraction of the full picture. The vast majority of accidents in the workplace are individual or small-scale. The International Labour Organization (ILO) have estimated that around a third of a million people a year in the world are killed in occupational accidents (including traffic accidents whilst working) (ILO 2011). If deaths when commuting to or from work and by illness caused at work are included, the figure rises to over 2.3 million (Tampere University 2014).

Personal injury

In addition to those risks encountered whilst travelling, working and congregating in public buildings, people also face a diversity of risks to their lives at home or at leisure. Electrical appliances and cooking facilities characteristic of modern living present another component of 'everyday danger' confronting an ever-increasing

TABLE 9.4 The top causes of accidental death in 2015

Form of accident	Deaths
Road traffic injuries	1,361,700
Falls	527,700
Drowning	323,800
'Mechanical forces' (e.g. guns, tools, suffocation)	200,600
Fires	176,000
'Foreign body' (e.g. choking)	151,600
Adverse effects of medical treatment	99,800
Animals	94,000
Poisoning	86,400
Environmental exposure to cold and heat	45,200
Other non-transport	134,200
Other transport	104,900
Total	3,305,900

Source: *Lancet* 2016.

proportion of the world's population. For example, the WHO estimate that over 300,000 people – mainly children playing – drown every year (Haagsma et al. 2016). Table 9.4 lists the most prominent causes of accidental death across all of the categories, and it is clear that many of these result from personal, domestic activities such as fires caused by deep fat fryers and children drowning in ponds. Again, domestic safety legislation has served to improve safety in the home in many countries but there is an observable tendency to accept the possibility of such 'mundane' ways to die.

The collateral damage of industrialization? The rise of accidental threats

Deaths by accident are very much a feature of the modern world. There have, of course, always been accidental deaths, but this form of threat to human life is closely associated with technological development and has risen in accord with industrialization and the onset of modernity. In fact it is possible to argue that accidents, in terms of their perception as such, did not exist for most of human history. The advent of modern science was significant in providing a means for comprehending unfortunate acts as something that could be explained and hence avoided. Green argues that: 'Before 1650, an accident was merely a happening or an event, and there appears to have been no space in European discourse for the concept of an event that was neither motivated nor predictable' (Green 1997: 196).

People are killed today in a variety of non-technological accidents, such as by drowning, but most accidental deaths are an unfortunate by-product of technological development. Health and safety legislation in developed countries has succeeded in reducing the potential hazards associated with transport, industrial production and the use of public buildings but, at the same time, people continue to travel more than ever and the industrial production and transportation of potentially hazardous substances continues to increase.

Smith posits that 1984 was a watershed year for technological disasters (Smith 2001: 322). As well as the Bhopal disaster, that year also saw a petroleum fire in Cubatao in Brazil kill 508 people and a petroleum gas explosion in Mexico City claim 452 lives. In total, more people were killed in major incidents in 1984 than in all technological disasters of the previous forty years. In particular, the three prominent disasters were in LDCs avidly pursuing industrial development. This served to demonstrate that, as with natural disasters, there was a socio-economic dimension to industrial accidents. The vast majority of such deaths prior to 1984 had been attributable to small-scale accidents in the developed world, giving credence to the notion that these were an unfortunate but inevitable form of collateral damage offset by the overall social gains to be had from sustained economic growth and mass consumerism. Two decades on, the 2013 Dhaka clothing factory disaster told a similar story. Bangladesh was the world's second largest clothing exporter and introduced a minimum wage and union rights only after this disaster. The scale of the problem in industrializing LDCs or 'emerging markets' now far outstrips that in the global North. The death rate for workers in advanced industrialized states is half that of India and China and construction workers in developing countries are ten

---

BOX 9.1 Warren Anderson

Warren Anderson was the Chairman of Union Carbide at the time of the Bhopal disaster in 1984. It is alleged that Anderson was directly involved in cost-cutting exercises and was fully aware of the safety shortcomings at the Bhopal plant. On flying to India from the USA after the disaster he was arrested for 'culpable homicide' but freed on bail. He returned to the USA and never faced justice even though he was subject to an extradition request by the Indian government. He was officially recognized by Interpol as an international fugitive and was even an absconder from justice within the USA, where he failed to appear in court on civil charges for compensation from the disaster. The fact that he was regularly tracked down by the press and pressure groups (particularly Greenpeace) at large homes in Florida and New York marked him out as an unusual sort of fugitive. The US and Indian governments did not appear to try particularly hard to bring him to justice. Union Carbide and the Indian government reached an out-of-court settlement over the disaster in 1989 in which $470 million, well below the original claim, was to be paid to victims and their families. The Indian government, mindful of the importance of economic links with the USA, tried to reduce the charges against Anderson to the non-extraditable offence of negligence, but this was rejected by the Indian courts and he remained 'on the run' from justice until a comfortable death in his nineties in 2014.

---

times more likely to die at work than their industrialized world counterparts (University of Bergen 2014).

The 1984 disasters also illustrated that technological accidents had become an international political economy issue in another dimension. It became clear on investigation that safety standards at Union Carbide's Bhopal plant were far more lax than at their home plant in West Virginia. The disaster gave ammunition to pressure groups and commentators concerned that globalization was a 'race to the bottom' in which MNCs would escape domestic safety constraints and seek out low-wage, low-safety sites for their operations. A similar backlash followed the 2013 Dhaka disaster when it became apparent that many leading Western retailers had sourced their garments from this creaking death trap.

An added transboundary and global dimension to workplace accidents comes from the disproportionate number of victims who are migrant labourers. Whilst confirmed figures are not available, reports have suggested a shocking death toll in the United Arab Emirates and Qatar, countries with two of the highest proportions of migrant workers in the world, and the latter in the spotlight due to a massive construction drive towards hosting the football World Cup in 2022. Over 400 Indian and Nepalese construction workers in Qatar (who make up around half of the total migrant workforce) died in both 2013 and 2014 (ITUC 2014). Adding climate change into this growing phenomenon of precarious migrant labourers working outdoors in some of the world's hottest countries has led the UNDP to estimate a steady rise in such deaths, as well as losses in productivity (UNDP 2016). Even in the country with what are regularly suggested to be the world's highest living standards and most liberal immigration policies, Norway, migrant workers are nearly three times as likely to suffer an accident at work as the working population as a whole (Langeland 2009).

Risky businesses – the idea of risk society

The inherent risks of modern living prompted sociologists in the 1990s to construct a new framework for thinking about both societies and accidents, encapsulated in the term 'risk society'. This idea posits that modern (or post-modern) society has gone beyond thinking of accidents as avoidable and accepts them as an inevitability. Hence insecurity becomes a part of life. Most of the conveniences and benefits of modern living come with some associated side-effects. The huge toll of fatalities on the road is largely tolerated by societies because of the gains to be had from personal mobility. The most rigorous health and safety legislation could not make working in a modern petrochemical plant or offshore oil platform entirely safe. The workers know this but accept the risk in exchange for monetary reward in excess of what they might be expected to receive in a safer occupation.

The gamble of taking on some degree of risk in order to achieve greater reward than attainable by safe behaviour is, of course, simple to understand in terms of individual behaviour and is as old as history. What characterizes today's 'risk society' as different from previous generations, though, is the social dimension of risk taking. Individuals can choose to play it safe by avoiding hazardous forms of transport or employment but may have to accept the possibility of a radiation leak from their local nuclear power plant. Such an individual would probably gain a pay-off from cheaper electricity but would be a largely involuntary participant in the deal and more vulnerable as well as wealthy, whether they like it or not. From the perspective of society at large, avoiding all risk can be costly and even increase insecurity. Leiss and Chociolko make this case in appealing for greater appreciation that the benefits to be had from developing new pharmaceuticals or pesticides outweigh the costs, even when this is calculated in human lives. 'We ask individuals and groups to abandon all unreasonably risk-averse stances and to recognize that our well-being as a society depends upon continuous risk-taking activity' (Leiss & Chociolko 1994: 16).

The perception of the social dimension of risk, then, is crucial in determining the political demands societies make of their authorities, beyond even the 'real' risk. Proponents of nuclear energy have long been irritated by the fact that the public in developed countries have demanded far greater restraints on this activity than on other power stations with worse accident rates. An irony of the backlash against nuclear energy after the 2011 Fukushima disaster is that it has led to a revival of electricity powered by coal, an industry which has a far worse accident rate. In this case, of course, the calculation is complicated by 'fear of the unknown' born not only of ignorance but of a genuine lack of clarity as to the hazard presented by nuclear radiation. A more clear-cut instance of rationality being distorted comes from contrasting public attitudes and government policy on transport safety. Travelling by rail is demonstrably far safer than travel by road. Statistics for the USA show that you are nearly twenty times more likely to die in a car accident than a train crash (and nearly 720 times more likely to die in a motorcycle crash!) (APTA 2016).[1] The sporadic though rare horror of train disasters compared to the steady background drip of car crashes compels governments to illogically favour the former in transport safety expenditure.

The leading exponent of the risk society paradigm, Ulrich Beck, has also advanced the thesis that risk society is increasingly a global social phenomenon.

> The new dangers destroy the pillars of the conventional calculus of security: damages can scarcely still be attributed to definite perpetrators, so that the polluter-pays principle loses acuity; damages can no longer be compensated financially – it makes no sense to insure oneself against the worst-case ramifications of the global spiral of threat.
>
> (Beck 1999: 142)

Securing those at risk in the world – international policy on accidents

The ILO and industrial accidents

The lead agency dealing with industrial accidents within the United Nations system is the International Labour Organization (ILO), which has a long history actually predating the UN. The ILO was founded in 1919 as part of the League of Nations system, absorbing the work of the International Association for Labour Legislation which had been set up in 1901. The ILO's 1929 *Prevention of Industrial Accidents Recommendation (R31)* incorporated a resolution of the previous year's International Labour Conference (ILC) that information be collated systematically on accidents and their causes. Numerous ILO conventions dealing with worker safety have been drafted and signed in the decades since, culminating in the 1993 Prevention of Major Industrial Accidents Convention (C174). Amongst the key requirements placed on ratifying states of this convention are:

- Article 4: the formulation, through consultation with stakeholders, of state safety policies.
- Article 16: the dissemination of information on safety measures on how to deal with an accident and prompt warning in the event of an accident.
- Article 17: siting hazardous installations away from residential areas.
- Article 22: ensuring the prior informed consent of importing authorities before exporting substances or technologies to other states prohibited for safety reasons in your own state.

These provisions are in accord with received wisdom on industrial safety and the domestic legislation of most industrialized countries, but many of them are ambiguous and the convention, as a whole, is surprisingly short for a legal document on such a broad, technical issue. A further limitation comes from the fact that it is also written into the agreement that the provisions do not apply to the nuclear industry, to military installations or to off-site transportation (except pipelines). Despite all of this, twenty years after the convention had entered into force in 1997 only eighteen states had ratified it.[2] This is, in part, due to the snail's pace of international legislation but it can also be seen that most governments do not pay much attention to international safety policy. The ratification rate for older ILO safety conventions is little better. The 1985 Occupational Health Services Convention (C161), which requires that a state's occupational health services advise employers and workers on safety, had, by 2017, been ratified by only 33 of the ILO's 187 member-states. This is particularly telling since, whilst many developed states can cite the fact that they have more thorough domestic legislation as a basis for not ratifying the Accidents Convention, the ILO consider that few non-ratifiers to C161 do have equivalent existing laws (Takala 1999: 4).

In order to improve ratification and increase the general awareness of occupational hazards, the ILO in 1999 launched the 'In Focus Programmes on Safety and Health at Work and the Environment' (known as 'SafeWork'), headed by Takala. SafeWork are unequivocal in their belief that injuries and deaths are not an inevitable side-effect of modern work. 'If all ILO member states used the best accident prevention strategies and practices that are already in place and easily available, some 300,000 deaths (out of the total of 360,000) . . . could be prevented' (Takala 2002: 6).

Chemical safety policy

The obvious hazard inherent in trading chemicals across borders has prompted the most extensive of all global regimes in the industrial safety sphere. Two similar regimes, developed in the 1980s and implemented in the 1990s around the principle of 'Prior Informed Consent', bear testimony to Beck's assertion in support of his risk society thesis that: 'In contrast to material poverty . . . the pauperization of the Third World through hazard is contagious for the wealthy' (Beck 1992: 44). The 1998 Rotterdam Convention[3] and 1989 Basle Convention[4] initiated effective international regulatory systems compelling the exporters of, respectively, chemicals or hazardous wastes to notify state authorities in the importing country if the material is restricted in the country of origin. These agreements provide some safeguard against the exploitative dumping of dangerous materials in countries poorly equipped to deal with them but also help wealthy countries feel surer that such dangerous substances will not revisit them in foodstuffs or pollution, in the 'circle of poison' effect.

Global regulation with regard to the use and production of, rather than trade in, hazardous chemicals is predictably less rigorous but has developed over time. The WHO have had a role in developing international labelling guidelines for pesticides as far back as 1953 (Hough 1998: 55–7). A plethora of international standards in this area were brought together in 2002 under the Globally Harmonized System of Classification and Labelling of Chemicals (GHS), co-managed by three

IGOs: the Organization for Economic Cooperation and Development (OECD), the United Nations Committee of Experts on the Transportation of Dangerous Goods (UNCETDG) and the ILO. As well as labelling standards this scheme includes data sheets for workers involved in chemical transport and guidance information for governments on how to implement the scheme. The system began the process of ratification in 2003 and by 2017 had been implemented by seventy-two states. It should be noted, though, that harmonized global standards are becoming more popular as much because they can facilitate trade by levelling the 'playing field' as because they enhance human security.

Nuclear power politics

As has been demonstrated, safety standards for the production of nuclear energy and the transportation of its constituent elements and by-products tend not to be included in general international policy on accident prevention. Instead, the responsibility for this lies with the International Atomic Energy Agency (IAEA), a forum set up by the UN in 1957 to coordinate policy on both military and civilian uses of nuclear power. The IAEA has an International Nuclear Safety Advisory Group which has coordinated the establishment of a range of 'Safety Principles' and a 'Code of Practice on the International Transboundary Movement of Radioactive Waste'. Prompted by the Chernobyl disaster and the end of Cold War secrecy, the IAEA codified their most extensive legal instrument to date in the 1990s with the Convention on Nuclear Safety, which came into force in 1996. The convention covers a range of issues including the siting and construction of power plants and emergency preparation. However, despite the implied strengthening of IAEA standards with the use of the term 'convention' in place of 'principles' and 'code of practice', this is not a robust piece of legislation. In the IAEA's own words: 'The Convention is an incentive instrument. It is not designed to ensure fulfilment of obligations by Parties through control and sanction' (IAEA 2012).

The high perception of risk attached to the production of nuclear power has made this a contentious issue of domestic politics in many countries but has also promoted a most literal form of spillover, inducing political cooperation between states. The Chernobyl disaster, more than Soviet–Western rapprochement, was the spur for the EC to launch the TACIS programme (Technical Assistance to the Commonwealth of Independent States) in 1991 which gave grants to most of the successor states of the Soviet Union and had a strong focus on the modernization of the nuclear industry.

On the other side of the coin, concerns over transboundary pollution from nuclear accidents have also served to sour relations between closely integrated countries. Chernobyl was also a key factor in instigating independence movements in Ukraine, where the plant was based, and in nearby Belarus. In both of these Slavic Soviet Socialist Republics anti-Russian nationalism was less of a spur for secession than the feeling of being treated as the USSR's industrial wasteland. Hence many of Ukraine's large Russian minority voted for independence. Further west, the desire of former USSR satellite states to integrate themselves into the European Union's integration project has also brought nuclear safety questions to the fore. The EU in

2002 persuaded Lithuania to close its Soviet-built nuclear plant, Ignalina, as a condition of membership, and in doing so agreed to provide substantial aid to assist in the project and compensate for the funding of alternative sources of energy production.

Whilst the 2011 Fukushima leak caused a backlash against nuclear energy, the industry that was once the *bête noire* of environmentalists has now come to be embraced by some as green, due to its relative attractiveness *vis-à-vis* fossil fuels in terms of mitigating climate change. Whilst this is defensible in terms of plant safety and carbon footprint, compared to the coal and gas industries, the more profound security threat posed by nuclear power is more long-term: securing future generations against a huge build-up of ultra-toxic waste (Blowers 2017).

Road safety

A WHO role in road safety, alongside their more traditional work on disease and sanitation, has gradually emerged since the turn of the century. A Five Year Strategy on Road Traffic Injury Prevention was launched in 2001 aiming to universalize proven accident-reducing practices such as alcohol limits for drivers, the use of seat belts and particular forms of speed controls and road design. A WHO steering committee on road safety has met since 2002 and, in collaboration with other UN agencies, and pressure groups such as the Global Road Safety Partnership (GRSP), released the World Report on Road Traffic Injury Prevention on World Health Day in 2004. The steering committee worked with the government of Oman to draft a series of UN General Assembly resolutions from 2003 to 2005 prompting the first UN Global Road Safety Week held in 2007. This paved the way for the launch of the UN Decade of Action for Road Safety in 2011, which does appear to have had some positive impact. The global total of deaths on the road has plateaued at around 1.25 million per year despite there being more vehicles on the roads, and thirty-three out of forty-six global North states have seen improved figures. Seventeen countries have amended their laws in accord with identified best practice in areas like drink driving and speed limits, and road safety has been incorporated in the Sustainable Development Goals (WHO 2015b).

Maritime safety

International maritime safety standards centre on the Safety of Life at Sea (SOLAS) Conventions, initiated in 1914 in the wake of the *Titanic* disaster. Measures declared mandatory for all ships on the high seas included reduced speed limits after the sighting of ice and lifeboat training for all crew members. In 1960 an updated version of SOLAS was adopted by the UN's Intergovernmental Maritime Consultancy Organization, which later became the International Maritime Organization (IMO). The IMO, based in London, is today the focal point for global maritime safety standards, such as the global Maritime Distress and Safety System, which from 1998 has ensured that any ship in distress can receive assistance even if it does not have a radio. As Table 9.1 indicates, safety in international waters has greatly improved, with most disasters now occurring domestically in overcrowded ferries in the global South.

Air travel safety

Global flight safety standards are much more embryonic than those covering sea travel. The International Civil Aviation Organization (ICAO), the relevant UN agency, has generally played a technical rather than regulatory role, with safety standards left to governments. However, in response to rising accident figures in the global South the ICAO worked with the airline industry in devising the Global Aviation Safety Roadmap, launched in 2006, which seeks to harmonize national and regional safety standards up to global North standards and share good practice. This roadmap metamorphosized into the Global Aviation Safety Plan which is now reviewed every three years by the ICAO, who also produce annual reports detailing levels of state compliance with its standards.

Personal injury

From the 1990s the WHO have also taken on board the task of highlighting and coordinating global action on reducing personal injuries. In 2002 a first ever World Congress on Drowning was hosted in Amsterdam and highlighted the need to work towards eliminating an estimated 80 per cent of deaths which are avoidable (mainly children) through better education on the causes of drowning and the use of life jackets and resuscitation techniques (World Congress on Drowning 2002). In 2014 a first report was produced by the WHO making recommendations on national water safety plans (WHO 2014). Similarly, a broader World Report on Child Injury Prevention, launched in conjunction with UNICEF, set out good practice in relation to burns, falls and poisoning (as well as drowning and road accidents) (WHO 2008).

Conclusions

Accidents are the most atypical of global security concerns and yet represent a much bigger threat to most people's lives than those most typical security concerns, war and terrorism. Most of you reading this are hundreds of times more likely to die in an accident than be killed by a soldier or terrorist. Security 'wideners' and even some human security advocates, whilst acknowledging that diseases, crime, environmental change and natural disasters can sometimes be matters of security, are reluctant to grant this status to accidents and man-made disasters. This reluctance seems to boil down to two objections: (1) there are no military or power politics dimensions; (2) they are not deliberate 'attacks' on countries or people.

Security wideners ignore accidents because there is rarely any scope for sending in troops to fight anyone or help clear up in the aftermath. However, such a line of argument makes sense only if you are to assume that security is a synonym for 'involves the military' rather than a description of what you are striving to provide for your people in political life. A further barrier to the 'securitization' of disasters for some is the absence of direct and deliberate human causation. Even MacFarlane and Foong Khong, whilst purporting to advocate human security, opine that natural disasters and accidents 'fail the "organized harm" test – tsunami waves, traffic accidents, the spread of viruses and crop failure are usually not organized by individuals to do their victims in' (MacFarlane & Foong Khong 2006: 275). For advocates of more expansive human security, though, there is a fatal fatalism in assuming that only direct and deliberate threats to life can be deemed worthy of security status. As discussed in previous chapters, securing people against such things is a political task accepted by industrialized governments from as far back as the late nineteenth century when 'social security' policies began to evolve in response to changing economic and social conditions. Accidents, hence, are actually no more unavoidable than other social systemic problems like war and crime, and people can be secured against them, at least to some degree. The human agency argument is flawed on two levels. First, there is human agency in most accidents. Human failings, whether at the state, corporate or individual level, account for most accidents and, hence, can be addressed in political actions. Second, must we deduce from this line of reasoning that anyone threatened or killed indirectly is not insecure? Are the 'collateral killings' of war or insurgency then not military or terrorist victims? Securing people against accidents has long been recognized as a task of responsible democratic government and, whilst that remains, there is compelling logic that globalization has now shifted some responsibilities to a wider level.

If there is a 'responsibility to protect' those imperilled by political violence why should there not be for those imperilled by their government's or host government's political negligence? Indeed it could be argued that the international community should feel a greater sense of responsibility when it comes to industrial accidents since they have become more functionally connected to these events in enjoying the fruits of this hard labour. The contemporary deaths of Chinese miners or Indian construction workers recruited to build skyscrapers for global finance firms and football stadia in the Gulf States should trouble Western consumers and governments as much as notorious domestic disasters did in the nineteenth and twentieth centuries.

This shift, though, has a long way to go. Global standards on the safety aspects of business and employment are limp when set against comparable standards for facilitating the trade in the produce of this process. The ILO and the IAEA do not have the same sort of authority in compelling states to protect workers and citizens living near areas of industrial production that the WTO has in compelling them to allow goods into their countries. Hence we see one reason why many political activists have come to view economic globalization as a dangerous exercise in unfettered liberalism, guided only by the profit motives of the global North. It is indeed telling that, whereas the idea of freeing up the movement of products, services and money is well established as a global norm, the notion of a free movement of the workers producing such common goods is barely conceivable. As Dauvergne says of accidents, the 'global jury of states is assigning no blame, no ethical responsibility, dismissing these deaths as mere accidents in the quest for global prosperity' (Dauvergne 2005: 44).

However, 'unfettered liberalism' is not the political system which has emerged from the political evolution of states which have industrialized and modernized and there is no reason to believe that it will be for the global polity. The industrialization of Western European and North American states prompted the emergence of policies to protect those put at risk by these social changes based both on compassion and pragmatism. An ideological consensus emerged in the late nineteenth century in support of the notion of state welfarism. The dangers associated with industrial employment and the economic uncertainties of trade prompted the emergence of interventionist Liberalism in place of its previous unfettered free market version and also paternal Conservatism and the birth of Socialism. The development of welfare systems in Western Europe, and to a lesser extent in the USA, arose from a blend of altruistic human security concerns and internal state security. Germany, under the arch-Conservative Bismarck, pioneered the idea of state protection for workers prompted mainly by the pragmatic realism that reform from above was the best means of preventing revolution from below. Bismarck's aim was not so much human security as state security: maintaining the unity of his newly-formed country which was witnessing some of the earliest manifestations of Socialist thought.

In addition, the precedent for freeing up trade between countries on a regional scale is that a levelling of an uneven playing field is a necessary precursor to achieving this. The issue may not arise for countries of a similar level of economic development, like the European Free Trade Association (EFTA) or the European Economic Community in its early years. The logic of spillover later dictated, however, that the EC embrace a social dimension alongside the 'Single Market' when it took on board the relatively poor states of Ireland, Portugal, Spain and Greece. States with poor safety standards are either (a) (from an economic perspective) giving themselves an unfair competitive advantage or (b) (from a social perspective) being exploited. Hence even the North American Free Trade Association (NAFTA), set up very much on an economic rationale without the idealism of the European integration project, featured from the start the 'North American Agreement on Labor Cooperation' (NAALC). The NAALC, centred on an industrial dispute resolution mechanism incorporating occupational safety, came into force alongside the main NAFTA agreement in 1994 to overcome the problem of Mexico's comparative advantage/ disadvantage compared to its wealthier partners to the north.

With the inexorable rise of a coherent global economic system, global society is now awakening, albeit slowly, to this need for worker safety standards. Incidents of workers or residents near industrial plants in LDCs being killed are no longer unfortunate problems unconnected with the relatively safe lives of people in the global North. Developed world consumers are functionally connected to these systemic failures as never before and increasingly aware of this fact. The rise in the global North of 'fair trade' products, in which the consumer pays a premium for goods imported from developing countries on the premise that the workers have not been exploited, and the 'anti-globalization' social movements bear testimony to this fact. What is needed, though, is not the abandonment of globalization but a more rounded notion of globalization which balances profits with responsibilities, as is broadly the norm in most developed democracies.

Such changes are slowly occurring. As with most of the areas of security considered in this book, the globalization of democracy and human rights offers hope for improving personal safety from accidents since more and more people are able to demand action from their governments. The fact that the unionization of workforces increases human security was highlighted by contrasting safety records in the construction of sports stadia for the 2012 London Olympics (no deaths and a strong union role) with the 2014 Russian Winter Olympics at Socha (sixty deaths and no prominent union role). If the Qatari World Cup construction industry is compared, the contrast is starker still (TUC 2014). In addition, recent evidence points towards the development of something of a 'union effect' on safety at the global level. Following up on pressuring the Bangladeshi government to legalize unions in the aftermath of the 2013 Dhaka disaster, a campaign by trade unions served to secure the release of unionists imprisoned on trumped-up charges in 2017.

Evidence is also now beginning to emerge of a globalization of a safety discourse. Whilst progress has been limited on the C174 and C161 conventions, ratifications for subsequent ILO conventions on occupational safety and health (OSH) have notably improved since most countries committed themselves to a 'national preventative safety and health culture' and the notion of a 'right to a safe and healthy working environment' at the 2008 Seoul Declaration on Safety and Health at Work (ILO 2011: 155, 187). International guidance has since been disseminated more effectively in a networking of the 'good safety is good business' message.

Securing people at work, at home, travelling or at leisure is for governments and societies, though, more than charity or even duty. A more secure and healthy workforce and society is more productive and contented. Four per cent of global GDP is estimated to be lost to accidents and around this amount was trimmed off the Japanese GDP by the single Fukushima disaster (ILO 2011). Exploiting workers and short-changing citizens is only profitable for so long when such people can be shown that there are alternatives. Disillusioned and angry workers have been a factor in nearly all revolutions. Welfarism suits both sides of the social contract. Health and safety is the dull stuff of politics and business but it is, nonetheless, 'life and death' both for members of society and for governments and has long been recognized as such in industrialized democracies. Globalization dictates that this can no longer be a purely domestic matter. With accidents, as with many of the other issues considered in this book, enhancing human security is not just altruistic; it makes economic and national security sense as well.

Key points

- Most man-made accidents (transport, structural, industrial or personal) are avoidable and, therefore, political matters.
- Most accidental deaths are linked to modern, industrialized living and are, to some extent, tolerated as inevitable.
- Industrialized countries have developed the capacity to contain accidents to some extent and less developed countries now bear the greatest burden of such deaths.
- Global policy on accidents has been subsumed by the rise of Economic Liberalism but demand for global safety standards, like those in developed countries, is growing through recognition that this is a global and not just a domestic matter.

Notes

1   Deaths per billion miles in the USA, 2000–2014: motorcycle 237.57, car/truck 6.53, train 0.33, bus 0.2.
2   The ratifiers are: Sweden (1994), Armenia (1996), Netherlands (1997), Colombia (1997), Estonia (2000), Brazil (2001), Saudi Arabia (2001), Albania (2003), Zimbabwe (2003), Belgium (2004), Lebanon (2005), India (2008), Luxembourg (2008), Bosnia-Herzegovina (2010), Slovenia (2010), Ukraine (2011), Russia (2012), Finland (2013).
3   The Rotterdam Convention on the Prior Informed Consent Procedure for Certain Hazardous Pesticides and Chemicals in International Trade. For an analysis of this convention see Hough (2000).
4   The Basel Convention on the Control of Transboundary Movements of Hazardous Wastes and Their Disposal.

 Recommended reading

Beck, U. (2009) *World at Risk*, Cambridge: Polity.
Blanton, R. & Peksen, D. (2017) 'Dying for Globalization? The Impact of Economic Globalization on Industrial Accidents', *Social Science Quarterly* doi 10.1111/ssqu.1267.
Dauvergne, P. (2005) 'Dying of Consumption: Accidents or Sacrifices of Global Morality', *Global Environmental Politics*, 5(3): 35–47.
Matthewman, S. (2015) *Disasters, Risks and Revelation: Making Sense of Our Time*, London: Palgrave.
Smith, K. & Petley, D. (2013) *Environmental Hazards: Assessing Risk and Reducing Disaster*, 6th edn, London and New York: Routledge (chapter 13).

 Useful web links

- International Atomic Energy Agency: www.iaea.org/
- International Labour Organization: www.ilo.org/global/lang—en/index.htm

Chapter 10

Criminal threats to security

> *No one country can effectively fight transnational organized crime within or outside its borders. Therefore, I submit, countries must relinquish some of their procedural or substantive sovereignty in order for the purpose for which sovereignty exists in the first place to remain intact.*
>
> Ronald Noble, Secretary-General of Interpol, 2003 (Noble 2003)

Introduction

Crime has always represented a threat to the security of ordinary people in all countries and, occasionally, to state institutions also. In recent years, however, this threat has changed in nature through utilizing the opportunities presented by globalization, undermining the capacity of governments to protect both their citizens and themselves and raising important questions about the nature of sovereignty. The use of legitimate sovereign force to uphold domestic law and order in the name of state and human security is universal and has a long history. Indeed, in many ways, this is the chief explanation for the gradual spread of sovereign rule from the dawn of the Westphalian system in the mid-seventeenth century.

In some countries state security has long been as much a domestic political issue as an international one. In Italy during the Cold War, for example, the domestic threat posed by political violence (most notably the Red Brigade) and criminal violence (most notably the mafia) dominated state security policy to much the same extent as the Soviet threat preoccupying the rest of Western Europe. This fact manifests itself in the existence and prominence in Italy of the paramilitary police force the *Carabinieri*, in contrast to its relatively modest military capabilities. This situation, though, has become typical as more countries have turned to paramilitary policing in recent years as a blurring of the distinction between internal and external security has prompted a commensurate blurring of the traditional roles of the military and police. In the USA, for example, the number of Special Weapons and Tactics (SWAT) police operations rose from 3,000 per year in the 1980s to around 40,000 per year in the 2000s (Kraska 2005).

Statistics are inevitably sketchy when dealing with an issue which is illegal, transnational and something many governments would prefer to downplay, but cross-border crime has undoubtedly grown worldwide over the last thirty years. The IMF estimated that the amount of criminally acquired money in the world grew from $85 to $5,000 billion between 1988 and 1998 (Kendall 1998: 264). This trend has continued and the global black market now accounts for over $2 trillion per year or 6 per cent of global GDP (UNODC 2011b). The true figure, though, is higher still since the UNODC do not take full account of tax evasion. A breakdown of the cost of some of the key forms of contemporary transnational crime is given in Table 10.1.

Most pertinent to the consideration of security is the fact that nearly half a million people per year are murdered (UNODC 2011a). As with the economic cost, this figure grew significantly in the 1990s. One of the most comprehensive and reliable studies of international crime, by the Council of Europe, showed that the number of convictions for completed homicide rose from 1.5 per 100,000 people in 1990 to 2.9 in 1996 (Council of Europe 1999: table 3.B.1.2). It is in the Americas and Africa, though, that life-threatening crime is most prevalent (see Table 10.2). The availability of firearms appears to be a major factor in explaining international variation

TABLE 10.1 The ten costliest forms of transnational crime

		Annual economic cost (US$)	Annual human cost
1	Corruption	1 trillion[a]	
2	Cybercrime	1 trillion[f]	
3	Counterfeits	968 billion[b]	
4	Drug trafficking	400 billion[b]	207,400 deaths[c]
5	Environmental crime (oil, wildlife, timber, fish)	175 billion[h]	
6	Human trafficking	150.2 billion[b]	11.7 million victims[b]
7	Stolen goods	20 billion[i]	
8	Maritime piracy	9.5 billion[e]	11 deaths, 1,000 hostages[e]
9	Arms trafficking	2.6 billion[b]	25,965 deaths[g]
10	Human organ trafficking	1.3 billion[b]	12,000 victims[b]
	Total	2.1 trillion (excluding tax evasion and accepting overlaps between crime types) of which 1.6 trillion is laundered[d]	

Sources: a Transparency International 2015. b Global Financial Integrity 2017. c UNODC 2016a. d UNODC 2011b. e IMO 2011. f UK FCO 2011. g Author's estimate extrapolated from the estimate that 15 per cent of small arms trade is illegal and small arms account for 173,100 criminal homicides (*Lancet* 2016). h. UNEP 2016. i Baker 2005.

TABLE 10.2 The top ten homicide rates by country

		Homicides per 100,000
1	Honduras	90.4
2	Venezuela	53.7
3	Belize	44.7
4	El Salvador	41.2
5	Guatemala	39.9
6	Jamaica	39.3
7	Lesotho	38.0
8	Swaziland	33.8
9	South Africa	31.0
10	Colombia	30.8
	Global average	6.2

Source: UNODC 2014.

Note: St Kitts & Nevis (33) and US Virgin Islands (57.6) are not included because the rate is distorted by tiny populations.

in homicide rates. Nearly three-quarters of all homicides in the Americas are committed by firearms, a rate over three times that of Europe (UNODC 2011a).

Two of the states of the Americas in the 'world homicide top ten', Colombia and Venezuela, epitomize the security threats posed by crime. In Colombia, criminal organizations (in tandem with violent political organizations), as well as providing a major human security threat to domestic and foreign citizens, have seriously undermined the capacity of the government to rule the country for half a century. In this time foreign troops have been called in to fight drugs barons whilst a large tract of Colombian territory was, for a number of years, conceded to 'narco-terrorists'. Years of political insecurity are reflected in marked criminal insecurity for Colombia and Colombians. Venezuela for many years was a political and criminal contrast to its neighbour but recent economic decline and political upheaval have seen the country descend into an even greater criminal quagmire, fuelled by a huge surge in illegal weapon imports. Colombia and Venezuela are extreme cases but in many countries throughout the world governments are threatened or undermined by armed groups terrifying their citizens, damaging their economy and corrupting their institutions.

As with many of the issues considered in previous chapters, though, there can be a danger of statecentricism in looking at crime from a security perspective. Governments often behave criminally as well as 'ordinary citizens' and organized crime syndicates. In addition to human rights abuses and political failings in securing citizens on a range of issues (as considered in previous chapters), 'kleptocracy' – fraud, corruption and nepotism carried out by governments – has and continues to undermine human security in many countries. Former presidents Suharto of Indonesia, Marcos of the Philippines and Mobutu of the Democratic Republic of the Congo are among many notorious heads of state who are believed to have syphoned off billions of their citizens' taxes for personal gain whilst their countries struggled with underdevelopment and conflict.

Global crime in historical context

Despite its recent rise to prominence and traditionally marginal role in international relations it should be remembered that several forms of global crime have a long history.

Narcotic drugs

The use, production and sale of narcotic drugs can be traced back to ancient history. Opiates were common in Ancient Greece (for example, their use is referred to by Homer), marijuana was in use in China over two millennia ago and coca was as much an integral part of life in the Inca civilization as it is in some parts of Andean South America today. The trading of opiates occurred within Asia for many centuries and from the mid-eighteenth century extended into Europe. This was, at the time, an entirely legal form of commerce since the use of opiates was not distinguished from the use of medicinal drugs or foodstuffs and was common among societal elites. When Imperial China did take steps to restrict the legality of opium in the mid-nineteenth century Great Britain twice took up arms against them (the Opium Wars of 1839–42 and 1856–8) in order to protect this trade between China and their colony, India.

The shift of positions of Western governments from fighting wars *for* drugs to the contemporary fighting of wars *against* drugs began in the latter part of the nineteenth century. By this time the use of opiates in Western Europe and the USA had begun to spread beyond that of literary and political elite social circles and come to be associated with working-class sloth and crime, prompting moves towards domestic prohibition. An international conference in Shanghai in 1909 initiated attempts to control the trade in opiates, culminating in the 1912 International Opium Convention. The League of Nations then made reference to the problem of narcotics in its charter and in 1920 established the Advisory Committee on Traffic in Opium and Other Dangerous Drugs (Bentham 1998: 90–2).

Whilst narcotics production, trading and consumption is a long-established global phenomenon, it has generally become more problematic over time. In 2014 an estimated 247 million people around the world took narcotic drugs, of which around 29 million suffered disorders as a result and 207,400 died (UNODC 2016a). The picture is becoming more complex as new synthetic 'highs' multiply, but a large part of this picture remains quite simple: heroin mainly from Afghanistan and cocaine mainly from Andean South America are being transported by criminal groups to a market chiefly found in Europe and North America.

Piracy

The menace caused to international commerce by the actions of pirates has, of course, a long and well-documented history and illustrates that threats to security from armed non-state actors are not a new phenomenon. Piracy is recorded as being of concern as early as the fourth century AD in the China Seas and gradually spread and grew through the centuries, becoming particularly rife in the Mediterranean from the sixteenth to the eighteenth century (Chalk 2000: 57). Again, though, it should be remembered that piracy is a crime that has not always been opposed by governments. Medieval European monarchs often supported 'buccaneers' in their endeavours if the victims were to be rival imperial powers.

The motivation for pirates to conduct robberies at sea rather than on land was that it made it harder for states to act against them. As such, piracy represents a classic concern of international law which, traditionally, is focused on tackling problems which do not fall under the direct jurisdiction of states. A series of international conventions were signed from the nineteenth century outlawing robbery on the high seas, culminating in the 1958 UN Convention on the High Seas, Articles 14–21 of which permit any state to try the perpetrators of such crimes regardless of the nationality of the criminal.

The success of these conventions has produced an unusual twist for international relations with the uncharacteristic effectiveness of international law enforcement diverting many of the criminals to take on domestic law enforcers instead. Modern-day pirates tend not to operate on the high seas, where they run the risk of encountering the full might of great naval powers, and prefer to challenge the sovereign authorities of less powerful states in ransacking ships in territorial seas, in anchorage or in the harbour. Hence, in recent years, the territorial waters off the Gulf of Guinea have emerged as a haven for maritime robbery, as international efforts have contained the most notorious contemporary pirates operating in the Indian Ocean around Somalia.

Slavery

As referred to in Chapter 5, international action against the age-old practice of slavery represents the first manifestation of human rights in international relations, with states acting to outlaw a crime for moral rather than economic reasons or the safety of their citizens. The rise of outrage in nineteenth-century Western Europe at the barbarism of using forced human labour, and of profiting from the trade in human cargo, translated itself into the diplomacy of the Concert of Europe. The 1815 Congress of Vienna saw the great powers of Europe acknowledge an obligation to make the international trade in slaves contrary to international law. A similar agreement was also made as part of the Treaty of Ghent between the USA and Great Britain in the same year. This obligation became official at the 1885 Treaty of Berlin and was codified in the 1890 Brussels Convention, producing the world's first piece of human rights legislation. Great Britain, on a number of occasions, took the step of enforcing this law by intercepting Arab slave ships off the coast of East Africa and freeing the captives (Robertson 2000: 14). As also discussed in Chapter 5, humanitarian interventions of this kind are still rare and highly contentious today. The act of slavery itself was made illegal under international law by the 1926 Slavery Convention which put slavers in the same category as pirates, subject to the jurisdiction of any state regardless of where the crime took place.

Forced labour, though, has not gone away and the Global Slavery Index estimates that 45.8 million people live in such conditions today. The North Korean government are believed to run huge labour camps filled with political opponents, and in Uzbekistan citizens are compelled annually to harvest cotton. In addition, the phenomenon is endemic in parts of society in India, China, Bangladesh and Pakistan (Global Slavery Index 2017). Contributory factors behind such 'cultures of slavery' include a lack of civil legal protection and the exploitation of refugees or trafficked people.

Smuggling illicit goods

Stealing is age-old and the subsequent movement of the proceeds of this across borders to evade domestic law enforcement and/or meet demands elsewhere is a similarly long-standing phenomenon. The high value of art and antiquities, for example, has for many centuries spawned a significant international black market. The trafficking of stolen goods persists today alongside similar movements of goods not stolen but produced or traded illegally. Interpol use the term 'trafficking in illicit goods' to cover: counterfeiting (trademark infringements), piracy (copyright infringements), smuggling of legitimate products (e.g. gold) and smuggling to evade tax (e.g. avoiding paying the tax on cigarettes).

'New' global crimes

Corruption

Corruption, of course, is not in any way new but it has become more pervasive and damaging as the criminals in some countries have become more organized at the same time as governments have got weaker. The pressure group Transparency International estimate that 68 per cent of states representing 6 billion of the world's people have a serious endemic problem with corruption, the worst of which are: Somalia, North Korea, Afghanistan, Sudan and South Sudan (Transparency International 2015). In four of these states internal sovereignty is weak owing to civil conflict undermining law, order and state institutions. The exception is North Korea where sovereign control is far from weak but the government itself is corrupt. In other cases organized crime has proven increasingly able to manipulate governments in states undergoing profound political and economic change. Godson and Williams use the term *mafiocracies* to encapsulate the problem of criminal syndicates buying into crucial aspects of state apparatus and winning political influence (Godson & Williams 2000: 113).

Arms smuggling

The illegal trade in weapons is also far from new but has greatly proliferated over the past thirty years. The supply side of the industry has come from the increased availability of weapons since the end of the Cold War (particularly from the former USSR) and the demand from the upsurge in insurgencies, terrorism and organized crime that has occurred at the same time.

Environmental crimes

Also not so much new but newly-prominent, most environmental crimes fall into two general categories: (a) wilful pollution, such as the dumping of toxic waste by corporations or the military destruction of land and water beyond the necessity of warfare (or ecocide – see Chapter 6); (b) the illegal exploitation or trade in wildlife and wildlife products. The black market in wildlife, like other international crimes, can be a case of trading goods that are illegal in themselves or smuggling legal goods for illicit profits. UNODC estimate that there are 900,000 shipments of wildlife cargo such as rosewood, which is not illegal to trade but is restricted in many domestic jurisdictions. This is facilitated by the falsification of documents and poor domestic legal implementation (UNODC 2016b). Other, longer-established and more clearly illicit trades continue in, for example, elephant tusks for jewellery, rhinoceros horns and pangolins for medicines, reptile and big cat skins for fashion items and turtles and apes for pets.

People trafficking

Distinct from the similar international crime of people smuggling, human trafficking is a phenomenon whereby people legally migrate but do so under the control of criminals who determine their movement and employment, including sometimes their sale to others. As such it is close to, and many would argue indistinct from, the slave trade. Essentially, human trafficking is a broader, more contemporary and subtler phenomenon than the slave trade since some of the victims may, at some level, consent to migrating and get paid for their labour. They are, though, still being controlled and exploited. It is estimated that 18 per cent of trafficked persons are for the purposes of forced labour (and hence indistinct from 'old-fashioned' slavery); 79 per cent are moved for sexual exploitation – most notably to work as prostitutes – and the vast majority of these are women (UNODC 2009). Whilst sex trafficking has grown hugely over recent decades it is not peculiar to the modern age and international efforts to prohibit 'white slavery' were initiated as far back as the late nineteenth century.

Human organ trafficking

More specific to the contemporary age is the trafficking of particular parts of people, most notably their livers and kidneys. This shocking phenomenon takes three principal forms: (1) victims are forced or deceived into giving up an organ; (2) victims agree to sell an organ but are not paid; (3) vulnerable people have an organ stolen whilst under medical treatment. Hence, in addition to the traffickers, the crime typically will include the corruption of hospital staff and/or the use of people to recruit vulnerable victims. As an illustration, in October 2016 police in Pakistan rescued twenty-four hostages in Rawalpindi who were due to have kidneys removed, who had been recruited for fake jobs. A contributory factor to the phenomenon illustrated by this episode is the rise of 'transplant tourism' that sees people travel to countries like Pakistan for operations owing to a shortage of legitimate organs in many countries (BBC 2017).

Cybercrime

The most clearly 'new' form of global criminality is cybercrime. This broad phenomenon has two dimensions: 'advanced cybercrime' refers to technologically-sophisticated attacks against hardware and software; whilst 'cyber-enabled crime' is the use of online technology to facilitate more traditional crimes, such as fraud, terrorism, theft and the luring of victims for sexual abuse. As with many international political issues, a lot of the focus has been on the potential national security implications of cybercrime but, up until now, the costs have been far greater for business and human victims. Online hacking has been deployed by governments, as the USA and Israel are alleged to have done in disabling the Iranian nuclear weapons programme with the *stuxnet* computer virus in 2010. Cyberterrorism has also attracted considerable attention, though, as yet, this does not appear to be as prevalent (in the advanced cybercrime form) as use of cybercrime by governments. However, the most significant proven dimensions of cybercrime concern 'cyber-enabled crime', particularly industrial espionage (by businesses and governments) and the theft from and defrauding of individuals. For example, by 2017 cybercrimes accounted for nearly half of all crimes committed in England and Wales, and the majority of these were online frauds (UK Office for National Statistics 2017).

Webs of deceit – the rise in prominence of transnational crime

As previously shown, the 1990s witnessed a significant rise in the scale of and political attention given to transnational organized crime. The ending of the Cold War and the onset of greater economic globalization can, in many ways, be seen to have created the conditions for a growing 'global underworld'. However, whilst international crime has become more prominent since the end of the 1980s, that is not to say that it was not apparent during the Cold War. To some extent, as with many issues, superpower military rivalry obscured the problem and led to 'a blind eye being turned' to very real problems like corruption and narcotics trading. It is incontrovertible that the superpowers were prepared to tolerate corrupt governments being involved with or even directing criminal operations if they were in charge of important military allies or client states.

The clearest illustration of a U-turn in tolerating crooked regimes can be seen with the USA's invasion of Panama in the dying days of the Cold War in 1989. One of the principal reasons for the breakdown in relations between the two countries, which led to the overthrow of the Panamanian government, was the refusal of President Noriega to yield to US demands to act to curb the flow of cocaine passing through his country on its way to their cities. Noriega's connections to the drugs underworld were well known to the Americans throughout the 1980s, as a military general until 1987 and as the president thereafter. At that time, though, this was not viewed in such a negative light since he had aided the USA in anti-leftist operations in Central America. The USA's security for the most part of the 1980s was construed almost entirely in terms of the Communist threat, which Noriega stood as a bulwark against, rather than the threat posed by cocaine addiction and related crime in US cities. By 1989 this was beginning to change.

The following phenomena help explain the globalization of crime since the end of the 1980s.

The rise of 'failed states'

Since the 1990s the term 'failed states' has come to be attributed to those countries where a single government could not be said to be in effective political control within its own borders beyond what could be understood as any sort of period of transition or temporary civil strife. In effect, such territories can be seen to be in a prolonged state of insurgency or general lawlessness. The preponderance of failed states increased after the ending of the Cold War partly because many such countries lost the patronage of either superpower in a New World Order where they ceased to hold such a strong military security attraction.

The classic case of the failed state is that of Afghanistan. Invaded by the USSR in 1979 Afghanistan became the focal point of the Second Cold War, with the USA providing substantial financial and military backing to the *mujaheddin* resistance fighters. The thawing of relations between the USA and USSR saw Soviet premier Gorbachev announce the withdrawal of troops from the bloody and intractable conflict in 1988. This ended the proxy war between the two superpowers but did not end the conflict in Afghanistan, where rival factions continued to fight out a civil war in the power vacuum created by the sudden loss of interest of the world's two most powerful states. The political legacy of this for the USA in terms of the rise of anti-American terrorist groups from the *mujaheddin* is well documented, but Afghanistan also rose again as a crucial haven for the global heroin industry. Ironically it was the toppling of the Taliban by the US-led invasion of 2001 that served to increase lawlessness in the country, and a resurgence in the export of opiates to the West, since that government had begun to clamp down on narcotics production (through concerns over domestic consumption).

Somalia represents another quintessential failed state, with much of the country existing in turmoil since the collapse of the Soviet-backed Barre government in 1991. Against this backdrop we can easily see how gangs of pirates were able to thrive off the coast in the 2000s and become a scourge of international cargo and tourist liners travelling through the region. The pirates themselves have even cited the lack of sovereign authority as a justification for their actions in seizing control of their country's waters from international criminals: 'We don't consider ourselves pirates. We consider pirates those who illegally fish in our seas and dump in our seas and carry weapons in our seas. Think of us like a Coast Guard' (Ali 2008).

Failed states are significant in international relations because they stand in contradiction to conventional notions of the sovereign state system. Sovereignty is traditionally viewed as the cement that holds together the state system and main-tains international order. The crucial component of the multi-faceted concept of sovereignty, enshrined in international law in the 1933 Montevideo Convention on the Rights and Duties of States, is that a sovereign state has a government in 'effective control'. The rise in cases where countries cannot be said to have a sovereign government in effective control – such as Afghanistan, Somalia or the Democratic Republic of the Congo (where 'blood diamonds' and other 'conflict minerals' are both a product and cause of prolonged civil war) – is, of course, a recipe for increased lawlessness in the world.

The rise of 'failing states'

Post-Cold War political change has also had criminal consequences because of the level of upheaval in the many countries that have undergone transition. Post-Communist change, in particular, has come at a cost as organized crime groups have often adapted better than governments to the new economic conditions internally and opportunities externally. Transition from a one-party state to a multi-party democracy, and from a centrally-planned economy to a more diverse mixed economy with private industries and shareholders, is not a smooth process. Poverty and social upheaval are always favourable conditions in which crime can thrive and even the more successful transition states of Central Europe have witnessed increased problems with black marketeers and illegal traders of various kinds. EU states have helped alleviate this for those joining the Union by providing policing advice and training to their eastern neighbours through aid and EU accession preparations. It is the former Communist countries further east which have found most difficulty in making the transition to capitalism and democracy and where crime has become most prevalent and of greatest concern to the rest of the world. Rapid, wholesale privatization programmes in countries without experienced businesspeople, shareholders and private bankers inevitably run the risk of leaving key industries in the hands of black marketeers and inscrutable individuals, as occurred in Russia in the 1990s with the rise of the 'oligarchs'.

The South African transition to democracy from racist authoritarianism has also led to crime becoming more organized (Shaw 2013). However, it is not democratization that is the problem so much as radical transition, as the recent descent of Venezuela from relatively well-ordered democracy to crime-ridden semi-dictatorship illustrates.

The increased volume of traded goods

The opportunities for trading in legal commodities are much greater than ever before in terms of costs, speed and the existence of global regulations favouring free trade over state protectionism. Such opportunities are also, however, present for the trading in illegal commodities. It is easier and cheaper for criminals to operate internationally, and the sheer volume of traded goods makes it difficult for state authorities to detect the movement of drugs, arms shipments and other illicit cargoes.

Drugs traffickers, for example, have come to make effective use of that very symbol of globalization, the internet, to boost their operations. Gangs are known to have used encrypted websites to communicate and share information on their activities whilst employing information technology experts as hackers to alter information held on customs databases and create phantom websites to put state officials off the scent of the real sites. A simple illustration of how modern technological aids to commerce can serve murkier purposes also comes with evidence that Australian drug traffickers have brazenly used the web service offered by legitimate couriers allowing customers to track the location of the goods they are having delivered (International Narcotics Control Board 2002: 2).

The growth of cross-border financial transactions

Ever-increasing cross-border financial flows can also present opportunities to international criminals as much as to international businesspeople. Large-scale criminal activity is usually accompanied by money laundering as crime groups seek to protect their ill-gotten gains from state authorities by moving the money around or investing it in legitimate businesses. This process is becoming increasingly globalized as criminal organizations learn to exploit the inadequacies of the sovereign state system by moving money from country to country. Investing the proceeds of crime into legitimate businesses in a state other than where the crime took place illustrates the nature of criminal globalization's challenge to the state system. A crucial aspect of a crime may not be construed as criminal in the country where it occurs and may even be considered to be a beneficial overseas investment. Transparency International have claimed that London's property boom of recent years has been partially fuelled by laundered money, with over 36,000 of the city's properties owned by companies with secretive offshore registrations taking advantage of relatively 'light touch' British regulations (Transparency Int. UK 2015).

The globalization of 'white collar crime' is another price that governments and individuals have paid for reaping some of the benefits of financial liberalization. Many governments – such as the USA and UK – consciously began taking a more 'hands off' approach to banking and financial services from the 1990s in order to accrue inward flows of investment. Whilst this bore many fruits for a while, such a voluntary relaxation of sovereign controls came to appear more questionable from 2008 when a global recession unfolded as a consequence of shoddy banking practices (see Chapter 4). Some bankers exploited the laxer regulatory environment, others went further and blatantly broke laws, feeling safe in the conviction that they would

---

BOX 10.1 Bernie Madoff

Madoff carried out what was surely the biggest fraud in history for over a decade as a seemingly-respectable Wall Street financier, conning at least US$18 billion from thousands of individuals and several leading banks. Exploiting the opportunities offered by the liberalization of US and Western financial markets, Madoff's firm, which employed several family members, operated an enormous version of an age-old scam: the 'Ponzi Scheme'. Under this form of fraud investors who cash in their stakes are paid not out of company profits but out of the sums invested by others. The deceit can be maintained for as long as only a few investors do cash in in the belief that there are big profits for long-term investment. The scam unravelled amidst the financial crash of 2008 (see Chapter 4) when banks began to question the veracity of Madoff's predicted dividends for investors, and he was arrested in 2009. He now resides in Butner jail, North Carolina, serving a 150-year sentence.

never be caught. A contender for the world's 'greatest' ever criminal thus emerged, not in Russia or Colombia, but on Wall Street in the guise of US financier Bernie Madoff (see Box 10.1).

Urbanization

The global trend towards urban living is a factor behind the rise of crime since city dwellers are statistically far more violent and lawless than their rural counterparts. The homicide rate in the urban municipalities of Brazil, for example, is over three times that of the rural municipalities (Small Arms Survey 2007: 230–1). Around one-sixth of the world live in urban slums, the majority of which are in the global South (UN-Habitat 2003). Deprived urban living is closely associated with the development of criminal gangs and this is a growing phenomenon in many megacities in both the global North and South. Whilst urban gang culture is not new, it appears to be globalizing not only via migration routes but through the global media. Hence the notorious Los Angeles *MS-13* in the 2000s became the biggest gang, and a significant societal and governmental menace, in Honduras and El Salvador, two countries with amongst the world's highest homicide rates (see Table 10.2) (Hagedorn 2008).

Criminal globalization

A key factor in the globalization of crime is the increased tendency for organized criminal groups to follow the lead of transnational corporations and set up operations in a number of other countries. Cheaper international travel costs favour criminals as much as they do other profit-seeking individuals. Godson and Williams describe how transnational criminal organizations can come to utilize a *home state* from where they direct operations, a *host state* where they carry out crimes or sell their produce, a *transportation state* where criminal activities will seek to ensure an unhindered passage of goods to the host state, and a *service state* in countries where favourably secretive banking laws allow for profits to be secured (Godson & Williams 2000: 115). Hence, a genuinely transnational operation can be established where, for example, a Colombian-based narcotics gang could secure access to markets in the USA by bribing Mexican officials to permit the transit of the drugs and then invest the proceeds in a Cayman Islands offshore bank account. The indirect human cost of such criminality can be huge. Over 40,000 Mexicans were killed between 2007 and 2012 in the context of internecine criminal wars based on the transit of South American narcotics into North America (BBC 2011).

At the 1994 United Nations Conference on Internationally Organized Crime, UN Secretary-General Boutros-Ghali referred to an 'empire of criminals' to highlight the problem of globally operating criminal gangs but also to illustrate the fact that many of these organized gangs were cooperating with other, likeminded groups to extend the reach of their operations. There is a long history of criminal gangs extending their influence into other countries but this, traditionally, had been in line with patterns of migration. Hence the mafia's influence in the US from the 1930s followed large-scale Italian migration. The 1990s, however, witnessed the increased formation of strategic alliances between transnational criminal organizations exploiting changing political rather than demographic circumstances. Russian 'mafiya' and South American cocaine cartels, for example, are known to have maximized their comparative advantages by engaging in extensive 'drugs for guns' deals (Williams 2001: 75–6). International criminal cooperation can sometimes even thrive where societal and governmental cooperation is absent. Serb and Albanian gangsters, for example, are known to have worked together extensively in human trafficking operations in the Balkans (Williams 2006: 198).

The size and organization of major criminal syndicates gives them the status of international political actors in conventional terms. The Russian-based Solntevkaya Bratva, for example, are believed to be worth $8.5 billion and have over 9,000 members (some highly educated), organized into distinct units in several countries including within the USA (Finley 2017: 372).

Criminal exploitation of political integration

Globalization not only provides criminals with the opportunities to widen their operations, it can also sometimes be seen to create new opportunities for crime. Political integration is a by-product of an increasingly interdependent world where states recognize the limitations on independent action in the global economy and work towards 'pooling' their sovereignty by creating new, wider economic and political communities with nearby states. By far the most extensive case of such political integration is in Europe with the European Union. The EU is very much a leap of faith since no comparable project has been attempted before and, as a result, merging together the economic activities of so many states has had some unintended side-effects.

The opening up of borders between the member-states of the EU from the late 1980s helped create a 'single market for crime' as well as business. The smuggling of drugs, stolen goods and people was particularly boosted by this, with crime syndicates exploiting laxer border controls in the south in the knowledge that their 'cargo' could move freely northwards to wealthier parts of the Union. The EU has responded to such developments through the establishment of a Justice and Home Affairs 'pillar' to accompany measures furthering economic integration and greater police cooperation, but the smuggling of illegal immigrants and contraband across weak spots on its vast borders remains a pressing concern.

The global consumption of criminal enterprise

Crime is always driven by both supply and demand and a key reason for its globalization is the existence of an international market for such products and services. The use of special US and UK military forces from the 1990s to take on Colombian drugs cartels marked a recognition of the state securitization of international crime, but the ever increasing flow of cocaine into those countries also showed the limitations of such an approach. At the same time as the American and British governments were dispatching troops to Colombia the Colombian government were dispatching diplomats and politicians to London and Washington to appeal for action to clamp down on the markets for the drugs. Rudimentary criminology recognizes that controlling crime is about tackling the demand as well as the supply side of the activities, but such strategies are difficult to implement when the traditional practices of international security politics are so focused on externalizing threats. Again there is a tendency in the North to see global problems as solely emanating from the global 'badlands', when much of the problem actually lies closer to home. The consumers of drugs, cheap pirated goods and sex worker services perpetuate these areas of global crime and these people generally reside in wealthy and apparently respectable countries.

Global crime fighting

Political global crime fighting

Interpol

Established in 1923, Interpol is the best known international response to the problem of transnational crime. Its membership is impressively universal with 190 member-states, each represented by delegates at the organization's headquarters at Lyon, France. Each member also hosts a National Crime Bureau (NCB) and these serve as the nodes in an information network to aid state police forces and promote cooperation amongst them. The 190 NCBs are linked by a computerized database which contains pooled information resources on known criminals and stolen goods, such as cars, to aid in the detection of transnational criminals and speed up the process of their extradition (although the process of extradition is still a bilateral matter between the governments concerned). In addition to this chief function of facilitating the exchange of information, Interpol also seeks to promote greater regional cooperation between police forces (as, for example, with the Mercosur countries: Brazil, Argentina, Paraguay, Uruguay and Venezuela) and acts as a 'value-added service provider' giving advice to governments on how to develop extradition agreements and to state police forces on updating their information technology resources. Interpol as an intergovernmental organization has a conventional decision-making structure. Each member-state is represented by a government-appointed delegate who attends an annual General Assembly, which votes by simple majority on the adoption of new procedures. The General Assembly also elects an Executive Committee of thirteen member-state delegates, which meets three times a year and prepares the agenda for the General Assemblies, as well as managing the implementation of decisions. Day-to-day administration is carried out by a permanent secretariat at Lyon headed by the Secretary-General, elected for a five-year term of office by a two-thirds majority of the General Assembly (Interpol 2012).

Despite proclaiming among its objectives that it aims to act 'in the spirit of the Universal Declaration of Human Rights' (Interpol Constitution, Article 2) Interpol has always sought to play a non-political role. Article 3 of its constitution makes this clear. 'It is strictly forbidden for the organisation to undertake any intervention or activities of a political, military, religious or racial character.' This somewhat contradicts the previous article since racial and religious persecution are amongst the crimes renounced in the Universal Declaration of Human Rights, but it would, of course, be impossible for an organization of this nature to maintain its broad membership without such a precondition.

Another limitation to the work of Interpol is its modest budget, derived from member-state contributions calculated on the basis of population and GDP. This point was clearly expressed by Secretary-General Ronald Noble: 'we have a multi-billion dollar problem being tackled by an organization running on just 30 million euros' (Interpol 2002). Sheptycki, with provocative irony, has argued that where Interpol has grown it has evolved like a series of protection rackets. As a largely informal arrangement, without an explicit treaty or fixed budget, Interpol inevitably 'chases the money' and tends to focus on illicit trade cases referred to it by state police in wealthy countries, rather than tackling global crime in the global interest. Hence issues uncomfortable for any particular state, such as the corruption of government officials or the dumping of toxic waste, rarely occupy the time of Interpol officers on temporary secondment from national jobs (Sheptycki 2003). Interpol is clearly a valuable resource to police forces around the world in arresting transnational criminals but, in its present guise, can only be a limited player in the development of global policies to arrest the rise of transnational crime. '[W]hat is needed is an agreed calculus by which to allocate policing resources in order for them to be efficiently and effectively targeted on criminal activities that cause social harm' (Sheptycki 2003: 53).

Europol

The rise in cross-border crime in the European Union, referred to earlier in this chapter, prompted the organisation in the early 1990s to instigate an Interpol-style institution of its own to coordinate the work of its member-state police forces. Europol was agreed upon at the 1992 Treaty on European Union (Maastricht Treaty), in line with the creation of a 'Justice and Home Affairs' dimension to the EU's political integration process, and came into being in January 1994. The 2008 Lisbon Treaty then brought Europol fully into the EU political system.

Like Interpol, Europol has a central database, The Europol Computer System (TECS), serving a system of offices in the member-states. Europol, though, has already outgrown its global 'parent'. Its budget for 2016 topped 100 million euros, nearly three times the amount it ran on fifteen years previously and much bigger than that of Interpol. In addition to a permanent secretariat in The Hague, Europol employs over 100 Europol Liaison Officers (ELOs) across all member-states, principally made up of experienced police and customs officers (Europol 2012b). Europol falls short of being a European police force but is more far-reaching than Interpol in terms of information-sharing.

The World Customs Organization

A similar body to Interpol, the World Customs Organization (WCO) aims to facilitate cooperation between customs officials and coordinate national customs procedures in order to combat illicit trade. Based in Brussels the organization is also near universal with 181 member-states and has been in operation for over sixty years but, like Interpol, is limited in what it can do in the face of increasingly sophisticated global criminals and variations in national capacity. By the WCO's own admission, 'efficient and effective performance is not spread evenly among all Customs administrations, or in all regions of the world' (WCO 2007).

United Nations

As with the EU, the role of the UN with regard to transnational crime originated in efforts to coordinate action against the narcotics trade before evolving into activities dealing with other realms of global criminal activity. The UN took over the management of the League of Nations' work on narcotics, as it did with many functional agencies established by its forerunner, with the League's Committee on the Traffic in Opium and Other Dangerous Drugs coming to be transformed into the Commission on Narcotic Drugs (CND). After a series of institutional reforms and an upsurge of concern on this issue in the 1990s, CND became part of the wider UN Office for Drugs and Crime (UNODC). This step marked a recognition by the UN of the growing significance of a range of transnational criminal operations, first evident in the sponsorship of a major conference in Naples in 1994 attended by government ministers from 136 states.

Legal global crime fighting

The 1994 Naples Conference initiated a Global Action Plan leading to the UN International Convention Against Transnational Organized Crime, adopted by the General Assembly in November 2000 and entering into force in 2003. Article 1 of the convention succinctly describes its purpose as 'to promote cooperation to prevent and combat transnational organized crime more effectively' (UN 2000: 1). Subsequent articles of the convention deal with a wide range of issues relating to transnational organized crime, which are summarized in Table 10.3.

A 'Conference of the Parties' has met regularly since 2003 to oversee the implementation and development of the 'TOC Convention'. The convention is a step

TABLE 10.3 UN Convention Against Transnational Organized Crime

Articles 2–4	definitions and scope of the convention
Article 5	criminalizing the participation in an organized crime group
Articles 8–10	corruption
Articles 11 & 12	punishment
Articles 13 & 14	international cooperation on confiscation
Article 15	jurisdiction
Articles 16 & 17	extradition
Articles 18–22	mutual legal assistance & investigative cooperation
Article 23	criminalizing the obstruction of justice
Article 24	witness protection
Article 25	victim protection
Article 26	encouraging public notification of crime
Article 27	law enforcement cooperation
Article 28	sharing information
Article 29	law enforcement training programmes (initiation or improvement)
Article 30	assistance to LDCs in implementing the convention
Article 31	prevention of organized crime at the domestic level
Articles 32–41	implementation

Protocols: 1 Trafficking in Persons. 2 Smuggling of Migrants. 3 Illegal Trading in Firearms.

forward in terms of providing the basis for greater international harmonization in tackling money laundering and corruption and is close to universal in its reach but, as with most intergovernmental arrangements of this kind, there are no enforcement measures beyond peer pressure. The compulsory sharing of information amongst parties has yet to happen, funding remains predominantly voluntary and implementation of the measures has been informal and sporadic. As with many international treaties, statecentricism has proved a barrier to international justice even though it might be imagined that fighting transnational crime was something all sovereign states could agree on. Governments, though, are not always on the right side of the cops versus robbers divide. As has been discussed, many governments are complicit in corruption, can benefit from illegal financial flows and are actively involved in cybercrime. Even human trafficking – for which a precedent for international action can be dated back to the 1902 Agreement for the Suppression of the White Slave Trade – struggles to unite all of the world's governments since countries of emigration often fear this being used as a pretext for crude anti-immigration policies.

Nevertheless, legal progress on tackling transnational crime continues and, as with human rights, a second generation of more specific treaties has begun to emerge from the platform provided by the TOC Convention. A UN Convention Against Corruption came into force in 2005 and in 2014 an Arms Trade Treaty was agreed by over ninety states, aiming to prohibit illegal small arms sales. Outside of the UN, the Kimberley Process has, since 2003, seen a certification scheme in place seeking to end the 'blood diamonds' phenomenon of African warlords profiting from the sale of these lucrative gems. There are weaknesses in the Kimberley Process, owing to corruption and uneven implementation, but this and other international regimes illustrate an increased international consensus on the need to act against global crime.

Military global crime fighting

The militarization of national crime-fighting, referred to at the start of the chapter, has also manifested itself internationally over the past thirty years. Most notably, in a follow-up to the Panamanian episode of the 'War Against Drugs', the prolonged Plan Colombia was initiated by the USA in 2001. This major foreign policy venture has seen over $10 billion spent in a range of operations including dispatching planes spraying the herbicide glyphosate (also a notorious human toxin) to destroy coca plantations and training and supporting the Colombian police and armed forces in the fight against narco-terrorists. This has tended to shift coca production to new locations but, overall, has not greatly affected the industry. However, the US support has possibly helped stabilize the country and improve its future prospects by contributing to the government being able to force FARC (who have often been part-funded by the cocaine industry) to the negotiation table in efforts to end the lengthy civil war.

As previously highlighted, international cooperation on piracy has often been robust and effective and this was most evident in recent military initiatives to combat thefts and kidnappings off the East African coast (chiefly Somalia). The Shared Awareness and Deconfliction (SHARE) military operation was launched in 2008 by a broad coalition of the most affected maritime states. SHARE is a non-hierarchical network featuring thirty-three countries (including – uniquely – all five UNSC permanent members), the EU and NATO and has succeeded in suppressing Indian Ocean piracy through successful naval cooperation. A clear mutual economic interest to act has made this 'coalition of the willing' relatively easy to assemble and coordinate.

Conclusions

Transnational crime, more starkly than any of the issues of global security politics, illustrates the limitations of the Westphalian system of sovereign states in protecting citizens' lives and livelihoods. Criminals used to exploit the lack of holism in domestic law enforcement by operating across (US) state boundaries or even (UK) county borders until such inappropriate decentralization was addressed politically. That situation has now arisen globally.

> States have become almost outmoded organizations: in effect, we are attempting to deal with a twenty-first century phenomenon using structures, mechanisms and instruments that are still rooted in eighteenth- and nineteenth-century concepts and organizational forms.
>
> (Godson & Williams 1998: 324)

There are, though, signs of hope in the fight against transnational crime. Global homicide rates have stabilized after rising through the 1990s and early 2000s, and international cooperation, whilst patchy, has reaped some rewards. Unprecedented military cooperation between the UN's 'big five' and many others has effectively defeated piracy off the Somalian coast. The war on drugs is far from won but global seizures of cocaine, opiates and cannabis doubled between 1998 and 2008 (UNODC 2016a: 22). In addition, whilst the picture varies across the world, most developed democracies have seen an unexpected decline in crime over the past decade, in spite of economic stagnation. The murder rate in the USA has dropped to a rate lower than for half a century and in Japan to pre-Second World War levels. Better policing is one factor behind this, with DNA profiling, databases of stolen cars and the ability to track mobile phones amongst ways in which IT advances have come to work against rather than for the criminals.

A further, less quantifiable but no less relevant change is positive normative progress. As historic crimes have come to be addressed and faced up to in many countries it has become apparent that societies have evolved and civilized and violence has become less tolerated. In many countries bullying and sexual abuse have come to be more acknowledged and exposed, and the perpetrators of this, rather than the victims, stigmatized (Eisner 2015). In the UK, for example, the sheer scale of child sex abuse cases from the 1970s and 1980s that have come to light over the past five years serves to illustrate that morality, as well as policing methods, has greatly progressed since this time.

This normative change is also becoming apparent on the international stage aided by global civil society. Mutual government interest is not enough to warrant action on some transnational crimes but moral pressure is beginning to have an influence in some of these cases. Kidney trafficking has struggled to find redress because, from a national interest perspective, health tourism is a source of income for some states and a means of remedying a shortage of organs for transplants for others. However, government lobbying and public campaigning by NGOs and medics have pushed governments like Pakistan (on the supply side) and Israel (on the demand side) to act in the face of a morally-indefensible phenomenon (Effrat 2013). NGOs have similarly helped fill the void of widespread government indifference to the illegal timber trade by being active in implementing certification schemes and providing intelligence on state violations (Elliott 2013).

Transnational crime has thrived in the opportunities presented by the profound economic, social and political changes that have been associated with globalization and the transition from a Cold War order over the last thirty years. However, as with other issues previously discussed like terrorism or health, this does not mean that globalization is the root of the problem. The world as a whole has gone through the sorts of changes that have seen crime rise in Russia, South Africa or – more recently – Venezuela. Evidence shows that crime flourishes in periods of national economic, social and political change but also that this can be addressed by coming to terms with new realities, learning how to combat new forms of criminality, and moral progress away from the acceptance or wilful ignorance of long-established bad practices. Political globalization can address the iniquities of purely economic globalization if states come to recognize this or are forced to address it by public pressure. Thus far crime has not prompted the same level of state response or public concern as health or terrorism, but this is beginning to change.

 Key points

- Internationally-operating criminal groups are not new but have become an increased threat to both human and state security by utilizing the opportunities offered by globalization and post-Cold War socio-political change.
- International political action to combat transnational crime has increased in recent years but much remains to be done to tackle a problem now beyond control by conventional inter-state politics.

 Recommended reading

Glenny, M. (2011) *Dark Market: Cyber Thieves, CyberCops and You*, London: Bodley Head.

Roth, M. (2017) *Global Organized Crime: A 21st Century Approach*, 2nd edn, Abingdon: Routledge.

Shelley, L., Picarelli, J. and Corpora, C. (2011) 'Global Crime Inc.', in Cusimano, M. (ed.) *Beyond Sovereignty: Issues for a Global Agenda*, Boston: Wadsworth Cengage: 141–69.

UNODC (2010) *The Globalization of Crime: A Transnational Organized Crime Threat Assessment*, Vienna: UN Office for Drugs and Crime.

Williams, P. (2011) 'Transnational Crime and Security', in Hughes, C. and Meng, L. (eds) *Security Studies: A Reader*, London: Routledge.

Useful web links

- Europol: www.europol.net/
- Interpol: www.interpol.int/
- United Nations Convention Against Transnational Organized Crime: www.unodc.org/unodc/en/treaties/CTOC/
- United Nations Office on Drugs and Crime: www.unodc.org/

Chapter 11

Towards global security?

> We are accustomed to regard the world as neatly divided into compartments called states . . . But this vision of the world divided into isolated compartments is not a true reflection of facts as they exist in a large portion of the earth today.
>
> Leonard Woolf (Woolf 1916: 216–17)

Thinking global: integration theories and global politics

Understanding global security necessitates ridding oneself of the preconception rooted in the traditional and still-dominant political culture that the security under consideration must be that of states, as determined by states. In an age when people's fates were inextricably linked to that of their governments, and the only significant cross-border interactions were military, diplomatic and economic exchanges between governments, this preconception was, to some extent, appropriate. That age, however, has now passed into history and the assumption that an individual's life is solely determined by their government is anachronistic. People in the twentieth century were dependent on their governments like no time before and like they will never be again. The diplomatic manoeuvrings of elected or self-appointed leaders did much to dictate the fates of a large proportion of the world's population in the age of total war. Many millions died and many millions of others were saved by their governments from death at the hands of other governments. Many of those same people were more directly still at the mercy of their governments, who could determine whether or not to murder them in order to enhance their own security.

War and politicide persist and the fates of many of the world's people continue to be determined by politics 'from above', but this is far from the full picture. Strokes of fate from outside of the traditional political world resulting from global technological, social or climatic change determine, to a far greater extent, whether people live or die in today's world. They also determined the fate of most people in 'yesterday's world', although this was obscured by governmental preoccupation with human threats they knew how to deal with. This is no longer so, on both counts. External state-based human threats have diminished and the capacity for governments acting unilaterally to safeguard their people against non-human foes is also in decline.

No life-threatening strokes of fate in today's world are, in fact, from outside of the realm of politics, even if they are outside the control of individual governments. Governments can imperil their own people without dragging them into wars against their interest or victimizing them for their own interests by failing to address, in concert with their fellow governments, global sources of human insecurity. Environmental degradation, transnational crime and infectious disease simply cannot be properly legislated against by a government acting in isolation. Life-threatening poverty and vulnerability to disease and disaster can be insured against by some governments, but this can be to the detriment of the security of other states' citizens. Economic cushioning, such as agricultural protectionism and exploitative market expansion, can come at the cost of the lives of those squeezed out. Optimizing global security is only possible by looking at the bigger picture.

Political integration

Recognition of the inadequacy of state and state-to-state politics in assuring the security of the world's people came early in the era of total war. The folly and horror of the First World War prompted a number of polemical works advocating world government in place of the sovereign system of states. British political socialists and pioneering IR Liberals John Hobson and Leonard Woolf wrote books advocating world government as a means of retreating from endemic war and imperialism (Hobson 1915; Woolf 1916). Woolf was a firm advocate of the League of Nations, which emerged after the Great War, whereas Hobson was highly dismissive of this organization as little more than a victors' club for a war of which he did not approve. Woolf was more positive, considering the League to be furthering the trend established in nineteenth-century international affairs, before the build-up to world war, of international organizations assuming the political stewardship of certain functions from governments.

Pre-dating Woolf and Hobson the US political theorist Paul Reinsch had also concluded from detailed analysis of nineteenth-century international political cooperation prior to its unravelling in the early part of the proceeding century that global governance was the future but in a subtler and less state-phobic form.

> [I]t is not so much the case that nations have given up certain parts of their sovereign powers to international administrative organs, as that they have, while fully reserving their independence, actually found it desirable, and in fact necessary, regularly and permanently to co-operate with other nations in the matter of administrating certain economic and cultural interests
>
> (Reinsch 1911: 14)

BOX 11.1 Leonard Woolf

This prominent literary and political writer formed part of the celebrated 'Bloomsbury Group' of intellectuals which included student friends from his days at Cambridge, including the philosopher Bertrand Russell, economist John Maynard Keynes and the feminist novelist Virginia Stephens, whom he later married.

Woolf resigned from a position in the Ceylon Civil Service due to his distaste of colonialism and was a conscientious objector during the First World War. The ideas which underpinned his most notable political work, *International Government*, were used by the British government in the talks leading up to the creation of the League of Nations, for whom Woolf later worked in a number of capacities.

Woolf, Hobson and Reinsch thus represented pioneers of two differing strands of political integration theory which were further developed, and partially applied, after the Second World War. Woolf and Reinsch's work was a source of inspiration for Functionalists, like David Mitrany, who favoured a gradualist, bottom-up approach towards world government in which ordinary people would rationally come to switch their loyalties from their states to international non-governmental bodies (Mitrany 1975). Hobson's route to world government was more direct and 'top down': the immediate creation of *supranational* agencies assuming control from governments of certain, clearly-defined political areas. World Federalism of this sort gained momentum with the failure of the League of Nations and the horrors that unfolded in the Second World War. The British and Indian premiers, Churchill and Nehru, both advocated this as a recipe for world peace, and the scientist Einstein, fearful in particular of the impact of atomic weapons on international relations, added his support. Advocacy for world Federalism receded as the Cold War reactivated the national interest and economic recovery provided more 'optimism' amongst states that sovereignty had not died alongside the millions of casualties of the Second World War. Churchill even backtracked on earlier support for Western European Federalism, leaving this venture to recent allies and adversaries across the English Channel.

Federalism has yet to happen in Western Europe, despite profound political integration for over sixty years, with Churchill's successors ultimately abandoning the project in the fear that it might one day happen. Elsewhere in the world the track record of sovereign states integrating into federations is not promising. Federalist ventures for a United Arab Republic linking Egypt, Libya and Yemen and a Federation of the West Indies collapsed altogether within a few years of their inauguration in 1958. It has been apparent since then that there is little prospect of a surrender/pooling (depending on your political perspective) of government sovereignty to a global federal authority. The European integration experiment, in fact, recognized from the start that governmental and public support for a United States of Europe had quickly evaporated as the shadow of the Second World War lifted and the European Communities (EC) were modelled on a modified version of Functionalist theory. Monnet, Spaak, Spinelli and the other founding fathers of the EC set about achieving a United Europe in a gradualist manner, starting with the European Coal and Steel Community in 1951, selected deliberately to act as a catalyst for political *spillover* into other sectors. Mitrany had little time for the EC, seeing it as a 'top down' plan which would simply replace a number of states with one bigger one, rather than fundamentally change international relations.

Neo-Functionalism was devised and embraced for the EC experiment for pragmatic rather than idealistic reasons. It was a half-way house between Functionalism and Federalism inspired by the fact that both theories appeared hopelessly utopian by the late 1950s. Federalism on a limited regional scale had failed to get off the ground and the functional international organizations which inspired Functionalism remained limited in influence and still controlled by governments. By the 1990s the continuation of integration without any real likelihood of a United States of Europe emerging from it, despite a revival of the direct approach to its achievement, prompted a new theoretical approach to explain what was happening. The Consociationalist theory of European integration contended that the states of the now restyled European Union would continue to merge economically and politically, inspired not by any holy grail of an idealized end-state but through pragmatic, economic necessity (Taylor 1991). Hence, from this perspective, the launch of a single EU currency did not mark the beginning of the end of sovereign member-states so much as the practical realization by the governments that this would speed up business and that, apart from the German mark, the national currencies were increasingly irrelevant on the global stage.

Neo-Functionalism and Consociationalism are theories very much designed to fit the European experience, but they have some currency when looking at the bigger picture and were foreseen by Reinsch. Consociationalism has global application to the development of the WTO and the numerous international regimes of common rules to which governments increasingly voluntarily commit themselves in order to ease the complications of dealing with modern economic interdependence. The United Nations does not have an equivalent of the European Commission to cultivate global integration from 'above', as Neo-Functionalists describe and advocate, but many initiatives from within its system have served to push forward the natural progress of spillover. Cases in point include the work of the International Law Commission in advancing human rights and establishing the International Criminal Court and the UNDP and Secretary-Generals in promoting human security, the Responsibility to Protect and the Sustainable Development Goals. UN decision-making remains intergovernmental, but there is no doubt that the myriad pro-grammes and specialized agencies under its umbrella are more than the sum of their formal governmental parts. Epistemic communities have established themselves in the various issue areas addressed in the preceding chapters, permitting global discourse to evolve beyond crude state-utilitarianism. Collective goods problems have begun to be addressed in the governance of global trade and environmental change and progressive normative change is evident in all issue areas to different extents.

BOX 11.2 **The specialized agencies of the United Nations**

- **FAO (Food and Agriculture Organization of the UN)**
- Works to improve agricultural productivity and food security.
- **IAEA (International Atomic Energy Agency)**
- Works for the safe and peaceful uses of atomic energy.
- **ICAO (International Civil Aviation Organization)**
- Sets international standards for the safety, security and efficiency of air transport.
- **IFAD (International Fund for Agricultural Development)**
- Mobilizes financial resources to raise food production in developing countries.
- **ILO (International Labour Organization)**
- Formulates policies and programmes to improve working conditions and sets international labour standards.
- **IMF (International Monetary Fund)**
- Facilitates international monetary cooperation and financial stability.
- **IMO (International Maritime Organization)**
- Works to improve international shipping safety and reduce marine pollution.
- **ITU (International Telecommunication Union)**
- Fosters international cooperation to improve telecommunications and coordinates usage of radio and TV frequencies.
- **UNESCO (UN Educational Scientific and Cultural Organization)**
- Promotes education for all and scientific and cultural cooperation.
- **UNIDO (UN Industrial Development Organization)**
- Promotes the industrial advancement of developing countries through technical assistance.
- **UNWTO (UN World Tourism Organization)**
- Serves as a global forum for tourism policy issues.
- **UPU (Universal Postal Union)**
- Establishes international regulations for postal services.
- **WHO (World Health Organization)**
- Coordinates programmes aimed at solving international health problems.
- **WIPO (World Intellectual Property Organization)**
- Promotes the international protection of intellectual property.
- **World Bank Group**
- Provides loans and technical assistance to developing countries to reduce poverty and advance economic growth.
- **WMO (World Meteorological Organization)**
- Promotes research on the Earth's climate and facilitates the global exchange of meteorological data.

This progressive evolution of global policy, though, is not cultivated only from within the UN system. Some governments have also attempted to sow the seeds of global governance within the UN system, guided by human security. The governments of Canada and Norway, the leading members of the Human Security Network, and also Japan have been most prominent in this regard. The UN Commission on Human Security was established in 2001 comprising twelve prominent international statespeople and thinkers, co-chaired by Indian economist Amartya Sen (see Box 4.1) and Japanese academic and former UN High Commissioner for Refugees Sadako Ogata. The Commission held five official meetings culminating in the production of their final report *Human Security Now*, after which it was succeeded by an eight-person Advisory Board chaired by Ogata. The report calls for multilateral, multi-layered governance in order to:

> build a protective infrastructure that shields all people's lives from critical and pervasive threats. That infrastructure includes institutions at every level of society: police systems, environmental regulations, health care networks, educational systems, safety nets and workfare programmes, vaccination campaigns and early warning systems for crises or conflict.
>
> (Commission on Human Security 2003: 132)

Generally better suited to the promotion of human security than governments, though, are pressure groups because of their transnational character, closeness to local populations, willingness to confront the political status quo and capacity for coalition-building (Michael 2002: 2). The Norwegian government has recognized this and worked extensively in international affairs with conflict resolution groups such as International Alert and developmental organizations such as the Aga Khan Foundation. Similarly, the Japanese government funds pressure groups furthering human-centred development through its Grant Assistance for Grassroots Human Security Projects (GGP) Programme. Over 1,000 European humanitarian and development-focused pressure groups were brought together in 2003 under

TABLE 11.1 Key recommendations of the Commission on Human Security

1. Protecting people in violent conflict
2. Protecting people from the proliferation of arms
3. Supporting the security of people on the move
4. Establishing human security transition funds for post-conflict situations
5. Encouraging fair trade and markets to benefit the extreme poor
6. Working to provide minimum living standards everywhere
7. According higher priority to ensuring universal access to basic health care
8. Developing an efficient and equitable global system for patent rights
9. Empowering all people with universal basic education
10. Clarifying the need for a global human identity while respecting the freedom of individuals to have diverse identities and affiliations

the umbrella of the Confederation for Cooperation of Relief and Development (CONCORD), and made human security the cornerstone of their campaigns, which have featured extensive lobbying of governments holding the EU presidency and notably succeeded in getting an increase in foreign aid pledges from the member-states in 2005. Similarly, human security was the theme of the 2003 Annual Conference of the 'World Association of NGOs' held in Bangkok and many pressure groups have individually indicated their support for the concept. In 2007 a campaign for the establishment of a United Nations Parliamentary Assembly was launched by NGOs such as the World Federalist Movement, former UN Secretary-General Boutros-Ghali, the European parliament and several hundred national parliamentarians seeking to democratize the UN and ensure it is formally structured in order to meet human as well as state interests.

> States and societies everywhere in the world increasingly confront forces far beyond the control of any one state or even group of states. Some of these forces are irresistible, such as the globalization of economic activity and communications. In the process, problems which can only be solved effectively at the global level, are multiplying and requirements of political governance are extending beyond state borders accordingly. Increasing decision-making at the global level is inevitable. In this process, however, democracy within the state will diminish in importance if the process of democratization does not move forward at the international level.
>
> Therefore, we need to promote the democratization of globalization, before globalization destroys the foundations of national and international democracy.
>
> (Boutros-Ghali 2007)

The UN and the League before it were always intended to be far more than intergovernmental talking shops and, from the start, sought to incorporate civil society as a way of enriching the international political agenda. The role of the UN's Economic and Social Council (ECOSOC) in giving consultative status to NGOs, formalizing cooperation evident under the League system, provides clear evidence of that.

Acting global: global solutions to global problems

A state-utilitarianist path to enhanced global security

Although contemporary international political practice marks a recognition of the fact that human and state security both rest on more than the preservation of sovereignty by force, it is clear from examining the issues of global security that this has not gone far enough. The 'cosmopolitan ethics' of Liberal IR scholars like Beitz and Liberal philosophers like Rawls found satisfaction in the late twentieth-century codification of international human rights law and deepening economic interdependence, as they confirmed that the individual was emerging as an entity in international politics from under the shell of the sometimes clumsy protection of the state (Beitz 1979; Rawls 1971).

Rawls's widely applied test of justice for a political system contends that inequality in the distribution of social goods can be considered fair if the least advantaged nonetheless gain increased social goods over time (Rawls 1971). The onset of political globalization from the mid-twentieth century has broadly been just according to this criterion since, in spite of the growing disparity between rich and poor, quality of life has improved for most people in nearly all countries. Near universal increases in life expectancy and HDI scores support this. Only two states – Syria and Swaziland – 'went backwards' in HDI between 1990 and 2015 (UNDP 2016). Chronic internal human security threats – from conflict in the former and HIV/AIDS in the latter – largely account for these anomalies.

When, in the 1990s, the changed international political environment facilitated the further advance of global justice and interdependence, it became apparent, however, that a continuation of 'twentieth-century Westphalian globalization' alone was not the solution to all of the world's ills. Despite major medical and technological advances in the decades after the Second World War, which had seen unprecedented global economic growth and a reduction in the health gap between North and South, it was clear by the end of the century that economic globalization was not enough to continue this improvement and even part of the problem. What was needed, however, was not the abandonment of globalization, increasingly advocated by a growing global social movement, so much as 'globalisation with a human spin' (Lee, Buse & Fustukian 2002: 279) or the democratization of globalization. The fact that the globalization of the value of economic gain had come without the commensurate globalization of the value of human security was at the root of global ailments becoming more apparent at the end of the millennium.

Frankman described the emerging global polity of the 1990s as 'hard democracy', a limited form of democratic representation dished out by political elites without properly empowering the stakeholders (Frankman 1997: 324). The term had originally been coined to describe the semi-democratization of some South American states in the 1980s by military dictatorships, driven by populist expediency rather than a genuine desire to free their citizens. Delving further back into history in trying to characterize the global political system at the start of the twenty-first century, a number of Realist thinkers have contended that Bull's cautionary 'new medievalism' has come to pass (Bull 1977: 254; Mathews 1997; Held et al. 1998: 85). This perspective argues that the complex overlap of competing jurisdictions and multiple levels of authority that increasingly mark the contemporary system is coming to resemble the chaotic politics of Europe before Westphalian order was imposed. The rise of anti-globalization and Eurosceptic sentiments in Western politics over the past two decades indicates that this is a message with increased public resonance.

A restoration of Westphalian order today, though, would not address the problems of global security. A measure of good governance is that it enhances human security, and it is clear that neither the state nor the partially globalized world order can claim to be achieving, or be able to achieve, this. Falk claims that there are three damnable indictments against 'inhumane' global governance: the 'global apartheid' of poverty, the persistence of the 'avoidable harm' of discrimination, and 'eco-imperialism' (Falk 1995: 47–78).

Keohane, a less radical Liberal than Falk or Mitrany, has suggested that there is now compelling evidence for five tasks to be assumed control of by a global level of governance:

1   Limiting the resort by states to large-scale violence.
2   Limiting the resort by states to exporting 'negative externalities' which arise from interdependence, such as pollution and protectionist 'beggar thy neighbour' economic policies.
3   The establishment of coordinated standards and language in global commerce. This would doubtless be controversial and initially costly but once agreed upon becomes efficient and in the interests of all.
4   A global facility for dealing with global 'system disruptions', such as economic depression.
5   A means of guaranteeing the protection of people against the worst forms of abuse by their states (Keohane 2002: 248–9).

In a similar vein and outside of the broad church of Liberalism, Wendt, notable for projecting his Neo-Realist instincts through a Social Constructivist filter, has made a state-utilitarian case for the inevitability of a world state within the next two centuries. Since the international system has gradually evolved from anarchy to a 'system of states' and then a 'world society', through the self-interest of states seeking to tame international war, he posits that further progress towards a world state is both inevitable and in the interests of even powerful states.

> [I]f the choice is between a world of growing threats as a result of refusing to recognize others versus a world in which their desires for recognition are satisfied, it seems clear which decision rational Great Powers should take.
>
> (Wendt 2003: 529–30)

Wendt and Keohane's prescriptions represent a more limited model of global governance than that generally advocated by world Federalists or Functionalists. They have some parallels with the Consociationalist approach to European integration or Reinsch's 'proto-functionalism', in that the suggested abrogations of state powers can largely be construed as being in the states' own interests since they are a means to the end of solving problems beyond their control. From such a state-utilitarian base more ambitious schemes proposed to aid global governance could eventually develop as state interests come to be redefined and non-state opinions become more influential.

Some proposals for future global governance, going beyond the state-utilitarianism of Consociationalism, have attracted significant levels of government support, even if they are still some distance from realization. The idea of a global 'Tobin Tax', named after the Nobel Prize-winning economist, has gained the official advocacy of many governments including in Brazil, France and Germany and has gained momentum since the onset of the 2008 recession. The tax would be a levy on cross-border currency speculation, the proceeds of which would be transferred to alleviate poverty and other global problems. Whilst the cynic could argue that this is still utilitarianism since transnational currency speculators are an economic threat to some states, the championing of another globally redistributive levy applied to international air travel by many developing countries and some developed world statesmen is even more obviously in the global rather than national interest.

Appropriate divisions of political responsibility vary over time as societies change and this needs to be acknowledged by responsible politicians if their aim is to serve their constituents' interests. The principle of subsidiarity underpins federal systems of government and has come to be a measure of the appropriate division of the responsibilities in the EU's part-federal political system. Subsidiarity is the guideline that decisions should be taken at the most appropriate level of governance for the satisfaction of the political goals at stake. Under this principle, decisions should be taken as closely to the local level as possible, with higher levels of authority only utilized when this is necessary and preferable. The logic of this premise can be seen outside of constitutional legal frameworks in a general political trend. The observable simultaneous decentralization and regional convergence of many democratic political systems in recent years serves to show that contemporary states are increasingly both too big and too small to satisfy the demands of their people in a number of policy areas. Governments are becoming aware of this but they are also, of course, sufficiently informed by the logic of self-preservation to resist the transfer of authority beyond that which serves their own interest.

In line with this trend towards regionalization there is a political logic that certain aspects of governance should be undertaken at the global level, since they simply cannot be satisfactorily carried out at even the regional inter-state level. The new medievalism problem, which has occurred as a result of the natural 'drift' towards multi-level governance, would also be resolved by a clear demarcation of responsibilities, in place of the ad hoc development of patchy international and global governance. The application of subsidiarity to global governance would not merely be about the sanctioning of ever-greater authority to remote institutions, of the form which has provoked a prominent 'anti-globalization' social movement. The decentralization of certain international political institutions and policies would also be a consequence, where it is clear that policies may be better formulated and implemented at the regional level. Howse and Nicolaidis, for example, argue that the principal target of anti-globalization activist anger, the World Trade Organization, would gain greater legitimacy if subsidiarity were applied to its operations. Through reform, more of its decisions could be taken at the state or regional level and a clear process found for resolving clashes between its rules and international environmental law, thus disarming the most significant criticisms of its workings (Howse & Nicolaidis 2003). Being answerable to a UN Parliamentary Assembly would also help bridge the democratic deficit.

In military politics the difficulties in getting global solidarity for collective security could be offset by the unambiguous delegation of such responsibilities to regional bodies like NATO or ECOWAS, as is already happening in what is often viewed a somewhat ad hoc and controversial manner. As discussed in Chapter 2, though, the notion of such an arrangement was around at the start of the UN's history but was overlooked during the Cold War. Chapter 8 of the UN Charter refers to 'the existence of regional arrangements or agencies for dealing with such matters relating to the maintenance of international peace and security as are appropriate for regional action'. Regional organizations, though, were barely in existence when these words were written in the 1940s and, when they did emerge, were never going to be able to work in tandem with all of the 'big five' at the UN. In 2006, on the basis of UNSC Resolution 1631 the previous year, the UN Secretary-General Kofi Annan produced the report *A Regional-Global Security Partnership: Challenges and Opportunities*, which stated that:

> The United Nations claims no monopoly on the settlement of disputes. There may be times when it would be better for other mediators such as those from regional partners to handle a given situation.
>
> (UNGA & UNSC 2006: 7)

Global ethics

The partial nature of global governance has served to inhibit functional spillover from occurring naturally. Clear injustice in a political system holds back its progress towards a better system by reducing the inclination of the disadvantaged to participate in the global discourse necessary for engineering improvement (Habermas 2001). Apel, like Habermas a Critical Theorist and firm believer in the existence of universalist ethics, has rationalized this setback in the progression of cosmopolitanist moral governance. Apel contends that the natural equilibrium between human actions and ethics, which had seen human rights policy develop alongside the proliferation of greater transnational interactions, has eroded due to the dark side of globalization becoming more apparent in poverty and environmental degradation. The dominance of Economic Liberalism in the global political discourse has hindered the development of the natural human ethic of social responsibility. Apel considers that for a more rounded 'planetary macro ethics' to emerge from the shadow cast by Economic Liberalism a global 'communications community' needs to develop, in which the private sphere of human values is able to take its place alongside the public sphere of profit-based rationality inherent in trading rules (Apel 1991). Hence the dark side of globalization necessitates permitting the full emergence of the light side, rather than a retreat from globalism.

> [T]he process characterized so far should only be considered a phenomenon of first-order globalization. It is a challenge to the philosophical reflection and thereby to a mobilization of moral responsibility for the establishment of a novel order of human interaction that could be called second-order globalization.
>
> (Apel 2000: 138)

Global ethics exist, and have gradually become more established, as evidenced by the development of human rights law, but they are undermined by the lop-sided nature of recent global political developments driven by economic gain (which, of course, has a light side as well as a dark side). Plenty of evidence shows that social responsibility is not absent in the political world so much as stifled by the focus on the freeing up of trade at the highest levels of governance. The reform of the World Bank, from being an advocate of 'unreconstructed liberalism' into a more socially-oriented set of institutions, is perhaps the clearest example of such normative change. The World Bank now routinely considers the environmental or social cost of any development project, as well as its economic viability, before granting it its seal of approval. This metamorphosis occurred through the development of a different epistemic community working within the system of organizations making up the 'bank' in response to pressure group criticism and necessitated by having to deal with the difficult socio-economic transition of former Communist countries in East Europe (Deacon, Hulse & Stubbs 1997: 198). Similar change has occurred in the UNDP as the normative shift from advocating 'pure' economic growth to more human-centred development has occurred amongst experts in the field. At the same time, international organizations clearly dedicated to welfare and social reform, such as the ILO, UNICEF and the office of the UN High Commissioner for Refugees (UNHCR), continue to propagate the ethos of co-responsibility in their work. As highlighted throughout this volume, human-focused approaches have come to evolve in the politics of all the issues of global security. An emergent global discourse has promoted the normative change that has seen principles like a right to health and a responsibility to protect and concrete aims such as the Millennium Development and then Sustainable Development Goals become established on the international stage, not directly equitable with national interests (see Box 11.3).

Global values of justice and co-responsibility are also evident in global discourse outside of the mainstream political sphere. Global sports bodies, for example, did more than inter-state politics to ostracize apartheid-era South Africa by banning the country from prestigious competitions such as the Olympic Games. Football's ruling body, the Federation of International Football Authorities (FIFA), has intervened in cases where minority nationals appear to have been discriminated against in the selection of 'national' sides. The spirit of 'fair play' underpinning these stances represents a good gauge of global morality since no hegemon or self-interest is behind the development of such rules. Where unrestrained human dialogue occurs, a code of ethics follows. Global political dialogue, however, became somewhat skewed by the rapid onset of economic globalization in the 1990s and the resultant ethics were distorted commensurately.

Globalization opens up both opportunities and problems in the same way that industrialization and the transition from Communism to Liberalism has in many states of the world. Twentieth-century Liberals in Europe recognized that Economic Liberalism alone was not sufficient to maximize individual freedom, prosperity and security in domestic politics and arrived at a consensus with Social Democrats and Conservatives on the need for a state role to help facilitate this. Hence today health and safety standards, welfarism and the notion of 'social security' are accepted as integral to the governance of most developed democracies. Similarly 'ecocentricism'

BOX 11.3 The Sustainable Development Goals

1 **No poverty** – address causes nationally & globally; increase resilience to climate change

2 **Zero hunger** – food security; increase productivity; address agricultural protectionism

3 **Good health & well-being** – combat communicable & non-communicable diseases

4 **Quality education** – literacy & numeracy; gender equality

5 **Gender equality** – tackle discrimination & violence; ensure reproductive rights

6 **Clean water & sanitation** – universal access to drinking water; combat pollution

7 **Affordable & clean energy** – universal access to energy; greater use of clean energy

8 **Decent work & economic growth** – economic growth for LDCs; labour rights; safe work

9 **Industry, innovation & infrastructure** – credit for small businesses; technology transfers

10 **Reduced inequalities** – social protection; financial regulation; trade reform; LDC inclusion

11 **Sustainable cities & communities** – safe, affordable housing; combat pollution & disasters

12 **Responsible consumption & production** – sustainability; chemical safety; tackle subsidies

13 **Climate action** – implement UNFCC; build adaptation; education

14 **Life below water** – tackle pollution, acidification & overfishing; co-management

15 **Life on land** – address deforestation, desertification & biodiversity

16 **Peace, justice & strong institutions** – reduce violence & crime; advance human rights

17 **Partnerships for the goals** – 0.7 per cent foreign aid target; complete Doha WTO Round

---

has often triumphed over 'anthropocentricism' in the environmental legislation of states such as the USA, who often appear to be driven only by the latter in global policy. Human co-responsibility and a respect for non-human life sometimes supersede economic and government self-interest in democratic domestic governance because people demand that to be the case. As Sen's 'entitlements thesis' convincingly argues, the democratic peace argument for enhancing military security can be applied, with greater rigor, to non-military security issues like famines and diseases

(Sen 1981). Democratic governments are compelled to be responsive to the needs of ordinary people whose security is imperilled, either directly or indirectly due to the pressure of the media or other concerned citizens, for reasons of their own self-preservation if nothing else. Ironically, it is in the realm of military politics that the limitations of state egoism have been most clearly acknowledged by governments in recent decades since dialogue and cooperation have proven to be the best means of breaking the security dilemma and the spiral of inter-state war once considered inevitable. Effective global governance, ultimately, serves national as well as human security.

Hence advancing human security need not be driven just by human compassion but by the same hard-headed conservative logic that prompted Bismarck to pioneer the world's first state welfare policies: the recognition that reform from above can prevent revolution from below. The Chinese government have come to compromise on their short-term economic growth in order to address pollution and climate change through a combination of coming to recognize the long-term economic necessity of doing so and concern that this is fomenting social unrest in their cities.

Discovering universal values as a path to maximizing global security

Good global governance, that which enhances human security, requires the restoration of the natural equilibrium between human actions and the ethics which guide them. This necessitates positive action to 'identify' the missing norms, which are in the interests of all but obscured from view. Hence, this approach takes a step further from the Communitarianism of Liberal philosophers like Rawls and IR scholars like Keohane and Wendt in going beyond the identification of common interests. '[A] genuine universalization principle of morality . . . must also be capable of preventing those factual forms of consensus that are reached at the cost of affected but absent parties' (Apel 2000: 152).

Showing that universal values are 'out there' is something that the UN Educational Scientific and Cultural Organization (UNESCO) has worked on since the 1980s when the organization's Universal Ethics Project initiated a process of identifying core universal values and principles. This process has seen the employment of both empirical and 'reflective' methodologies to find the ethics already out there, in addition to those which have as yet been unable to inform global policy and discourse. The culmination of this work was the 1999 Declaration of Human Duties and Responsibilities, whose drafters included the academic Richard Falk and prominent statesmen Bernard Kouchner[1] and Ruud Lubbers.[2] The reflective method permits one to 'derive ethical values and principles considered necessary in relation to the problems to be solved' (Kim 1999). Hence from the core empirical ethic of human survival other values can be deduced, since they contribute to the satisfaction of this. Examples include reciprocity, the prohibition of violence, truth-telling, justice and social responsibility. Hence the 1999 declaration reads as a charter for the advancement of human security. Amongst many articles, Articles 1 and 2 deal with the 'Right to Life and Human Security' and Articles 3 to 9 with 'Human Security and an Equitable International Order' (Kim 1999).

Similarly, attempts have been made to distil core values from the array of the world's religions, frequently cited as evidence of the relativism of human morality. The centenary 'Parliament of the World's Religions' in 1993 brought together representatives of 120 different faiths and produced a declaration drafted by Kung (a Swiss Catholic theologian). In the declaration two principles were espoused as universal: (1) every human should be treated humanely; (2) people should behave towards others as they would expect them to behave towards them. From this, more precise moral guidelines can be deduced such as: non-violence and respect for life, solidarity and just economic order, tolerance and truthfulness and equal rights between men and women (Kung & Kuschel 1993; Kim 1999).

'Identifying' missing norms is distinct from the hegemonic imposition of normative standards since inclusiveness is a prerequisite for allowing the normative dialogue to grow. Those who consider a political system to be fundamentally unjust will resist even the imposition of just norms. By identifying the common denominators of mutually beneficial living the functionalist imperative can be reactivated and good governance can evolve. Most democratic states needed some sort of push of this form, such as the codification of a constitution or a bill of rights, to assist in the evolution of gradually more just political systems. An important point here is to recognize that the 'creation' of normative ideas and principles today can affect future human behaviour. Even 'rational egoists' are less likely to overturn moral norms once they are established, unless for compelling tyrannical reasons, which will then be clearly understood as such (Keohane 2002: 259). If amoral action is against the norm it is less easily resorted to, even by the instinctively amoral actor. Reputation is important in international politics as evidenced by the mainstream acknowledgement of 'soft power'. Gradually over the last fifty years governments have less frequently violated global human rights standards or resorted to unjust wars because of the implications for their standing in the world. Similarly, MNCs have begun to act in a more socially and environmentally responsive manner through fear of the effects of naming and shaming and a general recognition that the moral climate in which they operate is changing. Human rights and justice cannot be undone as quickly as they are evolving so long as they are understood as the rights of all humanity and justice for all.

Across all of the issues of global security analysed through the preceding chapters we can see normative progress and the gradual appreciation of universal values. Sources of military tension persist and we remain far from in a condition of 'perpetual peace' but the twenty-first century is a huge advance from the imperialism and gunboat diplomacy of the nineteenth century or total war of the twentieth century. Terrorism is still a major concern but, again, hardly compares to the military threats of the past two centuries and has now spawned a commensurate level of international cooperation in response, also unimaginable in those eras. The persistence of global poverty and hunger is a stain on the global conscience but a consensus on the need for action on this has greatly advanced and, consequently, rates have fallen and look likely to continue to do so in spite of sluggish economic growth. A similar sort of consensus has been built in global environmental politics as evidenced by the 2015 Paris agreement on combating climate change at which oil exporters and one-time sceptics came to acknowledge the 'inconvenient truth'.

Human rights also continue to evolve, as does the notion of a 'right to health' and the need to address vulnerabilities to disasters and accidents. Transnational crime until recently was the most poorly addressed global security problem but the mutually reinforcing phenomena of global cooperation, learning and normative progress have begun to reap rewards in falling rates of criminality.

Conclusions

Throughout the world, governments increasingly have come to recognize their own limitations and see the Canute-like futility of a sovereign resisting the waves of globalization. This is partly a pragmatic appreciation that the world is changing and they must adapt or die but it is also a response to pressure from their constituents who recognize that their welfare and security needs are better met by different forms of governance. Hence there is a rational actor script by which global governance could be seen to continue to grow in the future. At some point in the future, though, that script comes to an ending not as happy as it could be for the people of the world as their security comes into conflict with government security once any meaningful remnant of sovereignty is faced with a curtain call. 'Rational' governments may come to accept new versions of a social contract more weighted to the interests of their citizens but few are likely to 'do the decent thing' and allow themselves to be submerged by the waves if that is what is in their citizens' best interests. Identifying the best interests of human beings thus needs to be done directly, rather than indirectly through intermediaries acting on their behalf but also according to their own interests. To ensure that this happens there is compelling evidence that global spillover needs to be 'cultivated' as a means of getting over the national interest barrier. The logic of Functionalism could then be reactivated and humanity be permitted to take up its rightful place at the centre of politics.

 ## Notes

1   A founding member of the pressure group Médecins Sans Frontières, former health minister in the French government and head of the UN's civil administration in Kosovo.
2   Former prime minister of the Netherlands and the UN High Commissioner for Refugees.

 ## Recommended reading

Keohane, R. (2002) *Power and Governance in a Partially Globalized World*, London and New York: Routledge.
Mitrany, D. (1975) *The Functional Theory of Politics*, London: Robertson.
Wendt, A. (2003) 'Why a World State Is Inevitable', *European Journal of International Relations*, 9(4): 491–542.
Yunker, J. (2011) *The Idea of World Government from Ancient Times to the Twenty-First Century*, Abingdon and New York: Routledge.

Useful web links

- Federal Union: www.federalunion.org.uk/about/
- UNESCO: www.unesco.org/
- United Nations Parliamentary Association: http://en.unpacampaign.org/
- UN Trust Fund for Human Security: www.un.org/humansecurity/

Glossary

Alter-Globalist: a position on globalization which is neither entirely pro or anti but reformist.

anarchy: lawlessness. In International Relations used to characterize the international state system in which no law supersedes the sovereign authority of the states.

anthropocentric: policies or actions carried out for human interests.

autarky: the aggressive pursuit of economic self-sufficiency.

authoritarian: non-democratic.

bilateral: involving two parties.

bipolar: dominated by two sides.

client state: a state sponsored by another (to, for example, fight a war).

codify: write down in law.

collective goods problem: a situation requiring a group (of, for example, states) to work together, rather than individually, in order to achieve an optimal outcome.

collective security: the world's states working together systematically in order to maintain peace.

conflate: mix together two ideas.

core and periphery: the progressive division of a country into two economic groupings due to the progressive accumulation of wealth by the elite.

defoliant: chemical used to strip leaves from trees and plants.

dialectic: the process of opposing ideas being debated until the truth emerges.

diplomatic immunity: the package of measures which give official state representatives legal privileges in the country in which they are serving.

diplomatic recognition: the process whereby one government acknowledges the legal existence of another government so permitting them to function as a sovereign entity in international law.

Eastern Bloc: the USSR's six East European satellite states during the Cold War: East Germany, Poland, Hungary, Czechoslovakia, Romania and Bulgaria.

ecocentric: policies or actions carried out for non-human interests.

emerging markets: states successfully undergoing economic development.

empirical: based on factual evidence (such as data).

endogenous: from within (a country).

epidemic: localized disease outbreak above the norm.

epidemiological: related to the study of disease.

epistemic community: transnational group of experts on a given subject.

epistemic consensus: broad agreement amongst an epistemic community.

epistemology: how you come to know something. The theory of establishing knowledge.

ethnocentricism: the tendency to consider one's own nationality as more significant or superior to others.

First World: collective term for the states of the developed, capitalist world during the Cold War.

fossil fuels: fuels produced from fossilized organic material (e.g. oil, coal and natural gas).

fundamentalism: ideology characterized by the revolutionary advancement of a religion.

global North: the world's developed and most wealthy states (which are principally in the northern hemisphere).

global South: the less developed countries (which are principally in the southern hemisphere).

gross domestic product (GDP): the sum total from all economic activity in a given country.

Grotian: a liberal, internationalist world view espousing the importance of a rigorous and moral-based system of international law. Named after the seventeenth-century lawyer Hugo Grotius.

gun boat diplomacy: the provocative display of military force (typically naval) intended to influence a target state without the resort to war.

Hegelian dialectic: historical process, associated with the writings of the philosopher Hegel, whereby an opposing thesis and counter-thesis (such as ideologies) clash until a new synthesized thesis emerges.

hegemony: the exercise, usually by a single state, of international dominance and leadership, particularly in economic relations.

herbicides: chemicals used to kill pest plants.

holistic: a systemic approach favoured on the basis that 'the whole is greater than the sum of its parts', making the understanding of the sub-units of a system insufficient.

Idealist: term applied to statesmen and academics of the 1920s and 1930s who advocated greater levels of international cooperation, epitomized by the creation of the League of Nations.

integration: the process whereby states merge some of their economic and political responsibilities into a wider political unit.

interdependence: the condition of inter-connectedness between actors in international politics which makes them reliant on each other.

intergovernmental organization (IGO): an international organization comprising government representatives of more than one country.

international non-governmental organization (INGO): an international organization comprised of private individuals rather than government representatives.

international regime: system of rules and policy-making procedures, either formal or informal, which influence the behaviour of actors in a particular international issue.

Iron Curtain: term applied to the tight border established by the USSR during the Cold War to isolate its allies in Eastern Europe from Western Europe.

liquidity: monetary reserves.

monetarist: economic policy that focuses on avoiding the excessive expansion of the money supply.

multilateral: involving more than two states.

multipolar: a political system with more than two dominant focuses of power.

neo-imperialism: the economic domination of a state by another without there being formal imperial control.

New Right: a strand of Conservative political thought favouring reduced state involvement in economic affairs. Rose to prominence in the 1980s in the Reagan and Thatcher administrations in the USA and UK, though its origins lie in Classical Liberalism of the nineteenth century.

nihilistic: extremely sceptical to the point of denying the existence of morality altogether.

non-combatant immunity: principle that civilians should not be targeted in warfare.

non-state actor: an organization with international political significance other than a state. A generic term for both INGOs and IGOs.

normative: moral-based.

ontological: enquiry into 'what there is' (ontology).

overpopulation: condition whereby a given state has a population in excess of its capacity to support them to an optimal level.

pandemic: widespread international outbreak of disease.

paradigm: general perspective on International Relations. A set of assumptions on how and why international political events occur in the way that they do.

positivism: value-free enquiry (the scientific method).

power capabilities: resources and attributes of a state which serve to determine how influential it can be. Includes natural resources, geographical location, population and level of economic development.

proxy war: war in which the participants are largely sponsored from afar.

realpolitik: amoral, self-serving political practice by states.

regime: (see 'international regime')

relativism: the assumption that something (such as morality) has no objective meaning and exists only in terms of someone's interpretation of it.

renewable resources: natural resources which are inexhaustible, such as wind power.

risorgimento nationalism: a form of nationalist ideology (originating in nineteenth-century Italy) which supports the principle of national self-determination for all nations, rather than just the advancement of one's own.

satellite state: a technically independent but effectively colonized state.

secular: description of a state where religion is separated from government.

security community: a group of states enjoying such good and close relations that they form a community in which war is unthinkable.

social construct: something which can be defined only in the subjective terms of the participants rather than by objective, empirical analysis.

social contract: the 'deal' in political theory whereby government legitimacy is maintained through the trade-off of them granting rights to their citizens in exchange for the imposition on them of certain duties.

social movement: broad societal movement seeking political change through mass activism rather than the party political process.

societal security: approach related to the perception of people that their society is under threat.

sovereignty: status of legal autonomy enjoyed by states so that their government has exclusive authority within its borders and enjoys the rights of membership of the international community.

spillover: the tendency for political integration in one area to provide the momentum for integration to occur in other, related areas.

statecentricism: analysis which is biased towards the roles and motivations of states over other actors in international relations.

statist: focused on the state.

structural adjustment: the package of conditions accompanying a loan given to a state, such as by the IMF. Such conditions typically entail monetarily conservative measures such as public spending cuts.

Structuralist: perspective which considers that individual behaviour is largely determined by the system in which the individual operates (as, for example, the behaviour of actors in the international system). Most (but not exclusively) associated with the Marxist paradigm of International Relations.

superpower: term applied to the USA and USSR during the Cold War because of their dominance of international relations, which superseded that of the *great powers* in earlier eras.

supranational: authority above the state.

symbiosis: the natural science process whereby two living organisms co-exist for their mutual benefit. Used in political science to denote situations when apparently contradictory aims (such as sovereignty and political integration) can both be simultaneously enhanced.

theocracy: political system in which religious leaders have ultimate power.

'the other': that which is distinguishable from 'the self' in the construction of social identities, such as nationality.

totalitarianism: autocratic rule in which the citizen is totally subject to the state.

total war: war in which civilians are targeted as well as military and state targets.

trade preferences: preferential terms of trade (e.g. lower tariff payments) granted to certain countries.

transnational: linking societies in different countries.

unilateral: one (state) alone.

utilitarian: driven by the aim of maximizing the utility of something. Term most used in International Relations in situations where governments cooperate to reap mutual material gains.

value-free: enquiry which is objective and not influenced by the enquirer's own opinions.

Westphalian: pertaining to the sovereign state system (named after the 1648 Treaty of Westphalia at which the concept of sovereignty is considered to have originated).

Bibliography

Abbasi, K. (1999) 'The World Bank and World Health: Changing Sides', Editorial, *British Medical Journal*, 318, 27 March: 365–9.

Abrams, A. (2001) 'A Short History of Occupational Health', *Journal of Public Health Policy*, 22(1): 34–80.

African Leadership Forum (1991) 'The Kampala Document: Towards a Conference on Security, Stability, Development and Cooperation in Africa', www.africaaction.org/african-initiatives/kampall.htm (accessed 23.7.03).

Ali, S. (2008) interview by J. Gettlem, *New York Times*, 30 September.

American Anthropological Association (1999) Declaration on Anthropology and Human Rights, AAA Committee for Human Rights, www.aaanet.org/stmts/humanrts.htm (accessed 12.3.03).

American Anthropologist Association (1947) 'Statement on Human Rights', *American Anthropologist*, 49(4): 539–42.

Ammann, A. and Nogueira, S. (2002) 'Governments as Facilitators or Obstacles in the HIV Epidemic', *British Medical Journal*, 324, 26 January: 184–5.

Amnesty International (2000) *Crimes of Hate, Conspiracy and Silence: Torture and Ill Treatment Based on Sexual Identity*, London: Amnesty International Report.

Anderson, B. (1991) *Imagined Communities: Reflections on the Origin and Spread of Nationalism*, London: Verso.

Annan, K. (1999) 'Statement by the Secretary General', in Ingleton, J. (ed.) *Natural Disaster Management. A Presentation to Commemorate the International Decade for Natural Disaster Reduction (IDNDR)*, Leicester: Tudor Rose.

Annan, K. (2002) video message for the '7th International Day of Commemoration for Workers Dead or Injured at Work' (Workers Memorial Day), ILO Headquarters, Geneva, 29 April.

Annan, K. (2004) 'A More Secure World: Our Shared Responsibility', *Report of the Secretary-General's High Level Panel on Threats, Challenges and Change*, New York: UN.

Anseeuw, W., Wily, L., Cotula, L. and Taylor, M. (2011) 'Land Rights and the Rush for Land. Findings of the Global Pressures on Land Research Project', Rome: International Land Coalition.

AP (2015) Associated Press, 10 December, https://apnews.com/3a42a7733a8b476889bb4b7b3be3560e/ap-count-over-2400-killed-saudi-hajj-stampede-crush (accessed 24/05/17).

Apel, K.O. (1990) 'The Problem of a Universalistic Macroethics of Co-responsibility', in Griffioen, S. (ed.) *What Right Does Ethics Have? Public Philosophy in a Pluralistic Culture*, Amsterdam: Vrije Universiteit Press: 23–40.

Apel, K.O. (1991) 'A Planetary Macroethics for Humankind', in Deutsch, E., *Culture and Modernity: East-West Philosophical Perspectives*, Hawaii: University of Hawaii Press.

Apel, K.O. (2000) 'Globalization and the Need for Universal Ethics', *European Journal of Social Theory*, 3(2): 137–55.

APTA (2016) *The Hidden Traffic Safety Solution. Public Transportation*, American Public Transport Association.

Arnold, M. and Merrick, P. (2001) 'Development for Disaster Reduction – the Role of the World Bank', *Australian Journal of Emergency Management*, 16(4): 34–6.

Ash, R. (2001) *The Top 10 of Everything*, London: Dorling Kindersley.

Ashdown, P. (2001) 'We Need Missile Defence', *Guardian*, 19 June.

Ashdown, P. (2011) Humanitarian Emergency Response Review, UK Department for International Development, www.dfid.gov.uk/emergency-response-review (accessed 20.9.11).

Atun, R. (2016) 'Economic Downturns, Universal Health Coverage and Cancer Mortality', *Lancet*, 388(10045): 684–95.

Aviation Safety Network (2017) 'Fatal Airliner Losses', https://aviation safety.net/statistics/period/stats.php?cat=A1

Ayoob. M. (1997) 'Defining Security: A Subaltern Realist Perspective', in Krause, K. and Williams, M. (eds) *Critical Security Studies*, Minneapolis: University of Minnesota Press: 121–46.

Baker, R. (2005) *Capitalism's Achilles Heel*, Hoboken, NJ: Wiley & Sons.

Balch, J., Bradley, B., Abatzoglou, J., Fusco, E. and Mahood, A. (2017) 'Human-Started Wildfire Expands the Fire Niche across the United States', *Proceedings of the National Academy of Sciences in the United States* doi:10.1073/pnas.1617394114.

Bankoff, G. (2001) 'Rendering the World Unsafe: "Vulnerability" as Western Discourse', *Disasters*, 25(1): 19–35.

Baylis, J., Wirtz, J., Cohen, E. and Gray, C. (2002) *Strategy in the Contemporary World*, Oxford: Oxford University Press.

BBC (2000) 'Drugs. A Global Business', *World News*, http://news.bbc.co.uk/1/hi/world/774301.stm (accessed 22.5.07).

BBC (2011) 'Mexican Drug-Related Violence', www.bbc.co.uk/news/world-latin-america-10681249 (accessed 8.10.11).

BBC (2016) 'Hajj Stampede: Iran Leader Says Saudis "Murdered" Pilgrims', *News*, 5 September, www.bbc.co.uk/news/world-middle-east-37274243 (accessed 30.03.17).

BBC (2017) 'Pakistani Police Rescue 24 from Organ Trafficking Gang', *News*, 24 January, www.bbc.co.uk/news/health-38722052.

Beck, U. (1992) *Risk Society: Towards a New Modernity*, London, New Delhi and Thousand Oaks, CA: Sage.

Beck, U. (1999) *World Risk Society*, Cambridge: Polity.

Becker, J. (2000) *Hungry Ghosts: Mao's Secret Famine*, New York: Free Press.

Beckett, M. (2007) 'Speech at the UN Security Council', 16 April, UK Foreign and Commonwealth Office Press Release.

Beitz, C. (1979) *Political Theory and International Relations*, Princeton: Princeton University Press.

Benatar, S., Daar, A. and Singer, P. (2003) 'Global Health Ethics: The Rationale for Mutual Caring', *International Affairs*, 79(1): 107–38.

Benedict, R. (1934) *Patterns of Culture*, Boston: Houghton, Mifflin Company.

Benjamin, D. (2000) 'Past Is Not Prologue. A Reunified Germany Is Big But Not the Bully That Some Had Feared', *Time Magazine Europe*, 156(15), 9 October, www.time.com/time/europe/magazine/2000/1009/benjamin.html (accessed 4.6.03).

Bentham, J. (1876) *Theory of Legislation*, translated from the French of Etienne Dumont by H. Hildreth, London: Trubner & Co.

Bentham, M. (1998) *The Politics of Drug Control*, Basingstoke: Macmillan.

Berger, S. (2017) *Measles: Global Status 2017*, Los Angeles: Gideon Informatics: 31–2.

Bernard, E. (1999) 'Tsunami', in Ingleton, J. (ed.) *Natural Disaster Management. A Presentation to Commemorate the International Decade for Natural Disaster Reduction (IDNDR)*, Leicester: Tudor Rose: 58–60.

Betts, R. (1997) 'Should Strategic Studies Survive?', *World Politics*, 50(1): 7–33.

Blaikie, M., Cannon, T., Davis, I. and Wisner, B. (1994) *At Risk: Natural Hazards, People's Vulnerability, and Disasters*, London and New York: Routledge.

Bloor, D. (1976) *Knowledge and Social Imagery*, London: Routledge & Kegan Paul.

Blowers, A. (2017) *The Legacy of Nuclear Power*, London: Routledge.

Bolivia (2011) *Law of Mother Earth*, Law 071.

Booth, K. (1991) 'Security in Anarchy: Utopian Realism in Theory and Practice', *International Affairs*, 67(3): 527–45.

Booth, K. (2005) *Critical Security Studies and World Politics*, Boulder, CO: Lynne Rienner.

Boutros-Ghali, B. (2007) http://en.unpacampaign.org/about/message-from-dr-boutros-boutros-ghali/ (accessed 31/05/17).

Brauch, H. (2003) 'Desertification: A New Security Challenge for the Mediterranean', in Kepner, W., Rubio, J., Mount, D. and Pedrazzini, F. (eds) *Desertification in the Mediterranean Region*, Dordrecht: Springer.

Britton, N. (2001) 'A New Emergency Management for the New Millennium?', *Australian Journal of Emergency Management*, 16(4): 44–54.

Brock, L., Geis, A. and Mueller, H. (eds) (2006) *Democratic Wars. Looking at the Dark Side of Democratic Peace*, Basingstoke and New York: Palgrave.

Brown, O. and McLeman, R. (2009) 'A Recurring Anarchy? The Emergence of Climate Change as a Threat to International Peace and Security', *Conflict, Security and Development*, 9(3): 289–305.

Brugha, R. and Walt, G. (2001) 'A Global Health Fund: A Leap of Faith', *British Medical Journal*, 323, 21 July: 152–4.

Brundtland, G. (1999a) 2000–1 Budget speech to WHA, March, A52/INF.DOC/2.

Brundtland, G. (1999b) Address to the Geneva Group–UN Directors, 'Changes at WHO', Geneva, 2 March.

Buccini, J. (2000) Chair of the 'Fifth Session of the International Negotiating Committee for an Internationally Legal Binding Instrument for Implementing International Action on Certain Persistent Organic Pollutants', Johannesburg, 4–9 December 2000.

Bull, H. (1977) *The Anarchical Society: A Study of Order in World Politics*, London: Macmillan.

Bullock, J. and Adel, D. (1993) *Water Wars: Coming Conflicts in the Middle East*, London: St. Dedmundsbury Press.

Burleigh, M. (1994) *Death and Deliverance: 'Euthanasia' in Germany 1900–1945*, Cambridge: Cambridge University Press.

Buse, K. and Walt, G. (2000) 'Global Public and Private Partnerships: Part II. What Are the Health Issues for Global Governance?', *Bulletin of the World Health Organization*, 78(5): 699–709.

Bush, G. (1991) *State of the Union Address*, Washington DC, 29 January.

Buzan, B. (1991) *People, States and Fears: An Agenda for International Security Studies in the Post-Cold War Era*, 2nd edn, Boulder, CO: Lynne Rienner.

Buzan, B. (1993) 'Societal Security, State Security and Internationalization', in Waever, O., Buzan, B., Kelstrup, M. and Lemaitre, P., *Identity, Migration and the New Security Agenda in Europe*, London: Pinter.

Buzan, B., Waever, O. and de Wilde, J. (1998) *Security: A New Framework for Analysis*, Boulder, CO and London: Lynne Rienner.

Canadian Department of Foreign Affairs and Trade (1999) 'Human Security: Safety for People in a Changing World', Concept Paper, 29 April, Ottawa.

Carlile, Lord, of Berriew (2007) 'The Definition of Terrorism', *Report by Independent Reviewer of Terrorism Legislation*, Presented to Parliament March 2007, London: UK Government.

Carson, R. (1962) *Silent Spring*, Harmondsworth: Penguin.

Carter, J. (1980) US President State of the Union Address, 23 January, Washington DC.

Castello-Cortes, I. and Feldman, M. (1996) *Guinness Book of World Records 1997*, London: Guinness.

Chalk, P. (2000) *Non-Military Security and Global Order*, Basingstoke and London: Macmillan.

Chan, M. (2016) 'WHO Director-General Briefs UN on Antimicrobial Resistance', Dr Margaret Chan, Director-General of the World Health Organization, remarks at a high-level dialogue on antimicrobial resistance with UN member-states, New York, 18 April.

Chapman, J. (1992) 'The Future of Security Studies: Beyond Grand Strategy', *Survival*, 34(1): 109–31.

Chellaney, B. (2001) 'India Paying for Its Soft Response to Terror', *Hindustan Times*, 13 December, www.hindustantimes.com/ (accessed 18.4.02).

Cheng, A. (2003) 'Fatal Accidents Fall Slightly on Roads, at Work', *South China Morning Post*, 17 April, www.china-labour.org.hk/iso/article.adp?article_id=4190&category_name= Health%20and%20Safety (accessed 5.6.03).

Chigwedere, P., Seage, G., Gruskin, S., Lee, T. and Essex, M. (2008) 'Estimating the Lost Benefits of Antiretroviral Drug Use in South Africa', *Journal of AIDS*, 49(4): 410–15.

Christopolos, I., Mitchell, J. and Liljelund, A. (2001) 'Re-framing Risk: The Changing Context of Disaster Mitigation and Preparedness', *Disasters*, 25(3): 185–98.

Clark, I. (2001) *The Post Cold War Order: The Spoils of Peace*, Oxford: Oxford University Press.

Clausewitz, C.V. (1976) *On War*, edited and translated by Howard, M. and Paret, P., Princeton: Princeton University Press.

Coch, N. (1995) *Geohazards: Natural and Human*, Englewood Cliffs, NJ: Prentice Hall.

Comfort, I., Wisner, B., Cutter, S., Pulwarty, R., Hewitt, K., Oliver-Smith, A., Weiner, J., Fordham, M., Peacock, W. and Krimgeld, F. (1999) 'Re-framing Disaster Policy: The Global Evolution of Vulnerable Communities', *Environmental Hazards*, 1: 39–44, http://jishin.ucsur.pitt.edu/publications/Reframing.htm (accessed 12.2.02).

Commission on Human Security (2003) *Human Security Now*, New York: CHS.

Conca, K. and Dabelko, G. (eds) (2002) *Environmental Peacemaking*, Washington DC: Woodrow Wilson Press.

Cornwell, R. (2002) 'The War of the Worlds', *The Independent Magazine*, 7 September: 6–11.

Council of Europe (1999) *European Sourcebook on Crime and Criminal Justice*, PC-S-ST (99) 8 DEF, Strasbourg.

Cox, M. (1981) 'Social Forces, States and World Orders', *Millennium*, 10(2): 126–55.

CRED (2011) *International Disaster Database*, Centre for Research on the Epidemiology of Disasters, Brussels, www.emdat.be/ (accessed 20.9.11).

CRED (2016) *Poverty and Death: Disaster Mortality 1996–2015*, Brussels: CRED https://www. preventionweb.net/files/50589_creddisastermortalityallfinalpdf.pdf

Cronin, A. (2009) *How Terrorism Ends*, Princeton: Princeton University Press.

Dalby, S. (2002) 'Security and Ecology in the Age of Globalization', *The Environmental Change and Security Project Report*, 8, Summer: 95–108.

Das, P. and Samarakera, U. (2008) 'What Next for UNAIDS', *Lancet*, 372: 2099–2102.

Dauvergne, P. (2005) 'Dying of Consumption: Accidents or Sacrifices of Global Morality?', *Global Environmental Politics*, 5(3): 35–47.

Davis, M. (2001) *Late Victorian Holocausts: El Nino Famines and the Making of the Third World*, London and New York: Verso.

Davson-Galle, P. (1998) *The Possibility of Relative Truth*, Aldershot: Ashgate.

Deacon, B., Hulse, M. and Stubbs, P. (1997) *Global Social Policy: International Organizations and the Future of Welfare*, London: Sage.

Despouy, L. (2002) *Human Rights and Disabled Persons*, Human Rights Studies Series, Number 6, Centre for Human Rights, Geneva (United Nations publication, Sales No. E.92.XIV.4). www.un.org/esa/socdev/enable/dispaperdes0.htm#_ftnref1 (accessed 13.3.03).

Deudney, D. (1990) 'The Case against Linking Environmental Degradation and Security', *Millennium*, 19(3): 461–76.

Deutsch, K. et al. (1957) *Political Community and the North Atlantic Area*, Princeton: Princeton University Press.

Dewan, T. (2015) 'Societal Impacts and Vulnerability to Floods in Bangladesh and Nepal', *Weather and Climate Extremes*, 7: 36–42.

De Wilde, J. (2008) 'Environmental Security Deconstructed', in Brauch, H. (ed.) *Globalization and Environmental Challenges*, vol. 3, Berlin: Springer: 595–602.

Disaster Center (2003) 'The Most Deadly 100 Natural Disasters of the Twentieth Century', www.disastercenter.com/disaster/TOP100K.html (accessed 18.8.02).

Donnelly, J. (2007) *International Human Rights*, 3rd edn, Cambridge, MA: Westview.

Dorrington, R., Bradshaw, D. and Budlender, D. (2002) 'HIV/AIDS Profile in the Provinces of South Africa – Indicators for 2002', Centre for Actuarial Research, University of Cape Town.

Downer, A. (2002) 'Advancing the National Interest: Australia's Foreign Policy Challenge', 7 May, www.australianpolitics.com/news/2002/05/02-05-07a.shtml (accessed 23.7.03).

Dreze, J. and Sen, A. (1991) *Hunger and Public Action*, Oxford: Clarendon.

Drouard, A. (1998) 'Eugenics in France and Scandinavia: Two Case Studies', in Peel, R. (ed.) *Essays in the History of Eugenics*, London: The Galton Institute: 173–207.

DTI (2003) 'Home Safety Network', London: UK Government Department of Trade and Industry, www.dti.gov.uk/homesafetynetwork/index.htm (accessed 12.5.03).

Dudley, N. (1987) *This Poisoned Earth: The Truth about Pesticides*, London: Piatkus.

Duffield, M. (2001) *Global Governance and the New Wars: The Merging of Development and Security*, London and New York: Zed Books.

Dupont, A. and Pearman, G. (2006) *Heating up the Planet: Climate Change and Security*, Lowry Institute Papers 12, Sydney: Lowry Institute.

Dyer, H. (2000) 'Environmental Security: The New Agenda', in Jones, C. and Kennedy-Pipe, C. (eds) *International Security in a Global Age – Securing the Twenty-First Century*, London and Portland: Frank Cass.

Easton, D. (1965) *A Framework for Political Analysis*, Englewood Cliffs, NJ: Prentice Hall.

ECDC (2017) 'Healthcare Associated Infections', European Centre for Disease Prevention and Control, http://ecdc.europa.eu/en/healthtopics/Healthcare-associated_infections/Pages/index.aspx (accessed 09.05.17).

Ecologist (1991) *FAO – Promoting World Hunger*, special edition, 21(2), March/April.

Economist (2001) 'Defence Folly', 8 September: 10.

Economist (2002a) 'Stop Denying the Killer Bug', 23 February: 69.

Economist (2002b) 'Economic Focus. A Voice for the Poor', 4 May: 93.

Economist (2002c) 'Mother Nature's Biological Warfare', 10 August: 42.

Economist (2010) 'Ploughing On', 1 July.

Economist (2014) 'Arms and the African', 20 November.

Ecuador (2008) 'Rights for Nature', Constitution, adopted 28 September.

Effrat, A. (2013) 'Combatting the Kidney Commerce: Civil Society against Organ Trafficking in Pakistan and Israel', *British Journal of Criminology*, 53(5): 764–83.

Ehrlich, P. (1968) *The Population Bomb*, New York: Ballantine.

Eisenhower, D. (1961) 'Farewell Address', Washington DC, 17 January.

Eisner, M. (2015) 'Why Violent Crime Is Plummeting in the Rich World', *New Scientist*, 4 February.

Elliott, L. (2013) 'Legality, Criminality and Agency beyond the State: Forest Governance, Illegal Logging and Associated Trade', *Comparative Research in Law and Political Economy*,

York University, Research Report No. 52/2013, http://digitalcommons.osgoode.yorku. ca/cgi/viewcontent.cgi?article=1294&context=clpe (accessed 12.4.17).

Encyclopaedia Britannica (2015) 'Bhopal Disaster', https://www.britannica.com/event/Bhopal-disaster.

Engdahl, W. (2012) *A Century of War: Anglo-American Oil Politics and the New World Order*, Palm Desert, CA: Progressive Press.

England, R. (2008) 'Is the Writing on the Wall for UNAIDS?', *British Medical Journal*, 336(7652): 1072.

Enloe, C. (1990) *Bananas, Beaches and Bases: Making Feminist Sense of International Politics*, Berkeley: University of California Press.

Euro-Atlantic Disaster Relief Coordination Centre (2002) Brussels: NATO www.nato.int/ eadrcc/home.htm (accessed 25.2.02).

Eurobarometer (2015) Internal Security Special Eurobarometer 432 Wave EB 83.2, April, Brussels.

Europol (2012a) *EU Terrorism Situation and Trend Report*, TEAT 2012, The Hague.

Europol (2012b) 'Europol at a Glance', www.europol.eu.int/index.asp?page=ataglance& language= (accessed 19.6.12).

Falk, R. (1971) *The Endangered Planet*, New York: Random House.

Falk, R. (1995) *On Humane Governance: Toward a New Global Politics*, Cambridge: Polity.

FAO (2002) 'FAO What It Is – What It Does', www.fao.org/UNFAO/e/wmain-e.htm (accessed 5.4.02).

FAO (2008) *Women and the Right to Food: International Law and State Practice*, Rome: Food & Agricultural Organization.

FAO (2011) 'Review of the State of World Marine Fishing Resources', FAO Fisheries and Aquaculture Technical Paper 569, Rome: FAO.

FAO/WHO (1992) 'Final Report of the International Conference on Nutrition', Rome, 5–11 December.

Feis, H. (1970) *From Trust to Terror: The Onset of the Cold War 1945–1950*, New York: Norton.

Ferris, E. and Petz, D. (eds) (2011) *A Year of Living Dangerously: A Review of Natural Disasters in 2010*, London: Brookings Institute.

Fidler, D. (1999) *International Law and Infectious Diseases*, Oxford: Clarendon.

Finley, L. (ed.) (2017) *Crime and Punishment in America: An Encyclopedia of Trends and Controversies in the Justice System. Volume 1: A–M*, Santa-Barbara: ABC-CLIO.

Floyd, R. (2010) *Security and the Environment: Securitisation Theory and US Environmental Security Policy*, Cambridge: Cambridge University Press.

Forster, A. and Wallace, W. (2001) 'What Is NATO for?', *Survival: The International Institute for Security Studies Quarterly*, 43(4): 107–22.

Fortna, V. (2008) *Does Peacekeeping Work? Shaping Belligerents' Choices after Civil War*, Princeton: Princeton University Press.

Frank, A.G. (1971) *Capitalism and Underdevelopment in Latin America*, Harmondsworth: Penguin.

Frankena, W. (1988) *Ethics*, 2nd edn, Englewood Cliffs, NJ: Prentice Hall.

Frankman, M. (1997) 'No Global War? A Role for Democratic Global Federalism', *Journal of World-Systems Research*, 3(2): 321–38.

Freedom House (2011) *Freedom in the World 2011*, Washington DC.

Fukuyama, F. (1992) *The End of History and the Last Man*, London: Hamish Hamilton.

Gaddis, J. (1997) *We Now Know – Rethinking Cold War History*, Oxford: Clarendon.

Galtung, J. (1969) 'Violence, Peace and Peace Research', *Journal of Peace Research*, 6(3): 167–91.

Garrett, L. (2007) 'The Challenge of Global Health', *Foreign Affairs*, 86(1): 14–38.

Genocide Watch (2003) http://www.genocidewatch.org/ (accessed 23.10.03).

Gentili, A. (1933) *De Jure belli libri tres*, Washington DC: J.C. Rolfe.

Gillies, R. (2004) 'The Real Reasons MSF Left Afghanistan', MSF Website, www.doctors withoutborders.org/publications/article.cfm?id=2068.

Gleick, P. (1994) 'Water, War and Peace in the Middle East', *Environment*, 36(3), April: 6–42.

Glenny, M. (2006) 'Boom Time for Crime Gangs', *The World in 2007, Economist*.

Global Alliance for Vaccines and Immunization, www.vaccinealliance.org/home/index.php (accessed 2.8.02).

Global Disaster Information Network, www.gdin-international.org/whats_GDIN.html (accessed 27.2.02).

Global Financial Integrity (2011) *Transnational Crime in the Developing World*, Washington DC: GFI.

Global Financial Integrity (2017) *Transnational Crime and the Developing World*, Washington DC: GFI.

Global Fund (2016) Global Fund to Fight Aids, Tuberculosis and Malaria, https://www.the globalfund.org/en/ (accessed 14.10.16).

Global Security (2007) *World Military Guide*, www.globalsecurity.org/military/world/ index.html (accessed 21.5.07).

Global Slavery Index (2017) www.globalslaveryindex.org/ (accessed 22.05.17).

Godlee, F. (1994) 'WHO in Retreat: Is It Losing Its Influence?', *British Medical Journal*, 30, 9 December: 1491–5.

Godlee, F. (1995) 'The World Health Organisation. WHO's Special Programmes: Undermining from Above', *British Medical Journal*, 10, 21 January: 178–82.

Godson, R. and Williams, P. (1998) 'Strengthening Cooperation against Transsovereign Crime: A New Security Imperative', *Transnational Organized Crime*, 4(3&4): 321–55.

Godson, R. and Williams, P. (2000) 'Strengthening Cooperation against Transsovereign Crime', in Cusimano, M. (ed.) *Beyond Sovereignty: Issues for a Global Agenda*, Boston: St. Martins: 111–46.

Goldstein, J. (2011) *Winning the War on War: The Decline of Armed Conflict Worldwide*, New York: Dutton.

Gorbachev, M. (1987) Speech at the Ceremonial Meeting on the Occasion of the Presentation of the Order of Lenin and the Gold Star to the City of Murmansk, Murmansk, 1 October.

Grau, G. (ed.) (1995) *Hidden Holocaust: Gay and Lesbian Persecution in Germany 1937–45*, London: Cassell.

Green, J. (1997) *Risk and Misfortune. The Social Construction of Accidents*, London: UCL Press.

Greene, O. (2001) 'Environmental Issues', in Baylis, J. and Smith, S. (eds) *The Globalization of World Politics: An Introduction to International Relations*, 2nd edn, Oxford and New York: Oxford University Press.

Grein, T., Kamara, K., Rodier, C., Plant, A., Bovier, P., Ryan, P., Ohyma, T. and Heymann, D. (2000) 'Rumors of Diseases in the Global Village: Outbreak Verification', *Emerging Infectious Diseases*, 16(2), March/April: 97–102.

Grotius, T. (1853) *De Jure Belli ac Pacis*, Cambridge: Wheelwall.

Haagsma, J. et al. (2016) 'The Global Burden of Injury: Incidence, Mortality, Disability-Adjusted Life Years and Tie Trends from the Global Burden of Disaster 2013', *British Medical Journal*, 22: 3–18.

Habermas, J. (2001) *The Postnational Constellation: Political Essays*, translated and edited by Pensky, M., Cambridge: Polity.

Hagedorn, J. (2008) *A World of Gangs: Armed Young Men and Gangsta Culture,* Minnesota: University of Minnesota Press.

Hagmann, M. (2001) 'Globalization How Healthy?', *Bulletin of the World Health Organization*, 79(9): 902–3.

Halliday, F. (1986) *The Making of the Second Cold War*, London: Verso.

Halliday, F. (2001) *The World at 2000: Perils and Promises*, Basingstoke and New York: Palgrave.

Halliday, F. (2002) *Two Hours That Shook the World. September 11, 2001: Causes and Consequences*, London: Saqi.

Hansen, L. (2000) 'The Little Mermaid's Secret Security Dilemma and the Absence of Gender in the Copenhagen School', *Millennium Journal of International Studies*, 29(2): 285–306.

Hardin, G. (1968) 'The Tragedy of the Commons', *Science*, 162: 1243–8.

Hardin, G. (1996) 'Lifeboat Ethics: The Case against Helping the Poor', in Aitken, W. and LaFollette, H. (eds) *World Hunger and Morality*, Englewood Cliffs, NJ: Prentice Hall.

Harman, G. (1996) 'Moral Relativism', in Harman, G. and Thomson, J. (eds) *Moral Relativism and Moral Objectivity*, Cambridge, MA: Blackwell.

Hazlitt, H. (1973) *The Conquest of Poverty*, New Rochelle: Arlington House.

Held, D., McGrew, A., Goldblatt, D. and Perratton, J. (1998) *Global Transformations: Politics, Economics and Culture*, Cambridge: Polity.

Henderson, E. (2008) 'Disturbing the Peace: African Warfare, Political Inversion and the Universality of the Democratic Peace Thesis', *British Journal of Political Science*, 39(1): 25–58.

Heymann, D. (2001) 'The Fall and Rise of Infectious Diseases', *Georgetown Journal of International Affairs*, 2(2): 7–14.

Hicks, J. (1992) 'DDT – Friend or Foe?', *Pesticide News, Journal of the Pesticides Trust*, 17 September: 14.

Hiller, D. and Nightingale, K. (2013) *How Disasters Disrupt Development. Recommendations for the Post-2015 Development Framework*, Oxford: Oxfam.

Hobson, J. (1915) *Towards International Government*, New York: Macmillan.

Homer-Dixon, T. (1994) 'Environmental Scarcities and Violent Conflict: Evidence from Cases', *International Security*, 19(1): 5–40.

Homer-Dixon, T. and Percival, V. (1996) *Environmental Scarcity and Violent Conflict: Briefing Book*, Population and Sustainable Development Project, American Association for the Advancement of Science and University of Toronto.

Horton, R. (2017) 'Offline: Global Health Security – Smart Strategy or Naive Tactics?', *Lancet*, 389 (10072): 892.

Hough, P. (1998) *The Global Politics of Pesticides: Forging Consensus from Conflicting Interests*, London: Earthscan.

Hough, P. (2000) 'Institutions for Controlling the Global Trade in Hazardous Chemicals: The 1998 Rotterdam Convention', *Global Environmental Change*, 10(2): 161–4.

Howard, R. (1995) *Human Rights and the Search for Community*, Oxford: Westview Press.

Howard-Hassmann, R. (2012) 'Human Security: Undermining Human Rights?', *Human Rights Quarterly*, 34: 88–112.

Howse, R. and Nicolaidis, R. (2003) 'Enhancing WTO Legitimacy: Constitutionalism or Global Subsidiarity?', *Governance*, 16(1): 73–94.

HRW (2012) *In the Name of Security. Counterterrorism Laws Worldwide since September 11*, Human Rights Watch, www.hrw.org/report/2012/06/29/name-security/counterterrorism-laws-worldwide-september-11 (accessed 22/05/17).

Hsiang, S., Meng, K. and Cane, M. (2011) 'Civil Conflicts Are Associated with Global Climate', *Nature*, 476: 438–41.

Hufbauer, G., Scott, J. and Elliott, K. (1990) *Economic Sanctions Reconsidered: History and Current Policy*, 2nd edn, Washington DC: Institute for International Economics.

Hughes, B., Kuhn, R., Peterson, C., Rothman, D. and Solorzano, J. (2011) 'Improving Global Health: Forecasting the Next 50 Years', in Hughes, B. (ed.) *Patterns of Potential Human Progress*, Boulder, CO: Paradigm.

Hultman, L., Kathman, J. and Shannon, M. (2014) 'Beyond Keeping Peace: UN's Effectiveness in the Midst of Fighting', *American Political Science Review*, 108(4): 737–53.

Human Rights Watch (2003) *Compounding Injustice: The Government's Failure to Redress Massacres in Gujarat*, 15(3), July, www.hrw.org/reports/2003/india0703/ (accessed 8.5.07).

Human Security Centre (2005) *Human Security Report*, www.humansecurityreport.info/ component/option,com_frontpage/Itemid,1/ (accessed 13.7.06).

Human Security Network (1999) 'A Perspective on Human Security: Chairman's Summary', 1st Ministerial Meeting of the Human Security Network, Lysøen, Norway, 20 May.

Humphreys, D. (2006) *Logjam: Deforestation and the Crisis of Global Governance*, London: Earthscan.

Hunger Project (1985) *Ending Hunger: An Idea Whose Time Has Come*, New York: Praeger.

Huntington, S. (1993) 'The Clash of the Civilizations?', *Foreign Affairs*, 72(3): 22–49.

IAEA (2012) Convention on Nuclear Safety, www-ns.iaea.org/conventions/nuclear-safety.asp (accessed 13.6.12).

ICAO (2011) *Implementing the Global Aviation Safety Roadmap*, Quebec: International Civil Aviation Organization.

ICC (2012) www.icccpi.int/php/show.php?id=home&l=EN (accessed 5.2.12).

ICIDI (1980) *North-South: The Report of the International Commission on International Development Issues*, London: Pan Books.

IFRC (2001) *World Disasters Report 2001. Focus on Recovery*, Geneva: International Federation of Red Cross and Red Crescent Societies.

IISS (International Institute for Security Studies) (2014) *The Military Balance 2014*, edited by J. Hackett, London: Routledge.

ILO (2002) SafeWork, *Global Estimates of Fatalities 2002*, www.ilo.org/public/english/ protection/safework/accidis/globest_2002/reg_world.htm (accessed 16.2.03).

ILO (2005) 'Decent Work – Safe Work', Report to the 27th World Congress on Safety and Health at Work, Orlando, 18–25 September, Geneva: International Labour Organization.

ILO (2011) *Introductory Report: Global Trends and Challenges on Occupational Safety and Health at Work*, XIX World Congress on Safety and Health at Work, Istanbul, 11–15 September: 155, 187.

ILO/WHO (2005) *World Day for Safety and Health at Work: A Background Paper*, Geneva: International Labour Organization.

IMF (2016) Jaumotte, F., Koloskova, K. and Saxena, S., 'Impact of Migration on Income Levels in Advanced Economies', *Spillover Notes*, Washington DC: International Monetary Fund.

IMO (2011) 'Piracy: Orchestrating the Response', background paper, www.imo.org/About/ Events/WorldMaritimeDay/2011/background/Pages/default.aspx.

Independent (2016) 'LGBT relationships Are Illegal in 74 Countries', 17 May, www. independent.co.uk/news/world/gay-lesbian-bisexual-relationships-illegal-in-74-countries-a7033666.html.

Ingleton, J. (ed.) (1999) *Natural Disaster Management. A Presentation to Commemorate the International Decade for Natural Disaster Reduction (IDNDR)*, Leicester: Tudor Rose.

Institute for Economics and Peace (2016) *World Terrorism Index 2016. Measuring and Understanding the Impact of Terrorism*, Sydney: IEP.

Intergovernmental Oceanographic Commission (2001) 'Eighteenth Session of the International Co-ordination Group for the Tsunami Warning System in the Pacific', ICG/ITSU-XVIII, Draft Press Kit, 8–11 October, Cartagena, Colombia.

Intergovernmental Panel on Climate Change (2007) *Climate Change 2007: The Physical Science Basis. Summary for Policymakers*, Geneva: IPCC.

International Federation of University Women (IFUW) (1999) 'International Convention on the Elimination of All Forms of Discrimination Against Women', www.ifuw.org/ advocacy/ia_cedaw.htm (accessed 5.4.03).

International Narcotics Control Board (2002) 'Report of the International Narcotics Control Board for 2001', E/INCB/2002/1, New York: United Nations.

Interpol (2002) 'An Overview. Foreword', www.interpol.int/Public/ICPO/Overview.pdf (accessed 4.8.05).

Interpol (2012) 'An Overview', www.interpol.int/ (accessed 14.3.12).

ISDR (2002a) 'ISDR Vision', www.unisdr.org/unisdr/aboutvision.htm (accessed 27.2.02).

ISDR (2002b) 'Living With Risk. A Global Review of Disaster Reduction Activities', Geneva: International Strategy for Disaster Reduction.

ISDR (2017) Sendai Framework, www.unisdr.org/we/coordinate/sendai-framework (accessed 12.4.17).

ITUC (2014) *The Case Against Qatar*, Brussels: International Trade Union Confederation.

Jacobs, G. and Aeron-Thomas, A. (2000) 'A Review of Global Road Accident Fatalities', TRL Report 44, Transport Research Laboratory, Crawthorne, UK, www.transport-links.org/transport_links/filearea/publications/1_771_Pa3568.pdf (accessed 15.9.11).

Jeggle, T. (1999) 'The Goals and Aims of the Decade', in Ingleton, J. (ed.) *Natural Disaster Management. A Presentation to Commemorate the International Decade for Natural Disaster Reduction (IDNDR)*, Leicester: Tudor Rose.

Jendritsky, G. (1999) 'Extreme Temperatures', International Decade for Natural Disaster Reduction (IDNDR) Programme Forum, Geneva, 5–9 July, www.unisdr.org/unisdr/forum/tempwmo.htm (accessed 13.2.02).

Jones, A. (2000) 'Gendercide and Genocide', *Journal of Genocide Research*, 2, 2 June: 185–211.

Kagan, R. (2003) 'Americans Are from Mars, Europeans Are from Venus', *Sunday Times News Review*, 2 February: 1–2.

Kaiser, R. (1997) 'Chinese Leader Urges US to Seek "Common Ground"', *Washington Post*, 19 October: A1.

Kaldor, M. (2007) *New and Old Wars: Organized Violence in a Global Era*, Cambridge: Polity.

Kamradt-Scott, A. (2016) 'WHO's to Blame? The World Health Organization and the 2014 Ebola Outbreak', *Third World Quarterly*, 37(3): 401–18.

Kant, I. (1970) 'Perpetual Peace: A Philosophic Sketch', in Reiss, H. (ed.) *Kant's Political Writings*, 2nd edn, Cambridge: Cambridge University Press.

Kaplan, R. (1994) 'The Coming Anarchy', *The Atlantic Monthly*, 273: 44–76.

Kegley, C. and Wittkopf, E. (2006) *World Politics: Trend and Transformation*, 7th edn, New York: St Martin's/Worth.

Kendall, R. (1998) 'Responding to Transnational Crime', *Transnational Organized Crime*, 4(3&4): 269–75.

Kennan, G. (1984) 'Soviet-American Relations: The Politics of Discord and Collaboration', in Kegley, C. and Wittkopf, E. (eds) *The Global Agenda*, New York: Random House: 107–20.

Kennan, G. (1985) 'Morality and Foreign Policy', *Foreign Affairs*, 64: 205–18.

Kennan, G. ('X') (1946) 'The Sources of Soviet Conduct', *Foreign Affairs*, 25(4): 566–82.

Keohane, R. (2002) *Power and Governance in a Partially Globalized World*, London and New York: Routledge.

Keohane, R. and Nye, J. (1977) *Power and Interdependence: World Politics in Transition*, Boston: Little, Brown.

Ker-Lindsay, J. (2000) 'Greek-Turkish Rapprochement: The Impact of Disaster Diplomacy?', *Cambridge Review of International Affairs*, XIV(1), special section, *Disaster Diplomacy*, edited by Kelman, I. and Koukis, T.: 214–94.

Kevles, D. (1995) *In the Name of Eugenics: Genetics and the Uses of Human Heredity*, Cambridge, MA and London: Harvard University Press.

Kim, Y. (1999) 'A Common Framework for the Ethics of the 21st Century', Paris: UNESCO Division of Philosophy and Ethics.

Kissinger, G., Herold, M. and De Sy, V. (2012) *Drivers of Deforestation and Forest Degradation. A Synthesis Report for REDD+Policymakers*, Vancouver: Lexeme Consulting.

Kitchin, C. (2001) 'Early Discoveries', part of feature: 'Focus: Asteroids', *Astronomy Now*, 15(1): 54–5.

Klare, M. (2007) *Blood and Oil: The Dangers and Consequences of America's Growing Dependency on Imported Petroleum*, New York: Owl.

Koivusalo, M. and Ollila, E. (1997) *Making a Healthy World: Agencies, Actors and Policies in International Health*, London and New York: Zed Books.

Kolko, G. and Kolko, J. (1972) *The Limits of Power: The World and United States Foreign Policy, 1945–1954*, New York: Harper & Row.

Korey, W. (2001) 'Revisiting the U.N.'s Genocide Convention', *Forward*, 10 August, www.forward.com/issues/2001/01.08.10/oped2.html (accessed 12.3.03).

Kortunov, S. (1998) 'Is the Cold War Really Over?', *International Affairs: A Russian Journal of World Policy, Diplomacy and International Relations*, 5: 141–54.

Kraska, P. (2005) 'Researching the Police-Military Blur: Lessons Learned', *Police Forum*, 14(3).

Kung, H. and Kuschel, K.-J. (1993) *A Global Ethic: The Declaration of the Parliament of the World's Religions*, New York: Continuum.

Kunkel, K., Pielke, R. and Changnon, S. (1999) 'Temporal Fluctuations in Weather and Climate Extremes That Cause Economic and Human Health Impacts: A Review', *Bulletin of the American Meteorological Society*, 80(6): 1077–98.

LaFeber, W. (1991) *America, Russia and the Cold War 1945–1990*, New York: McGraw-Hill.

Lancet (1995) 'Fortress WHO: Breaching the Ramparts for Health's Sake', 345, 28 January.

Lancet (2016) 'Global Burden of Disease 2015', 8 October.

Langeland, B. (2009) *Work Related Accidents and Risks among Migrant Workers*, European Working Conditions Observatory, Norway, www.eurofound.europa.eu/ewco/2009/07/NO0907019I.htm (accessed 22.6.12).

Laqueur, W. (1990) 'Reflection on the Eradication of Terrorism', in Kegley, C. (ed.) *International Terrorism: Characteristics, Causes, Controls*, New York: St Martin's Press: 207–12.

Laurance, J. (2006) 'Climate Change Blamed for Legionnaire's Disease Surge', *Independent*, 18 October: 4.

Lee, K., Buse, K. and Fustukian, S. (2002) *Health Policy in a Globalizing World*, Cambridge: Cambridge University Press.

Leiss, W. and Chociolko, C. (1994) *Risk and Responsibility*, London and Buffalo: McGill-Queen's University Press.

Lemkin, R. (1944) *Axis Rule in Occupied Europe: Laws of Occupation – Analysis of Government – Proposals for Redress*, Washington DC: Carnegie Endowment for International Peace.

Levy, M. (1995) 'Time for a Third Wave of Environment and Security Scholarship?', *The Environmental Change and Security Project Report*, 1, Spring: 44–64.

Lewis, J. (2005) 'Statement to the US Senate Committee on Environment and Public Works', 18 May, http://epw.senate.gov/hearing_statements.cfm?id=237817 (accessed 8.5.07).

Libiszewski, S. (1995) 'Water Disputes in the Jordan Basin Region and Their Role in the Resolution of the Arab-Israeli Conflict', ENCOP Occasional Paper No. 13, Zurich/Berne: Centre for Security Policy and Conflict Research/Swiss Peace Foundation.

Lichfield, J. (2015) 'Côte d'Azur Urbanisation Blamed as Floods Kill at Least 16 People', *Independent*, 5 October: 21.

Lim, S. et al. (2012) 'A Comparative Risk Assessment of Burden of Disease and Injury Attributable to 67 Risk Factors and Risk Factor Clusters in 21 Regions, 1990–2010: A Systematic Analysis for the Global Burden of Disease Study 2010', *Lancet*, 380: 2224–60.

Lippmann, W. (1943) *US Foreign Policy*, London: Hamish Hamilton.

Lomberg, B. (2001) *The Sceptical Environmentalist*, Cambridge: Cambridge University Press.

London School of Hygiene and Tropical Medicine with Save the Children (2002) *New Products into Old Systems: The Initial Impact of the Global Alliance for Vaccines and Immunizations (GAVI) at Country Level*, London: Save the Children.

Lopez, G. and Cortright, D. (2002) 'Smarting under Sanctions', *The World Today*, 58(3): 17–18.

Loretti, A. (2000) 'The Health Sector in Disaster Reduction and Emergency Management', keynote address for the session 'Managing and Preparing for Disasters', International Public Health Congress, Health 21 in Action, Istanbul, 8–12 October.

Lynn-Jones, S. and Miller, S. (1995) *Global Dangers: Changing Dimensions of International Security*, Cambridge, MA and London: MIT Press.

MacFarlane, N. and Foong Khong, Y. (2006) *Human Security and the UN: A Critical History*, Bloomington: Indiana University Press.

Mackenstedt, U., Jenkins, D. and Romig, T. (2015) 'The Role of Wildlife in the Transmission of Parasitic Zoonoses in Peri-Urban and Urban Areas', *International Journal for*

Parasitology: Parasites and Wildlife, 4(1): 71–9, www.sciencedirect.com/science/article/pii/S2213224415000085.

Malthus, T. (1798) *An Essay on the Principle of Population*, London: J. Johnson.

Mandelbaum, M. (1999) 'A Perfect Failure', *Foreign Affairs*, 78(5): 2–8.

Marsh, G. (1965) *Man and Nature* (reprint), Cambridge, MA: Harvard University Press.

Marshall, M. and Gurr, T. (2005) *Peace and Conflict 2005*, Maryland: Center for International Development and Conflict Management.

Martine, G. and Guzman, J. (2002) 'Population, Poverty, and Vulnerability: Mitigating the Effects of Natural Disasters', *Environmental Change and Security Project (ECSP) Report*, 8, Summer: 45–68.

Maruthappu, M., Watkins, J., Noor, A., Williams, C., Ali, B., Sullivan, R., Zeler, T. and Alun, R. (2016) 'Economic Downturns, Universal Health Coverage and Cancer Mortality in High-Income and Middle-Income Countries, 1990-201: A Longitudinal Study', *Lancet*, 388 (100450): 684–95.

Mathew, R., Barnett, J., McDonald, B. and O'Brien, K. (eds) (2010) *Global Environmental Change and Human Security*, Boston: MIT.

Mathews, J. (1989) 'Redefining Security', *Foreign Affairs*, 68(2): 162–77.

Mathews, J. (1997) 'Power Shift', *Foreign Affairs*, 76(1): 50–66.

Matin, N. and Taher, M. (2000) 'Disaster Mitigation in Bangladesh: Country Case Study of NGO Activities', Report for Research Project, *NGO National Disaster Mitigation and Preparedness Projects: An Assessment of the Way Forward*, ESCOR Award no. R7231.

Mazzini, G. (1862) *The Duties of Man*, London: Chapman and Hall.

McCormack, T. (2008) 'Power and Agency in the Human Security Framework', *Cambridge Review of International Affairs*, 21(1): 113–28.

McDonald, M. (2002) 'Human Security and the Construction of Security', *Global Society*, 16(3): 277–95.

McEwen, F. and Stephenson, G. (1979) *The Use and Significance of Pesticides in the Environment*, New York: John Wiley & Sons.

McGee, K. (2003) 'Unintentional injury', Department of Injuries and Violence Prevention, World Health Organization, email (21.2.03).

McGilvray, D. and Gamburd, M. (2010) *Tsunami Recovery in Sri Lanka: Ethnic and Regional Dimensions*, London: Routledge.

McMichael, A., Campbell-Lendrum, D. and Kovats, S. (2004) 'Global Climate Change', in Ezzati, M.J., Lopez, A., Rodgers, A. and Murray, C. (eds) *Comparative Quantification of Health Risks: Global and Regional Burden of Disease Due to Selected Major Risk Factors*, Geneva: World Health Organization.

McMurray, C. and Smith, R. (2001) *Diseases of Globalization: Socioeconomic Transition and Health*, London: Earthscan.

McNeill, W. (1989) *Plague and Peoples*, Toronto: Doubleday.

McSweeney, B. (1996) 'Identity and Security: Buzan and the Copenhagen School', *Review of International Studies*, 22(1): 81–93.

McSweeney, B. (1999) *Security, Identity and Interests: A Sociology of International Relations*, Cambridge: Cambridge University Press.

Mearsheimer, J. (1990) 'Why We Will Soon Miss the Cold War', *The Atlantic Monthly*, 226(2): 35–50.

Mearsheimer, J. (1995) 'The False Promise of International Institutions', *International Security*, 19(3): 5–49.

Mearsheimer, J. (2001) *Tragedy of the Great Powers*, New York: Norton.

Meddings, D. (2005) 'After the Emergency. Injury, Health Systems and Data Collection', World Health Organization, www.survivorconference.org/ppt/13_Meddings.ppt.

Michael, S. (2002) 'The Role of NGOs in Human Security', Working Paper no. 12, submitted to the UN Commission on Human Security.

Mill, J.S. (1863) *Utilitarianism*, London: Frasers.

Mitchell, D. (2008) 'A Note on Rising Food Prices', Policy Research Working Paper 4682, Washington DC: World Bank Development Prospects Group.

Mitchell, J. (ed.) (1996) *The Long Road to Recovery: Community Responses to Industrial Disaster*, Tokyo, New York and Paris: UN University Press, www.unu.edu/unupress/unupbooks/uu21le/uu21le00.htm (accessed 12.2.03).

Mitrany, D. (1975) *The Functional Theory of Politics*, London: Robertson.

Morgenthau, H. (1972) *Politics among Nations*, 5th edn, New York: A. Knopf.

Morgenthau, H. (1982) 'Another "Great Debate": The National Interest of the United States', in Vasquez, J. (ed.) *Classics of International Relations*, Englewood Cliffs, NJ: Prentice Hall.

Morkevičus, V. (2015) 'Power and Order: The Shared Logics of Realism and Just War Theory', *International Studies Quarterly*, 59(1): 11–22.

Mueller, J. (1989) *Retreat from Doomsday: The Obsolescence of Major War*, New York: Basic Books.

Murray, C., Lopez, A., Mathers, C. and Stein, C. (2001) 'Global Burden of Disease 2000 Project: Aims, Methods and Data', Global Programme on Evidence for Health Policy Discussion Paper No. 36, Geneva: World Health Organization.

Murray, K., Ruktanonchai, D., Hesalroad, D., Fonken, E. and Nolan, M. (2013) 'West Nile Virus, Texas, USA, 2012', *Emerging Infectious Diseases*, 19(11), https://wwwnc.cdc.gov/eid/article/19/11/13-0768_article.

Myers, N. (1993) *Ultimate Security: The Environmental Basis of Political Stability*, New York: W.W. Norton.

Nakajima, H. (1997) 'Global Disease Threats and Foreign Policy', *Brown Journal of World Affairs*, 4(1): 319–32.

Narrain, A. (2001) 'Human Rights and Sexual Minorities: Global and Local Contexts', *Law, Social Justice and Global Development*, electronic journal, http://elj.warwick.ac.uk/global/issue/2001–2/narrain.html (accessed 10.4.03).

National Intelligence Council (USA) (2000) 'The Global Infectious Disease Threat and Its Implications for the United States', NIE 99–17D, www.cia.gov/cia/publications/nie/report/nie99-17d.html (accessed 8.2.02).

NATO (2013) *Environmental Security*, www.nato.int/cps/en/natolive/topics_49216.htm.

Natsios, A. (1999) 'The Politics of Famine in North Korea', Special Report, Washington DC: US Institute of Peace, www.usip.org/oc/sr/sr99082/sr990802.html (accessed 2.4.02).

Netherlands (2006) *Policy Agenda 2006*, Ministry of Foreign Affairs.

Neumann, P. (2007) 'Negotiating with Terrorists', *Foreign Affairs*, 86(1): 128–39.

Newman, E. (2010) 'Critical Human Security Studies', *Review of International Studies*, 36: 77–94.

Newman, G. (ed.) (1999) *Global Report on Crime and Justice*, United Nations Office for Drug Control and Crime Prevention, New York: Oxford University Press.

NGDC (2002) 'Tsunami Event Database', National Geophysical Data Center, http://wist.ngdc.noaa.gov/nndc/servlet/gov.noaa.nndc.idb.ShowDatasetsServlet?dataset=101327&search_look=7&display_look=7 (accessed 16.9.02).

NGDC (2003) 'Natural Hazards Data', www.ngdc.noaa.gov/seg/hazard/hazards.shtml (accessed 20.6.03).

Noble, R. (2003) 'Interpol's Way: Thinking beyond Boundaries and Acting across Borders through Member Countries' Police Services', speech delivered at Tufts University, Boston, 1 March, www.interpol.int/Public/ICPO/speeches/SG20030301.asp (accessed 20.7.03).

Norks, R. and Gleditsch, N. (2007) 'Climate Change and Conflict', *Political Geography*, 26(6): 627–38.

NRDC (National Resources Defense Council) (2006) 'Global Nuclear Stockpiles 1945–2006', *Bulletin of the Atomic Scientists*, 62(4): 64–7.

Nye, J. (1990) *Bound to Lead: The Changing Nature of American Power*, New York: Basic Books.

Nye, J. (2005) *Understanding International Conflicts: An Introduction to Theory and History*, London: Pearson.

OECD (2014) 'Is Migration Good for the Economy?', *Migration Policy Debates*, https://www.oecd.org/migration/OECD%20Migration%20Policy%20Debates%20Numero%202.pdf (accessed 5/2/17).

Ó Gráda, C. (1999) *Black '47 and Beyond: The Great Irish Famine in History, Economy, and Memory*, Princeton: Princeton University Press.

Oneal, J. and Russett, B. (1997) 'The Classic Liberals Were Right: Democracy, Interdependence, and Conflict 1950–1985', *International Studies Quarterly*, 41(2): 267–94.

O'Neill, S. (2001) 'Secret Group That Exports Fanatical Brand of Terror', *Telegraph*, 27 September, www.telegraph.co.uk/news/main.jhtml?xml=/news/2001/09/27/whunt127.xml (accessed 2.7.03).

O'Reilly, A. (2003) 'A UN Convention on the Rights of Persons with Disabilities – the Next Steps', paper presented at the General Assembly Meeting of Rehabilitation International Arab Region, 8–9 March, Kingdom of Bahrain, www.rehab-international.org/un/steps.html (accessed 9.4.03).

Osborn, F. (1948) *Our Plundered Planet*, New York: Grosset & Dunlap.

Ottoson, D. (2007) *State Sponsored Homophobia. A World Survey of Laws Prohibiting Same Sex Activity between Consenting Adults*, International Lesbian and Gay Association.

Oxfam (2002) *Cut the Cost. Patent Injustice: How World Trade Rules Threaten the Health of Poor People*, Oxford: Oxfam.

Paddock, W. and Paddock, P. (1967) *Famine 1975*, London: Weidenfeld & Nicolson.

Palme, O. (1982) *Common Security: A Programme for Disarmament*, London: Pan Books.

Pape, R. (2005) 'Soft Balancing against the United States', *International Security*, 30(1): 7–45.

Paris, R. (2001) 'Human Security: Paradigm Shift or Hot Air?', *International Security*, 26(2).

Paul, T. (2005) 'Soft Balancing in the Age of US Primacy', *International Security*, 30(1): 46–71.

Peiser, B. (2001) 'Impact Scares and How to Avoid Them', in 'Focus: Asteroids', *Astronomy Now*, 15(1): 64–5.

Peterson, P. and Sebenius, J. (1992) 'The Primacy of the Domestic Agenda', in Allison, G. and Treverton, G. (eds) *Rethinking America's Security: Beyond Cold War to New World Order*, New York: W.W. Norton & Co.: 57–93.

Petterson, T. and Wallensteen, P. (2015) 'Armed Conflicts 1946–2014', *Journal of Peace Research*, 52(4): 536–50.

Pettman, J. (1996) *Worlding Women: A Feminist International Politics*, London: Routledge.

Pirages, D. and Runci, P. (2000) 'Ecological Interdependence and the Spread of Infectious Disease', in Cusimano, M. (ed.) *Beyond Sovereignty: Issues for a Global Agenda*, New York: St Martin's Press: 177–93.

Potter, J. (1992) *The Sultana Tragedy: America's Greatest Maritime Disaster*, Gretna, LA: Pelican.

Power, S. (2002) *A Problem from Hell: America and the Age of Genocide*, New York: Basic Books.

Prescott, E. (2003) 'SARS: A Warning', *Survival*, 45: 207–26.

Preston, S. (1975) 'The Changing Relationship between Mortality and Level of Economic Development', *Population Studies*, 29(2): 231–48.

Prevent Genocide (2003) 'Key Writings of Raphael Lemkin on Genocide', www.preventgenocide.org/lemkin/ (accessed 1.4.03).

Price-Smith, A. (2001) *The Health of Nations: Infectious Diseases, Environmental Change, and Their Effects on National Security and Development*, Cambridge, MA: MIT Press.

Prins, G. (2002) *The Heart of War: On Power, Conflict and Obligation in the Twenty-First Century*, London and New York: Routledge.

Prins, G. and Stamp, R. (1991) *Top Guns and Toxic Whales: The Environment and Global Security*, London: Earthscan.

Putin, V. (2004) 'Terror in the Moscow Subway', *MOSnews*, www.mosnews.com/mn-files/subway.shtml (accessed 11.5.07).

Ramonet, L. (1998) 'The Politics of Hunger', *Le Monde*, 1 November, http://mondediplo.com/1998/11/01leader (accessed 3.4.02).

Ramsey, P. (1968) *The Just War: Force and Political Responsibility*, New York: Scribner's.

Rasmussen, M. (2001) 'Reflexive Security: NATO and International Risk Society', *Millennium Journal of International Studies*, 30(2): 285–309.

Rawls, J. (1971) *A Theory of Justice*, Cambridge, MA: Harvard University Press.

Reinsch, P. (1911) *Public International Unions, Their Work and Organization: A Study in International Administrative Law*, Boston: Ginn & Co.

Rennie, D. (2002) 'How Soviet Sub Officer Saved the World from Nuclear Conflict', *Telegraph*, 14 October.

Reuveny, R. (2007) 'Climate Change-Induced Migration and Violent Conflict', *Political Geography*, 26(6): 656–73.

Reza, A., Mercy, J. and Krug, J. (2001) 'Epidemiology of Violent Deaths in the World', *Injury Prevention*, 7: 104–11.

Risse, T. (1995) 'Democratic Peace – Warlike Democracies? A Social Constructivist Interpretation of the Liberal Argument', *European Journal of International Relations*, 1(4): 489–515.

Robertson, G. (2000) *Crimes against Humanity: The Struggle for Global Justice*, 2nd edn, London: Penguin.

Rogers, P. (2000) *Losing Control: Global Security in the Twenty-First Century*, London and Sterling, VA: Pluto Press.

Rosaldo, R. (2000) 'Of Headhunters and Soldiers: Separating Cultural and Ethical Relativism', *Issues in Ethics*, 11(1), www.scu.edu/ethics/publications/iie/v11n1/relativism.html (accessed 1.5.03).

Rose, R. and Shiratori, R. (eds) (1986) *The Welfare State East and West*, New York: Oxford University Press.

Rosenau, J. (1980) *The Study of Global Interdependence*, London: Frances Pinter.

Rosenau, J. (1990) *Turbulence in World Politics: A Theory of Change and Continuity*, Princeton: Princeton University Press.

Rostow, W. (1960) *The Stages of Economic Growth*, Cambridge: Cambridge University Press.

Ruggie, J. (1998) *Constructing the World Polity: Essays on International Institutionalization*, London and New York: Routledge.

Rummel, R. (1994) *Death by Government*, New Brunswick, NJ: Transaction Publishers.

Rummel, R. (2003) 'Freedom, Democracy, Peace; Power, Democide and War', www.hawaii.edu/powerkills/welcome.html (accessed 1.2.03).

Russett, B. and Oneal, J. (2001) *Triangulating Peace: Democracy, Interdependence and International Organisations*, New York: Norton.

Russett, B. and Starr, H. (1996) *World Politics: The Menu for Choice*, 5th edn, New York: Freeman.

Russia (1996) *Environmental Security of Russia*, issue 2, Moscow: Security Council of the Russian Federation, 13 October.

Salehyan, J. (2008) 'From Climate Change to Conflict: No Consensus Yet', *Journal of Peace Research*, 43(3): 315–26.

Sambanis, N. (2008) 'Short and Long Term Effects of United Nations Peace Operations', *World Bank Economic Review*, 22(10): 9–32.

Saul, H. (2015) 'ISIS Leader Resurfaces', *Independent*, 15 May, www.independent.co.uk/news/world/middle-east/isis-leader-abu-bakr-al-baghdadi-resurfaces-in-audio-urging-supporters-to-join-terror-group-10251955.html (accessed 16.5.17).

Schabas, W. (2000) *Genocide in International Law: The Crime of Crimes*, Cambridge: Cambridge University Press.

Schabas, W. (2001) *An Introduction to the International Criminal Court*, Cambridge: Cambridge University Press.

Schlesinger, A. (1967) 'The Origins of the Cold War', *Foreign Affairs*, 46(1): 22–52.

Schmid, A. (1983) *Political Terrorism: A Research Guide to Concepts, Theories, Data Bases and Literature*, Amsterdam: North Holland Publishing.

Schweller, R. (2001) 'The Problem of International Order Revisited', *International Security*, 26(1): 161–86.

Seale, P., Shellenberger, S. and Spence, J. (2006) 'Alcohol Problems in Alaska Natives: Lessons from the Inuit', *American Indian and Alaska Native Mental Health Research: The Journal of the National Center*, 13(1): 1–31.

Sen, A. (1981) *Poverty and Famines: An Essay on Entitlement and Deprivation*, Oxford: Clarendon.

Sen, A. (1999) 'Democracy as a Universal Value', *Journal of Democracy*, 10(3): 3–17.

Sharma, S. (2010) 'Assessing Diet and Lifestyle in the Canadian Arctic Inuit and Inuvialuit to Inform a Nutrition and Physical Activity Intervention Programme', *Journal of Human Nutrition and Dietetics*, 23, special supplement, 7 September: 5–17.

Shaw, M. (2013) 'Organized Crime in Africa', in Reichel, P. and Albanese, J. (eds) *Handbook of Transnational Crime and Justice*, London: Sage.

Sheptycki, J. (2003) 'Global Law Enforcement: A Protection Racket', in Edwards, A. and Gill, P. (eds) *Transnational Organized Crime: Perspectives on Global Security*, London and New York: Routledge: 42–58.

Short, J. (2012) *Globalization, Modernity and the City*, London: Routledge.

Simmons, I. (1996) *The Fortean Times Book of Life's Losers*, London: John Brown.

Simon, S. (2002) 'The ASEAN Regional Forum Views the Councils for Security Cooperation in the Asia Pacific: How Track II Assists Track I', *National Bureau of Asian Research Analysis*, 13(4), www.nbr.org/publications/analysis/vol13no4/ARF%20views%20CSCAP.html (accessed 12.6.03).

Singer, P. (2001) 'Corporate Warriors: The Rise of the Privatized Military Industry and Its Ramifications for International Security', *International Security*, 26(3): 186–220.

Singh, J. (1998) 'Against Nuclear Apartheid', *Foreign Affairs*, 77(5): 41–52.

SIPRI (2008) *The Effectiveness of Foreign Military Assistance in Natural Disaster Response*, Stockholm: Stockholm Peace Research Institute.

SIPRI (2016) 'Global Nuclear Weapons: Downsizing but Modernizing', https://www.sipri.org/media/press-release/2016/global-nuclear-weapons-downsizing-modernizing (accessed 18.4.17).

SIPRI (2017) *Trends in World Military Expenditure 2016*, Stockholm: Stockholm International Peace Research Institute.

Sleeman, J. (1930) *Thug or a Million Murders*, London: Sampson, Low, Marston & Co.

Small Arms Survey (2007) *Small Arms Survey 2007. Guns and the City*, Geneva: SAS.

Smith, A. (1776) *An Inquiry into the Nature and Causes of the Wealth of Nations*, London: Methuen.

Smith, A. and Flores, A. (2010) 'Disaster Politics: Why Earthquakes Rock Democracies Less', *Foreign Affairs*, 15 July.

Smith, D. (1994) 'Dynamics of Contemporary Conflict: Consequences for Development Strategies', in Græger, N. and Smith, D. (eds) *Environment, Poverty, Conflict*, Oslo: International Peace Research Institute (PRIO), Report 2/1994: 47–89.

Smith, K. (2001) *Environmental Hazards: Assessing Risk and Reducing Disaster*, 3rd edn, London and New York: Routledge.

Smith, R. (2002) 'A Time for Global Health', Editorial, *British Medical Journal*, 325, 13 July: 54–5.

Smith, R., Corvalan, C. and Kjellstrom, T. (1999) 'How Much Global Ill Health Is Attributable to Environmental Factors?', *Journal of Epidemiology*, 10(5): 573–84.

Snyder, J. (2000) *From Voting to Violence: Democratization and Nationalist Conflict*, New York: Norton.

Somavia, J. (2000) *Decent Work, Safe Work*, Geneva: ILO Safework, www.ilo.org/public/english/protection/safework/decent.htm (accessed 13.2.03).

Sonmez, S., Apostopoulos, L., Tran, D. and Dentrope, S. (2011) *Human Rights and Health Disparities for Migrant Workers, Health and Human Rights*, 13(2).

Sopoanga, S. (2002) 'Statement by Tuvalu', Johannesburg: World Summit on Sustainable Development, 2 September.

Sprout, H. and Sprout, M. (1971) *Toward a Politics of the Planet Earth*, New York: Van Nostrand Reinhold.

Stanton, G. (2002) *Genocides, Politicides, and Other Mass Murder since 1945, with Stages in 2002*, GenocideWatch, www.genocidewatch.org/genocidetable.htm (accessed 21/3/03).

Starr, J. (1991) 'Water Wars', *Foreign Policy*, 82, Spring: 17–36.

START (2015) *Mass Fatality Coordinated Attacks Worldwide and Terrorism in France*, National Consortium for the Study of Terrorism and Responses to Terrorism.

Stern, G. (2000) *The Structure of International Society*, 2nd edn, London: Pinter.

Stern, N. (2006) Stern Report on the Economics of Climate Change, UK Government, www.hmtreasury.gov.uk/independent_reviews/stern_review_economics_climate_change/stern_review_report.cfm.

Stott, R. (1999) 'The World Bank: Friend or Foe to the Poor?', *British Medical Journal*, Editorial, 318, 27 March: 822–3.

Sukhdev, P. (2008) *Economics of Ecosystems and Biodiversity*, Berlin: Helmholtz Association.

Swiss Re (2012) *Natural and Man-Made Catastrophes in 2011*, Sigma study 2/2012.

Takala, J. (1998) *Global Estimates of Fatal Occupational Accidents*, 16th International Conference of Labour Statisticians, ICLS/16/RD 8, Geneva: ILO.

Takala, J. (1999) *Introductory Report of the International Labour Office*, 15th World Congress on Occupational Safety and Health, 12–16 April.

Takala, J. (2002) *Introductory Report: Decent Work. Safe Work*, 16th World Congress on Safety and Health at Work, Vienna, 27 May.

Tampere University (2014) *Global Estimates of Occupational Accidents and Work-Related Illnesses 2014*, Tampere: Tampere University of Technology (commissioned by the ILO).

Tatham, C. and McCleary, R. (1992) 'Just Cause? The 1989 US Invasion of Panama', in McCleary, R. (ed.) *Seeking Justice: Ethics and International Affairs*, Boulder, CO and Oxford: Westview Press.

Taylor, P. (1991) 'The European Community and the State: Assumptions, Theories and Propositions', *Review of International Studies*, 17: 109–25.

Thomas, C. (2000) *Global Governance, Development and Human Security*, London: Pluto Press.

Tickner, A. (1992) *Gender in International Relations*, New York: Columbia University Press.

Tickner, A. (2001) *Gendering World Politics. Issues and Approaches in the Post-Cold War Era*, New York: Columbia University Press.

Tran, M. (1999) 'I'm Not Going to Start Third World War for You Jackson Told Clark', *Guardian*, 2 August.

Transparency International (2015) *Corruption Perceptions Index 2015*, Berlin: TI.

Transparency International (2017) *Transnational Crime and the Developing World*, Berlin: TI.

Transparency Int. UK (2015) *Corruption on Your Doorstep: How Corrupt Capital Is Used to Buy Property in the UK*, London: TIUK.

Truong, T. and Gasper, D. (2011) *Transnational Migration and Human Security*, Heidelberg: Springer.

TUC (2014) *Stronger Unions*, http://strongerunions.org/2014/02/08/sochi-winter-olympics-rights-suspended-workers-dead/ (accessed 23.1.17).

Twigg, J. (2001) 'Physician, Heal Thyself? The Politics of Disaster Mitigation', Benfield Greig Hazard Research Centre Working Paper, www.bghrc.com/DMU/WorkingPapers/BGHRCWorkingPaper1-2001.pdf (accessed 21.7.02).

UK FCO (2011) 'Cyber Crime', *Global Issues*, http://www.fco.gov.uk/en/global-issues/cyberspace/ (accessed 25.6.11).

UK Government (2003) 'DIY Accidents', Department of Trade and Industry, www.dti.gov.uk/homesafetynetwork/dy_stats.htm (accessed 4.6.03).

UK Office for National Statistics (2017) *Crime Survey of England and Wales*, www.crimesurvey.co.uk/index.html (accessed 4.3.17).

Ullman, R. (1983) 'Redefining Security', *International Security*, 8(1): 129–53.

UN (2000) 'United Nations Convention Against Transnational Organized Crime', www.uncjin.org (accessed 2.5.02).

UN (2017) 'Next Month's Ocean Conference Eyes Cutting $35 Billion in Fisheries Subsidies – UN Trade Officials', *UN News Centre*, 10 May, www.un.org/apps/news/story.asp?NewsID=56725#.WRr-jLc5Xct (accessed 10.5.17).

UNAIDS (2009) 'What UNAIDS Does', http://unaids.org/about/what.asp (accessed 25.2.09).

UNAIDS (2016) 2016–2021 Unified Budget, Results and Accountability Framework, www.unaids.org/sites/default/files/media_asset/20160531_UNAIDS_PCB38_16-10_Revised_UBRAF_EN.pdf.

UNDP (1993) *Human Development Report. People's Participation*, Oxford: Oxford University Press.

UNDP (2002) *Human Development Report. Deepening Democracy in a Fragmented World*, Oxford: Oxford University Press.

UNDP (2003) *Human Development Report. Millennium Development Goals: A Compact amongst Nations to End Human Poverty*, Oxford: Oxford University Press.

UNDP (2006) *Human Development Report. Beyond Scarcity*, Oxford: Oxford University Press.

UNDP (2016) *Climate Change and Labour: Impact of Heat in the Workplace*, Climate Vulnerable Forum, United Nations Development Programme, www.ilo.org/wcmsp5/groups/public/—dgreports/—dcomm/documents/genericdocument/wcms_476051.pdf.

UNEP (2000) *Assessing Human Vulnerability Due to Environmental Change. Concepts, Issues, Methods and Case Studies*, Nairobi: UNEP.

UNEP (2002) *GEO 3: Global Environmental Outlook*, http://geo.unep-wcmc.org/geo3/ (accessed 3.10.02).

UNEP (2011) *Human Development Report. Sustainability and Equity. A Better Future for All*, Oxford: Oxford University Press.

UNEP (2012) 'South Sudan Joins Montreal Protocol', www.unep.org/Documents.Multilingual/Default.asp?DocumentID=2666&ArticleID=9010&l=en (accessed 12.5.13).

UNEP (2016) *The Rise of Environmental Crime*, Nairobi: UNEP.

UNFPA (2012) *Sex Imbalances at Birth*, Bangkok: UNFPA Asia and Pacific Regional Office.

UNGA & UNSC (2006) *A Regional-Global Security Partnership: Challenges and Opportunities*, Report of the Secretary-General, 28 July, A/61/204–S/2006/590.

UN-Habitat (2003) *The Challenge of Slums. Global Report on Human Settlements*, United Nations Human Settlements Programme, London: Earthscan.

UNHCR (2017) www.unhcr.org/uk/figures-at-a-glance.html (accessed 13.4.17).

United Nations General Assembly (2006) 'Unity Against Terrorism: Recommendations for a Global Counter-Terrorism Strategy', 27 April, A/60/825.

United Nations Security Council (2000) Resolution 1308, 17 July, S/RES 1308.

University of Bergen (2014) *Occupational Health in Developing Countries*, https://www.futurelearn.com/courses/occupational-health-developing-countries/0/steps/13075.

University of North Dakota (2002) *Volcano World*, http://volcano.und.nodak.edu/vwdocs/volc_images/southeast_asia/indonesia/tambora.html (accessed 3.10.02).

UNODC (2005) *World Drug Report*, Vienna: UN Office for Drugs and Crime.

UNODC (2007) *World Drug Report*, Vienna: UN Office for Drugs and Crime.

UNODC (2009) *Global Report on Trafficking in Persons*, Vienna: UN Office for Drugs and Crime.

UNODC (2010) *The Globalization of Crime. A Transnational Organized Crime Threat Assessment*, Vienna: UN Office for Drugs and Crime.

UNODC (2011a) *Global Study on Homicide. Trends, Context Data*, Vienna: UN Office for Drugs and Crime.

UNODC (2011b) Overview of Global and Regional Drug Trends and Patterns, Vienna: UN Office for Drugs and Crime.

UNODC (2014) *Global Study on Homicide*, Vienna: UN Office for Drugs and Crime.

UNODC (2016a) *World Drug Report*, Vienna: UN Office for Drugs and Crime.

UNODC (2016b) *World Wildlife Crime Report*, Vienna: UN Office for Drugs and Crime.

UNSC (2007) Letter Dated 5 April from the Permanent Representative of the United Kingdom of Great Britain and Northern Ireland to the United Nations Addressed to the President of the Security Council, S/2007/186.

Uppsala/PRIO (2010) *Armed Conflict Dataset*, www.prio.no/Data/Armed-Conflict/UCDP-PRIO/.

Upton, M. (2004) 'Global Health Trumps the Nation State', *World Policy Journal*, Fall: 73–78.

USA (1983) 'United States Code', Title 22 section 2656f(d).

USA (1994) *National Security Strategy Document*, Washington DC.

Uvin, P. (1994) *The International Organization of Hunger*, London and New York: Kegan Paul.

Waever, O., Buzan, B., Kelstrup, M. and Lemaitre, P. (1993) *Identity, Migration and the New Security Agenda in Europe*, London: Pinter.

Wallace, C. (2002) 'Chain Reaction', *Time*, 11 February: 18–20.

Wallerstein, I. (1979) *The Capitalist World Economy*, Cambridge: Cambridge University Press.

Walt, C. and Buse, K. (2000) 'Partnership and Fragmentation in International Health: Threat or Opportunity?', *Tropical Medicine and International Health*, 15(7): 467–71.

Walt, S. (1991) 'The Renaissance of Security Studies', *International Studies Quarterly*, 35(2): 211–39.

Waltz, K. (1959) *Man, the State and War*, New York: Columbia University Press.

Waltz, K. (1979) *Theory of International Politics*, Reading, MA: Addison-Wesley.

Waltz, K. (2000) 'Structural Realism after the Cold War', *International Security*, 25(1): 5–41.

Waltz, K. (2012) 'Why Iran Should Get the Bomb', *Foreign Affairs*, 91(4): 2–5.

Walzer, M. (1978) *Just and Unjust Wars*, London: Allen Lane.

Warren, M. (1985) *Gendercide: The Implications of Sex Selection*, Totowa, NJ: Rowman & Littlefield.

WCO (2007) 'About Us', www.wcoomd.org/home_about_us.htm (accessed 3.2.07).

Weir, D. (1987) *The Bhopal Syndrome: Pesticides, Environment and Health*, London: Earthscan.

Weiss, R. (2002) 'War on Disease', *National Geographic*, February: 5–31.

Wendt, A. (2003) 'Why a World State Is Inevitable', *European Journal of International Relations*, 9(4): 491–542.

Werner, D. (2001) 'Whatever Happened to "Health for All?"' *New Internationalist*, 331, January/February: 22.

WFP (2002a) *Mission Statement*, Rome: World Food Programme.

WFP (2002b) 'WFP in 2000: A Quick Glance', Rome: World Food Programme, www.wfp.org/aboutwfp/facts/2000.html (accessed 5.4.02).

WFP (2002c) 'Introduction', Rome World Food Programme, www.wfp.org/aboutwfp/introduction/overview.html (accessed 5.4.02).

WFP (2009) 'Hunger', World Food Programme, http://www.wfp.org/hunger/stats (accessed 28.6.09).

WFP (2011) *WFP Management Plan 2012–2014. Executive Summary. Follow up Briefing*, 5 October, Rome: World Food Programme.

WFP (2017) 'Zero Hunger', www1.wfp.org/zero-hunger (accessed 19.3.17).

White, M. (2001) 'Wars of the Twentieth Century', *Historical Atlas of the Twentieth Century*, http://users.crols.com/mwhite28/war-list.htm (accessed 6.6.03).

White, M. (2004) '30 Worst Atrocities of the Twentieth Century', http://users.erols.com/mwhite 28/atrox.htm9.

White House (USA) (1994) 'National Security Strategy of Engagement and Enlargement', Government Printing Office, Washington DC, July.

Whittow, J. (1984) *The Penguin Dictionary of Physical Geography*, London: Penguin.

WHO (1998) 'Fifty Years of the World Health Organization in the Western Pacific Region', Report of the Regional Director to the Regional Committee for the Western Pacific, www.wpro.who.int/public/policy/50TH/50_toc.htm (accessed 1.8.02).

WHO (1999a) Executive Board 103rd Session, 18 January, EB103/9.

WHO (1999b) *World Health Report*, part 1, 'Health and Development in the Twentieth Century', Geneva: WHO.

WHO (2000a) *Transport, Environment and Health*, edited by Dora, C. and Phillip, M., Copenhagen: WHO Regional Office for Europe European Series no. 89.

WHO (2000b) *World Health Report 2000*, Geneva: World Health Organization.

WHO (2001) 'Small Arms and Global Health. WHO Contribution to the UN Conference on Illicit Trade in Small Arms and Light Weapons', 9–20 July, WHO/NMH/VIP/01.1, Geneva: WHO.

WHO (2002a) 'Roll Back Malaria', www.who.int/rbm (accessed 12.9.02).

WHO (2002b) *World Health Report 2002*, Geneva: World Health Organization.

WHO (2002c) *World Report on Violence and Health*, Geneva: World Health Organization.

WHO (2003) *Structure of the WHO*, www.who.int/aboutwho/en/structure.htm (accessed 1.8.02).

WHO (2004a) *World Health Report 2004*, Geneva: WHO.

WHO (2004b) *World Report on Road Traffic Injury Prevention*, Geneva: World Health Organization.

WHO (2006) 'Violence Against Women', Factsheet, www.who.int/mediacentre/factsheets/fs 239/en/.

WHO (2008) *World Report on Child Injury Prevention*, Geneva: World Health Organization.

WHO (2011) *Global Burden of Disease 2008*, Geneva: World Health Organization.

WHO (2012a) *Global Health Expenditure Atlas*, Geneva: World Health Organization.

WHO (2012b) www.who.int/about/en/.

WHO (2014) *Global Report on Drowning*, Geneva: World Health Organization.

WHO (2015a) 'Global Health Observatory Data. Malaria', www.who.int/gho/malaria/en/ (accessed 23.11.15).

WHO (2015b) *Global Status Report on Road Safety*, Geneva: World Health Organization.

WHO (2016a) *Global Report on Diabetes*, Geneva: World Health Organization.

WHO (2016b) *World Health Statistics. Suicide*, Geneva: World Health Organization.

WHO (2016c) 'Violence Against Women' Factsheet http://www.who.int/mediacentre/factsheets/fs239/en/ (accessed 20.06.2016).

WHO (2016d) *World Health Statistics 2016*, Geneva: WHO.

WHO (2017) *Global Health Observatory. Data on Road Safety*, Geneva: World Health Organization, www.who.int/gho/road_safety/mortality/rate_text/en/.

Who's Who in the Twentieth Century (1999) Oxford: Oxford University Press.

Wight, M. (1978) *Power Politics*, edited by Bull, H. and Holbraad, C., Leicester: Leicester University Press.

Wilkinson, P. (1986) 'Fighting the Hydra: International Terrorism and the Rule of Law', in O'Sullivan, N. (ed.) *Terror, Ideology and Revolution*, vol. 1, Oxford: Wheatsheaf: 205–24.

Wilkinson, P. (1990) 'Fighting the Hydra: Terrorism and the Rule of Law', in Kegley, C. (ed.) *International Terrorism: Characteristics, Causes, Controls*, New York: St Martin's Press: 253–8.

Wilkinson, P. (2011) *Terrorism versus Democracy: The Liberal State Response*, Abingdon: Routledge.

Williams, P. (2001) 'Transnational Criminal Networks', in Arquilla, J. and Ronfeldt, D. (eds) *Networks and Netwars: The Future of Terror, Crime and Militancy*, Santa Monica, CA: RAND: 61–97.

Williams, P. (2006) 'Strategy for a New World: Combating Terrorism and Transnational Crime', in Baylis, J., Wirtz, J., Cohen, E. and Gray, C. (eds) *Strategy in the Contemporary World*, 2nd edn, Oxford: Oxford University Press: 192–208.

Williams, P. and Woessner, P. (2000) 'Gangs Go Nuclear', *World Today*, December: 7–9.

Wilson, N. and Thomson, G. (2005) 'Deaths from International Terrorism Compared with Road Crash Deaths in OECD Countries', *Injury Prevention*, 11: 332–3.

Win/Gallup (2014) *Win/Gallup International Annual Survey 2013*, Sofia: Gallup.

Wirtz, J. (2002) 'A New Agenda for Security and Strategy?', in Baylis, J., Wirtz, J., Cohen, E. and Gray, C. (eds) *Strategy in the Contemporary World: An Introduction to Strategic Studies*, Oxford: Oxford University Press: 309–27.

Wisner, B. (2000) 'Disasters. What the United Nations and Its World Can Do', *United Nations Chronicle*, online edn, 38(4), www.un.org/Pubs/chronicle/2000/issue4/0400p6.htm (accessed 13.8.02).

Wolf, A. (2007) 'Shared Waters: Conflict and Cooperation', *Annual Review of Environmental Resources*, 32: 241–69.

Woolf, L. (1916) *International Government*, New York: Brentano's.

World Bank (1991) *World Development Report*, Oxford: Oxford University Press.

World Bank (1993) *World Development Report: Investing in Health*, Washington DC.

World Bank (2003) *World Development Indicators Database*, www.worldbank.org/data/databytopic/GNIPC.pdf (accessed 25.6.03).

World Bank (2009) *The Sunken Billions*, Washington DC: World Bank Publications.

World Bank (2011) *Conflict, Security and Development. World Development Report 2011*, http://wdr2011.worldbank.org/fulltext (accessed 4.1.12).

World Bank (2017) *Military Expenditure*, http://data.worldbank.org/indicator/MS.MIL.XPND.GD.ZS (accessed 21.2.17).

World Congress on Drowning (2002) www.drowning.nl/csi/drowning.nsf/index/home/$file/home.htm (accessed 29.4.03).

World Meteorological Organization/United Nations Environmental Programme (2006) *UNEP/WMO Scientific Assessment of Ozone Depletion: 2006*, Global Ozone Research and Monitoring Project, Report no. 50, Geneva: WMO.

Wyn-Jones, R. (1999) *Security, Strategy and Critical Theory*, Boulder, CO: Lynne Rienner: ch. 4, www.ciaonet.org/book/wynjones/wynjones04.html (accessed 14.3.03).

Yuval-Davis, N. (1997) *Gender and Nation*, London: Sage.

Zakaria, F. (1997) 'The Rise of Illiberal Democracy', *Foreign Affairs*, 76(6): 22–43.

Index